THE BUILDINGS OF ENGLAND

BE35

WORCESTERSHIRE

NIKOLAUS PEVSNER

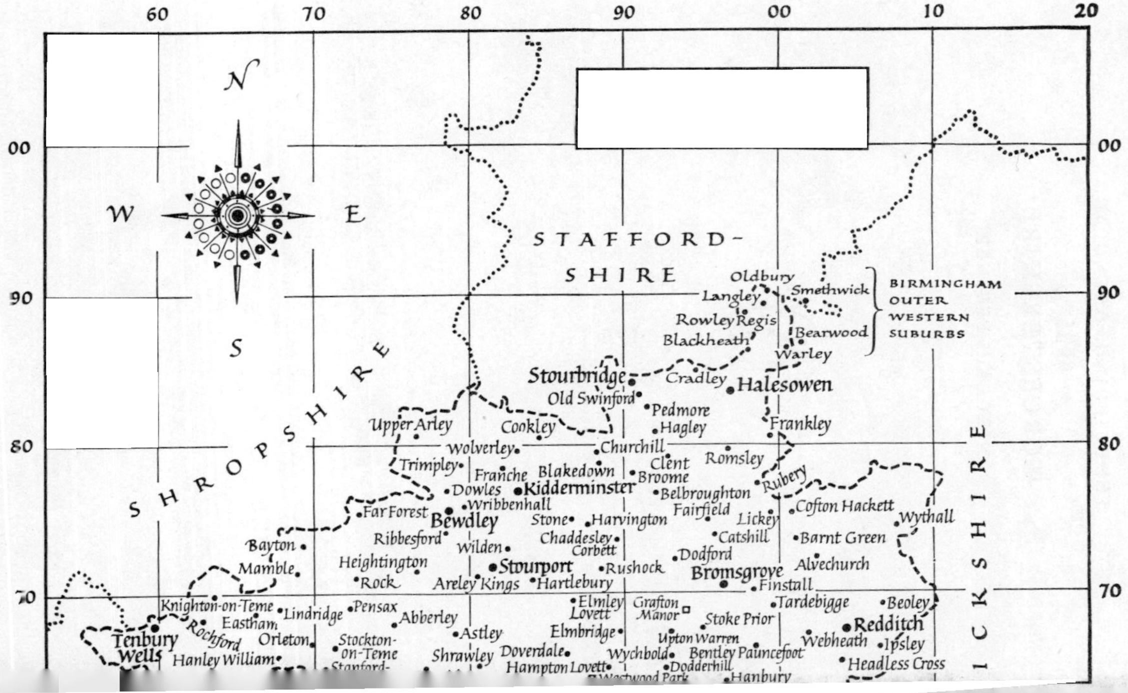
60
70
80
90
00
10
20
00
90
80
70
N
W
E
S
STAFFORD-
SHIRE
SHROPSHIRE
BIRMINGHAM
OUTER
WESTERN
SUBURBS
ICKSHIRE
Oldbury
Langley
Smethwick
Rowley Regis
Blackheath
Bearwood
Warley
Stourbridge
Cradley
Halesowen
Old Swinford
Pedmore
Upper Arley
Cookley
Hagley
Frankley
Wolverley
Churchill
Clent
Romsley
Trimpley
Franche
Blakedown
Broome
Rubery
Dowles
Kidderminster
Belbroughton
Wribbenhall
Fairfield
Cofton Hackett
Far Forest
Bewdley
Stone
Harvington
Lickey
Wythall
Ribbesford
Chaddesley Corbett
Catshill
Barnt Green
Bayton
Wilden
Dodford
Alvechurch
Mamble
Heightington
Stourport
Rushock
Bromsgrove
Rock
Areley Kings
Hartlebury
Finstall
Knighton-on-Teme
Pensax
Elmley Lovett
Grafton Manor
Tardebigge
Beoley
Eastham
Lindridge
Abberley
Stoke Prior
Redditch
Rochford
Astley
Elmbridge
Tenbury Wells
Orleton
Stockton-on-Teme
Upton Warren
Webheath
Ipsley
Hanley William
Shrawley
Doverdale
Wychbold
Bentley Pauncefoot
Headless Cross
Hampton Lovett
Dodderhill
Hanbury

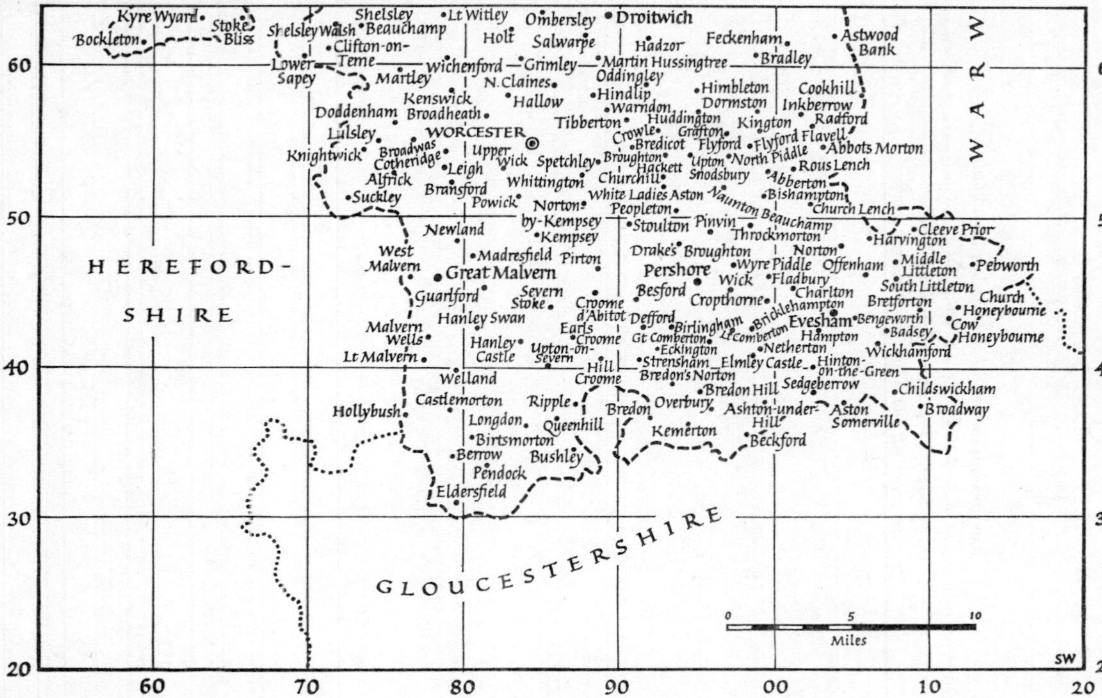
Kyre Wyard
Bockleton
Stoke Bliss
Shelsley Walsh
Shelsley Beauchamp
Lt Witley
Ombersley
Droitwich
Holt
Salwarpe
Hadzor
Feckenham
Astwood Bank
Clifton-on-Teme
Lower Sapey
Wichenford
Grimley
Martin Hussingtree
Bradley
Martley
N. Claines
Oddingley
Himbleton
Cookhill
Kenswick
Hallow
Hindlip
Dormston
Inkberrow
Doddenham
Broadheath
Warndon
Huddington
Kington
Radford
Tibberton
Lulsley
WORCESTER
Crowle
Grafton
Flyford Flavell
Broadwas
Bredicot
Flyford
Abbots Morton
Knightwick
Cotheridge
Upper Wick
Spetchley
Broughton Hackett
Upton Snodsbury
North Piddle
Rous Lench
Alfrick
Leigh
Churchill
Abberton
Suckley
Bransford
Whittington
White Ladies Aston
Naunton Beauchamp
Bishampton
Powick
Norton by-Kempsey
Peopleton
Church Lench
Newland
Kempsey
Stoulton
Pinvin
Throckmorton
Cleeve Prior
Harvington
West Malvern
Madresfield
Pirton
Drake's Broughton
Norton
Middle Littleton
Pebworth
Great Malvern
Pershore
Wyre Piddle
Offenham
Wick
Fladbury
South Littleton
Guarlford
Severn Stoke
Croome d'Abitot
Besford
Cropthorne
Charlton
Bretforton
Church Honeybourne
Hanley Swan
Defford
Birlingham
Bricklehampton
Evesham
Bengeworth
Cow Honeybourne
Malvern Wells
Earls Croome
Gt Comberton
Lt Comberton
Hampton
Badsey
Hanley Castle
Upton-on-Severn
Eckington
Netherton
Wickhamford
Lt Malvern
Strensham
Elmley Castle
Hinton-on-the-Green
Hill Croome
Bredon's Norton
Welland
Bredon Hill
Sedgeberrow
Childswickham
Castlemorton
Ripple
Overbury
Ashton-under-Hill
Aston Somerville
Broadway
Hollybush
Bredon
Longdon
Queenhill
Kemerton
Beckford
Birtsmorton
Berrow
Bushley
Pendock
Eldersfield
HEREFORD-SHIRE
GLOUCESTERSHIRE
WAR
Miles
SW

The publication of this volume has been made possible by a grant from
THE LEVERHULME TRUST
to cover all the necessary research work

THE BUILDINGS OF ENGLAND

Worcestershire

BY

NIKOLAUS PEVSNER

*

PENGUIN BOOKS

Penguin Books Ltd, Harmondsworth, Middlesex, England
Penguin Books, 625 Madison Avenue, New York, New York 10022, U.S.A.
Penguin Books Australia Ltd, Ringwood, Victoria, Australia
Penguin Books Canada Ltd, 41 Steelcase Road West, Markham, Ontario, Canada
Penguin Books (N.Z.) Ltd, 182–190 Wairau Road, Auckland 10, New Zealand

—

First published 1968
Reprinted 1977

—

—

ISBN 0 14 071035 3

—

Made and printed in Great Britain
by William Clowes & Sons, Limited, London, Beccles and Colchester
Set in Monotype Plantin

To

Sir Gordon Russell

this small token of admiration

and gratitude

CONTENTS

Map References

*

The numbers printed in italic type in the margin against the place names in the gazetteer of the book indicate the position of the place in question on the index map (pages 2–3), which is divided into sections by the 10-kilometre reference lines of the National Grid. The reference given here omits the two initial letters (formerly numbers) which in a full grid reference refer to the 100-kilometre squares into which the country is divided. The first two numbers indicate the *western* boundary, and the last two the *southern* boundary, of the 10-kilometre square in which the place in question is situated. For example Ripple (reference 8030) will be found in the 10-kilometre square bounded by grid lines 80 and 90 on the *west* and 30 to 40 on the *south*; Hanbury (reference 9060) in the square bounded by grid lines 90 and 00 on the *west* and 60 and 70 on the *south.*

The map contains all those places, whether towns, villages, or isolated buildings, which are the subject of separate entries in the text.

FOREWORD

The preparation for this volume was in the experienced hands of Miss Jennifer Sherwood; so I need hardly say that it left nothing to be desired. The text of my illegible handwriting was converted into type with her sleep-walking precision by Miss Dorothy Dorn, and Mrs Judith Tabner coped without complaint with the extensive correspondence. My companion, driver, helper, and dogsbody on the journey was Mr Neil Stratford. He also never complained, although it must soon have become sadly clear to him that he would not have enough time to work with thoroughness on the Norman sculpture which was his foremost interest. In order to write what he liberally contributed to my book he decided to retrace his steps (or tyre-marks) later, and the result is evident in many places. Mr F. W. B. Charles contributed the introduction to, and gazetteer of, timber-framed houses. They are therefore done better and more throughly than in any preceding volumes. The geology is, as before, the work of Professor Terence Miller; for the essay on building materials (amongst other things) I am grateful to my friend Alec Clifton-Taylor. Prehistory once again was covered by Mr Derek Simpson, Roman remains by Professor Barry Cunliffe.

The information contained in the gazetteer should be comparatively satisfactory as far as I could base it on the Victoria County History (VCH), *though for secular buildings its coverage varies and can be weak. Weaker throughout is what has been published on those places which, until 1931, were in Gloucestershire.*

As in previous volumes, I have to thank the National Monuments Record (here abridged NMR*), former National Buildings Record, for their liberality – the study of their seventy-seven boxes of Worcestershire photographs was an essential part of my work – the Ministry of Housing and Local Government* (MHLG) *for placing at my disposal their lists of buildings of architectural and historic interest, Mr Peter Ferriday* (PF) *for putting on permanent loan at my office his index of Victorian church restorations, and Mr Geoffrey Spain* (GS) *for providing me with lists of Victorian buildings mentioned in the architectural journals. The abbreviation* GR *refers to the Goodhart-Rendel index of Victorian churches, the abbreviation* TK *to Sir Thomas Kendrick's index of Victorian stained glass, now in the library of the Victoria and Albert Museum.*

I am extremely grateful also to the librarians of Worcestershire, and in particular Mr J. C. Hayward of the Worcester City Libraries, Mr C W. T. Huddy of the Evesham Public Library, Mr N. H. Parker of the Malvern Public Library, Mr A. H. Huskinson, the Smethwick Borough Librarian, and Mr H. White, the Stourbridge Borough Librarian.

I want to express my gratitude too to Sir Gordon Russell for help on Broadway, to the Dean of Worcester for help on the cathedral, to Mr P. A. Barker for help on the history of Worcester, to Mr J. Matley Moore for help on the Greyfriars and the walls of Worcester, and to Mr W. A. Peplow for allowing me the use of the proofs of his catalogue of church plate in the Archdeaconry of Worcester. Unfortunately the Archdeaconry of Dudley has not yet been completed in manuscript by Mr Peplow.

I am also grateful to Mr George Sayer for help on Malvern College, to Avoncroft College, Bromsgrove for allowing Mr Stratford and myself to stay for about a week, and to the Rev. W. C. Duker, Mr T. Nicolls, the Rev. C. F. Pilkington, and Mr J. Rollins. Rectors, vicars, and owners or occupiers of houses have helped me in various ways, by allowing me access to houses, by answering questions, and by reading proofs and commenting on them.

The principles on which the following gazetteer is founded are the same as in the thirty-four volumes of the Buildings of England which precede it. I have myself seen everything that I describe. Where this is not the case, the information obtained by other means is placed in brackets. Information ought to be as complete as the space of the volume permits for churches prior to c.1830 and all town houses, manor houses, and country houses of more than purely local interest. Movable furnishings are not included in secular buildings, though they are in churches. Exceptions to the latter rule are bells, hatchments, chests, chairs, plain fonts, and altar tables. Royal arms, coffin lids with foliate crosses, and brasses of post-Reformation date are mentioned occasionally, church plate of after 1830 only rarely. Village crosses are omitted where only a plain base or stump of the shaft survives. As for churches and chapels of after 1830, I had to make a selection, and this is dictated by architectural value or by significance otherwise in the light of architectural history. The same applies to the secular buildings of the C 19 *and* C 20.

Finally, as in all previous volumes, it is necessary to end the foreword to this with an appeal to all users to draw my attention to errors and omissions.

INTRODUCTION

BY NIKOLAUS PEVSNER

THE scarcity of Roman remains in Worcestershire which Professor Cunliffe reports (p. 44) is exceeded by the almost total absence of ANGLO-SAXON remains. The Cropthorne cross head 6
and the Lechmere Stone at Severn End, Hanley Castle, are the only pieces which must be recorded in this introduction. The former is of the C9, the latter of the C9 or the C11, the former of high quality and wonderfully preserved, the latter barbaric, but all the more impressive for that. The two sum up the Anglo-Saxon alternatives: one a Renaissance rather than continuation of the highly accomplished style of the Ruthwell and Bewcastle Crosses of the late C7, with scrolls inhabited by birds and beasts and with such classical motifs as the Greek key; the other along the Celtic lines of ferocious stylization. Apart from these, Worcestershire has just a few odd parts of crosses with interlace (Frankley, Rous Lench, Stoke Prior), and a few turned capitals of Oswald's Worcester Cathedral of 961 etc. re-used in the slype.

Worcester was a monastic cathedral. Whenever it was originally 4 &
founded, Oswald introduced or re-introduced Benedictine p. 296
monks. The other great Benedictine abbeys were Pershore and Evesham, and Malvern was of considerable importance too. Pershore was founded *c.*689, Evesham in 714, Malvern *c.*1085. Of Malvern we have the church, with outstanding Norman and Perp work, and the Great Gate of Evesham abbey church, just one lump of stone, though the plan has been recovered by excavation, and in addition the entrance to the chapter house, the isolated Late Perp 'clocher' or campanile, a Norman gate, a fragment of the great C14 gate, and two strangely placed parish churches. Of Pershore only the E part of the church survives, of Worcester too much to enumerate here. There are not many other monastic houses. Little Malvern Priory was Benedictine too. What is preserved is half the church and the prior's lodging. Bordesley Abbey near Redditch, founded in 1138, was Cistercian. Nothing is preserved. Whiteladies, founded *c.*1250 just N of inner Worcester, was a Cistercian nunnery. The E wall of the church is all that is left us. The other nunnery in Worcestershire, Cookhill, presents us with no more than a few fragments of the church.

That leaves Halesowen, founded in 1218 for Premonstratensians, and having kept fragments of chancel, S transept, and refectory, and the Greyfriars at Worcester, established in 1239, but of which the remaining timber-framed house in Friar Street, probably the guest house, is as late as *c*.1480. Of the Blackfriars at Worcester nothing is preserved, nor anything of the Austin Friars at Droitwich. To this list of monastic establishments one may add Stanbrook Abbey, Powick, Anglo-Catholic, begun in 1878, and Glasshampton Monastery, Astley, also Anglo-Catholic, which established itself in a Georgian stable range in 1918.

7 Of NORMAN work, the crypt of Worcester Cathedral is a complete survival of the 1080s. With its about fifty short columns with their block or single-scallop or single-trumpet-scallop capitals and with its plain groin-vaults, it represents to perfection the mood of those determined and ruthless years. Of the same date approximately must be the slype, S of the S transept. The crypt allows us to reconstruct the plan of the E end. It must have had an ambulatory without radiating chapels, i.e. the same pattern as Jumièges, and chapels E of the transepts. It also must have had a gallery extending over these chapels. This was the same at
9 Pershore. The Pershore transept in all probability had a four-tier elevation, i.e. a small triforium and a clerestory, as was, it seems, the case also at Tewkesbury. The case is not proven, and it is possible that there was no clerestory in these buildings and a tunnel-vault instead, as was done so often in France. In this context it should be said that evidence at Halesowen parish church seems to suggest a mid-C12 tunnel-vault in the chancel. Pershore nave, again as at Tewkesbury (and Gloucester), had high round
8 piers, 25 ft at Pershore. The piers at Malvern are round too, though not so high. These parts are probably in both places of *c*.1120, and the (re-tooled) foliage trails of the capitals of the arch to the S transept chapel at Worcester give us approximately the same date. Again of that time must be the memorable Worcester
10 chapter house. It is round, with a high central column, and must always have been vaulted. It is the ancestor of all the centrally planned – though polygonal – chapter houses in England. Evesham also has at least a reminder of those early decades of Norman architecture: the Cemetery Gate of some time between 1122 and 1149, but looking rather earlier than 1122.

As regards Norman work in parish churches, Worcestershire is one of the richest of all counties. Mr Neil Stratford, who studied it in detail and on whose results the following is based, counted work in nearly half the pre-Georgian churches, i.e. in about ninety. As in the cathedral and the abbeys and priories, two phases can at once be distinguished, *c.*1120–50 and *c.*1175–1200 and after. The earlier has simple capitals, mostly block or single-scallop, and big roll mouldings. Ornament is relatively flat. The later has as its hallmark trumpet-scallop capitals or finely decorated multi-scallop capitals and often already crockets or even early stiff-leaf.* Similarly the arches may already go pointed. But the morphological logic of unmoulded–round, single-step–moulded–round, and so on to pointed, is not at all consistently kept, and earlier and later forms mix. Of the early style is a characteristic group with blank arcading, simple or interlaced, above slightly projected doorways (Stockton-on-Teme, Bockleton, Knighton-on-Teme, Eastham, Stoulton‡), and another, mid-century, with figured capitals (Holt, Rock). Of the later style there is too much to attempt any enumeration here.§

The date of the later type is indicated by work at Worcester after the crossing tower had fallen in 1175. The replacements that went on in the S transept included the ornamental motifs of the later type, such as zigzag at r. angles to the wall and a little higher up, i.e. later, keeled shafts for intended vaulting, and stiff-leaf
capitals. At Worcester also, the W end of the nave dates from the 12
last quarter of the century. It is odd in certain details, but goes closely with the transept. The S aisle is in fact rib-vaulted; the shafts for the nave vaulting were an afterthought of shortly after the beginning. The principal arches are pointed.

A few of the parish churches are of interest in plan or elevation. Powick had E chapels to the transepts like the greater churches, Bredon has a Late Norman rib-vaulted porch, Astley
has curious buttresses, in section semicircular above, but below 11
of two semicircles with a spur between. Crossing towers were quite frequent (Beckford, Bredon, Dodderhill, Halesowen, Pershore Abbey, Pirton, Ripple). It is remarkable how large some of the Norman Worcestershire parish churches were. Examples are Halesowen, Bredon, Broadway, Kempsey, Powick, Ripple, and Rock. Another remarkable thing is the amount of surviving NORMAN SCULPTURE.** It is not easily dated but seems to go

* Dodderhill, consecrated in 1220, still has trumpet scallops.

‡ Cf. the interlaced arcading of the Worcester chapter house and on the E wall of Halesowen parish church.

§ To put the Pirton Stone into a footnote is an admission of defeat. Is it 14
Early Norman ? And what was it made for anyway ? Comments must be looked up on p. 244.

** Readers must be referred to the more detailed account by Mr Neil Stratford on p. 44.

from *c.*1130–40 to the late C12. Little is of high quality, and
much is iconographically baffling. By far the finest quality is that
17 of the two lecterns of Crowle and Norton, strongly influenced by
Italian ambones, though English. The Norton lectern belonged in
all probability to Evesham Abbey, where a Lectorium for the
refectory was provided by an abbot who ruled in 1160–91. Any
date earlier than 1190 must be excluded. Both the lecterns have
a figure in the middle and leaf scrolls l. and r. Also clearly in-
13 fluenced by Italy is the S doorway at Beckford (tympanum on two
head corbels – via Ely?); English and directly influenced by
France is the small Chartresque head of a queen at Defford. The
15 seated Christ in a niche at Rous Lench must be mid-C12 and also
has international connotations. On the other hand, the Anglo-Saxon past rears its head in the two barbaric tympana of Romsley and Pedmore, both with Christ in Majesty, but one with angels holding his glory, the other with the Signs of the Evangelists. But while these are iconographically French motifs, Romsley has a border of loose interlace around,* and at Pedmore the almond-shaped glory starts and ends as monster-heads. Other tympana are at Beckford with Christ, his cross-staff on a dragon, and a devil leashed, at Ribbesford with an archer and two quadrupeds, Beckford again with a cross and a rose, a bird, and two quadrupeds, at Netherton with a fine big winged dragon, at Rochford with a Tree of Life, and at Little Comberton with a cross and four big, fat whorls. In addition, several churches have re-set small oblong panels with the lamb and cross, quadrupeds, a centaur, etc. (Earls Croome, Eastham, Elmley Castle, Ribbesford, Stockton). It is not known what their original function was.

In the context of Norman sculpture NORMAN FONTS must be considered. Signally many are preserved. Undecorated ones are not listed in the gazetteer, but even counting only the decorated ones, one reaches the two-dozen mark. Nearly all are round. A number of them have no more ornament than a band or two of rope-moulding or plait or zigzag, or blank arches (Broome, Pinvin, Stoke Bliss). The Pershore font has seated figures in the blank arcading. Other fonts have just rosettes or a medallion with the lamb and cross (Rock, Inkberrow, Bricklehampton). The

* Romsley is the place where St Kenelm, King of Mercia, was murdered in 819. The church and two others (Clifton-on-Teme and Upton Snodsbury) are dedicated to him. The only three other rare dedications in the county are St Godwald (Finstall), St Cassian (Chaddesley Corbett), and St Eadburga of Pershore (Abberton, Broadway, Leigh).

most ornate of all is at Chaddesley Corbett, in style an outlier of 16
Herefordshire. The motifs are four dragons. At least as impressive are the four mighty dragons on the base of the Elmley 18
Castle font, but they must be early C13. Big monster-heads are the motif at Holt, where the date is the mid C12. Earlier still seem to be the two figures of the Overbury font, and early also must be the snaky Viking interlace on the Halesowen font.

Medieval SCULPTURE in Worcestershire reached its climax in the EARLY THIRTEENTH CENTURY. The monuments, all of *c.*1220–30, are the beautiful, though damaged, large seated Christ in the refectory of Worcester Cathedral, the so-called Standing 20
Christ at Leigh, which is really a funerary slab, and the marvel- 19
lous Purbeck marble monument to King John in the cathedral. 21
The Purbeck monument to Bishop William of Blois † 1236 is almost as fine, and there are in the cathedral other C13 Purbeck monuments to bishops and to ladies.*

William of Blois, just mentioned, began the chancel of the cathedral in 1224. It is of course the major monument of EARLY 22
ENGLISH ARCHITECTURE in the county. It is large, of eight bays, with a pair of E transepts, and has a triforium and quad- 24
ripartite vaults with a longitudinal ridge-rib. There is plenty of Purbeck marble and plenty of sculpture, much of it Victorian. It is more conventional than Lincoln, but possesses for that very reason a reposeful though cool perfection. The feature nearest to Lincoln is the syncopation of the triforium, where the rhythm 23
of the arcading towards the choir is different from that of the blank background arcading. The E end of Pershore was begun 27
some twenty years earlier than that of Worcester and consecrated in 1239. The progress of the building is not easy to unravel. Work started at the E and ended at the E. The plan incidentally is odd, with an ambulatory but two square-ended chapels l. and r. of the former Lady Chapel, all three facing due E. In addition there are a N and a S chapel as vestigial E transepts. The chancel itself has rich stiff-leaf capitals, and the wall-passage taking the place of a triforium is architecturally pulled together with the clerestory much higher up, resulting in a two-tier elevation on the pattern of St Davids and Llantony. The E chapels and what

* Coffin lids with foliated crosses are only occasionally listed in the gazetteer, but one at Halesowen deserves a note. It shows a kneeling figure in profile below a crucifix. It is incidentally also worth a note that Bishop Carpenter, who died in 1476, still chose (or had chosen for him) a plain foliated cross as his memorial. It is at Alvechurch.

remains of the Lady Chapel are alone distinguished by a display
of Purbeck shafting.

In parish churches the demand must have been all but satu-
rated when the E.E. style set in. There is little to note here: parts
25 of St Andrew at Droitwich of *c.*1200 etc., the noble chancels of
Overbury and Kempsey of *c.*1250, the former rib-vaulted, and
the entry arch to the chapter house vestibule of Evesham Abbey
with an order of seated and an order of standing figurines,
perhaps of *c.*1260. Such figurines occur in the chapter house
entrance of Westminster Abbey and the S portal of the Lincoln
Angel Choir.

Nor is the DECORATED STYLE more frequent. In parish
churches there is very little indeed, and for really rewarding
work one must go to Pershore and Worcester. Of parochial jobs
two are datable: Dodderhill with a consecration in 1322 and
Broadwas with the institution of a new chapel in 1344. Chad-
32 desley Corbett has a delightful chancel, Fladbury a vaulted
porch. But go to Pershore and you find the revaulting of the
chancel and the rebuilding of the crossing tower after a fire
26& which had taken place in 1288. If the vault of Pershore with its
28 liernes opening and closing along the ridge in a scissor-like pat-
tern is really as early as *c.*1290–1300, it is, with St Stephen's
Chapel in the Palace of Westminster and the chancel of Bristol
Cathedral, the earliest lierne-vault in England. The vault achieves
full harmony with the parts below, which had been consecrated
in 1239. The crossing tower is a very beautiful piece. It has
plenty of ballflower, and so probably dates from about 1310–20
33 or so. At Worcester the rebuilding of the nave began at the NE
end *c.*1320. It was carried on speedily and consistently so that by
the 1370s the vaults were complete. Imperceptibly in the years of
the third quarter Dec changed into Perp. The rebuilding of the
cloister had started a little later than that of the nave, and work
34 finished only in the C15. But one can see in the earliest, the E,
range how the reticulation motif of the Dec style, prominent in
the embrasures of the windows, stands side by side with the
Perp detail above the entry to the chapter house. The nave can
be called Dec without hesitation. The general elevational theme
is continued from the chancel, an interesting and typically Eng-
lish case of deliberate conformity. The result is a very satisfying
harmony between builds separated by a century. The piers are
complex, the arches complex, the windows have Dec tracery. The
details, however, differ between N and S and make it clear that
the N side was built almost completely before work started on the

S side; for in the latter the rich Dec band of nobbly foliage in the
capitals is replaced by single thin, emphatically Perp capitals,
and in the upper part this Perp thinning can also be observed.*
The vault of the nave is still remarkably simple, with ridge-ribs,
but even without tiercerons. These and lierne ribs appear in the S
transept and the crossing-tower vaults‡ and also in the cloister
vaults from the start. There are bosses of interest in all these
vaults, the best figural ones in the cloister S range. Purely Dec
was the Guesten Hall, which survives only as a ruin, and Dec also
is the refectory with its large, even windows and the pretty vault
over the former reading pulpit. The seated Christ of *c.*1220–30 20
on the E wall is surrounded by a bold C14 'reredos'.

Before continuing with the Perp style it may be useful to
round up CHURCH FURNISHINGS and funerary monuments
from where we have left them to where we have reached now.
There is not much to record. A few beautiful pieces of STAINED
GLASS of the C14 (Kempsey in the first place and also Birtsmor- 36
ton, Bredon, St Peter Droitwich, Mamble, Sedgeberrow, Warn- 35
don), a beautiful painted female saint of the same time at Kyre
Wyard, the remains of a yet somewhat earlier cycle of WALL
PAINTINGS at Pinvin, an excellent small piece of SCULPTURE 30
at All Saints Evesham, of *c.*1300 some fine heraldic TILES,
again of the early C14, at Bredon, and the silver-gilt mid-C13
PATEN with the *manus dei* at Worcester Cathedral. For MONU-
MENTS there is more to be said. Purbeck marble Ladies at Wor-
cester Cathedral have been mentioned before. The earliest and
best of them is of *c.*1250. The earliest Knight – his legs not yet
crossed – is at Malvern (*c.*1250 at the latest). An early cross-
legged one, of *c.*1280, is at Pershore, and then there are, as every- 29
where, plenty with crossed legs – an exceptionally late one at
Alvechurch. The best late C14 monument in Worcestershire is
the Beauchamp Tomb in the cathedral with its two recumbent
effigies. It may well be *c.*1400. The tomb-chest of Bishop
Giffard † 1302, also in the cathedral, is noteworthy for its deli-
cately carved allegorical reliefs. For reasons of the quite excep-
tional composition, an early or mid C14 coffin lid at Bredon 31
deserves attention. It has a cross and at its top two frontal busts.

The PERPENDICULAR STYLE has not much quantitatively in
the county, but some of what there is, is of the highest order.
That is true of the crossing tower of the cathedral, of 1374, of the 4

* However, the window tracery is flowing and not yet Perp at all.

‡ But externally the crossing tower has Perp detail on its lower, Dec details on its higher stage.

N porch completed in 1386, and of the very grand, if quite irre-
gular, windows in the transepts. But the most complete impres-
37 sion of Perp is to be had at Malvern. Here, from *c.*1420 onwards,
38 the nave was remodelled and the chancel rebuilt. There are few
monastic establishments in England which did so much at so late
a date. Inspiration from Gloucester is evident. At Evesham
Abbot Lichfield (1514–39) built in the most sumptuous manner
a fan-vaulted chapel in All Saints (while he was still prior), a fan-
40 vaulted chapel in St Lawrence, and the campanile or *clocherium*
39 with its two main walls panelled all over and its two other walls
almost completely bare. The panelling has its parallels in the
gatehouse and the porch at Malvern. Of other buildings in this
41 context Romsley has a specially attractive slim W tower, Church
Honeybourne and Hampton have porches with transverse stone
ribs or arches, a type more usual in such counties as Nottingham-
shire and Derbyshire, Little Malvern Priory received at the hands
of Bishop Alcock, i.e. in 1480–2, a new chancel and the upper
parts of the crossing tower, and Kidderminster built itself a very
ambitious parish church. It is a pity that it is so drastically re-
newed – almost as drastically as the whole exterior of the cathe-
dral. Kidderminster has at its E end – an exception in a parish
church – a three-bay-long Lady Chapel. The arcade piers of the
nave are octagonal, with concave sides, a Cotswold motif. It also
occurs at Rock, and there is dated 1510. Other Perp arcades
worth comment are octagonal with, in the diagonals, one hollow
(Bredon, Evesham All Saints, Pebworth – new in 1528), or even
two hollows (North Claines), or quatrefoil with each foil being
of three sides of an octagon (e.g. St John in Bedwardine Wor-
cester). Ribbesford has an arcade entirely of timber, and of
49 timber also are the porches of Huddington and Romsley.

This is the place to introduce the important part played by
TIMBER in Worcestershire. Mr Charles has written his own piece
on this on pp. 52 ff., and so we need here only to remember the
salient facts. Worcestershire has one completely timber-framed
church of the mid C14 (with Dec detail). This is Besford. It is a
type of which Shropshire has examples too (Melverley, Halston).
Of roof-timbering in parish churches the best example is Shelsley
Walsh, with foils above the collar-beams. Like Shropshire,
Worcestershire also has timber towers as well as bell-turrets over
48 the W end of the nave. The former are Pirton, Dormston,
Kington, Warndon, and Cotheridge. To the latter belong
Knighton-on-Teme, Mamble, White Ladies Aston, and Himble-
ton. The heavy internal bracing of both types is impressive. The

Pirton tower has two aisles, like Essex towers such as Margaretting, but the diagonal braces of the main posts are like huge cruck blades. Several other churches rely on beams to carry the bell-turret (note the finely decorated beam at Peopleton which is all that is left of the original bell-turret structure). Yet others have a whole timber-framed cross-wall inside the nave of the church, as if it were the wall of a house. This is so at Bayton, Bransford, Knighton-on-Teme, and Mamble. At Martley there is instead a timber-framed tympanum between nave and chancel. The technique, to say it once more, is that of TIMBER-FRAMED HOUSES, fully dealt with by Mr Charles. An important element is CRUCKS, most monumentally displayed in the grand timber-framed BARN at Leigh Court, probably of the early C14, and the grand stone barn of Middle Littleton, mid C13 despite documentary evidence for the end of the C14. The Leigh Barn is over 150 ft long, Middle Littleton 136 ft, and third in size is the aisled Bredon Barn, 124 ft. Barns at Holiday Farm Berrow, Rectory Farm Grafton Flyford, and Pirton Court have crucks. In timber-framing, with the basic distinction between wall units and roof units, it has been established chiefly in Herefordshire that heavy, square framing precedes framing with emphasis on closely spaced studs. Close-studding came into fashion *c.*1400, probably much earlier in church towers. In Worcestershire the large curved or elbowed wall-braces, obtained by cleaving (not the straight sawn ones), precede close-studding and were often combined with it through the C15, but curved forms become rare in the C16. Close-studding however persists till the very end. Rectangular panels were always the normal framing method, but their proportions change, tending to become more vertical in later times, and from the mid C16 straight wall braces and such ornamental motifs as herringbone strutting were introduced. Concave-sided lozenges, fleurs-de-lis, and other shapes, obtained by letting in between the studs a panel of solid board carved in relief, came later still. The ornamental period was Elizabethan and Early Jacobean. The best example of the curved wall-brace period is the west front of Besford church. Examples of close-studding are the very complete Booth Hall at Evesham, 52
the front range of Besford Court, Huddington Court of the early
C16 (with the richly decorated brick chimneystacks of the Henry 53
VIII type), Eastington Hall Longdon, Salwarpe Court, the Greyfriars at Worcester, and the Commandery at Worcester. Internally the roof construction is the most rewarding element. The roof of the former chapel at Woodmanton Farm, Clifton-on-Teme,

is a timber wagon vault and can be connected with a date 1332. Churches show a slight preference for such single-framed or rafter-type roofs over the double-framed or purlin-type roofs that are characteristic of timber-framed buildings. But the roof
50 of the Guesten Hall of Worcester Cathedral now in Holy Trinity is of the latter type and dates from 1326. It has three tiers of purlins on each roof-slope and cusped wind-braces between each tier. Cusped wind-braces are in the roofs of Hyde Farm, Stoke Bliss too, which are of *c.*1300, if not earlier. Early C14 also is Little Malvern Court, the prior's lodging of the priory. This has a spere-truss and a roof with trefoils in the top triangles of the trusses. Cofton Hall and originally the Commandery at Worcester have (or had) hammerbeam roofs. Other roofs of interest are in the rectory at Martley (*c.*1300) and Tickenhill Manor, Bewdley (C15).

As *ensembles*, the Commandery and the Greyfriars are the most interesting. The Commandery was a hospital, the Greyfriars is really the guesthouse of the Franciscan establishment. The hall
51 in the Commandery has a timber-framed oriel window and an upper room with painting to which we shall return in a moment. The Greyfriars has a lower and an upper hall, the latter with a twelve-light window. The whole façade is 69 ft long and has two cross-gables at the ends, the l. one above an archway which leads into a small courtyard.

The earliest dated example of the kind of ornamentation which characterizes the last stage of timber architecture is the former Hop Pole Inn at Bromsgrove. The date is 1572, quite an early date for its concave-sided lozenges and its fleurs-de-lis.* The most complete and finest timber-framed Elizabethan manor
54 houses are perhaps Mere Hall Hanbury of *c.*1560 and Dowles Manor House outside Bewdley, the latest – and this is indeed a surprisingly late date – is Fairfield House, dated 1669. But this is anticipating, and we must return to the C14 and C15.

STONE HOUSES of before the C16 are very rare. There are in fact only the fine C14 Abbot's Grange at Broadway with hall, solar, and the three doorways to the former kitchen, buttery, and pantry, Prior's Manse, also at Broadway, with just one original doorway, Grange Farm House at Bretforton, with a tunnel-vaulted undercroft with transverse arches, and the Bishop's Palace at Worcester which, though it appears early C18 from the

* It must however be noted that in a wall painting of *c.*1500 at Molesworth in Huntingdonshire a timber-framed house appears in the background with concave-sided lozenges.

street, contains the great hall and extensive rib-vaulted under-
crofts of the late C13. CASTLES, it is strange to report, do not
exist at all, except for the C14 tower of Holt Castle. The hall and
solar behind it are a C15 addition.*

The interest in, and quality of, late medieval domestic archi-
tecture is matched by the interest and quality of FUNERARY pp.
MONUMENTS. The best are either of brass (Strensham † 1390, 274, 205,
Strensham † 1405, Kidderminster † 1415, Fladbury † 1445) or of 155.
alabaster (Bromsgrove † 1450, Martley c.1460, Stanford-on-Teme 42
† 1493). Their dress helps to date them. But the finest monuments
by far are both sculpture and architecture: the late C15 monu-
ment to a lady in Kidderminster parish church and – in a class 43
of its own – Prince Arthur's Chantry in Worcester Cathedral. 44
This was begun in 1504 and has high walls with windows and
panelling, a large number of statuettes, many of them unmutilated
by the iconoclasts, a lierne-vault inside, and a very rich reredos,
but no effigy on the tomb-chest.‡

This is the one major piece of Late Perp enrichment in the
cathedral. One has to go to Malvern to see first-class CHURCH
FURNISHINGS of the C15 and early C16. For STAINED GLASS
and tiles Malvern is among the most important churches in
England. The glass, considering its date of c.1460 to c.1500, is 46
more complete than anywhere else in the country, and its quality
is high, though C15 glass nowhere achieves, or aims at, the jewel-
like colour of the C13 and the intensity of emotion of the early
C14. It is all rather cooler and more matter-of-fact, and scenes
from the lives of Christ or Saints suffer from being hard to make
out. But the totality of enclosure in pictures remains.§ The
TILES of Malvern are entirely without English parallel. Some p.
twelve hundred have been counted of about ninety patterns. 164
They include, against the back wall of the stone choir screen walls,
the only wall tiles in England. The patterns are attractive – shields,
letters, ornamental motifs – and very many parish churches have
them as well. Malvern has STALLS too, with MISERICORDS. In
the latter respect Worcestershire is lucky. The set of 1379 in the
cathedral and the C15 set at Ripple are among the best we have.
At Ripple the Labours of the Months are paramount among the 47

* Dudley Castle has recently been transferred to Staffordshire.

‡ The delightful canopy with a fortified city in the cathedral comes from 45
the pulpit.

§ Little Malvern Priory has much glass of the same period too. Otherwise what has remained is mostly bits and pieces, though more than can be counted.

scenes represented. For PAINTING there is one remarkable survival, but not in a church: it is the room in the Commandery at Worcester which has religious paintings of *c.*1500, including the Trinity which is painted on the ceiling. SCREENS are on the whole minor. Worcester Cathedral has one of stone, not outstanding, and those of wood in the county are mostly of one-light divisions. Shelsley Walsh and Little Malvern have kept the rood beam or part of it, and Besford the rood-loft parapet. At Pershore is a handsome stone REREDOS, and that is all.

Take in the ELIZABETHAN AND JACOBEAN AGE, and you will not get more – with two exceptions. One is CHURCH PLATE. There, of before the Reformation hardly anything has survived: apart from the C13 paten already mentioned, only a C15 bronze Censer at Ripple and two Patens of *c.*1500, at Cofton Hackett and Great Witley. Then the Reformation and the struggles which followed led to a total stop in the purchasing or giving of plate. So much was destroyed moreover that, when the Elizabethan Settlement finally came, the need for new plate, especially a cup and a cover paten, was so great that the makers for a few years enjoyed the boom of all time. Here are the figures.* 'Mid-C16'
59 one, 'Elizabethan' one, 1570 eight, 1571 sixty-three (ten of them doubtful), 1572 one, 1573 one, 1576 two (one doubtful), 1577 three, 1578 one. Of the pieces of 1571 seventeen are signed *H. W.* The other lavish pieces are PULPITS, again understandable in Elizabethan, Jacobean, and especially Laudian England. Many average ones survive, with the usual squat blank arches and with panels with arabesques, or flowers, or dragons, or just lozenges. Naunton Beauchamp still has linenfold side by side with loose leaf panels and is therefore probably mid-century. Broadway, Cow Honeybourne, Kidderminster (Unitarian Chapel), and Ipsley are the most sumptuous. Stoke Bliss is dated 1631, Broadway 1632. These are Laudian dates, though the style is still purely Jacobean, and the COMMUNION RAIL at Castlemorton still has the Jacobean motif of flat openwork balusters and yet the dates on it are 1683 and 1684.

This conservatism applies not only to a Jacobean survival, but even more to a Gothic survival. Here is a list of the few CHURCHES AND CHAPELS of the late C16 and the C17: the Sheldon Chapel at Beoley of the late C16 with the elementarized Perp of its E window, the Berkeley Chapel of 1614 and much else at Spetchley, the chancel at Ashton-under-Hill of 1624 with its Perp intention

* A cup counts one, a paten counts one, but a cup with paten also count one.

and incorrect, quite entertaining execution, and the still Perp
work of 1674 on central tower, chancel, and N chapel at Hanley
Castle. The material here is brick, but BRICK had of course ap-
peared in the county much earlier, e.g. at Warndon Farm and
in the chimneystack of Huddington Court before 1500. 53

Take DOMESTIC ARCHITECTURE of between 1540 and 1620,
and you will find that brick is perfectly at home by the mid C16.
Examples are The Nash Kempsey of *c.*1540–50, Madresfield
Court of *c.*1546–93, and Grafton Manor of 1567. All three have
crow-stepped gables. The porch and the parlour window of 55
Grafton Manor are among the best things of that moment in
England, of an interest in classical motifs which grew less when
the Elizabethan style had developed into something more of its
own, and when the influence from the Netherlands had got a
firmer hold on England. Worcestershire has only one major
country house of that time, Westwood Park, with its compact 67
Jacobean core of the Chastleton type and its unique four wings
attached radially to the corners about 1660–70, yet still detailed
in the Jacobean tradition. The house has an ornate porch and a
delightful gatehouse. Westwood Park is of brick, the other best
Jacobean houses are of oolitic limestone, i.e. they are in the
Cotswolds or near by. They are the Lygon Arms at Broadway,
and Woollas Hall, Eckington, at the foot of Bredon Hill. Both
have asymmetrical façades, that of the Lygon Arms more
convincingly composed. Woollas Hall has its hall screen and a
wooden chimneypiece. There are many chimneypieces of this
age in houses: Dormston Manor; St Peter's Manor Droitwich;
Hanbury Hall from Tickenhill Manor, Bewdley; The Nash 58
Kempsey; Madresfield; and – specially gorgeous – Westwood
Park. The Nash at Kempsey also has two charming plaster ceil-
ings with chains of ogee reticulation units. Other Elizabethan and
Jacobean plasterwork is at the Lygon Arms Broadway (*c.*1620)
and, quite modest, in Portershill North Claines, Pirton, and a
house at Friar Street, Worcester. A ceiling painted with a straw-
berry pattern is at No. 32 Friar Street. Elizabethan wall paintings
survive at Dowles Manor House and in greater profusion at p.
Harvington Hall, an informal, very picturesque Elizabethan 193
brick house. The paintings are of *c.*1570, and some of them are
extremely elegantly drawn, with nothing of the usual English
coarseness.

This comparative scarcity of Elizabethan and Jacobean houses
of consequence is in contrast to the wealth of FUNERARY MONU-
MENTS. They illustrate all phases, all types, and all moods,

starting with an alabaster monument at Bromsgrove of *c.*1550,
where no Renaissance features are introduced yet, and continuing
56 with the date of death 1561 in a tablet at Bengeworth, where we
find the characteristic elegant Renaissance details which were
later as a rule either coarsened or anyway overlaid with Nether-
landish strapwork, caryatids, and the like. The tablet at Broms-
grove has no figures at all, not even an effigy. Of the same year of
death, 1561, is a Blount monument at Mamble, where the effigy –
a rare case in the Elizabethan Age – is replaced by a skeleton.
Another Blount monument, again of the same year of death, at
57 Astley shows the way from the Early Elizabethan classicism to
the more rigid, more Mannerist stylization which is one trend
of the mature Elizabethan style. That style in its full panoply
is represented e.g. by the Freake Monument at Worcester
Cathedral, † 1591, which has incidentally the rare distinction of a
signature, though we do not know who *Anthony Tolly* was. The
tomb-chest and back arch here are standard elements. In many
of the more lavish Worcestershire monuments they are combined
with columns l. and r. and a top cornice with shields, obelisks,
or the like. Examples are two Sheldons † 1570 and 1613 at
Beoley, and – one of the finest – the double tomb of two gener-
61 ations of Sandys at Wickhamford with the date of death 1626.
The type goes on till after 1632, see the Russell Monument at
Strensham, † 1632. The material here is alabaster, and as a rule
alabaster produced the best results. That is clearly shown in a
comparison of the clumsy wooden monuments to members of the
Walsh family at Stockton-on-Teme † 1593 and at Shelsley
Walsh † 1596 with the later Washbourne Monument at Wichen-
ford of 1632, or also of the stone monument of 1594 at Bockleton
with the alabaster tomb-chest with effigies at Malvern † 1589, or
the perfect Berkeley Monument † 1611 at Spetchley, or the
equally perfect Reed Monument † 1611 at Bredon, or the Savage
62 Monuments † 1631 at Elmley Castle and at Inkberrow. The latter
monument has a detail which deserves to be noted: the underside
of the canopy is decorated with cusped quatrefoils – a case of
Gothic Revival rather than Survival. The same is true of the
underside of the canopy at Wickhamford († 1626) and of the low
wooden rail round the alabaster effigy at Besford († 1576), where
the motif is the reticulation unit. Besford also has a memorable
Late Elizabethan monument, that to another member of the
Harewell family, which is a painted triptych with a kneeling figure
and surrounding it religious and allegorical scenes and inscrip-
tions. Kneeling effigies seen in profile are one of the standard

types of Elizabethan and Jacobean funerary art. There are many of them in the county. If two are to be singled out, they may be the Hanford Monument at Eckington († 1616), quite possibly by *Epiphanius Evesham*, and the Moore Monument in Worcester Cathedral († 1613), where three men kneel in the front and three women behind them and the recess has been given a fan-vault with pendants – another case of chosen Gothicism.*

The latest dates of death so far referred to are 1631 at Elmley Castle and Inkberrow and 1632 at Strensham and Wichenford.
But of † 1631 also is the tablet to Humfrey Pakington at 63
Chaddesley Corbett, and that has (once again) no figures at all and is entirely classical in its elements. The same is true of tablets of † 1633 at Bushley and † 1639 at Ribbesford. So the Inigo Jones revolution, or, if you like, the CAROLEAN STYLE, had reached Worcestershire comparatively early.

In DOMESTIC ARCHITECTURE it came much later. Gabled stone houses went on for a long time. A monumental example is Tudor House at Broadway of 1660, which, as against the Lygon Arms, is symmetrical, or nearly so. Also, though it still has mullioned windows, it has replaced the traditional individual hood-moulds of the windows by drip-courses running through. In dated small houses one can watch these changes as follows. A house in Broadway dated 1687 still has mullioned windows and gables. Houses at Conderton, Beckford of 1675 and Barnt Green of 1678 still have mullioned windows but a symmetrical arrangement, and this is so in cottages at Broadway even as amazingly late as 1718 and 1722. On the other hand, in Childswickham House of 1698 the windows, of course also symmetrically arranged, have mullion and transom crosses, and that can be regarded as the late C17 standard. They usually come with hipped roof and represent the final turn from the informal to the formal.

The gables so far referred to have been straight-sided or stepped. But shaped gables also appear, though surprisingly late.
At Westwood Park they are of after 1660, and so they seem to be 67
at Bell End Farmhouse Belbroughton, at the Great House Knighton, at The Grove Stoke Bliss, and a house at Stockton-on-Teme. The first Dutch gable, i.e. shaped gable with a pediment on top, is at Severn End, Hanley Castle. The date is 1673, i.e. some forty years after its introduction to London.

* In Worcestershire as against other counties these monuments with kneelers were specially favoured about 1610–20: Badsey † 1617, Cropthorne 1646 (an
exception), Hanbury † 1627, Leigh † 1615, Leigh † 1639, Norton † 1613 (this 60
also could be by *Evesham*), Salwarpe † 1613, All Saints Worcester † 1621.

Altogether Worcestershire was conservative. Take the splen-
68 did, high, and symmetrical Foley Hospital at Old Swinford. It was founded in 1670, six years before Wren began Trinity Library, and yet still has straight-sided gables. The elaborate portal has the capricious details characteristic of work away from court and nobility in the fifties and sixties, the kind of details now usually called Artisan Mannerism. You have to go to the porch
69 which leads into the great hall of the Bishops' Palace at Hartlebury which was built in about 1680 and also to the Berkeley Hospital at Worcester, founded in 1697, to get on to the Jones–Pratt–May–Wren style, or to Dresden House, Evesham of 1692 with its symmetrical classical fenestration, its hipped roof, and its restraint in all decoration (except for the gloriously over-sized iron brackets l. and r. of the doorway). Interior work of this new style is the staircase at Westwood Park rising straight up to the upper floor in two parts with an intermediate landing between
71 and the splendid plaster ceiling in the upper hall. Staircase and stucco must be work of *c.* 1675–80 and are not at all retarded, though the radial wings to which reference has already been made were still entirely pre-classical.

In FUNERARY MONUMENTS, as we have seen, the change towards the classical ideal came in the 1630s, not in the 1680s and 1690s. What happens in the last two-thirds of the century is that certain monuments stay classical and shed what had still been impure in the thirties, while others go Baroque. The former trend is best illustrated by three memorials to bishops of Worcester, all entirely architectural, without any figures and with hardly any ornamental details. The dates of death are 1675, 1683, 1689. On the other hand the road to the Baroque was opened with greater pomp and circumstance than nearly anywhere in England with
64 the monument to the first Lord Coventry at Croome d'Abitot. He died in 1639, and if this was indeed made shortly after his death, it is the ancestor of the most frequent and characteristic type of monumental memorial about 1700, that with the effigy semi-reclining and standing or seated figures l. and r., or, to make it more Baroque, on only one side. *Grinling Gibbons*'s Coventry Monument of 1690 also at Croome belongs to the type, and the figures are dull, as so much of Gibbons's figure work is.* Other
65 semi-reclining effigies are at Elmley Castle (the first Earl of Coventry, made *c.*1700–5 for Croome) by *William Stanton*, where again two large figures stand l. and r., at Strensham † 1705 by

* Another monument by him, at Clifton-on-Teme † 1688, is good in the garlands, but not specially interesting otherwise.

Edward Stanton, where the wife of the deceased sits at his head, at Bengeworth † 1709, and so on, right into the Georgian years, with monuments with semi-reclining effigies at Hanbury † 1722 83
by *Edward Stanton* and *C. Horsnaile*, where Justice sits at Thomas Vernon's feet, and Hampton Lovett † 1727, by *Joseph Rose*.

Other types of monuments need only a passing reference. One major tablet at Croome d'Abitot, to be attributed confidently to *Kidwell*, has large, white caryatids l. and r., and the date of death is 1686. The monument to Olave and Elizabeth Talbot † 1681 66
and † 1689 at Salwarpe has no effigy but two charity girls against the tomb-chest. Smaller tablets often have twisted columns – they start already in one with the date of death 1650, at Clent – or a gristly cartouche surround (Peopleton † 1682), or columns with pediments, sometimes open and curly, and garlands of the Gibbons type. The major standing monuments – and of course already some of the first half of the C17 too – are of a size and especially height beyond anything medieval – except for Prince Arthur's Chantry – and, as they were placed in the parish churches belonging to the estates, they tend to choke the buildings.

For it was rare for the CHURCHES to be built with a view to the monuments. One such case in the EIGHTEENTH CENTURY is Great Witley, where *Rysbrack*'s spectacular monument to the first Lord Foley stands at the right distance and with the right unobstructed view in the chapel of his house, a chapel of large parish church size. It is not known who designed it – maybe it was *Gibbs*. It was consecrated in 1735 and has a quiet, restrained exterior, but a gloriously Baroque interior, thanks to *Bellucci*'s 78&
ceiling paintings, *Joshua Price*'s stained glass, and the gold on 79
white papier-mâché decoration. Paintings and glass were bought when princely Chandos' Canons was sold up in 1747, and the decoration was probably moulded from the decoration there. The result is the most Italian and most Baroque church interior in England. Great Witley has a W tower and arched windows. That is the same with the four parish churches which Worcester built between 1730 and 1770. They are externally all of the same type, though St Nicholas by *Hollins*, 1730–5, and St Swithun by the 75
Woodwards of Chipping Campden, 1734–6, have no aisles, and All Saints, probably by *R. Squire*, 1739–42, and St Martin by 77
Anthony Keck, 1768–72, have aisles, the former with Tuscan columns and a segmental plaster tunnel-vault, the latter with unfluted Ionic columns, each with a piece of entablature, and a flat ceiling. The towers of All Saints and St Swithun are Perp, and in 1751 the Perp tower of St Andrew received a new spire with a

Corinthian capital instead of a finial. St Nicholas has an ambitious
façade towards the main street of Worcester, St Swithun, All
Saints, and St Martin have fully developed E façades. In the
villages and small towns there are more Georgian churches, all
simple rectangles in plan and all with round-arched windows and
W towers. In chronological order they are as follows: Stourbridge
76 1728-36, with Tuscan columns and an odd panelled vault, Smeth-
wick (Birmingham suburbs) 1728, much more modest, Bewdley
81 1745–8, by *Thomas Woodward*, with Tuscan columns and a
plaster tunnel-vault, Upton-on-Severn 1756–7, of which only a
80 small fragment and the stately tower remain. The tower with its
octagonal top stage and cap by *Keck*, 1769–70, is a fine and
unexpected landmark. Croome d'Abitot 1763, perhaps by
Lancelot Brown, is of great architectural interest far beyond county
concerns, not so much because of its Gothick interior, delightful
as this is, but because of the archeological exactitude of its ex-
terior, which might well deceive the casual passer-by. The atti-
tude is one which comes in as a rule only gradually in the 1820s.
Of 1768–9 is Stanford-on-Teme by *James Rose*, where the tracery
is, in contrast to Croome, of the usual Y and intersecting varieties
which were the favourite of the Georgians, before archeological
interest made itself felt. 1772 is the date of Wolverley, also by an
unknown architect and the complete contrast to Croome. This is
frankly Georgian, and in spite of substantial size unashamedly
utilitarian: red brick, arched windows, a square W tower, and
plain arches also in the arcades between nave and aisles – not an
attractive but a convinced, determined building – proto-Brutalism,
as it were. *F. Hiorn* in 1777, and now in contrast to Wolverley,
gave Tardebigge a decidely Baroque steeple. Hanbury of 1793
has pointed windows and windows with Y-tracery. After that
there is nothing of note till the 1820s.

The NONCONFORMIST denominations had made a good appearance with the Presbyterian church at Bewdley of *c.*1680, with its two apsed ends. The same theme was taken up in the chapel of the Countess of Huntingdon's Connexion at Worcester, which is of 1804 and 1815. The Unitarian Chapel at Evesham of 1737 has an ashlar-faced front, with giant pilasters, the Presbyterian church at Stourbridge of 1788 a plain three-bay front with a three-bay pediment such as was going to be early C19 standard. No other early Nonconformist chapels need be recorded here.

For CHURCH FURNISHINGS, few churches can be so complete and so pretty as St Swithun at Worcester, though the pulpit and

the font at Croome d'Abitot are individually as fine as any. 86
Robert Adam himself had to do with the interior of the church. The furnishings of Great Witley have already been discussed. That leaves nothing of special interest except the wrought-iron altar-table with marble top at Birtsmorton and the wrought-iron sword rests in All Saints and St Swithun at Worcester. 82

MONUMENTS on the other hand are plentiful. *Rysbrack*'s enormous Lord Foley of before 1743 at Great Witley must be number
one, though *Roubiliac*'s Bishop Hough of 1746 in Worcester 84
Cathedral is as fine in quality and more sophisticated in composition. Everything here is Rococo in the sense not so much of ornament as of subtly calculated asymmetry, resulting in a general zigzag movement through the whole monument. The other *Roubiliacs* in Worcestershire are less sensational, one at Hanbury, the other at Hagley, designed by *Sir Charles Frederick*. The first Rococo, i.e. asymmetrical, cartouche, incidentally, is as early as 1718 (date of death) in a monument at Birtsmorton with semi-reclining effigy. Bishop Hough is reclining no longer; he is seen rising, or drawn up, to the higher spheres. *Prince Hoare*'s Bishop Maddox † 1759 was no doubt made in opposition to Roubiliac. The large female figure is decently draped and phlegmatic. Of sculptors of the late C18 and the early years of the C19, *Wilton* is represented by an exquisite Adamish monument in Worcester Cathedral of *c.*1775–80, *Nollekens* by two monuments with the busts in which he excelled, one † 1774 in Worcester Cathedral, designed by *Adam*, the other † 1797 at Ombersley. *Thomas Scheemakers* has an extremely good monument at Powick († 1786), and *John Bacon* a beautiful piece with Benevolence and Sensibility by an urn at Astley († 1793). His earlier work in St Swithun at Worcester is not memorable, his later one in the cathedral († 1803) again very delicate. Bacon was also the chief designer for Mrs *Coade*'s factory of moulded sculpture in artificial stone, and the two reliefs of Agriculture and Navigation, dated 1788, on the gatepiers of the former Perdiswell Hall outside Worcester have all the characteristics of his elegant, somewhat florid style of drapery. *Thomas Banks* was a heavyweight,
compared with Bacon, and his monument at Halesowen of 1797 91
shows that. *Bacon Jun.* has two tablets † 1801 and 1806 at Astley and one ambitious monument in the cathedral which is the type of the memorials in St Paul's Cathedral to those killed in the Napoleonic wars. Sir Henry Ellis in fact fell at Waterloo. The two *Flaxmans* (Wolverley † 1801, Broome † 1804) are not outstanding. *Westmacott*'s more intimate approach is demonstrated

in the fine figure of a resting pilgrim on a tablet in Malvern Priory (*c.*1830). *Chantrey* ends this chapter. His white seated or kneeling female figures in profile, in relief, or in the round, pure and classical and at the same time sentimental, can be seen in the cathedral (1825), at Tardebigge (1835), and at Hanbury (1837). *Peter Hollins*'s monuments at Malvern († 1811 and † 1836) are in the same mood. Hollins worked at Birmingham. The local Worcester monumental carvers were *William Stephens* (born 1737), his son *Joseph Stephens the Elder* (born 1773), and his grandson *Joseph Stephens the Younger* (born 1808), and they could do very good work (e.g. Kempsey † 1790 by William). *Thomas White* (*c.*1675-1748) was a Worcester man too. His tablets are not up to much, but he was important as an architect. *Richard Squire* (1700–86), whom we have found as the probable designer of All Saints, Worcester, made monuments as well. The *Ricketts* family worked at Gloucester, the *King* family at Bath.

EIGHTEENTH CENTURY HOUSES in Worcestershire are a large chapter. With the porch of Hartlebury Castle, Dresden House, Evesham, and the Berkeley Hospital the Wren style had
70 established itself. Hanbury Hall of 1701 is the finest example of it in the county. The stone decoration of the centre makes it likely that *Talman* was the designer. The paintings inside are *Thornhill*'s,
72 an early job of his. They are on the whole better than those of Verrio and Laguerre, the favourites of court and nobility. There is also original plasterwork (and an outstanding overmantel of *c.*1750). The rather more Baroque, i.e. less restrained, style of the Smiths of Warwick and others working in the same vein in the West Country is represented by Ombersley Court of 1723–6, a work of *Francis Smith*, and by a number of anonymous houses, some quite ambitious, such as Tutnall Hall Tardebigge, Overbury Court, and the Bishop's Palace at Worcester. Overbury Court also has a grand entrance hall and three beautifully panelled rooms. Far more exuberant is what *Thomas White* did (or probably did) at Worcester, the spectacular and a little over-
73& done Guildhall of 1721–3 and Britannia House of *c.*1725 (Ottley
74 School) with his seated Britannia in the raised centre of the parapet. Apsidal hoods over doorways with carved decoration are a Queen Anne fashion. The White House at Suckley has a specially pretty one. Typical of Early Georgian houses is the segment-headed window. Two houses on the river bank at Upton-on-Severn have them, one in conjunction with a Gibbs surround to the doorway (a motif also surviving from the former church at Upton, which, as we have seen, dated from 1756–7), the other

with a Venetian window which is a mid-C18 motif in Worcestershire too, as we shall see presently.

Palladianism, including an Inigo Jones revival, started in London already in 1715–20. It reached Worcestershire late. The paramount examples are Croome Court of 1751–2 by *Lancelot Brown* or *Sanderson Miller* and Hagley Hall of 1754–60 by 87
Sanderson Miller, both chaste and correct, and both with the corner erections with pyramid roofs which Inigo Jones had introduced at Wilton and Kent had taken up at Holkham. It is curious that these two most purely architectural houses should be by a garden designer and by the Gothick specialist in the county. On the other hand both indeed have more PARK FURNISHINGS than any other, though the Picturesque in layouts and sentimental buildings had been introduced a little earlier in Shenstone the poet's The Leasowes Halesowen. Not much survives either of the house or of the garden furnishings. At Hagley the most important pieces are the Castle by *Sanderson Miller*, be- 89
gun in 1747, and the Temple of Theseus by *James Stuart* of 1758, the first reproduction of a Greek Doric temple front in all Europe. Stuart and Nicholas Revett had been in Athens in 1751–5, but their *Antiquities of Athens* did not begin to appear until 1762. Sanderson Miller's first efforts at a medieval revival belong to Edgehill in Warwickshire, his own estate, and the years 1744–5. Hagley also has a rotunda. Croome d'Abitot has a rotunda by *Adam* called the Panorama Tower and other garden temples by him (he worked for Croome from 1760) and by others, a second rotunda, a grotto, Dunstall Castle, which looks very much like Miller's, and other minor follies. All this belongs to the years of the sixth earl, who also built Broadway Tower in 1800, a nine- 90
cornered folly tower with three turrets. The Fish Inn on Broadway Hill was a summer house belonging to another estate; it is classical in an entirely playful way and must be earlier than the tower. Another tower, Leicester Tower, is in the grounds of Abbey Manor, Evesham. Castle Bourne, Belbroughton has a ruined castle with two towers, Pull Court, Bushley a smaller artificial ruin.

Of the motifs of Croome and Hagley, the one which became most popular in Worcestershire is the Venetian window. It was used not, as in the Palladian mansions, as a rare, significant accent, but all over façades, just to make them more ornate. A typical case in a town is No. 61 Broad Street at Worcester, one bay wide, four storeys high, with nothing but Venetian windows and, incidentally, on the top a (later?) domed little belvedere with

pointed windows. Another, on a smaller scale, is Perrott House, Pershore. This has very fine plasterwork inside which may well have been designed by *Adam*, who was busy for Croome Court at the same time. In Croome Court not much of original interiors
88 is preserved, but Hagley has a series of extremely fine ones.

An amusing and historically telling variation on the theme of the Venetian window is the Gothick Venetian window, i.e. the tripartite window whose raised arched middle part is given an ogee arch. Often this motif is accompanied by ogee gables or a parapet treated as ogee gables. The examples are a house at Bromsgrove, Broome House N of Bromsgrove, a house at Stourbridge, a house in Arch Hill Square at Kidderminster, Tudor House at Chaddesley Corbett, Pool House at Astley, and the refronting of the E side of an early C18 house at Worcester (now the Department of Health). Unfortunately not one of these houses is dated. About 1770 is likely.

Georgian houses with less to distinguish them are to be found in all towns and in the country. Worcester still has a few streets where they easily dominate, and the five-bay brick houses in the county can hardly be counted and are not even all included in the gazetteer. The best Georgian ensembles in the county are Bewdley and Stourport, the first with its bridge, waterside
3 street, and the short Load Street running straight to the church, the second built in the place where the Staffordshire and Worcestershire or Trent and Severn Canal reached the Severn, once a port with warehouses and now a boating centre. Which ought to be called the finest villages of Worcestershire will always remain a matter of personal choice. Everybody will have Broadway among its first three, with an exceptionally long main street and hardly anything out of place – in fact some say: too little that is out of place, or at least too little that is left alone. Other villages which rank high are Ombersley and Chaddesley Corbett, both with main streets too, Overbury and Cropthorne with a more complex structure, and the curious Wolverley with the church on a steep hill and the little square down below dominated by the
93 Gothic and oddly monumental Sebright School of 1829.

The Sebright School is a reminder that PUBLIC BUILDINGS have so far been neglected. Nothing but the Worcester Guildhall and the almshouses at Old Swinford near Stourbridge have been mentioned. The C18 and early C19 saw quite a number go up: the pedimented brick Infirmary at Worcester by *Keck*, 1767–70, and the brick House of Industry also at Worcester, by *Byfield*, 1793–4 (who in 1791 had designed the handsome new assembly

room in the Guildhall), forerunner of the later workhouses (1838
at Martley and Bromsgrove, both also brick, and both still class-
ical), the small towns halls of Bewdley, 1808, and Upton-on-
Severn, 1832, both undetached terrace houses, and then the fine
Grecian ashlar-faced Shire Hall at Worcester by *Charles Day* and
Henry Rowe of 1834–5. In domestic architecture Grecian purity
had been preceded by the beautiful ashlar-faced Spetchley Park, 92
begun in 1811 and designed by the little known *John Tasker*, and
by Strensham Court of 1824. Public buildings also the BRIDGES
must be called. *Telford*'s Bewdley Bridge of 1795–8 is still stone
and of Georgian classicity, while his bridges of Bushley, Holt,
Powick, and Smethwick are iron (1826–37), and with the use of 95
iron for such purposes we are on the way into the VICTORIAN
AGE.

Victorian CHURCHES must be taken first. Here the stylistic
development is most easily recognized and most fully documented. The classical Georgian churches were first replaced by
the type of rather pinched Gothic which is usually called the Commissioners' type and which is characterized by aisleless buildings
with galleries, short chancels, rather thin W towers, and high
and thin windows, separated by thin buttresses. *H. Eginton*,
a local architect, built this kind of church (Catshill 1838, St
Michael Broadway, his best work, 1839,* Trimpley 1844), and
Blore's Bushley of 1843 as well as *Thomas Rickman*'s Catholic
Our Lady at Redditch of 1834 also belong here. But Rickman was
largely responsible for the acquisition of a greater degree of
archeological scholarship and its application to church design.
His Ombersley of 1825–9 and Hartlebury of 1825 etc. show this. 94
But earlier than these is the amazingly accurate and substantial
St George at Kidderminster by *Francis Goodwin*, built as early
as 1821–4. Equally amazing is the seriousness and Perp exactitude of the little-known *Thomas Jones* in his church at Pensax of
1832–3.

The Catholics could now begin to build on a larger scale. St
George at Worcester is one example, Rickman's Our Lady another, *Charles Hansom*'s quite lavish, not at all starved church at
Hanley Swan of 1846 a third.

The Nonconformists kept for a long time to their Georgian
type in order not to appear churchy. Their big mid-century
chapels turned Italianate, and a variety of Italianate chapels
from simplicity to Baroque lavishness can be seen well at

* But the vault must be later.

Smethwick and Oldbury. But chapels looking exactly like churches are characteristic only of the last third of the century. The change takes place in Worcester between the Congregational Church of 1858 and the Baptist Church of 1863–4.

Where the Church of England for some reason did not want to go Gothic, they had patent reasons not to be Italian, and so for a short time they chose Norman. The great fashion for Norman was in the forties, but St Clement at Worcester is an example of neo-Norman as early as 1822–3. Its architect, *Thomas Lee Jun.*, must have been one of the first in the whole of England to make that choice. Or was the design by the otherwise unknown *Thomas Ingleman*?

The change from Commissioners' Gothic to a fully understood, archeologically correct Gothic is connected with the name of *A. W. N. Pugin.* Worcestershire has no church by him, only the very modest school at Spetchley of 1841. Pugin regarded Perp, until then the most usual phase to be imitated, as debased, and pleaded for what his Church of England supporters, the Ecclesiologists, called Second Pointed or Middle Pointed, i.e. the style of the late C13 and the early C14, from geometrical to freer but not yet flowing tracery. Among those whom Pugin convinced at once was (Sir) *George Gilbert Scott.* From about 1841 he designed in a competent Second Pointed. In Worcestershire his principal work is the – terribly drastic – restoration of Worcester Cathedral, taken over from *Perkins.* The only original church of his is the late Stourport parish church, designed in 1875 and built by his son, *John Oldrid Scott.*

In contrast to those who wanted to build convincingly-medieval churches are those who refused to give up their own personalities and believed in the possibility of a Gothic at once ancient and modern. *William Butterfield* was the leader in that trend. His Alvechurch of 1859–61 and his Sedgeberrow of 1867–8 are typical of his style and his idiosyncrasies, especially in their interiors. *Henry Woodyer* also belongs here. His St Michael's College at Tenbury of 1856 etc. with its crazily steep dormers, and even the roofs of the large, much quieter church to go with the college, are proof of that. His St Stephen Redditch of 1854–5 is less interesting. An example of this trend at its most intransigent is the elder *Bidlake*'s group of church, school, and parsonage at Stourbridge of 1860, all done in engineering bricks.

The leading Victorian architects, other than Scott and Butterfield, are less well or not at all represented in Worcestershire. *G. E. Street* did quite a lot, e.g. the large, restrained parish church of Hagley in 1858–65, but only his St Peter Great Malvern of 1863–6 shows the hard and bold style of his early and most personal years. *Arthur Blomfield*'s Upton-on-Severn of 1878–9 is large and competent and has a fine steeple.

Local architects played a much greater part in the C19 than they have a chance to play now. Eginton has already been mentioned. Others are *F. Preedy* (buildings with dates of 1856–86), *William J. Hopkins* (1820/1–1901), and *Henry Rowe Jun.* (buildings 1876–1909).

The last quarter of the century is characterized by greater refinement, but also greater licence. It is the time on the one hand of William Morris and of Bodley and Pearson – not represented in Worcestershire churches – on the other of the Arts and Crafts and of, say, Sedding. The first of the two directions is indicated in the county by *A. E. Street*'s church of 1892 at Smethwick (Birmingham suburbs), *Temple Moore*'s addition to St Stephen at Redditch of 1893–4, *Comper*'s early Holy Name at Malvern Link of 1893, with its complete furnishings, and *W. H. Bidlake*'s tower of Wythall church, which is of 1903. A thorough job of 101
Arts and Crafts furnishing, all by minor Birmingham craftsmen, is the private chapel of Madresfield Court of 1902. Church architecture at its best at the moment before abandoning historicism is (Sir) *Aston Webb*'s large St George at Worcester of 1893–5, Gothic, but not imitated from any one building or phase of style (he had built the fine outer N aisle at North Claines already in 1886–7), also *G. H. Fellowes Prynne*'s new St Martin at Worcester of 1903–11, and emphatically *Arthur Bartlett*'s Dodford of 1907–8, with its excellent Arts and Crafts detail, especially the round transept window, and its delightful composition round a small courtyard. The only TWENTIETH CENTURY church later than these which may here be referred to is *Denys Hinton*'s St Paul Smethwick of 1965–6, with its clever use of the ruin of its predecessor.

On VICTORIAN CHURCH FURNISHING little need be said. Worcester Cathedral has plenty, most of it done to *Scott*'s designs. His sculptors were *James Forsyth** of Worcester and *R. L. Boulton* of Cheltenham.‡ They appear in churches in the county as well. High Victorian reredoses with figures in relief and mosaic, High Victorian round stone pulpits, and High Victorian

* His brother *William Forsyth* moved to Worcester in 1875 and worked in and around the town as well.

‡ There were quite a number of other members of the *Boulton* family in the sculpture business.

metal screens are easily recognized. But the chief High Victorian contribution is STAINED GLASS. Much is by *Hardman* of Birmingham, much by others including *Capronnier* of Brussels (1870, 1871, 1882), whose work shows how superior average English Victorian work was to average Continental. The best glass of the sixties is a window by *Lavers & Barraud* of 1862 in Worcester Cathedral, severely and quite personally stylized, and *William Morris*'s glass of *c.*1863 at Rochford. He and *Burne-Jones* also did glass of 1875 at Ribbesford, and the whole of Wilden church, thanks to Arthur Baldwin, has Morris glass, a unique case, though all done from earlier designs after Morris's and Burne-Jones's deaths. It need hardly be said that it is more convincing than anybody else's.

The Baldwins were steel magnates in Worcestershire, and it is characteristic that industrial riches now begin to be reflected in large mansions. The showiest of them all in the county, Château
100 Impney outside Droitwich of 1869–75, was built for John Corbett of the Stoke Prior salt works who developed Droitwich into the resort it became. Not that the nobility stayed behind in commissioning large houses: Witley Court was rebuilt for Lord Ward, Madresfield Court for Earl Beauchamp, Hewell Grange Tardebigge for the Earl of Plymouth.

But an account of SECULAR VICTORIAN ARCHITECTURE must begin with the spread of Worcester in the early C19. Britannia Square, begun *c.*1820, Lansdowne Crescent, Lark Hill, St George's Square are places where white stuccoed or red brick so-called Regency houses, often semi-detached, were put up. A little later, thanks to canal and railway, industry began to fill the area of Shrub Hill. The red and yellow brick factories, classical to Italianate, but of course essentially utilitarian, date from *c.*1850. Commercial buildings are not very prominent at Worcester, but some are very fine, first and foremost *Elmslie*'s Lloyds Bank of 1861–2, Italian Renaissance handled with great *finesse*.*

It is odd that the same *Elmslie* should have been responsible both for the railway station and for the two big Gothic hotels of Great Malvern, the Imperial Hotel and the Link Hotel, of 1860–62; the first is now converted into the Girls' College, and the second is no longer a hotel either. Malvern had started its career as a spa about 1810, and there is a nucleus of mostly stuccoed, Georgian, classical building of 1810–45, culminating in the large former Priessnitz House. The railway came in 1858, and plenty of villas – Tudor, Italianate, and, on a larger scale, Gothic –

* Mr Bryan S. Smith tells me that Elmslie settled at Malvern about 1854.

went up. Bargeboards are followed by shaped gables, and they occasionally by embattled turrets. Malvern College received its very large Gothic or Early Tudor main building in 1863. The architect of this competent and impressive job was *Charles Hansom*. It no longer suffered from the imposed, grim puritanism of mid-century scholastic architecture. But the finest building of Malvern College by far is the Library, done in 1924 by 102
Aston Webb, the architect who had done so well at St George's Worcester. His free treatment of Gothic and Tudor motifs has an ease and felicitous details not often matched at that moment.

Worcestershire provided a bumper crop of COUNTRY HOUSES. The first to be mentioned is Norton Park, Bredon's Norton of 1830, an amazingly early example of Tudor as against Gothic Revival. The first on a large scale is *Blore*'s Pull Court, 96
Bushley of 1836–46, in a competent and monumental, symmetrical Jacobean. The grandest of all is *Samuel Dawkes*'s Witley Court, Great Witley of *c.*1859–61, now a spectacular ruin. It is 98
Italianate with long, truly gigantic giant porticoes but extremely restrained in ornamental detail, no doubt to keep in harmony with the church of the 1730s. Only the curved wing towards the orangery takes as its pattern something more Baroquely Italian. The sumptuous terraces are by *W. H. Nesfield*, who had established himself in collaboration with Barry as the provider of Italian as against Anglo-Picturesque settings. The 26-ft-high fountain is by *James Forsyth*. Reticently Italianate, and very 99
spacious also, are some merchants' villas, such as the present St James's School at West Malvern and Wheatfield at Powick. The rebuilding and sweeping enlargement of Madresfield Court was placed in the hands of *P. C. Hardwick* and begun in 1863. He was not the most disciplined of architects, and the result has variety but it is curiously scattered. Château Impney by the French 100
architect *Tronquois*, it can't be denied, is thoroughly debased, yet its exuberance is catching. *Bodley & Garner*'s Jacobean Hewell Grange, Tardebigge of 1884 etc. is the very opposite: 97
disciplined, knowledgeable, and yet not simply imitative – although Garner was to bring out the standard work on English domestic Tudor architecture (1911). The importance of Quattrocento motifs and passages must be emphasized. The contrast between this substantial mansion and Blore's so much thinner Pull Court of fifty yeats before – both inspired by the same style – is instructive.

Meanwhile, on a smaller scale, Philip Webb and *Norman Shaw* had created a more freely historicist, more elegant and delicate type of country house. What Shaw could do is well illustrated by his gate lodges for Madresfield, and especially the dovecote of 1867 there, and by his later, i.e. more Baroque, village hall at Overbury (1895–6). *Voysey*, inspired by the Webb–Shaw style but some twenty years younger, built his first country house in Worcestershire: Bannut Farmhouse at Castlemorton of 1890, still with the black and white gables he was soon to abandon, but already in all essentials in his sensible, pretty style. Voysey appears at his best with the gatehouse cottages of 1901 at Madresfield.

There are only a few buildings of the TWENTIETH CENTURY in Worcestershire which would justify inclusion in this introduction, two of before the First World War and five of after the Second World War. Messrs Kay & Co.'s offices at Worcester of 1907 by *J. W. Simpson & Maxwell Ayrton* is original for its date and combines boldness with functional soundness, and *Randall*
103 *Wells*'s Besford Court of 1912 is one of the most imaginative and dramatic examples of a monumental, very freely historicist style one usually connects with Lutyens exclusively.

As regards RECENT BUILDINGS, my five are the following. A very good, sound school by *Yorke, Rosenberg & Mardall* at Wribbenhall of 1954–5, and the equally good and sound new office block for Henry Hope's at Smethwick (Birmingham Suburbs) by *J. H. D. Madin & Partners* of 1963–4, these two faithful to the laws of functionalism and appearance laid down earlier in the century; and, in the more varied and less exacting idiom of today, the central development scheme at Worcester by *Shingler Risdon Associates*, as acceptable as architecture as it is unacceptable as town planning. Very much of today are the remaining two recent buildings: *Richard Sheppard, Robson & Partners'* Institute of Horticulture at Pershore with its sharp diagonals and its unexpectedly rising truncated cylinder and other motifs welcomed today, and their more severe Technical College at Worcester, which asserts itself self-confidently, close to the cathedral. It hurts a little, but one should accept it if one has faith in the validity of architecture in the C20.

FURTHER READING

The main source of information is of course the *Victoria County History* (VCH). It came out in four volumes from 1901 to 1924 and is complete for the county.

Of older sources, the Survey of Worcestershire by Thomas

Habington begun in 1586 was published only in 1895–9 in the *Worcestershire Historical Society Publications*, but made use of by T. R. Nash for his *Collections for the History of Worcestershire* of 1781–2. The Prattington Collection of drawings in the library of the Society of Antiquaries dates from 1810 and consists of 35 volumes. The best architectural account of Worcester Cathedral is of course Robert Willis's, published in the *Archaeological Journal*, XX, 1863. The archeological periodical of the county is the *Transactions of the Worcestershire Archaeological Society*. The *Transactions* and *Proceedings of the Birmingham Archaeological Society* contain Worcestershire material too. For houses *Country Life* (*C.L.*) is, as in all counties, the best place to go to.

PREHISTORY

BY DEREK SIMPSON

BEFORE the Iron Age there is virtually nothing in the form of field monuments to indicate the presence of prehistoric settlement in Worcestershire, although stray finds attest to occupation extending back some 100,000 years. If there is nothing on the ground, however, a great deal can be seen and is currently being recorded from the air. These new sites are concentrated on the Avon gravels and indicate intensive settlement from Neolithic times. The majority of the sites recorded on aerial photographs do not show sufficiently precise morphological characteristics to enable them to be ascribed to any particular culture or period without excavation. Until many have been examined, the earlier prehistory of the area must be reconstructed from occasional finds.

The earliest evidence of human settlement in the county is provided by a number of Lower Palaeolithic hand-axes of Acheulean type from the 100 ft gravel terrace of the Severn at Worcester. For the succeeding Mesolithic period of the early post-glacial phase finds are again scanty. Flint axes termed 'Thames picks' have been found at Hallow and Worcester, and the characteristic diminutive flint tools or microliths, used as arrowtips or barbs in composite weapons, are recorded from the Clent Hills, Stone, and Tutnall (Tardebigge), although in each case with an admixture of later flint forms.

Recent aerial reconnaissance has revealed the earliest monumental remains of the prehistoric period in the form of two elongated rectangular ditched enclosures, termed cursuses, at Charlton and Norton, at the former site with a circular ditched structure symmetrically placed over its S end. The function of these monuments is uncertain, but in view of their association elsewhere in Britain with long barrows, long mortuary enclosures, and henges, the first two demonstrably sepulchral and the latter ceremonial in intent, it is reasonable to assume that the cursus was similarly associated with funerary ritual. Other evidence for primary Neolithic settlement (from *c.* 3000 B.C.) comes exclusively from stray finds. Of these the most interesting are the ground and polished stone axes which indicate widespread commercial activities. Axes from factories in Cornwall have been found at Hagley and Longdon, from the Great Langdale, Westmorland, factory at Race Course Farm, Stourbridge and Tunnel Hill, Chadbury, and from the Graig Lwyd factory in North Wales at Oldfield Farm, Ombersley. Flint axes from various localities in the county are further evidence for trade. These implements are concentrated in the Severn valley and indicate the route along which they must have travelled from the chalk lands of Wessex. It is uncertain whether the axes were traded as finished products or simply in the form of flint nodules or rough-outs. A number of flint-knapping sites in the county make it clear, however, that some of this material was imported in its raw state. The most important of these is at Tardebigge (Tutnall and Cobley), where material has been picked up in four neighbouring fields. Other working sites are known at Hoarstone (Bewdley), Stone, and Hanley William. The evidence is largely in the form of cores and waste flakes, but a number of finished implements, including scrapers and leaf-shaped arrowheads, have also been found.

For the complex period of the Late Neolithic in Britain there are scant remains in our area. A number of crop-marks probably fall into the category of henges, but none have been excavated. Sherds of grooved ware were recovered from a probable storage pit revealed during gravel-digging at Broadway, and Beaker pottery from Bredon and gravel pits in Hill and Moor and Kempsey parishes attest to penetration of the region by the valleys of the Avon and Severn. To the latter cultural group one may also ascribe the archer's wrist guard from Aldington (possibly a settlement site), a fragmentary flint dagger from Diglis Lock, Worcester, and bronze flat axes from Claines, Cropthorne, and Kidderminster parishes.

These varying Neolithic cultural traditions, but sparsely represented in Worcestershire, were to amalgamate to produce a more uniform Bronze Age society from the C17 B.C. Many of the circular ditched crop-marks on the gravels must mark the sites of ploughed-out round barrows of this period, but this awaits confirmation by the spade. There are no longer any round barrows in the county which can be seen by an observer on the ground, although a number are mentioned in records of the C18 and 19. The most interesting was a group of barrows on Clent Heath, Clent opened in the C18 which covered cremation burials, one in an urn. A second urn was found beneath a cairn on Worcester Beacon during work for the Ordnance Survey. The only other known Bronze Age vessel from the county is an unusual collared urn with polypod base. The pot contained a cremation but was not covered by any form of mound. The later Bronze Age is represented entirely by stray finds of metalwork – axes, spearheads, and swords – concentrated in the valley of the Severn and its tributaries. All these objects are isolated finds, and no example occurs of the great metalworkers' hoards known from elsewhere in Britain at this period.

It is only in the Iron Age (from *c.* 550 B.C.) that any notable monuments survive. They are the great hillforts of Bredon, Conderton (Beckford), Woodbury (Great Witley), Wychbury (Hagley), and the fragmentary earthworks recently discovered in Worcester. Whether communal refuges in time of unrest or permanent hill-top defensive settlements, they represent only one category of Iron Age monument and one facet of contemporary life. Of the open settlements belonging to peasant communities in the area we know little. A series of circular huts at Broadway produced Iron Age B pottery, and surface material scattered over a considerable area at Badsey suggests an extensive settlement. Most recently an oval stock enclosure, discovered from the air, has been excavated at Beckford. Among the finds from the latter site were sherds of Iron Age B duck-stamped pottery. Similar ware was found at Badsey and in the hillforts of Bredon and Conderton and indicates a movement into the area from the SW by way of the Severn. From the S again came the final incursion of Iron Age peoples in the early C1 A.D., by the tribe of the Dobunni with their capital at Bagendon in Gloucestershire. Their presence is marked by the distribution of their gold and silver coinage, by occasional finds of wheel-turned pottery, and perhaps too by the violent end to occupation at Bredon hillfort and the massacre of many of its defenders. Their dominion was short-lived however, and within a generation control had passed to Rome.

THE ROMAN OCCUPATION

BY BARRY CUNLIFFE

WORCESTERSHIRE is not renowned for its Roman remains, for the county lies on the borders of potentially hostile Wales, and for much of the C1 and C2 it must have been subjected to military control. Forts are known at Droitwich, Grimley, and possibly Worcester and Clifton-on-Teme. Only Droitwich can definitely be dated to the C1, but the others are likely to be of this date too, belonging to the campaigns which led to the subjugation of the Welsh tribes. The early C2 saw an uneasy peace, but this seems to have been shattered *c.*155 by a Welsh uprising which may have caused the burning of part of the settlement at Worcester and initiated the second refortification of the Droitwich fort. It is hardly surprising that under these conditions civilian development was retarded.

The C3 and C4 were more peaceful: both Droitwich and Worcester developed extensive settlements, roads were well looked after, and a few villas arose among the peasant settlements of the Severn and Avon valleys. But no signs of expansive romanization are yet known, and it seems that there was little surplus wealth in the area, although the valleys offered adequate farmland, and industries such as salt production (Droitwich), iron-smelting (Worcester), and tile-making (Leigh Sinton) would have provided a subsistence level sufficient for the relatively large population.

NORMAN SCULPTURE

BY NEIL STRATFORD

WORCESTERSHIRE is not rich in good Norman sculpture. Survivals are often piecemeal, and chronology must remain controversial. There is only one fixed date available, the cathedral crypt of between 1084 and 1092. In the smaller churches nothing is likely to be earlier than *c.*1120. This early C12 lacuna however can be paralleled in many other counties. In the cathedral the slype has early bulbous capitals. They may be re-used Anglo-Saxon material or evidence of the so-called Saxo-Norman overlap. The slype also has block capitals. Among the block capitals of the crypt (some with billet on the abacus) a few have an elegant concave shape, unparalleled elsewhere and curiously prophetic of the trumpet scallops of nearly a hundred years later. Block capitals also occur in the gatehouse at Evesham, where they seem certain to be of between 1122 and 1149, and probably to be shortly after 1122. Here the shafts are grouped in three, the earliest known case of a motif typical of the Transitional style of the late C12 in the West of England. The loss of Evesham Abbey causes the greatest gap in our knowledge of Norman sculpture in the county. At Pershore we are more fortunate. A variety of decoration survives in transepts and crossing, including simple volute, block, and scallop capitals and one pair with interlace and six busts. But the finest capitals of *c.*1120–40 are those of the E arch of the S transept in the cathedral, block capitals decorated with acanthus foliage of the Winchester type, a dragon and an angel. Their connexions are the Canterbury crypt and Romsey. Enough also remains to suggest large areas of diapered wall, as in other buildings of the first half of the C12 (cathedral, S aisle gallery). During this phase the cathedral masons built in alternate courses of green and white stone, as slightly later in the chapter house too.

The decoration of the second quarter of the century in smaller churches is with one exception confined to fairly plain doorways and arches with a heavy roll and simple cross patterns. In the NE of the county one team of masons worked at Stockton-on-Teme, Eastham, Knighton-on-Teme, and Martley. Bockleton of the 1160s still belongs to this group. Plain doorways with a heavy roll are also at Childswickham, Grimley, and Stoulton. Several of this whole group of doorways (Eastham, Grimley, Knighton, Martley, Stoulton) are set in a projection of the wall, a feature which evidently became popular, cf. Abberley, Astley, Beckford, Bockleton, Hampton Lovett, Holt, Pirton, Rochford, and Rock. In addition four of these doorways (Bockleton, Eastham, Knighton, Stoulton) are topped by blank arcading of a more or less elaborate form. At Ribbesford a richer decoration, including a tympanum carved with a hunting scene, must date from about 1140–50. Entirely on its own in the county is the Christ in Majesty of *c.*1140 at Rous Lench, the only ambitious early figure 15
to survive. It is close to the Prior's Door at Ely (also of *c.*1140) and may be the work of a sculptor from Northamptonshire. The tympanum at Rochford has a tree, a motif frequent in the West of England. A crude tympanum at Pedmore, a fragment by the same hand at Chaddesley Corbett, and a tympanum at Romsley (with the only example of beakhead in Worcestershire) all probably date from the fifties. The Romsley tympanum shows influence from the Herefordshire School. Romsley as well as Pedmore

suffers from the carver's naïve incomprehension of the iconographical models.

Sculpture of *c.*1160–80 is on the whole more lavish. This applies especially to zigzag. In the first half of the century zigzag was applied simply to the outer face of an order, or to both outer and inner faces so that a lozenge shape results. The zigzag may be decorated with bobbins (Pedmore), pellets (Halesowen), diamonds (Bayton, Chaddesley Corbett), etc. The earliest example of outward-pointing zigzag is of *c.*1150 (Rochford), but this motif only becomes popular in the third quarter (Astley, Beckford, Castlemorton, Earls Croome, Pirton, Queenhill, Rock, Shelsley Walsh). At Halesowen and Holt an order is decorated with more than one range of zigzag applied in steps. Already shortly before 1150 zigzag begins to be used elsewhere than on arches (e.g. the window heads of Rous Lench); cf. the later Holt and jambs at Astley, Beckford, and Rock. In the S of the county the zigzag is usually furrowed, i.e. has alternately concave and convex ribs. At Holt (*c.*1160–75) zigzag is treated for the first time with slight undercutting. From then onwards undercut zigzag develops an astonishing range of patterns (Worcester Cathedral, Bredon, Eckington, Elmbridge, Netherton, Shrawley). At this final stage of its evolution zigzag may even be found set diagonally to the wall (Worcester Cathedral, Bredon, Bricklehampton).

For other sculptural decoration we must return to *c.*1150. The county now appears divided into two distinct areas, N and S, divided by a line across at about the latitude of Worcester. In the N (Astley, Bockleton, Holt, Rock N doorway) there are close connexions with Herefordshire and Shropshire. The Rock chancel
16 arch and the Chaddesley Corbett font, both of *c.*1160, must in fact be the work of Herefordshire carvers. They mark the high point of sculpture of this period in Worcestershire. The S is less clearly defined. Beckford alone (*c.*1160–75) survives with its sculpture nearly intact. This includes a tympanum with the Harrowing of Hell and another with a strange Adoration of the Cross. The ornamental repertoire has much in common with Bricklehampton, Eldersfield, Pendock, Pirton, etc., but adds some Italianate features. Earls Croome (*c.*1155–60) until the C19 had a richly arcaded W front. The chancel arch and N doorway have capitals with foliage of a type unique in Worcestershire.

Among the elaborate Norman FONTS, Chaddesley Corbett of course leads qualitatively. There are leaves at Bayton and Rock, grotesque heads at Broome and Holt, and historiated decoration at Halesowen, Overbury (cf. Coleshill, Warwickshire), and Pershore.

The TRANSITIONAL phase opens with the building of the two W bays of the cathedral *c.*1180–5 and the similar work in the infirmary passage and – of *c.*1200 – in the upper parts of the S transept. Sophisticated patterns of undercut zigzag belong to this phase (*see* above). So do trumpet-scallop capitals. Their first appearance may be as early as *c.*1175 (on the Pershore font). Not earlier than 1185 purely French crocket capitals are introduced, and the S transept of the cathedral has early stiff-leaf as well. Three other features should be noted: the use of groups of three shafts (cf. above), the use of foliage paterae (in the spandrels of the gallery in the cathedral W bays; cf. e.g. Lady Chapel, Glastonbury), and the use of continuous edge-roll mouldings together with orders on shafts with capitals (Bredon, Bricklehampton, Dodderhill, Ripple, Shrawley). Farther N three churches have trumpet-scallop and stiff-leaf capitals side by side but no undercut zigzag (Dodderhill, Droitwich St Andrew, Stoke Prior). Undercut zigzag goes on in the area of Worcester until after 1200, a date when the motif was still in use only in the West of England. However, reactionary and progressive forms mix in such unexpected ways that dating must be hazardous. E.g. in the chancel at Pershore as late as *c.*1220, the extreme form of trumpet scallop known as cornucopia capitals is still used with entirely post-Norman work. Similarly capitals at Bretforton with heads and a dragon inspired by the Wells Cathedral transept are probably as late as *c.*1215–20.

Finally the two most interesting pieces of C12 sculpture to survive: the two lecterns at Crowle and Norton, the latter from 17
Evesham Abbey. Italian-looking in the supporting figures, made of an exotic stone (marble ?) which was possibly imported, they are nevertheless absolutely native in style and foliage. Heavy restoration lessens their value in a period from which large-scale figure sculpture has rarely survived. Their date seems to be *c.*1190–1200, and their closest parallels are to be found among the capitals at Wells.

GEOLOGY

BY TERENCE MILLER

Worcestershire sits neatly like a shallow basin rimmed by the hills of three uplands. Down and through the centre of the basin runs in a surprisingly narrow valley the Severn, with its principal tributaries the Teme, the Stour, and the Warwickshire Avon.

Of the three uplands only two can be considered genuine parts
1 of the county. On the W the Malvern Hills, continuing N across the Teme as the Abberley Hills and Woodbury Camp; in the NE the Clent and Lickey Hills forming an outer margin to the sloping plateau of the Birmingham district, with a narrow extension S of Redditch carrying the ancient Ridgeway. The third member of the trio, the main front of the Cotswolds, lies beyond the county boundary, except where a tongue is pushed onto the crest above Broadway. However, a forward outpost, or outlier, of the Cotswolds, Bredon Hill, does come into Worcestershire and provides a dramatic accent in the low ground along the S open side of the basin.

This 'framed basin' is rather closely under geological control. The striking range of the Malverns, rising sharply 1200 ft above the Severn plain, is an inclined slice of ancient pre-Cambrian metamorphic rocks. These gnarled and fractured masses with a partial cover of Lower Palaeozoic rocks to the W (in Herefordshire) and northward through the Abberley Hills, emerge from beneath the Devonian Old Red Sandstone which underlies the upper Teme valley between Knightsford Bridge and Tenbury. This corner of the upland frame is completed by the Coal Measures of the Forest of Wyre between the Teme and the Severn at Bewdley. The same Coal Measure strata, mainly grey sandstones and shales with some red and brown claystones and ironstones, and the famous fire-clay of the Swinfords, also form part of the north-western upland, where they just reach down into Worcestershire from their main outcrop as part of the South Staffordshire coal-field and the 'Black Country'. The geological base of this great midland complex of heavy industry originally lay in the availability at close quarters of ironstone, coal, and limestone.

The main high ground here is along the line of the Clent and Lickey Hills. This ridge is composed mainly of Permo-Triassic rocks somewhat younger than the Coal Measures, but at Bilberry Hill and near Rubery there are Cambrian quartzites and Silurian sandstone, with a small patch of even older rocks. The curious rounded hill shapes of the Lickeys are caused by gravels overlying more easily eroded soft sandstone slopes.

Of the true S rim of Worcestershire, the Cotswolds, only a narrow sector – above Broadway – actually lies within the county. South and Central Worcestershire, therefore, is essentially a low undulating plain based on soft red marls and siltstones of Triassic age which lie in a horseshoe along the front of the Malverns, on both sides of the Severn round by Worcester and Droitwich, and then turning S again, by Redditch, almost as far as Evesham. Sandwiched with the rather soft, weak rocks are some sandstones, red and buff in colour, which have been quarried E of Stourport and around Bromsgrove. These sandstones produce minor ridges in the landscape and give lighter and drier soils than the surrounding marls of the plain. Where the sandstones stand up as minor cliff-like features, as at Kinver Edge and near Blakes Hall, cave-dwellings have been excavated and occupied until comparatively recent times. The prevailing redness of the soil is expressed in place-names like Redmarley d'Abitot (Gloucestershire).

Red rocks are often interpreted as the products of ancient deserts. This is not invariably a valid interpretation, since there is no necessary connexion between redness and ancient temperatures. However an ancient hot climate can be firmly inferred if there are deposits of salts that could only be produced by solar evaporation of enclosed or semi-enclosed bodies of water. Such salt deposits are to be found interbedded in the red Triassic sandstones and marls below the Droitwich–Stoke Prior area. Droitwich 'Spa' depended on the brine pumped up from the salt layers, and the more ancient importance of the deposits is suggested by the name 'Upper Saltway' given to what is certainly a Roman, and possibly a pre-Roman line of road.

Within the central horseshoe from near Droitwich to the county boundary S of Bredon Hill, the country on either side of the Bow Brook is on Lower Jurassic (Lias) clays and muddy limestones with a good deal of superficial sand and gravel – particularly round Pershore and Evesham – scattered about for good measure. On the centre line of this tongue lies in upward stratigraphic order a remnant of the Middle Jurassic Inferior Oolite limestone, a brown shelly rock with 'fish-roe' texture, and broken bits of sea-lily stems. This is the outlying Cotswold island of Bredon Hill, whose scattered and rubbly upper slopes provide evidence of the severity of the British climate in glacial times.

Worcestershire is not outstandingly rich in building stone within its own boundaries (cf. pp. 50 ff.). Red, yellow, and buff Devonian and Coal Measure sandstones have been quarried in the N and NW, but the commonest stone is the red and yellow Triassic sandstone of the Bromsgrove district. For the rest, an abundance of clays and marls – Triassic, Lias, and Glacial – in the centre and S of the county, together with plenty of timber, results in a great range of warm red brick and timber combination in buildings. In the Middle Ages Malvern and Droitwich were well known for ornamental tiles such as may still be seen in the priory church at Malvern. The thin, blue-hearted Liassic limestone bands were at one time used for paving and roofing. They were for both purposes unsatisfactory, being in the one case too easily broken and worn, and in the other too thick and heavy.

BUILDING MATERIALS

BY ALEC CLIFTON-TAYLOR

TODAY Worcestershire is emphatically a brick county, and this is nothing new; red brick has been the predominant building material of every Worcestershire town for more than two and a half centuries. Mixed in among the brick buildings a few towns, notably Evesham, Droitwich, Upton-on-Severn and Tenbury, preserve a decreasing but still appreciable quantity of half-timbering, but others, like Pershore, Bewdley, Stourport, Bromsgrove and Worcester itself, owe most of their character to their brick architecture. Large brickworks were started in Claines parish just N of Worcester soon after 1700, and many of the county's clays make excellent bricks. Worcestershire even has, in the extreme N around Dudley, deposits of those clays employed in the C19 to make the specially strong blue bricks known as 'engineering bricks' and usually associated with Staffordshire. The craft of brickwork does not display during the Georgian period in Worcestershire the virtuosity and refinements to be found in the counties of the South-East, but none the less the best examples afford considerable pleasure. Brick buildings are usually roofed with red tiles.

Next in importance to brick comes half-timbering, of which a great deal still survives in country districts all over the county. It forms the subject of a special section by Mr F. W. B. Charles which follows this one. Worcestershire half-timbering is now almost all of the 'black-and-white' kind characteristic of every county of the West Midlands. The framework, always of oak, was originally left in its natural state, but later it was blackened with tar or pitch or even paint, probably as a preservative against the weather; at the same time the plaster infilling was limewashed. Worcestershire 'black and white' in juxtaposition with Georgian brickwork can look strident, but in a village street or in

isolation across the fields these black-and-white houses have undoubted charm. So popular did they become that when later the lath and plaster infilling gave place to brick nogging, as it frequently did, this was also carefully whitened; and not content with that, in the Victorian period houses built entirely of brick would sometimes be given a deceptive black-and-white covering intended to simulate half-timbering. The genuine half-timbered buildings are usually earlier than any in brick; visible cruck construction is rare* and nearly everything is of the post-and-truss type, sometimes, as at Mere Hall, Hanbury, and Middle Beanhall, 54
Bradley, culminating in serried gables of lively exuberance. For timber-framed buildings straw thatch is the traditional roofing material, and is still used for cottages when it can be obtained; but today those who can afford to do so usually rethatch with Norfolk reed or the long straw from the South-West known as wheat reed.

Where a Worcestershire building is of stone, as most of the churches are, there is a strong likelihood that this will be one of the New Red Sandstones. In Worcestershire, as elsewhere, these display considerable colour variations and are, of course, by no means always red; sometimes the colours are most delightful, as for example at Martley, where the church tower is a rich red ochre, dusted with blue-grey lichen, while the walls present an enchanting blend of pink, fawn and grey-blue. Unhappily these sandstones seldom weather well and evidences of decay are frequent; the history of the cathedral is indeed a story of incessant refacing, which explains its new-looking appearance and regrettable absence of patina. The Bunter sandstones of North Worcestershire make very poor building stones and have usually been rejected for this purpose; the Keuper sandstones, which are widely distributed over the county, are better, but by no means always reliable. A little Devonian Old Red Sandstone can be seen in buildings on the western edge of the county (e.g. the church at Clifton-on-Teme), while close to the northern fringes Carboniferous sandstone of good quality has been quarried from the Coal Measures.

Limestones are wholly absent from the N half of Worcestershire, but three varieties were used farther S. At Broadway all the older buildings are of Inferior Oolite, the lovely honey-coloured limestone of the Cotswolds; so that lithologically one feels that Broadway ought really to belong to Gloucestershire. This is

*Cf. Mr Charles's contribution, p. 54.

Worcestershire's show-piece, and her only one, in the field of building stones, although oolite can be seen at Overbury, Conderton, and other villages on the flanks of Bredon Hill, where at one time it was also quarried. In the south-eastern portion of the county Blue Lias is the prevailing stone; more often grey or buff than blue, this is a stone which weathers no better than the New Red Sandstones, and is less amenable than they, since it is usually obtainable only in rather small pieces that cannot be ashlared: Blue Lias is not a freestone.

Finally there is, on the W side of the valley of the Teme NW of Worcester, a limestone which is not very common in England: tufa. This stone is formed from accumulations of calcium carbonate deposited by spring water bubbling forth from some older limestone, in this case Devonian, a thin bed of which occurs along the perimeter of the broad Old Red Sandstone area that stretches away to the W, to cover most of Herefordshire. As it dries out and hardens, tufa assumes that characteristic 'frozen sponge' appearance which can be well seen at the church of Shelsley Walsh and on the tower of Clifton-on-Teme. In its rather more compact form, known as travertine, this stone is familiar enough in Italy, but in England it occurs at a handful of places only.

TIMBER-FRAMED BUILDINGS

BY F. W. B. CHARLES

THE tradition of timber-framing gave Worcestershire her towns and villages, farms and mills, at least some of her lesser churches, and, of course, her great monastic roofs, halls and tithe barns. Carpentry however is a technical subject, and the buildings cannot be adequately described in terms of the historic styles of architecture. Dating mainly depends on observing constructional details – not made easier, particularly in houses, by alterations as well as layers of wallpaper and plaster. Indeed, until the demolition gang moves in, many buildings can scarcely even be recognized as timber-framed.

The two structural types most general in Worcestershire are the 'cruck' and the far more numerous 'post-and-truss' buildings. The cruck frame consists of two huge limbs of oak, curved in shape, or elbowed, which extend from the base of the outer side walls to the ridge of the roof. A pair of cruck-blades is obtained by splitting the main branch and trunk of the oak tree so that each blade exactly matches the other. The blades of the internal frames of a building are always perfectly symmetrical, even though the outer ones, seen in the gable walls, sometimes have unmatched blades. The method of erecting a cruck building is by *rearing*. That is, the components of each frame, previously

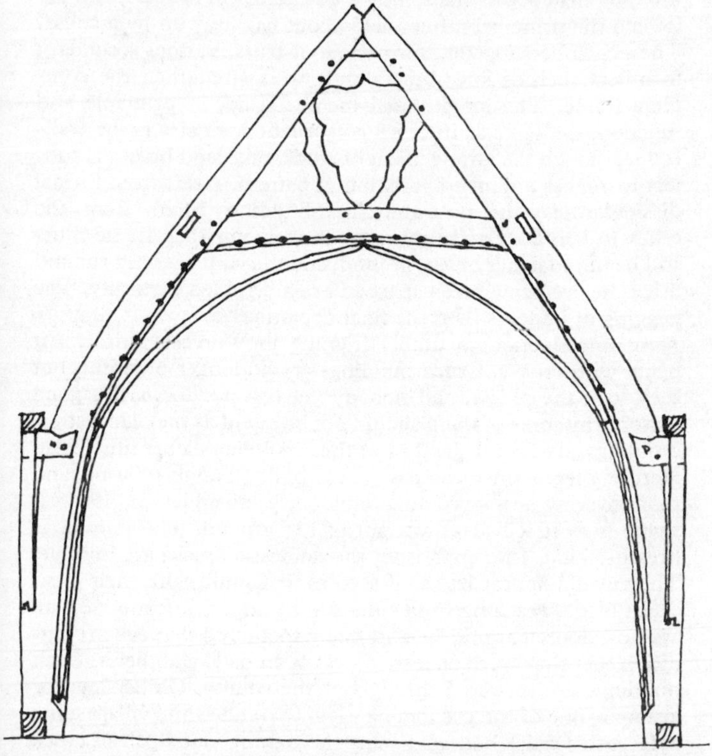

Cruck Truss

wrought and numbered in the carpenter's yard, are laid out on the building plot, jointed, and pegged to make a rigid frame, which is then raised through ninety degrees with the feet of the blades resting on the sill beam. As it is reared a tenon projecting from the bottom of the blade engages a mortice already cut in the upper surface of this beam. Indeed no timber simply rests on or against another one. The longitudinal members – wall-plates, purlins and wind-braces – are used to locate and secure each frame as it is reared. Post-and-truss construction as found throughout Worcestershire and in all the West Midlands is very closely allied to cruck building. Of the many variations of this form, the most common consists of posts on either side of the building held across the top by a tie-beam. On to this beam are jointed the principal rafters held about half-way up by a collar. These members together form the roof-truss. Various secondary members such as knee-braces and struts strengthen the complete frame. The longitudinal members are, in principle and function, the same as in cruck construction, so also is the wall-frame, though the arrangement of studs, rails, and braces is subject to almost unlimited variation of pattern. Apart from formal dissimilarities, the post-and-truss building differs from the cruck in being erected timber by timber, but each frame must still be put together on the ground, and the joints exactly cut and fitted, before being taken apart and re-assembled vertically. The pegging of joints is then the final operation.

An introduction to timber-framing in Worcestershire must begin with crucks. Cruck buildings are no longer plentiful, but they look the oldest, and nobody yet has put forward a good reason why some of them should not be as old as the oldest stone buildings. By far the greatest of them is Leigh Court tithe barn. Hardly altered since the day it was built (though its walls and roof-covering are becoming ominously dilapidated), its vast shape is as if it had grown out of the ground. The interior is breath-taking. In comparison, the domestic crucks are humble. They would appear less so if seen as first built, with their great cruck blades reaching from sill beam to ridge. Unfortunately all are now floored at mid-height, many so altered that even recognition that they were once medieval open halls is difficult. Such buildings are scattered throughout the county. Ombersley, for example, one of the predominantly black-and-white villages, has at least two cruck houses. Facing the roundabout a pair of cruck blades can just be discerned amidst the superimposed Victorian timbering. The other gable confirms one's suspicions. Two slender blades go the whole height. The house is a medieval four-bay cruck, originally with a two-bay hall open to the roof and a two-storey bay at each end. The central truss spanning the hall can be glimpsed through a crack in a partition at the top of the stairs. It might be a revelation to those who believe that crucks represent a kind of peasant architecture to see the quality and finish of these timbers. The other house, more easily recognizable, is farther up the road on the opposite side. Instead of four bays, this had three bays in the hall range and a cross-wing of two storeys. The third bay of the hall range disappeared some time ago, leaving only the two. These are large cruck houses, though scarcely comparable with some Welsh examples or several that have survived in Shropshire, including, of course, Stokesay Castle, the largest cruck hall in existence.

In the design of four-bay houses with a two-bay open-roofed hall in the middle, the truss demarcating the bays was the architectural centrepiece. Such a truss was recently rescued from a row of C18 cottages in Bromsgrove and is now at the Avoncroft Museum of Buildings. The upper bay contained the dais. The screens passage occupied about a third of the always shorter lower bay. The hearth was also in the lower bay, set to one side. In several cruck halls, as well as those of post-and-truss construction, a 'mantel-beam' spanned the central truss about 6 ft above the floor, and a wattle and daub or timber-framed chimney-stack (there is also one of these at Avoncroft) stood on the mantleshelf. The two end bays beyond the hall were always two-storeyed. At the upper end was the first-floor solar and ground-floor parlour or cellar, which went underground later but always remained at the upper end. A few cruck houses, such as the White House at Peopleton, have a solar cross-wing instead of the upper bay. At the lower end was the service bay with a storeroom or possibly sleeping room over. As at Ombersley, there was sometimes a cross-wing at the lower end. The kitchen was outside, and the well often survives to help in its location.

'Base-crucks' are a grander version of cruck construction. The blades are stopped half-way up the roof and connected by a collar-beam and powerful knee-braces to make a rigid frame capable of being reared. At the same time, base-crucks only differ from aisled buildings in that cranked blades, instead of straight posts, support the roof-plate. The Middle Littleton tithe barn has frames of both types, and its roof structure is probably the oldest in the county, *c.*1260 by carbon-14 analysis.* At each end is an aisled bay, and the eight intervening bays are of base-cruck construction with the feet of the cruck blades set high above the floor in the stone walls. The numerous inserted posts now give the appearance of botched aisled construction throughout, but the effort needed to visualize the interior as it was is worth while. Bredon barn should be closely compared with Middle Littleton.

* *See Journal of the Society of Architectural Historians*, vol. XXV, 1966, pp. 221–39.

It is as splendid, and, owned by the National Trust, in much better condition. It is the only completely aisled timber structure in the county. Its date, pending confirmation of carbon-14 analysis, could also be C13.

Of domestic base-crucks, only two have been discovered in Worcestershire. One of these, a farmhouse called the Hyde at Stoke Bliss in the far W of the county, is now entirely cased in stone, but the timber structure is practically intact. The original

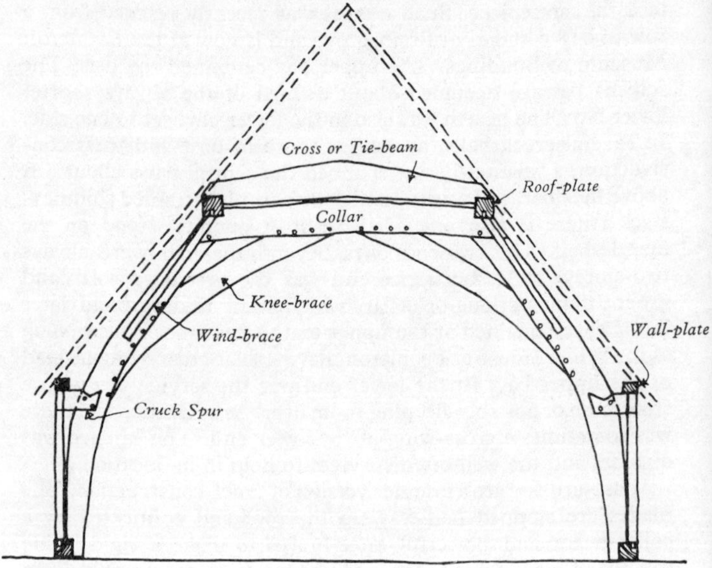

Base Cruck Arch

house was a hall and cross-wing with a stupendous Gothic-arched base-cruck truss dividing the two bays of the hall. Everything about the building – the laborious structural method, the huge timbers and their heavy cusping and moulding – points to an early date. The other house, Rectory Farm at Grafton Flyford, is sadly depleted, but the all-important central truss survives. This house must have been similar to the now classic, fully restored base-cruck hall of West Bromwich Manor House in Staffordshire. The Hyde has more in common with Amberley Court in Herefordshire. The date of all of them is probably *c.*1300, if not earlier. The little two-bay solar wing of the Hyde is hardly less remarkable than the hall – certainly of the same date. The C16 jettied four-bay stable and granary building opposite the house is also unique in Worcestershire.

Now to the greater medieval roofs, excluding church roofs. The type of roof typical of the region is the purlin roof with open collar-truss or tiebeam-truss – frequently both within the same building. Cusping of struts and wind-braces is the normal decoration, generally less vigorous than in Herefordshire and Shropshire. Intermediate trusses in each bay are characteristic of buildings with framed rather than stone walls. Wind-braces springing from these, as well as the main trusses, form a continuous Gothic arcading throughout the length of the building. In the roof of Holy Trinity Worcester, *c.*1320, which until the middle of the last century was at the Guesten Hall of the cathedral, the cusped and curved wind-braces set between each tier of purlins are a tour de force. No roof can quite compete with this, but the refectory at Little Malvern Court has a roof of the same type and date, though much smaller and less ornate. The other typical Worcestershire roof of grand scale was that at Great Malvern Priory, destroyed in the last century and the only one of which the hall was wholly timber-framed. What is left of St Wulstan's Hospital at Worcester, the so-called Commandery, also includes a timber-framed hall. But its roof, a hammerbeam roof of *c.*1500, is not only alien to Worcestershire but to timber-framed structures in general. Hammerbeam roofs need masonry walls to resist their thrust. Although this roof is ornamentally impressive, the plain structural logic of the more native collar- or tiebeam-trusses is more satisfying. Until destroyed in 1962, Chorley House, Droitwich, exemplified this type of roof, as well as C14 curved wall-brace design, better than any building in Worcestershire.

Domestic post-and-truss halls of the C14 and C15 are scarce. There are more solar wings of this period, alongside hall-parts of much later date. Probably the original halls were of cruck construction, which could not be adapted to take a first floor when this became fashionable. The typical plan was still the two-bay hall, generally with solar and services cross-wing at each end. Each was a separate structure, even though built at the same time. Martley rectory has every feature one might expect to find in the earliest of post-and-truss houses. The supporting members of each frame are enormous; the roof members almost flimsy – reminiscent perhaps of unframed post-hole construction, which

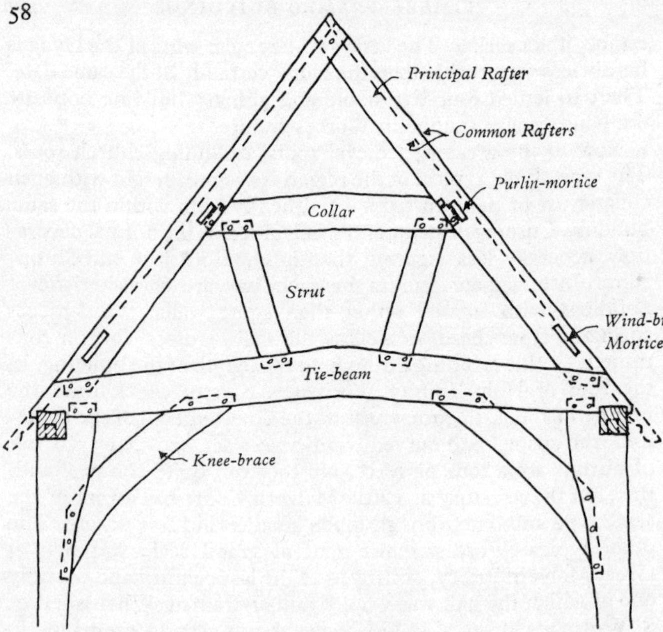

Medieval Tie-beam Truss

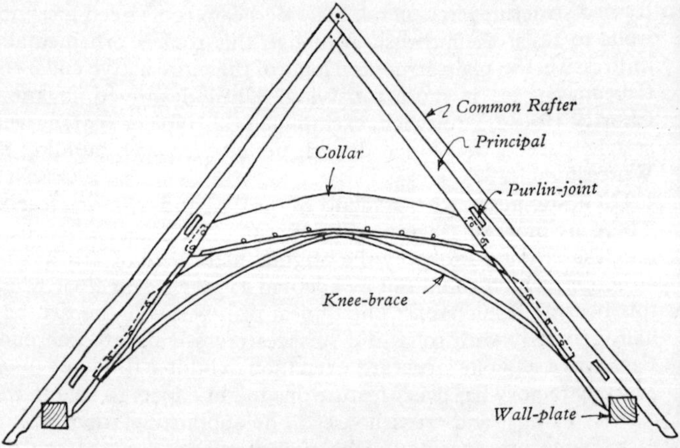

Intermediate Collar Truss

was probably the normal method of building houses when timber-framing first spread to the countryside. The struts between tiebeam and collar have none of the structural economy and refinement that normally determine the form of every component in a roof truss. These struts are like misplaced timbers of cruck construction. The solar wing is not only structurally separate from the hall, but separated from it by some 5 ft. This also points to an early date. Probably Martley rectory was a first attempt to design an important house, as opposed to the great halls and town buildings, in the 'modern movement'. If so, its date may be early C14.

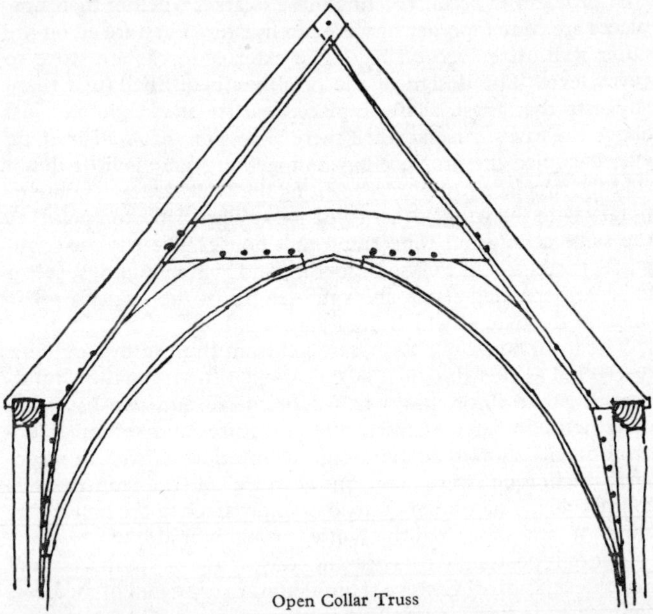

Open Collar Truss

The solar of 38 High Street, Droitwich, is a classic of *c.*1400. It is of three bays with an open collar-truss. All the timbers are heavily moulded, the wall-plate brattished, and there are two tiers of strongly cusped wind-braces. The ground-floor parlour has ceiling beams as richly carved as the roof timbers. Another three-bay solar of slightly later date is that of Shell Manor, Himbleton. Later still, *c.*1500, are those of Salwarpe Court and Throckmorton Court Farm – the last with an exceptionally complete and large hall range. By this time buildings were acquiring the skeletal appearance of Tudor architecture. The heavy curved wall-braces following the natural grain of the timber were on their way out. The close-timbered barn at Throckmorton still has them, but they are diminutive in comparison with those of earlier buildings. Similarly the cusping of the trusses in Throckmorton's solar wing has lost the structural discipline of earlier examples. It is overdone and the edges have no chamfer. By contrast, the moulding of the tiebeam, posts, and wall-plate of the great chamber is elaborate and faultless. The shallow ogees are wholly in character with Perp.

A problem in reconstructing these solars is whether their fireplaces are contemporary or were put in later. They are all on the outer wall of the second bay. The external stacks are stone to eaves level. The design of the brick shafts of Shell (of *c.*1600) suggests that these shafts replaced earlier smoke outlets just above the eaves. Also at Shell there is no sign that wall-framing ever occupied the fireplace bay. Altogether, there is little doubt that the fireplace structure, excepting the brick shafts, is contemporary with the wing. Other evidence at Throckmorton points to the same conclusion concerning that house. The enclosed fireplace, therefore, like close timbering and rich mouldings, seems to have depended more upon the length of the owner's purse than on the date at which the house was built.

The town house of *c.*1475, rescued from Bromsgrove and now re-erected as first designed at the Avoncroft Museum of Buildings at Stoke Prior, has a half-floored hall and two-bay solar wing, jettied over the street. These features and several structural details show that the design of interiors as well as structural technique were well in advance of the conservative countryside. The timber-framed chimneystack in the hall is certainly of later date than the house, probably mid C16.

The only post-and-truss peasant house of the C15, a successor of the crucks, is Shell Cottage, Himbleton. Every detail of medieval hall design is there in miniature – the architectural central truss, screens passage, wind-braces, door-heads, even solar and service bays, but these are single-storey outshuts at each gable of the hall.

The towns, particularly Worcester, Bromsgrove, Evesham, and Upton-on-Severn, must still have substantial vestiges of medieval buildings behind their C16 and C17 street-front framing or later brickwork. Friar Street, Worcester, in fact still looks medieval. Greyfriars, splendidly restored in the 1940s after a long struggle against the demolishers, is an important building in every sense, not least as a dating milestone. None of its details, except the obvious Elizabethan staircase, windows, and other additions and alterations, would contradict *c.*1480, the date now generally accepted. Most significant, the upper chambers were ceiled at that date. The ceiling construction of elegantly moulded beams exactly follows that of the first floor. Nor is there reason to doubt that the fireplaces were also contemporary with the original building.

A word about churches. The W end of the timber church at Besford is the best example, now that Chorley House has been destroyed, of C14 curved wall-brace design. This church is a little gem. In comparison the C15 timber arcading at Ribbesford
is huge and impressive. The little steeples of Dormston, Warn- 48
don, Kington, Pirton, and Cotheridge, and many porches are also worth a look. The former, though generally attributed to the late C15 or C16, could easily be contemporary with their churches. The latter are invaluable as first lessons in timber construction, and in summing up changes of style. Compare, for example, C14 Dormston with C16 Romsley. The earliest porch would seem to be Warndon's. Its archaic structure of two slabs of oak, forming an arch exactly following the grain, *could* be contemporary with the church, C12!

Few of Worcestershire's large, well-kept halls and courts of the first half of the C16 are accessible to the public. But one of
them, Huddington Court, with the finest and probably earliest 53
brick chimneyshafts in the county, does not conform to the hall and cross-wing plan. It is a large four-bay range, like the early crucks, but much taller, of two storeys throughout, and with an upper-floor hall occupying the two centre bays. This may have been the solar range of the originally much larger building. Of smaller scale and later in date, Middle Beanhall Farm, Bradley, before its ornamental front of 1635 was added, was of the same type. Harvington Hall near Kidderminster also has an upper hall, but C16 alterations, converting the house into a warren of priest-holes, and more at the end of the C17, have destroyed its original character. Harvington, however, is the cross-wing type. A still later house showing the persistence of the four-bay range is Stone House at Elmley Lovett, *c.*1640. Another unusual type is Manor Farm at Feckenham, early C16, which has a three-bay hall range with the solar in the jettied end-bay and a service cross-wing at the lower end.

The last of the larger halls is at Birtsmorton Court. The hall was rebuilt *c.*1580 of enormous timbers perhaps from the earlier building. Internally it was in the new fashion with moulded plaster ceiling and a gallery round three sides supported on round timber columns. But not only the screens passage was retained, for the new trusses above the ceiling are as fine open collar-trusses as many of medieval date. The rest of the house, like most of these larger houses, has been so often altered and rebuilt that even its medieval solar is scarcely recognizable. The last of the free-standing solars is at Pirton Court, a great three-bay, three-storey block of the decorative style. Alas, all the decorative, as well as structural, timbers were taken out a few years ago and its character completely destroyed. The rest of the house, like Birtsmorton, is a picturesque jumble of every period.

Timber-framing was a technique always advancing towards economy in the use of the oak tree and in methods of getting the building up. The last hundred years of the tradition, *c.*1570–1670, produced the earliest farmhouses designed for modern living. These 'yeoman' houses had rooms, fireplaces, staircases, and glazed windows. They faced the fold surrounded by the barn, stables, and buildings for cider-making, malting, baking, and so on. The barn is generally all that remains, and cattle have transformed the cobbled fold into a sea of mud. The house is generally the best preserved, but few original windows have survived, and white-painted brick and plaster, and black paint or pitch on the timbers, a most unwelcome 'improvement' of the last century, have destroyed more than its originally natural colour. Lane House near Redditch is an exception, not only in this respect. Its three-bay, two-storey plus attic range, jettied at each end, is perhaps a direct development of the medieval solar. The hall has become merely a rear wing – on its way to final relegation as the 'servants' hall' of the C18 and C19. Dormston Moat Farm, dated on the front tiebeam 1663, has the same plan. Both these houses still have the extremely functional, as well as ornamental, 'weatherings' – bracketed pent-roofs built out about 18 inches at each storey height all around the building. Wattle and daub panels protected by these weatherings are better by far than 9 inches of brick. Most houses lost them in the last century and were given only 4½ inches of brick instead. Lower Tundridge Farm on Leigh Brook, Suckley, almost in Herefordshire, is the largest of these three-bay 'solar' houses. Its rear service wing makes the complete house L-shaped instead of T-shaped, as Lane House. Moreover, its solar's middle bay, the largest of the three at Lane House, is the smallest at Lower Tundridge. It has become the staircase hall, flanked by the main rooms with symmetrically placed windows. Thus the step from timber-framing to Georgian merely consisted of a skin of brickwork.

Other farmhouses more directly followed the medieval hall plan with three-bay hall range and unenlarged solar cross-wing. The service bay in these houses had become the kitchen. The hall, still with its door at the lower end, was the main living part or 'house-place'. Its large fireplace was built back-to-back with the parlour fireplace in the cross-wing. There were also fireplaces in the upper rooms. The complete fireplace structure thus filled the original upper bay of the hall, though the bay was reduced in length as compared with its medieval prototype. The range or cluster of four brick shafts at the junction of the hall and cross-wing roofs is a common enough sight in any part of the county. Tardebigge Farm, Keys Farm, and Warndon Farm – the last a practically untouched example of brickwork of *c.*1600 with stone mullioned windows – are splendid examples of this house type.

The towns were also rebuilt during this period, but unlike the rebuilding of towns in the second Elizabethan age, the first

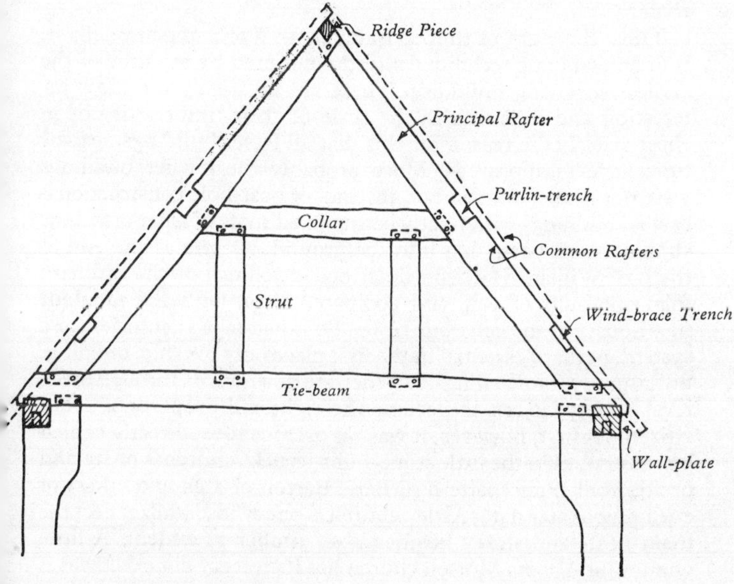

Seventeenth Century Tie-beam Truss

Elizabethans did not destroy all the past. Many medieval houses were simply brought up-to-date. Nash House in New Street, Worcester (recently well restored, though a five-storey timber-framed shot tower, probably unique in all England, was lost in the process), is the best of the new style of *c.*1600. The Bailiff's House at Bewdley, dated on the doorhead 1610, is of the same type, though a storey lower. In these buildings the whole front block, including the attic, consisted of rooms overlooking the street. Fireplaces and chimneystacks were ranged along the rear wall, so also was a passage or gallery giving access to the upper rooms. Heavy, carved console brackets supported the jetties; decorative timber-work was more rife in the towns than in the countryside, though it can be found everywhere; the main windows had ovolo-moulded mullions and transoms, planted on the face of the wall panel and also bracketed beneath the sill; barge-boards, rare at every period in the countryside but more prevalent in towns, were also richly carved; but perhaps best of all was the framing and moulding of the floor beams and joists. Some of the ceilings thus produced must have compensated the Elizabethans for the disappearance of their predecessors' supreme open roofs.

Thus, the story of timber-framing, as Worcestershire tells it, is of an elaborate technique already mastered by the time of the earliest surviving buildings. These are invariably the most interesting and imposing in the scale of their timbers, if not in sheer size. Is the reason for this that all lesser buildings of their time have disappeared? More probably the lowlier buildings were not timber-framed but, instead, of post-hole construction – that is, buildings with lightly constructed roofs of alder or willow supported on posts dug into the ground. As late as the end of the C16 William Harrison described dwellings of the ordinary folk, not built of oak, and compared them with the fabulous new houses of the *nouveaux riches*. So it had taken centuries for a system, perhaps essential in the first place only for ship-building, but a luxury for dwellings, to penetrate downwards through medieval society, at last to become the right and property of every citizen. At first, however, it was *the* architecture, directly copied by masons, as in the little stone-built 'cruck' churches of Ireland or the wall-frame pattern of Earls Barton church and others of even much later date. Astley church is one whose walls reflect the main posts and storey height rail of timber precedent. A little window at Abbots Morton church has its tracery cut exactly as if by the carpenter's fret saw. Herringbone masonry perhaps derives from filling square panels with stone. The bay system of building is entirely the carpenter's. And, lastly, even if the great masons 'invented' Gothic, the carpenters confronted by the huge limbs of oak trees could have framed their tithe-barn roofs in no other conceivable way. So the gulf fixed between stone and oak architecture is as much a myth as the idea that houses were built of old ships' timbers. And the sooner done away with, the sooner it will be realized that pulling down a cruck 'cottage' may be historically and architecturally little better than destroying a Saxon (or should I say, Celtic?) church. The trouble is that after the mutilations of centuries so few timber buildings can be seen for what they were.

WORCESTERSHIRE

★

ABBERLEY 7060

ST MARY. 1850–2 by *J. J. Cole*, rebuilt with few alterations by the same architect after a fire in 1876. It is a stately church outside the village, of buff stone, with a SW steeple and aisles. The style is later C13. The arcades have polished columns and stiff-leaf capitals. The chancel is given its due prominence by marble shafts along the walls, and detached in front of the one-light windows. To the S chapel two two-light openings with cinquefoils in the spandrels, a favourite Victorian motif. The carving of the capitals was done by *Earp*. – PLATE. Paten on foot of 1714.

OLD CHURCH. In the village centre. Only the chancel is roofed, but the lower courses of the nave and W tower walls have also been kept and the S doorway. This is Norman, with a tympanum the bottom of which is segmental. The doorway is placed in a projection of the wall (cf. Stoulton and many other places). The rest is too badly weathered for recognition. The E respond of the S arcade indicates a C13 aisle. The present entry to the chancel is Norman (one order of colonnettes; zigzag arch) and was once a doorway into the nave on the N side. In the chancel is a Norman N window. The chancel E end is clearly a C13 lengthening. – MONUMENTS. Mrs W. and Mrs G. Walsh, the latter † 1679. A double monument of black and white marble, with three columns and a joint segmental pediment.

(RECTORY. A pre-Reformation hall-house with solar and service wings. The W side of the solar wing still shows its timber-framing. The hall roof survives above the upper floor which was put in in the first half of the C16. N of the hall a building of stone, originally separate, perhaps the first kitchen. It may date back to the C14. Canon J. S. Leatherbarrow)

Opposite the church a later C17 house with shaped gable-ends. The bricks are already laid in Flemish bond. Also JAYLANDS, an C18 brick house of three bays, the mid-windows stressed, e.g. on the first floor by a decorated lintel. One-bay pediment. On the road from the village to Astley, i.e. to the SE

(Firleigh, of ashlar, three bays with a central Venetian window and), Town Farmhouse, of *c.*1600 with two gabled cross wings with decorated bargeboard and finials. The r. gable has an overhang on brackets.

Abberley Hall, 1 m. sw. By *Dawkes*, built for Joseph Jones, *c.*1846. The house is entirely Italianate, in the way of Barry's Mount Felix at Walton-on-Thames of 1835–9, with the typical asymmetrical tower with open top stage. The tower is placed in the angle between the main block and the service wing. The main block has arched ground-floor windows, with blank shell pediments; top balustrade; deep porte-cochère. To the garden nine bays with a five-bay Ionic veranda. In 1883 *St Aubyn* built, at a distance opposite the entrance side, the amazing clock tower, very high and visible against the sky for miles around. Red, rock-faced lower stages, top of buff stone with projecting polygonal angle buttresses ending in pinnacles. Between them octagonal top stage with lucarne gables into the short spire. The tower was built by John Joseph Jones in memory of his father.

9050

ABBERTON

St Eadburga.* 1881–2 by *W. J. Hopkins*. Not a small church. w tower, and nave and chancel in one. The ornate w and e windows are typical of Hopkins. The interior is faced with yellow bricks, and there is some patterning in dark green and red brick. – font. Late Norman, round, with one band of arrowheads and one of zigzag. Very similar to the font at Wyre Piddle. – reredos. Early Victorian, of wood, now under the tower. – plate. Cup and Cover Paten, by *H. B.*, 1571; Salver Paten, by *S. R.*, *c.*1670.

Abberton Hall. Timber-framed and later encased in brick. Splendid stone chimneybreast, dated 1619, and three star chimneys of brick.

ABBEY MANOR *see* EVESHAM

0050

ABBOTS MORTON

2 A village predominantly of black and white houses and cottages of astonishing variety. The village layout consists of the church on its hill at one end of the street, the more important houses at the same end, giving place towards the lower end to the peasant

* Of Pershore.

houses and cottages built end-on to the street on long narrow plots. Several houses show how their timber frames were altered, probably at the end of the C17, bringing their elevations up to date or raising the roofs.

ST PETER. W tower, nave and chancel. The W tower has a late C14 W window with pretty tracery, the chancel a Dec E window and a straight-headed early C16 S window of three lights with quite uncommonly pretty tracery (cf. Broadway old church). The N transept is Dec too. Charming, unrestored interior with nice roofs and a plaster tympanum over the chancel arch. – COMMUNION RAIL. Jacobean, with sturdy, vertically symmetrical balusters. – BENCHES. Two plain ones with moulded top rails in the porch. – STAINED GLASS. In the N transept N window C15 and C18 glass, in the E window Flemish medallions, one dated 1590. – PLATE. Cup by *H. W.*, 1571.

ALDINGTON *see* BADSEY

ALFRICK 7050

ST MARY MAGDALENE. Long nave and lower chancel, timber bell-turret. In the nave one Norman S and one N window; and a Norman W window. Other windows are of all medieval centuries: nicely profiled cusped lancets of *c.*1300, a Dec E window with reticulation and two pretty, straight-headed Perp windows. The N transept and vestry added by *Aston Webb*, when he was young, in 1895 (PF). – PULPIT. Plain; Jacobean. – SCREEN. C15 dado with Victorian tracery. – STAINED GLASS. Many panels, round and oblong, of Netherlandish glass of the C16 and C17. – PLATE. Chalice by *H. W.* and Paten of 1571.

ALVECHURCH 0070

There was a house of the bishops of Worcester at Alvechurch, but it was pulled down in 1780. The more recent development is due to the Birmingham–Worcester Canal. Wharves are 2 m. N, at Hopwood, close to where the canal leaves the Westhill Tunnel.

ST LAURENCE. Norman S doorway. The capitals of the colonnettes odd, with a bundle of three lines at the corners converging into a small volute. Hood-mould with saltire crosses. C13 chancel, though the external details are mostly C19. But the vestry doorway inside has a continuous roll with a fillet and some dogtooth. Dogtooth and fillets also in the SEDILIA. The N aisle has one Perp and two Dec windows. The W tower has a date 1676, see the parapet details. Can the W doorway and the broad arch towards the nave also be C17? They both have continuous chamfers. But this description, singling out what is old, has falsified the true impression, which is of a Victorian brick building, red with white bands. Inside, this impression is strengthened so much that the architect is at once recognized. *Butterfield* rebuilt the church in 1859–61. The interior is of stone and red brick with white brick lozenges. The N arcade has round piers with round multi-scallop capitals, the S arcade round piers and E.E. moulded capitals. The chancel chapel arcades are typical Butterfield. Two bays, and in the spandrel a large octofoiled roundel with brick patterns. – STAINED GLASS. The E window of 1873 typical of *Gibbs*, Butterfield's favourite. – MITRE, in the chancel above the bishop's chair. Of wood. For the connexion with the bishops see above. The date of the mitre is not known.* – MONUMENTS. In the chancel Perp niche with ogee arch and buttress shafts, partly C19. – In the N chapel larger Dec niche with ogee arch and buttress shafts. The arch is cusped and crocketed. Under it effigy of a Knight, cross-legged but according to the dress late C14. The head with the visor half-down lies on a pillow held by two angels. The effigy is specially interesting from the point of view of armour. – Bishop Carpenter of Worcester † 1476. Coffin lid with a foliated cross – still! But the flowers inside the cross head betray the real date. Chalice and shield l. and r. of the cross shaft. – Brass to Sir Philip Chatwyn † 1525, a 28½ in. figure, quite good. – Edward Moore † 1746. Tablet with two pilasters and a round-arched centre. Fine Rococo cartouche at the foot. – In the churchyard MEMORIAL CROSS to Baroness Windsor, 1861 (*see* Tardebigge). Big, Gothic, heavily detailed.

RECTORY. 1872 by *Butterfield*. Big, of brick and half-timbering.

SCHOOL, School Lane. Probably 1856, by *Butterfield*, with additions. The schoolhouse on the l. is typical, with its half-hips and set-offs to chimneys.

Alvechurch has a vestigial central square with, alas, the A road running along it. At r. angles to the W rises BEAR HILL. Several nice houses and one more than nice: THE OLD HOUSE, timber-framed with two cross-gabled wings. Close

* The Rev. P. Blakiston thinks it is Victorian.

studding, big diagonal braces. In the upper parts decorated with concave-sided lozenges and ogee struts. The date is probably late C16.

ARELEY KINGS 8070

St Bartholomew. Of 1885–6 by *Preedy*, except for the S tower, which is Dec below (see the mouldings of the entrance arch) and Perp above, and the chancel, which has a Norman S window and an E window of *c.*1800. – Font. The base Norman with an inscription 'Tempore La. . amanni santi'. This refers to Layamon, the author of *Brut*. He died in 1200 and was priest at Earnley-by-Severn which may well mean Areley. – Sculpture. Small figure with an hourglass. From a sundial made in 1687. – Plate. Cover Paten 1570; Cup 1571.

Rectory. To the E a flat brick front, Jacobean, with three gables, looking a little stunted because of a Georgian parapet. To the churchyard a Georgian four-bay façade. (Magnificent staircase.) The summer house at the end of the garden is dated 1728. It is still a gabled house, but the brickwork is of course now in Flemish bond.

Church House, S of the church.* Timber-framed and small. Also to the S a beautiful view into the hills by the Teme.

Areley House, ¼ m. ESE. Late C18. Ashlar-faced. Five bays, two and a half storeys, with a three-bay pediment and a porch of pairs of unfluted Ionic columns. The entrance hall has a screen of two columns and behind it is an oval room represented outside by a big bow.

(Hermitage, 1 m. SE, in the parish of Astley. A whole system of apartments and cells on two levels, cut into the sandstone cliff by the Severn. As early as 1538 Bishop Latimer said it could 'lodge 500 men, as ready for thieves and traitors as true men'. VCH)

ASHTON-UNDER-HILL 9030

St Barbara. Unbuttressed W tower, begun in the C13. Norman nave, see the simple S doorway with one order of colonnettes and a roll moulding in the arch. In the S porch are re-set Dec window heads. The nave S windows are a mixture, including a four-light Perp window. The N aisle seems Victorian, but the arcade of four bays with octagonal piers and

* Or was it the priest's house? Canon Leatherbarrow has raised the question.

four-centred arches is Perp. The only really interesting feature of the church is the chancel, dated 1624. It shows how vague Jacobean Gothicism could be. The priest's doorway e.g. has a leaf frieze up the very arch, and the E window curious tracery with carved fishes in the spandrels. – FONT. Elaborate Perp piece. Octagonal, with fleurons in quatrefoils and leafy knobs coming out of the underside. – PLATE. Chalice and Paten Cover of 1578; Credence Paten, unmarked.

VILLAGE CROSS. C15, complete, except for the very top, which is replaced by a sundial.

Several worthwhile farmhouses.

7060

ASTLEY

11 ST PETER. The S wall of the nave shows that here someone about 1160 or so wanted to build lavishly, even if on the small scale of a parish church in a village. The wall is horizontally divided by a string course and by an eaves corbel frieze with heads and paired heads, and vertically by buttresses whose section above is semicircular but below of two semicircles and a spur between, as in Norman rib-vaults. Three windows are placed in this framework. The S doorway is set in a slightly projecting piece of wall (cf. Stoulton and other places). It has two orders of colonnettes with zigzag decoration (mostly the work of the restorers) and zigzag in the arch. In the chancel also are Norman windows, and the chancel arch consists of a pair of demi-columns and one recessed shaft E, one W. Decorated scallop capitals, single-step arch. The N arcade of three bays is Norman too, but later: circular piers with round trumpet-scallop capitals, octagonal abaci, single-step arches. That leaves the Perp W tower, whose arch to the nave has concave sides, as has also the thin capital-band, the Perp N chapel with an arch to the nave which is clearly interfered with, and the N aisle, which dates from *c.*1838. – FONT. Very odd and certainly not Norman, as the VCH says. The eight sides have each a big rising tulip-petal, as it were, and the top is heavily moulded. It is probably Perp, though unusual. – PULPIT. Jacobean, with the common broad blank arches. – MONUMENTS. Walter Blount † 1561 and wife. Recumbent
57 effigies. The tomb-chest with pilasters and kneeling children, the girls in closely pleated skirts, very Mannerist in this. – Robert Blount † 1573 and wife. Recumbent effigies. The tomb-chest still with balusters and wreaths, an Early Renaissance scheme. In the wreaths Tudor roses. – Samuel Bowater

† 1696 and Anne Bowater † 1687. Both cartouches, rather out of date for the late C17. – Sir Thomas Winford † 1702. Standing monument of white marble. Urn in a recess with looped-up curtains. Obelisks r. and l. with putto heads halfway up. – Sarah Winford † 1793. By *Bacon* and very similar to his monument in Bristol Cathedral. Benevolence with a pelican and Sensibility with flowers stand l. and r. of a pedestal with a wreathed urn looking outward. – Harriet Winford † 1801 and Sarah Freeman † 1806, both by *Bacon Jun.* Both with a seated pensive female figure by an urn, but the details differ just about enough.

ASTLEY HALL, ¾ m. E. Elizabethan to Jacobean with a symmetrical three-bay centre. The porch is of the Grafton type, but at the top are shaped gables. Lord Baldwin was born at Bewdley and died in Astley Hall.

(ASTLEY MILL, ½ m. WSW. A small C17 timber-framed water mill on a very high weir. Picturesque, with its external wheel and most of the internal machinery still intact. FWBC)

POOL HOUSE, ⅞ m. NE. A delightful late C18 Gothick façade set in front of a C17 house the character of which reveals itself round the corner. Mullioned and cross windows, star-topped chimneys, and two shaped gables. The façade is of three bays and has three even ogee gables with quatrefoils set in, ogee-headed windows, and four ogee Venetian windows. The doorway has a curious stepped hood, not at all Gothic but not correctly classical either.

GLASSHAMPTON MONASTERY, ¾ m. SSW. The noviciate of the Society of St Francis of Cerne Abbas. In 1918 the early C19 stables of Glasshampton House were converted for the Society of the Divine Compassion to start a Cistercian house within the Church of England. Handsome brick range with angle turrets with pyramid roof and a centre with pediment and lantern. The centre window is tripartite with a blank segmental arch over.

ASTON SOMERVILLE 0030

CHURCH. W tower, nave and chancel. The tower was started in the C13 – see the responds of the arch towards the nave. C13 also the chancel, the priest's doorway in fact rather *c.*1200. Perp E window. Much else Dec. A one-bay S chapel has been demolished. – FONT. A very odd piece. Is it Norman, cut down and re-tooled? – PULPIT. With Jacobean woodwork. – SCREEN. Perp, of one-light divisions. – STAINED GLASS.

Bits in a N aisle window. – PLATE. Chalice and Paten Cover of 1572; Alms Plate of 1681; Flagon of 1701. – MONUMENT. Later C13 effigy of a Knight in chain mail. A very tall figure.

ASTWOOD BANK

0060

ST MATTHIAS AND ST GEORGE. 1884 by *W. J. Hopkins*, in a conventional Dec. The N tower has never gone beyond the base storey. The nave was rebuilt in 1911 by *W. G. St J. Cogswell*. The playful tops of the long paired lancets betray the date externally. Otherwise one may well be reminded of the Commissioners' churches of a hundred years before. Pair of very high W lancets. Internally the piers without capitals are again typical of the early C20. Are they influenced by Bidlake of Birmingham? They are oblong octagons in section with short main sides and very long diagonals or chamfers.

BADGE COURT *see* ELMBRIDGE

BADSEY

0040

ST JAMES. Norman nave. Before the restoration of 1885, the present N window was in the S wall. Jamb of another N window. Norman N doorway. The lintel has a rope-frieze, the arch flat zigzag. Perp ashlar-faced W tower. Dec chancel. – FONT. The stem is early C14 and has excellent leaf capitals. – PULPIT. With linenfold panels. – PLATE. Cup, *c.*1571. – MONUMENTS. Richard Hoby † 1617. Two kneelers facing one another. On the prayer-desk a skull. Kneeling children below (facing W, not E, because her children are from a first husband). Two columns and two flat arches. An hourglass in relief between them. – William Jarrett, 1685. White marble tablet in rich surround.

MANOR HOUSE. A sick-house for the monks of Evesham Abbey. It was granted in 1545 to Sir Philip Hoby of Bisham. Late C16. Stone below, but above timber-framing with lively lozenge or herringbone patterns. The masonry is probably older.

SEWARD HOUSE. C17; stone. Recessed centre and two gabled wings. The windows of the one C17, of the other C18.

BLAKESMERE. Late Georgian. Ashlar. With two shallow upper bows.

STONE HOUSE. A beautiful later C17 stone house with slightly recessed centre and two gables. All windows of the cross type and already of classical proportions. String courses running through instead of hood-moulds. They only survive in the gables.

SILK MILL COTTAGES, at the E end of the village. Brick, two storeys, ten bays, Dated 1864. (The old MILL HOUSE itself is dated 1711. The mill closed about 1845–50.)

ALDINGTON MANOR HOUSE, ¾ m. NW. A fine ashlar-faced early C19 house with a recessed centre filled on the ground floor by a Tuscan porch. Giant pilasters at the angles of the wings.

BARBOURNE *see* WORCESTER, p. 334

BARNT GREEN

0070

ST ANDREW. 1909–14 by *A. S. Dixon.*

BARNT GREEN HOUSE, beyond the railway. Timber-framed. Dated *c.*1602 by the MHLG. The date refers to the r. part only. Two gables with decoration of concave-sided lozenges. Close studding below. Most of the chimneys are new.

LONGMEAD, formerly SANDHILLS FARMHOUSE, E of the church. Dated 1678. This is interesting, as it is a house which still has mullioned windows, but has them now symmetrically arranged: 3–2–3 lights above, 3–doorway–3 below. Porch with long, thin, attached columns and closed sides. The house is ashlar-faced.

BAUGHTON *see* EARLS CROOME

BAXTER MEMORIAL *see* WOLVERLEY

BAYTON

6070

ST BARTHOLOMEW. W tower of 1817 with arched bell-openings and windows with Y-tracery. Plain Norman S doorway. Zigzag arch, also lozenges broken round the angle (cf. Chaddesley Corbett).* The E window and other restoration is of 1905. The timber-framed wall between nave and chancel also of 1905. Fine roof with tie-beams, collar-beams, and wind-braces. – FONT. Drum-shaped, Norman, similar to the font at Rock. With beaded long scrolls and a rope-moulding. Short stem, with long, ribbed leaves.‡ – PULPIT. With Jacobean

* Mr Stratford reminds me that Noak reports a figured tympanum at Bayton. Its disappearance is particularly sad, as it might have cast some light on the relation between Bayton, Rock, and Chaddesley Corbett.

‡ Mr Stratford compares with Linley in Shropshire and abaci at Leominster in Herefordshire.

panels. – PLATE. Cup of 1656; Cover Paten with illegible hallmark.

SCHOOL HOUSE. E of the church. 1810. Single-storeyed, of brick. Six pointed windows with Y-glazing bars.

SHAKENHURST, 1¼ m. W. The front is dated 1798. It is of red brick, two and a half storeys high. Two canted bay windows and a three-bay centre between. Ionic porch with broken pediment. The back of the house seems early C17.

BEANHALL FARMHOUSES *see* BRADLEY

BEARWOOD *see* BIRMINGHAM OUTER WESTERN SUBURBS

9030

BECKFORD

ST JOHN BAPTIST. Nave, central tower, former S transept and chancel. Large Norman S doorway, originally in a wall projection. Two orders of columns and an outer vertical band of zigzag at r. angles to the wall, including the furrowed zigzag of e.g. Malvern Priory. Very decorated scallop capitals of the folded variety (cf. Eldersfield). The tympanum is supported on two corbels each with two heads, an Italian motif (cf. Ely
13 Cathedral). In the tympanum a cross with, above the arms, a roundel l., a bird r., and below two quadrupeds. The arch has much zigzag also at r. angles to the wall. In the S wall also a Norman window and a jamb-shaft of another, larger one. The Norman N doorway is not in its original state. It includes now two beast's heads of the Malmesbury type. The tympanum represents the Harrowing of Hell. Christ in the middle, his cross thrust into the mouth of the dragon. His other hand holds Adam (?) on a leash (cf. the tympanum of Quenington Gloucestershire and Shobdon Herefordshire). On the lintel a kind of honeysuckle frieze. The W wall of the nave shows traces of Norman fenestration. The present W window is Perp. The central tower was begun at the same time as the church. The W arch is Norman, like the doorways. Decorated scallop capitals, zigzag arch. The main l. shaft has a centaur placed across (again an Italian motif; cf. W doorway, S. Ambrogio, Milan) and two human heads set horizontally. The base of the shaft has a spur which bears a human head. The E, N, and S arches of plain chamfers and the springers for a rib-vault are E.E., and so are the upper parts of the tower, except for the top with the bell-openings (intersecting tracery), which must

be C18.* The chancel is E.E. Paired lancets and three E lancets with two roundels over in plate tracery.‡ – FONT. Octagonal, Perp, with fleurons in quatrefoils. – BENCH ENDS. Traceried panels. – PLATE. Chalice and Paten Cover, 1576; Credence Paten, 1719. – MONUMENT. Richard Wakeman † 1662. Tablet with strange and elegant vertically halved balusters l. and r. Open segmental pediment.

BECKFORD HALL. The house stands on the site of a priory of Augustinian canons founded in 1128. Of this buttresses survive now in the cellar. The house itself is Jacobean. It has a flat front with seven even gables. Most of the windows are Victorian, and there are large Victorian additions as well.

ENCLOSURES. In the fields to the E of the village and N of the Carrant Brook a series of rectangular enclosures in the gravels has been discovered by aerial photography. A number of these have been excavated, revealing a complex structural and cultural history beginning in the C2 B.C. with duck-stamped ware of south-western type.

At CONDERTON, 1 m. NW, is a stone house with the date 1675. It is interesting as showing how the Jacobean type develops into the classical type by gradual symmetrization. Each window here still has its hood-mould.

DANES CAMP, 1½ m. NNE of Conderton. This elongated earthwork occupies a steep-sided spur with strong natural defences. The first earthwork, built in the C2 BC., was a comparatively slight univallate structure enclosing the whole of the spur – an area of some 3 acres. There are entrances on the S and the middle of the N side. In the C1 B.C. the defended area was reduced to 2 acres by the construction of a stone-faced rampart on the S end of the spur. Occupation during this phase was probably permanent, as a series of storage pits and circular huts with stone footings occupy the interior.

BELBROUGHTON 9070

HOLY TRINITY. In the S aisle is a Norman window. It is totally renewed, but the S doorway contains some original Norman fragments. The PISCINA inside the aisle is a good, re-set C13 piece with a pointed trefoiled head. The priest's doorway

* It can hardly be 1622.

‡ The above treatment of the Norman parts of the building incorporates comments made by Mr Neil Stratford. He also points out that Italian motifs in English sculpture could have reached England by way of the Rhineland as easily as direct. Mr Stratford dates Beckford *c.*1160–75 and stresses how different its decoration is from anything farther North.

in the chancel with its continuous roll-moulding must be Norman again, even if late, but the chancel windows are Dec. There is indeed inside an ogee-headed N recess. The SEDILIA, although round-arched, are of course not Norman; they must be Late Perp. The whole N wall is of 1894–5, in spite of its irregular, partly old fenestration. Old also the doorway. It has an ogee head and is Dec. The N arcade is medieval too. With its slender piers and continuous chamfers it is probably Perp. The S arcade is certainly Late Perp (although parts are Victorian). For the concave-sided octagonal piers one has the Kidderminster parish church as a pattern. The chancel arch goes with these piers. – FONT. Octagonal, Perp, a standard job with quatrefoils and a flower in each. – PULPIT. Jacobean. The top frieze has dragons – a Norman reminiscence. – LECTERN. With re-used parts of the same design. – COMMUNION RAIL. Jacobean. – PAINTING. A female Saint at the E end of the S aisle towards the N. – STAINED GLASS. Old parts in a N aisle window. – S aisle E by *Kempe*, end of the C19. – Chancel S by the same, 1905. – PLATE. Restoration Cup; Salver of 1701; Cup of 1809.

RECTORY, E of the church. Five bays, C18. The middle three bays half a storey higher.

CHURCH HOUSE, S of the church. Late C18 Gothic. Three bays, cemented. The first-floor windows have four-centred arches. Above them quatrefoils and above them ogee gables.

SCHOOL, opposite this. Gothic, 1876, nothing special.

BRADFORD HOUSE, ½ m. S. Ashlar, H-shaped, and probably later C17. In the two gables oval openings. The Venetian doorway with a steep pediment is no doubt much later.

LYDIATE, opposite the former. Five-bay brick house of three storeys with a steep pediment and in it a keyed-in oval window. This is probably early C18. The doorway with its broken pediment is Later Georgian.

DRAYTON HOUSE, 1 m. SW. Brick. Seven bays, two storeys, hipped roof, windows with keystones, heavily detailed doorway. Is it early C18?

GROVE HOUSE, at the S end of Drayton hamlet. Brick, of five bays, the windows also with keystones. Doorway with Doric pilasters and pediment.

BELL HALL, at Bell End, 1⅛ m. E. In the garden a Norman CHAPEL. The side windows have remained Norman, but the E and W windows are plain, mullioned C17 pieces. The doorways are Norman too and quite simple.

BELL END FARMHOUSE, E of the former. Derelict at the time of writing. Later C17 probably, with two shaped gables and an oval opening in the third, straight, gable.

CASTLE BOURNE, 1⅝ m. E. Attached to the house is a late C18 folly castle with two round towers connected by a short length of wall. Quatrefoil windows and under the embattled top blank leafy cross-shapes. The connecting link with the house is a wall with three arches, the middle one wider and four-centred.

BELL END *see* BELBROUGHTON

BENGEWORTH

0040

ST PETER. 1870–2 by *T. D. Barry* of Liverpool. The cost was £3,550 (GS). Yet it is a large building with a prominent S steeple. Granite arcade columns inside. Large, graceless E window of five lights. – PLATE. Cup and Paten Cover by *R. C.*, 1627; small Cup and Cover by *R. C.*, 1636. – MONUMENTS. Thomas Watson † 1561. Quite a small tablet, but 56
typical of the elegance of classical detail in some of the earliest Elizabethan work. Two short columns, fine foliage frieze, pediment with a skull. Strapwork panel. – John Deacle † 1709. Large, standing marble monument. He is seen seated or half-reclining on the ground. Back wall with pilasters and open segmental pediment. Inscription on a piece of drapery.

OLD CHURCH, Church Street. Only the lowest stage of a S tower survives. Diagonal buttresses. Entrance with two continuous chamfers.

(VICARAGE, 49 Broadway Road. Built in 1866. Gothic of the type which Canon Leatherbarrow nicely calls 'fit for Tractarians to live in'.)

SECONDARY SCHOOL, Four Pools Road. By *Richard Sheppard & Partners*, 1954–6. Very good, with light engineering bricks and some wood slatting. Low and of varied outline.

PORT STREET is the main street. It leads down to Evesham Bridge and is continued by Bridge Street, Evesham. The more interesting houses are all away from the bridge and near the new church. Opposite it LANSDOWN, a handsome stuccoed early C19 house with giant fluted Ionic angle pilasters, and a Greek Doric porch. Its STABLES are low and unstuccoed. Then two cottages with doorway hoods on iron supports. Farther on, opposite, the POST OFFICE with flat (late) Venetian windows and finally an ashlar-faced terrace of houses

(58–64) with very curious, wilful detailing of the ground floor. There are wooden posts, but, instead of capitals, oblong fluted boxes.

Along the river runs WATERSIDE. Here is FAIRWATER, a handsome gabled and pebble-dashed house, not by *Lutyens*, and the HOSPITAL, Late Georgian, long, of brick, with a three-bay pediment.

BENTLEY PAUNCEFOOT

9060

ST MARY. Red brick; 1874–5. Built at the expense of Lord Windsor.

KEYS FARMHOUSE. T-planned house of *c.*1600, with a hall range consisting of the fireplace bay, hall, and kitchen bay, all of two floors and attic. Also a solar cross-wing. The latter is close-timbered below with square panels above. The front of the house part is close-timbered on both levels.

BEOLEY

0060

ST LEONARD. The earliest piece is the C12 chancel arch, unmoulded, and on the most elementary imposts. Then follows the S arcade, early or mid C13, and the N arcade of about 1300. One of the piers of the S arcade has a round core and two detached shafts with shaft-rings in the diagonals. The N arcade has a little nailhead and typical quatrefoil piers in two versions. The W tower and N aisle are Perp. Heavy decoration of the W doorway and the N doorway with its niche over. In the S aisle a C17 dormer, restored. The N (Sheldon) chapel is late C16, with a very characteristic five-light E window. The lights end straight, and there is simplified panel tracery above – i.e. an elementarized Perp conceit. – FONT. Circular, with four big female heads on the underside. What is the date? Can it really be Norman? – SCULPTURE. Small Norman relief of an abbot in mass vestments. One arm is raised. – PAINTING. Italian Trecento Crucifixion with the Virgin and St John. Said to have been bought at Rimini *c.*1929. – STAINED GLASS. In the N chapel E window part of a canopy; in a S aisle window minor bits. – MONUMENT. A C13 coffin lid with a foliated cross is in the Sheldon Chapel. – The two principal monuments are between the chapel and the chancel. They are to William Sheldon † 1570 and his wife and to Ralph Sheldon † 1613 and his wife. They are the same in type but different in all details. Tomb-chests with arched canopy, columns l. and r., and top achievements. Both are of stone, not alabaster. William Sheldon started the first English tapestry workshops (at Barcheston and Bordesley). – In the Sheldon Chapel are set in blind arcading the tomb-chests with back-wall achievements of two other Sheldons, made in 1600 and 1601, again identical in type and different in all details. – Many more Sheldon tablets in the chapel, e.g. † 1663 and † 1684. – In the churchyard base of a CROSS with blank quatrefoils.

BEOLEY HALL. The house, three-storeyed, stuccoed, and at the time of writing in poor repair, could, with its projecting wings, be late C17 or early C18. But the E wing was partly rebuilt in 1791 by *John Sanders*, and this rebuilding was an architecturally more ambitious job – two-storeyed, though to the same height as the former three, and with only three wide bays to the E. Porch of four Tuscan columns. Tripartite windows with blank segmental arches l. and r., a handsome vase and garland arrangement on the parapet. Several reliefs of Pompeian or Wedgwood type. Inside a staircase behind a screen of two columns and with a round skylight, and a large room with a honeysuckle frieze in the Adam tradition. The bow windows on the S side must date from *c.*1791 too, but they were originally only one-storeyed.

BERROW

7030

ST FAITH. Norman nave and chancel. The N doorway has one order of colonnettes and a single-stepped arch. The chancel was lengthened in the C14. The S arcade is Perp but much pulled about. Dec to Perp W tower with square higher stair-turret. The arch to the nave has two continuous chamfers. – FONT. Norman, of cauldron shape, with one rope and one beaded rope pattern. – PULPIT. C17. The panels have a simple flower in the middle. – PLATE. Salver Paten, 1682; Chalice, 1714; Flagon and Almsdish by *Humphrey Payne*, 1749.

HOLIDAY FARM, ½ m. W. The BARN, unattractive externally at the time of writing, has splendid cruck trusses inside. It is assigned to the C14.

BESFORD

9040

ST PETER. This is the only timber-framed church in Worcestershire. Comparison would have to look to Shropshire (Melverley, Halston). The framing is in very large squares (nearly

5 ft), and yet the date can hardly be later than the mid C14 – see the ogee-headed N doorway and the W window with a quatrefoil in a roundel in the spandrel between two ogee-headed lights.* The thin bell-tower with traceried bell-openings and spire must be *Hopkins*'s, who restored the church in 1880–1. Apart from the squares there are bold diagonal braces. The S porch is also timber, but probably C15. The chancel with E.E. windows is by Hopkins. Internally, the timber posts carry tie-beams which carry queen-posts. There is also the complete ROOD LOFT parapet with fleurons in quatrefoils and a top cresting. The handsomely carved vine foliage below was no doubt the top of the SCREEN. Only the part nearest the N end is original. – COMMUNION RAIL. Jacobean. Very heavy balusters. – PANELLING in the nave, also C17. – HELMET. With an animal as the crest. – PLATE. Cup by *R. F.* and Cover Paten by *R. D.*, the latter dated 1590. – MONUMENTS. Richard Harewell † 1576 aged fifteen. Recumbent alabaster effigy with a thin low wooden railing around. The railing stands on the stone tomb-chest. It consists – very curiously – of horizontal reticulation units. The tomb-chest has on the front a small arched panel with a frontal little child. Back wall with wooden panelling and decoration. – Another member of the Harewell family, probably fourth quarter of the C16. Painted triptych with movable wings (cf. Burford, Shropshire). On the outside shields, two of them held by large figures of angels. When opened it shows the deceased kneeling and smaller figures and scenes above, l. and r., which are, alas, largely destroyed or damaged. Above him was Christ in Majesty on the rainbow. Below was a child playing at a tank. In the 'predella' is the dead body of a child and l. and r. two putti, one with a flower, the other blowing bubbles. On the inner wings were Father Time and Death with a dart and beneath the following inscription (abridged):

Of Harewell's blodde ere conquest made
Knowne to descende of gentle race,
And sithence linckt in jugall leage
With Colles whose birth and vertues grace,
An Impe entombed heere dothe lie,
In tender years berefte of breath;
Whose hope of future virtuous lyfe
Was plaine forshewed by lyfe and death.

* But Mr Charles pronounces in favour of the late C14 and attributes the screen to that time as well.

A Childe he seemde of graver years,
And childishe toies did quyte dispise:
He sought by yealdinge parents due,
And serving God to clime the skies
But prickte with percing plagues of death
For mercie still to God he cryde.
Soo lyvde he with the love of men,
Soe deere in sight of God he dyed.

– Sir Edward Sebright † 1679. Twisted columns and an open segmental pediment. In the 'predella' the small kneeling figures of two daughters who died aged two and five.

BESFORD COURT. Besford Court has not only a very good timber-framed range of *c.*1500, but also extremely good work of 1912 behind, the best of that just pre-modern date in the county. The W front is quite flat. In it a gateway with a flat-topped arch and the original door. Above it an oriel and gable, the gable with decoration in timber of *c.*1600. All the rest is the typical close vertical studding of the C15 and early C16. The ground-floor windows are renewed and with their pediments no doubt also represent *c.*1600. There is a timber-framed wing running E from the N end, and the S side of the front range continues with two gables. After that the work of 1912 sets in. It is by *Randall Wells* (1877–1942), one of the most interesting architects of that moment in England. He started as Clerk of Works to Lethaby at Brockhampton church in 1901–2 and clerk and partner to E. S. Prior at Roker church and Kelling Place. The two churches are among the best of their years in Europe. Wells's S front of Besford Court is neo-Tudor and no mistake about it. But the way he organized the façade is admirable. Three canted bay windows on the ground floor only and two first-floor oriels in carefully chosen relation to the bays below. The fenestration with its mullions and transoms also is broken in just one place by two arched tripartite windows. To the E the canted apse of the chapel projects. This is in an imitation-Romanesque which is – in contrast to the rest – uninspiredly imitative. But the real thrill of the house is the interior. Through the gateway one enters a straight passage with low cloister openings to the l. to show the timber studding of the range referred to. To the r. in a bold sweep – of Lutyens inspiration – the main staircase curves up to the upper floor. At the end of the 103
passage is a spacious courtyard with a cloister on the ground floor and a gallery on the upper floor. The cloister has two round-arched openings with a roundel above, again a little

too conventional a motif, the gallery has on the W side large round arches, on the other side just small two-light windows. A secondary staircase, also curved, is in the SE corner of the cloister. In the middle of the E range is the chapel, the nave covered by very impressive closely placed transverse stone arches on double forward-curving corbels – all this a South French motif. Wells was as remarkable in his choice of patterns as in his treatment of those he had chosen. The main hall of the house has bold transverse stone arches across, a motif used by Norman Shaw.

BEVERE *see* NORTH CLAINES

7070

BEWDLEY

Bewdley in the C15 and C16 was a more important town than it is now. Its charter was given by Edward IV in 1472. Leland writes that 'the whole towne glittereth, being all of new buildings'. Prince Arthur resided for a while at Tickenhill Manor, there were several local industries in the C16 to C18, and much of the carrying trade on the Severn was centred on Bewdley. Stourport in the late C18 did much to change this, after Bewdley had made it known that they did not want the Worcestershire and Staffordshire Canal to end at Bewdley. Yet, quiet as it now is, or because it is now quiet, Bewdley is the most perfect small Georgian town in Worcestershire, and it is not too late to preserve it as such. There is only one danger spot so far. Gordon Cullen has shown how the town ought to be looked at and cared for. It has three visual blessings: a riverside street, a wide river crossed by a fine bridge, and a short wide street continuing that bridge and ending in a Georgian church.

ST ANNE. The W tower is of 1695–6, the body of the church of 1745–8. The architect of 1745–8 was *Thomas Woodward* of Chipping Campden. The tower is of rougher stone than the rest, but in style there is no clash between the two periods. The church has five arched windows each side and a Venetian window in the E facing down the street. Top balustrade. The tower windows are also arched, but the forty years' difference in time comes out in the different surrounds. Inside are giant
81 Tuscan columns carrying a plaster tunnel-vault and straight ceilings in the aisles. The chancel is lower, and the chancel arch segmental. Galleries at the W end. – PULPIT. Contemporary with the church. With a little discreet inlay. – PLATE.

Cup, Paten, and Flagon of 1637; two Patens of 1759. – There are no monuments at all left in the church.

For CHAPELS and PUBLIC BUILDINGS *see* the Perambulation.

PERAMBULATION. Start on the BRIDGE, which is by *Telford* and dates from 1795–8. It cost £9,000. Three beautiful segmental arches with rusticated extradoses. Small land arches. Substantial stone balustrade. Along the approaches on both sides slimmer cast-iron balustrading. At the Bewdley end of the bridge one can take Load Street straight on, but one should perhaps first walk along the river. SEVERNSIDE is a perfect river-bank street, as good in its minor way as the Brinks at Wisbech. The individual houses of the N part are of no special interest. Along the S part there are Nos 5–6, late C17, of brick, RIVER HOUSE of five bays with a shell-hood on carved brackets over the doorway and the central window crowned by a far-projecting pediment, then a gap which is a sign of danger, and all care should be taken to ensure a good (and modern) infilling, then the THURSTON HOTEL of three bays with the middle recessed and provided with a doorway with Tuscan columns and a pediment, echoing the two bigger pediments of the two projecting bays, and so finally No. 27, timber-framed, with a slight overhang and two gables. Oriels on the first floor on little brackets. What makes Severnside so attractive is the directness in the relation between the houses and the river, without trees or even a railing.

LOAD STREET leads from the bridge to the church. It is, as has 3
already been said, a short, wide street, closed at the end by the six-bay side of the largest Georgian house in Bewdley and by the E view of the church, subtly (though by chance) out of axis. No. 5 is stuccoed and only one and a half bays wide. The main bay has a blank giant arch. No. 6 is of five bays with decorated lintels and two canted ground-floor bay windows. Opposite, No. 71 is of four bays with a two-bay pediment and Venetian windows in the first and fourth bay. Then No. 66 with a shop front of Tuscan columns and some cast-iron foliage in the fascia. Opposite is the TOWN HALL, 1808, probably by *Sympson*. Three bays, tall open rusticated arched ground floor. Giant Doric pilasters above in a rhythm of 1–2–2–1.* Next to the town hall is the POST OFFICE, a fine C16 house of timber-framing with two gabled wings and a recessed gabled centre. Overhang and all close studding.

* CORPORATION PLATE. Two silver Maces of the early C18.

Opposite a six-bay brick house of three storeys with decorated keystones. Then the GEORGE HOTEL, of four bays stuccoed, and Messrs WEATHERHEAD, with a fine, very lively timber-framed front. The decoration includes concave-sided lozenges and also squares with lobes coming out of the middles of the sides. The six-bay black and white house which follows is in fact painted imitation of timber-framing. On the other side one has now reached Nos 15–18, one three-and-a-half-storeyed brick house of six bays to the N and nine to the W. The half-storey has arched windows. To the W is a three-bay pediment. The first-floor middle window has pilasters and an open pediment, the window above that a Gibbs surround. By the church the street splits, and there are no more important houses (except for a timber-framed three-storey building that can be glimpsed at the foot of Park Lane just beyond its narrow entrance into Load Street. But this will have gone by the time of publication, and instead a wide road entrance will carry the eye to spec houses clambering up the hillside; FWBC).

So turn E to walk the HIGH STREET, a narrow street, not straight, and with shops only at its W end. Nos 69–68 of 1610 is the best timber-framed house at Bewdley, with concave-sided lozenge patterns above and three dormers. Doorway with carved spandrels and corbels.* No. 67 is timber-framed too and, at the time of writing, derelict. Then, lying quite far back, the church of the HOLY FAMILY (R.C.), built *c.*1680 as the PRESBYTERIAN CHAPEL, oblong with both ends rounded. Arched windows. Curved W gallery. Opposite, No. 12 lies back a little too and stands on its own. It is of *c.*1775, of five bays. Doorway with broken pediment on Tuscan columns. Again on the other side a good group with the MANOR HOUSE of 1607‡ but refaced Georgian with rusticated quoins of even length and a small doorway with segmental pediment. The METHODIST CHURCH is of 1795. Three bays, stuccoed, with arched windows and a doorway with broken pediment. The HIGH STREET ALMSHOUSES are externally of 1860 but have the foundation plaque of 1693.

* A splendid two-storey-and-attic house, jettied at each floor. Heavy Jacobean console brackets support the jetties. The first-floor windows are original with ovolo-moulded mullions, planted on the face of the wall-frame. The plan is of three bays with a wide gallery at the back for the lateral fireplace and staircase (FWBC).

‡ The piece of timber with the date is put up on the wall of the neighbouring house.

LOWER PARK is the continuation of the High Street. No. 15 is a five-bay brick house. The doorway has a segmental hood on carved brackets. Lord Baldwin was born here. Opposite a five-bay house on its own, Tuscan doorway with pediment. The SAYERS ALMSHOUSES were founded in 1763 but look Victorian. The FRIENDS' MEETING HOUSE lies behind older houses and is a plain two-bay cottage. The interior fitments are well preserved, and the graveyard deserves a visit.

A little farther out KATESHILL HOUSE, mid-C18, of five bays with a pedimented Venetian doorway, and then WYNTERDINE, built in 1758. Bow windows and a Tuscan porch. The house is stuccoed and has inside 'a delightful series of curved rooms' (G. Beard).

TICKENHILL MANOR is reached by continuing in the line of Park Lane up the hill. The house is of nine bays with a short, probably recent, projecting wing. Its exterior is of *c.*1740 and quite plain, but inside are the roof timbers of a C15 hall. The house became a royal manor under Edward IV and remained one in the C16, when the Council of the Marches often met at Tickenhill. (In the grounds is supposed to be an ICE HOUSE, 8 ft in diameter and as much as 28 ft high.)

BIRLINGHAM 9040

ST JAMES. The W tower, which is Perp, stands forward beyond the S aisle of the church. The church itself is by *Benjamin Ferrey* and dates from 1871–2. The tower has a higher stair-turret, the top of which is probably also of the time of the rebuilding. The new building has competently handled geometrical tracery and also one segment-headed imitation-Dec window. Of the old church a Norman arch was re-erected as the entrance to the churchyard. It was the chancel arch and has one order of shafts, single-scalloped capitals, and zigzag at r. angles to the wall in the arch. – LECTERN. A life-size stone angel with the Bible open at the beginning of *Acts*. By *Theodore Pfyffers*. – SCULPTURE. In the porch two corbel-heads. – PLATE. Chalice, 1655; Paten by *I. C.*, 1667; Salver Paten by *Humphrey Payne*, 1742.

(PARSONAGE. The surviving plans are dated 1774. Canon J. S. Leatherbarrow)

BIRMINGHAM OUTER WESTERN SUBURBS 9080

The area here taken together is now mostly the new County Borough of Warley. It consists of Smethwick, Oldbury, Rowley

Regis (these three now called Warley), and in addition Langley, Cradley, and Blackheath. As they are really Birmingham, the user would only be confused by the boundaries which he can nowhere notice. All these parts of Birmingham have new high housing, and it is nowhere of special architectural distinction, though much of it may be of interest to those who follow the industrial production of the components of housing.

CHURCHES

In alphabetical order of places.

ST MARY, Bearwood Road, Bearwood. 1888 by *J. A. Chatwin.* Brick, without a tower. The interior shows the bricks too. Short round stone piers. – STAINED GLASS. The E window by *Kempe*, 1887.

ST PAUL, Long Lane, Blackheath. 1869 by *Hopkins*. Brick, large, but without tower, with short round piers carrying Early Gothic capitals and a clerestory in the most curious rhythm. How is one to account for it?

ST PETER, above the High Street, Cradley. In a fine position. Built in 1789 for the Countess of Huntingdon's Connexion. Square with arched windows and galleries inside (remodelled in 1933). The W tower is a Gothic addition of 1876. It is of darker brick and has a bell stage with pairs of shafted lancets. The shallow and wide apse is later still. It was built in 1933.

(ST JOHN EVANGELIST, Cradley. 1855–6 by *Preedy*.)

ST PHILIP, High Park Road, Cradley Heath. By *Alfred Pilkington*, 1893. Brick and brown terracotta. Round-arched details and an odd façade with a kind of low bastions l. and r. of the portal. Short marble-faced chancel with, against the E wall, an upper blind colonnade. The transepts are two bays deep from W to E and two bays long from N to S. The tall columns are used in pairs, with thick shaft-rings.

ST LUKE, Upper High Street, Cradley Heath. 1847 by *William Bourne*. The apse of 1874. Pebbledash and lancet windows. The three W doorways are set in columned arcading.

ST MICHAEL, Causeway Green Road, Langley. 1890–1. Brick, without a tower. Lancets and geometrical tracery.

HOLY TRINITY, Trinity Street, Langley. Disused. 1852. Stone, with a bellcote. Late C13 tracery.

CHRISTCHURCH, Church Street, Oldbury. 1840 by *Johnson*. Alterations of 1867. Brick, with a NW tower. Pairs of lancets along the sides. Inside wooden galleries squeezed under the arcade arches. Short, square-ended chancel.

ST FRANCIS XAVIER (R.C.), Pinfold Street, Oldbury. 1865. Recently given up.

ST GILES, Church Road, Rowley Regis. 1923 by *A. S. Dixon* and *H. W. Hobbis*. Red brick with a square W tower.

OLD CHURCH, Uplands and Church Road, Smethwick. 1728. Brick, with a W tower and round-arched windows. The nave is four bays long. – MONUMENTS. Several Georgian tablets, especially one of † 1760 with a pretty Rococo cartouche at the foot.

ST MATTHEW, Windmill Lane, Smethwick. 1855 by *Joseph James*. Stone, with bellcote.

ST MICHAEL, Crocketts Lane, Smethwick. By *A. E. Street*, 1892. Brick, without a tower. Lancet style. Impressively wide nave. There is a transeptal N addition, but without any interruption of the arcade. The arcade is the best thing in the church. Square, slightly chamfered piers and arches taking in the triplet lancets of the clerestory. The arcade arches themselves are surprisingly not pointed but round.

ST PAUL, St Paul's Road, West Smethwick. The old church is largely demolished. But *Denys Hinton & Associates* in rebuilding in 1965–6 left the steeple and part of the N wall and a funny turret now inside, and made the wall with its window the boundary between the street and a forecourt. It is a handsome solution.

ST STEPHEN, Cambridge Road, Smethwick. 1900–2 by *F. T. Beck*.

HOLY TRINITY, Birmingham Street, Smethwick. 1838, but rebuilt in 1887–8 by *F. Bacon* of Newbury. Of the church of the thirties remains the W tower with spire and possibly the aisle windows (pairs of lancets) which, if this is so, are re-set in the new aisles. The W windows of the aisles have geometrical tracery of 1887–8. Six-light E window. Wide nave and round piers.

OUR LADY AND ST HUBERT (R.C.), Bleakhouse Road, Warley. 1935 by *G. Drysdale*. Brick basilica with round-arched windows and a SE campanile. The interior has square, marble-faced piers, unmoulded arches, and narrow passage aisles. Apse.

NONCONFORMIST CHAPELS

They are in chronological order.

WESLEYAN CHAPEL, Church Street, Oldbury. Inscribed WESLEY 1853, four-square and red.

SIKH TEMPLE, High Street, Smethwick. Formerly CONGREGATIONAL. 1853–4. Italianate, brick and stucco. Two doorways; four giant pilasters, thinly rusticated, support a pediment.

WESLEYAN CHAPEL, New Street, Smethwick. 1855–6 by *G. B. Nicholls*.

BAPTIST CHAPEL, Regent Street, Smethwick. 1877. Brick. A more elaborate and expensive version of the Sikh Temple. Pompous Baroque. Giant pilasters and other details in stone. In addition a two-tier Jacobean frontispiece with a double doorway.

METHODIST CHURCH, Regent Street, Smethwick. 1887. Modest Lombard Renaissance; of three bays. Round-headed doorway with gable, three-light window with a segmental head with pierced quatrefoil and carved foliage. Acanthus string course and quatrefoils either side of the doorway.

METHODIST CHURCH, Waterloo Road, Smethwick. 1896 by an architect called *Harper*. Of the Church-of-England type. Gothic, with a NW steeple; geometrical tracery.

WARLEY WOOD METHODIST CHURCH, Abbey Road, Smethwick. 1928 by *Moss* of *Crouch, Butler & Savage*. Massive walls, tiny windows, steeply pitched roof with dormers. Low aisles and squat W tower. Simplified Perp details; rather arty.

THE CENTRES IN ALPHABETICAL ORDER

This includes Public Buildings. Nowhere is a true perambulation possible.

HADEN HILL
between Cradley and Blackheath

HADEN HILL HOUSE. Halesowen Road. Brick, with stepped gables and canted bay windows. An odd motif is short lengths of blank pointed arches above windows. Also occasionally plain blank triangles. The date is probably the first half of the C17. The SW side is better preserved than the front. Brick DOVECOTE.

OLDBURY

In the MARKET PLACE the MUNICIPAL BUILDINGS, 1890 by *Wood & Kendrick*, red brick, with a corner tower, in a vaguely Norman-Shaw–1630–50 style. Much more rewarding the TALBOT HOTEL, stuccoed, symmetrical, of about 1840 or so, with a Tuscan entrance *in antis.* In CHURCH STREET the former COURT HOUSE (now Police), 1816. Five bays, two storeys. Brick, with all the windows set under arches. On the opposite side THE BIG HOUSE, early C18, of four bays and three storeys, rather blunt, but with a doorway with open curly pediment.

In BURY HILL PARK is a KEEPER'S COTTAGE, transferred from a different site. It is by *Voysey*, a comfy-looking job, with a big hipped roof and Voysey's customary buttresses.

SMETHWICK

In the HIGH STREET the LIBRARY, built as the Public Hall in 1866–7 by *Yeoville Thomason*, very poor Gothic. Turn l. to the end of High Street and along part of the Oldbury Road. To the N in ROEBUCK LANE two bridges across the old and the new canal. The OLD CANAL was built by *Brindley* in 1768–9 to carry coal from Wednesbury to Birmingham. The SUMMIT BRIDGE is of 1789. *Telford* in 1826 built the NEW CANAL. By him is the GALTON BRIDGE of 1829. It is of iron and has a span of 150 ft. Just one arch, in the details identical with his bridge of 1828 at Holt. Turn E along Dartmouth Road to reach HALFORD'S LANE, for the large metal window factory of HENRY HOPE. Their new office building by *John H. D. Madin & Partners* of 1963–4 is excellent, with its bold staircase tower interrupting the even curtain walling. At the S end of the High Street is the COUNCIL HOUSE, 1905–7 by *Fred J. Gill* of Smethwick. Two storeys with central attached portico and a high cupola. The style might be called a free, somewhat Baroque William and Mary. The material is brick and Bath stone.

Yet further S, at the end of BEARWOOD ROAD, in Lightwoods Park is LIGHTWOODS HOUSE. Brick, five bays and two storeys. The upper windows have pilasters with intermittent square blocks and segmental pediments with coarse shell motifs. The enclosed porch has columns also with square blocks, and the blocks are continued as bands. It is all very restless and looks Early Georgian. But there is supposed to be a brick inside, inscribed 1789.

WARLEY

At CAUSEWAY GREEN a PRIMARY SCHOOL of 1951–2 by *Yorke, Rosenberg & Mardall.* A difficult site led to much changing of levels. Combined chimney and water tower.

8030 BIRTSMORTON

ST PETER AND ST PAUL. A Dec church with a Perp W tower. Dec the nave windows, Victorian Dec the E and transept N and S windows. – COMMUNION TABLE. Mid-C18, of wrought iron, with a marble top, graceful and very unecclesiastical-looking. – EMBROIDERY. The purpose of the piece with the Hastings arms and the date 1693 is not known. – STAINED
36 GLASS. Many fragments of the late C14 and C15 in many windows, the best in a chancel S window. This includes the very rare representation of the Baptism of St Christopher. – PLATE. Cup and Cover by *Thomas Heard*, 1571; Almsdish by *R. W.*, *c.*1693. – MONUMENTS. Tomb-chest with many kneeling figures but without effigy. Probably the tomb of Jane Nanfan in memory of her three husbands. The first was an Arundel, and the kneeling bishop would in that case be Bishop Arundel of Chester, her son. This would date the tomb to *c.*1500. – Bridges Nanfan † 1704. Small tablet signed by *White* of Worcester. Nothing special. – This alone is not enough reason to attribute to him the excellently carved monument to Admiral William Caldwall † 1718. Semi-reclining effigy, on the tomb-chest his flagship. Reredos background, with a multitude of nautical instruments. Top a cartouche already asymmetrical, i.e. Rococo, and military trophies.

BIRTSMORTON COURT. An eminently picturesque house placed in a wide moat. The prospects are varied on every side. The architectural history is far from clear. The archway on the N side built of stone and with a segmental arch is clearly C14, and the range to its E has a stone base too and may be as old. The E range of the house has disappeared, leaving the irregular courtyard open. The S range contains the hall. Its entrance is heavily timbered. It leads into the screens passage. The hall itself has a big fireplace in its S wall. To the outside the chimneybreast in its lower part is again of stone. To the W of the hall is the Parlour with fine panelling with Corinthian pilasters and a ceiling with beams and plasterwork. A second room has a ceiling of the same period. The period is that of Giles Nanfan, i.e. 1572 and after, whereas the C15 or early C16 belongs to either Sir John Nanfan († 1446) or Sir Richard († 1506). Externally the S side is especially picturesque.*

*The solar cross-wing is medieval with once jettied S gable. The original roof has gone, and externally the wing is entirely of C18 and C19 brickwork and windows. The hall with enormous wall-posts and Elizabethan windows

BISHAMPTON

9050

ST PETER. Perp W tower, the rest by *Preedy*, 1870–1. He used, however, ancient parts such as the late C12 S doorway and the simpler N doorway. The S doorway has one order of colonnettes with trumpet scallop capitals and a moulded arch with a keeled roll. An animal head above the apex. The N doorway has a continuous roll. Also old one Norman S window. – FONT. Of cauldron shape; late C12. Decoration of crosses, rosettes, and rope mouldings (cf. Bricklehampton and South Littleton). – HOURGLASS STAND. Of iron; by the pulpit. – ARCHITECTURAL FRAGMENT. Small part of a stone screen from Worcester Cathedral, with one reticulation unit. – PLATE. Shell-shaped Paten by *Thomas Maundy*, 1634; Cup and Salver Paten by *Thos. Wynne*, 1778.

In the village street, on the E side, is a stately, symmetrical timber-framed house, dated 1629. Two projecting gabled wings. Square panels and brick infilling. Some diagonal and some curved struts.

(COURT FARM, next door, is very much older. It was once a cruck hall with solar cross-wing, but is now entirely cased in brick. The inserted floor of the upper hall bay has richly moulded beams. FWBC)

BLACKHEATH *see* BIRMINGHAM OUTER WESTERN SUBURBS

BLACKSTONE ROCK *see* STOURPORT

BLAKEDOWN

8070

ST JAMES. By *G. E. Street*, 1866, but the bell-turret not by him, and the aisle of 1905. Thus little of his remains, other than the uncoursed stone walling.

(HARBOROUGH HALL. Timber-framed with Jacobean ceilings. The VCH mentions two priest holes.)

BLAKES HALL *see* WOLVERLEY

---

opposite a lateral fireplace was panelled up to the screens gallery. The gallery, supported by circular oak posts, was continued across the chimneybreast and round the upper end of the hall. The walls above the gallery, and also the ceiling, are heavy geometrically moulded plasterwork. The trusses, still in the medieval tradition, were, however, never open to the hall. Structure, plan, and details all point to *c.*1580. The rest of the house, consisting of a service bay continuous with the hall and a stone and timber-framed service wing, is too much altered to be of interest (FWBC).

5060

BOCKLETON

ST MICHAEL. C17 or early C18 W tower, Norman nave, and E.E. chancel.* Norman the buttresses, the (enlarged?) windows, and the doorways. The S doorway has two orders of colonnettes with decorated scallop capitals, and in the arch two thick rolls. Crenellation and a lozenge chain on the hood-mould. Above blind arcading of five interlaced arches, the arches with billet decoration. The N doorway is of the same *parti*, yet richer, and different in the details. Both doorways are set in a projecting piece of wall (cf. Stoulton and other places).‡ The chancel has two-light windows with pointed-trefoiled heads. The E window is of *Woodyer*'s restoration of 1862 and showy. – STAINED GLASS. E window by *Kempe*, *c.*1905. – PLATE. Two Patens of 1719; Flagon of 1727; Cup, probably C18. – MONUMENTS. Is the round-arched nave N recess connected with a former (C16?) monument? – Richard Barneby and wife. Put up in 1594. Sandstone. Two elaborately carved recumbent effigies, a helmet between their heads. Tomb-chest with caryatids. Also larger caryatids l. and r. carrying obelisks which frame the back wall. Against it kneel the children. The top is – oddly enough – a pediment of two double curves – as if it were much later. On them a boy blowing bubbles and Father Time. – Charles Baldwyn † 1706. Standing monument without an effigy. Predominant 'reredos'. – William Wolstenholme Prescott. By *Woolner*, 1867. White marble. Recumbent effigy. On the tomb-chest a relief of a young man holding the hand of an older dying man. The young man died of a fever caught while attending to the old man, who was his gamekeeper. – The LYCHGATE is C15 work, perhaps from a porch.

BOCKLETON COURT (Camp School). 1866–9 by *Henry Curzon*. Neo-Jacobean, of brick.

(BOCKLETON COURT FARM, the old manor house, close by the church, has Jacobean plasterwork in a room on the first floor, and a Jacobean overmantel. VCH)

BORDESLEY ABBEY *see* REDDITCH

BRADFORD HOUSE *see* BELBROUGHTON

* The Rev. E. Burgoyne tells of Saxon foundations in the churchyard on the N side.

‡ These places date from *c.*1125–50, Bockleton from *c.*1160–70 (cf. Rock N door), remarks Mr Stratford.

BRADLEY 9060

ST JOHN BAPTIST. 1864–5 by *W. J. Hopkins*. On its own and very pretty to look at with its tower at the E end of the nave N wall and its broach spire. Rose window in the W wall. Inside some red stone patterning. – PULPIT. Stone, round, typically High Victorian. – PLATE. Chalice and Cover, by *H. W.*, 1571.

BEANHALL FARMHOUSES, $\frac{1}{2}$ to $\frac{3}{4}$ m. N, spaced out at a distance E of the S–N road. Three timber-framed C16 houses, the most interesting the middle one, though the lower (N) and upper (S) look more picturesque. The Lower Farmhouse has close studs and windows of four and five lights in the W wing, the Middle Farmhouse a specially good W front also with close studding. The attic gables and the porch go with the date 1635 on a rain-water head.* (Inside the Middle Farmhouse is a wooden Jacobean fireplace.) Both Lower and Middle Farmhouse have brick star-chimneystacks.

BRANSFORD 7050

ST JOHN BAPTIST. Carefully restored by *Robert Potter* in 1957 etc. Nave and chancel in one and timber bell-turret. One small early C13 S lancet. The S doorway with its plain ogee arch is of course C14. The bell-turret part of the nave is separated from the rest by a C17 timber-framed wall. In this tower space some of the original supports of the turret remain. Fine single-framed wagon-roofs. – COMMUNION RAIL. Jacobean. – PAINTINGS. Found during the restoration and re-covered for financial reasons except for one small area. – (STAINED GLASS. The canopy work in a nave N window may be of *c.*1400.) – PLATE. Cup by *H. W.* and Cover Paten by *I. F.*, 1571; Chalice by *R.S.*, 1664.

BREDICOT 9050

ST JAMES. A late C13 church, much restored in 1843. It is unknown whether the tracery of the windows, Y and intersecting, represents the early or the late date. It goes with both. Victorian bellcote. – TILES. C15, in the porch. – PLATE. Cup and Cover Paten, 1571.

* The house itself is older. It is of the upper-floor-hall type, probably going back to *c.*1500. The new front is an attempt to copy the fashionable long gallery. The four gables had continuous windows which, however, only lighted a low attic. The extreme lower end of the original building was a smoke bay later incorporated in the kitchen (FWBC).

9030 BREDON

ST GILES. An impressive and varied large church. Long Norman nave, central tower with a slim recessed spire, chancel, and a fine E.E. S chapel with high-pitched roof. The nave is entered by a vaulted Norman N porch, something extremely rare in parish churches. The entrance arch has one order of columns with reeded capitals and an arch with zigzag set diagonally as well as at r. angles to the wall. The vault has diagonal ribs (two rolls and a hollow between) standing on shafts with trumpet-scallop capitals. The inner doorway starts with a rounded inner order and then has two orders of colonnettes. Zigzag at r. angles to the wall in the arch. Above the porch entrance runs a zigzag course. One Norman window W of the porch. The S doorway is similar to the N, but the capitals here have trumpet scallop and the arch a band of lozenges connected by straight lines. There is a Norman window W of this doorway as well. The W doorway is again similar, but the window above it is Perp. The W front has two square pinnacles (cf. Tewkesbury) shafted in two tiers at the angles. The whole nave has kept its plain corbel-table. Inside, the three doorways have – oddly enough – inner segmental arches with a roll-moulding. To the same build belongs the W arch of the tower. Trumpet-scallop capitals again and an arch with zigzags forming lozenges broken round the angle. The arch here is pointed. All this work must be of *c.*1190 and is attributed by Willis to the master of the W bays of the nave of Worcester Cathedral.* Next followed the S chapel or aisle. Two bays, quatrefoil piers, and arches of one step and one rounded step as they are in the doorways. That looks early C13, but the beautiful windows can hardly be earlier than *c.*1250. Pairs of lancets with trefoiled heads. To the W a quatrefoil opening over. Inside there are detached shafts behind the lancets of each pair. In the S wall three low, plain tomb recesses. The Norman chancel was

*Mr Stratford notes the following features of common Worcestershire occurrence: continuous mouldings alternating with normal arch orders on shafts (cf. W bays of the cathedral, Ripple, Bredon's Norton, Shrawley, etc., and also St Mary Shrewsbury), beast-head label-stops (cf. Ripple etc.), and advanced zigzag varieties (cf. Eckington, Netherton, St Mary Shrewsbury etc.). Zigzag set diagonally occurs early in the C13 in the Hereford crypt and also in the triforium of the W bays of the cathedral. Zigzag enfolding a roll is to be found in the same W bays, and moreover at Holt and in Salop and Herefordshire. The capitals again correspond to the cathedral bays. Willis is thus fully vindicated, and the date at Bredon is probably *c.*1190 at the earliest.

replaced *c.*1300–10, see the tracery of the side windows, the chancel arch, and the SEDILIA and PISCINA. Nothing here would indicate a later date. The upper parts of the central tower also could be as early as 1300. Dec N aisle windows, but Perp N arcade. The piers have a core with eight polygonal shafts. – FONT COVER. Jacobean, with nice scrolls up the edges. – COMMUNION RAIL. Jacobean, with long pendants between the balusters. – PAINTING. Original red trellis painting in the chancel. – TILES. In the chancel. An extremely interesting set, all heraldic, and all early C14. The families represented include Berkeley, Despenser, Mortimer, Hastings, and also Bishop Trillek of Hereford (1344–60), who had been rector of Bredon. The tiles face the chancel steps and are thus probably in their original position. – STAINED GLASS. In a N chancel window 35
two small female saints, very fine. Early C14. – PLATE. Cup of 1667; Paten probably of 1667; Paten of 1779. – MONUMENTS. In the chancel N wall Easter Sepulchre with crockets and ballflower decoration. In the recess heavy blue-stone tomb lid with a cross and much decayed ballflower. – On the chancel S wall extremely fine coffin lid with a cross with lopped-off 31
branches and above the arms two busts, husband and wife, of the early to mid C14. – To the r. of this, Late Perp tomb recess with the effigies of husband, wife, and child. Depressed arch and fleuron frieze along the straight top. – Giles Reed † 1611 and wife. Superb alabaster monument with effigies between columns. The arch above the effigies is coffered. Outside the columns lower, square-topped side-pieces for the children to kneel in. Superstructure with obelisks and two putti and yet higher centre again with obelisks. – Bishop Prideaux of Worcester † 1650. Brass inscription, mitre above, shields in the corners.

Round the church is an exceptionally fine group of buildings. To the N the RECTORY, Elizabethan, stone. Gabled porch with pilasters. Big cross gables at the ends of the front. Good stone gatepiers. Large C18 brick STABLES.* Also a separate cottage (E) which once belonged to the rectory. This has a two-storeyed gabled stone porch with a re-set C15 window. To the NE of the rectory is the OLD MANSION, C17, brick, with dormers and mullioned windows, as far as they are original. To the W of the church the MANOR HOUSE, C18, stone, of five bays, with

* In the 1880s the then rector, a relative of the Dukes of Portland, enlarged the rectory to more than eighteen room : He had fifteen servants (Canon J. S. Leatherbarrow).

singularly uncouth detail: three-bay segmental or rather basket-arched pedimental gable, and porch of Tuscan columns with a pediment of the same shape. W of the manor house the splendid TITHE BARN, C13 or early C14 throughout, 124 ft long, with aisles and two porches. In one of the porches is an upper room with a fireplace. This is the only aisled barn in the county, but quite unlike those of lowland England. The main frames were reared; hence the cross-beam connecting the aisle post about 6 ft below the tie-beam. S of the church is a nice OBELISK milestone of 1808.

The village street is uncommonly enjoyable. Among the houses HANCOCK'S ENDOWED SCHOOL of 1845 must be mentioned. The REED ALMSHOUSES of 1696 are modest, one-storeyed, of stone, with two projecting wings.

MITTON FARMHOUSE, $2\frac{1}{8}$ m. SW, is a late C17 brick house with hipped roof. (In it an uncommonly good Jacobean stone chimneypiece.)

9030

BREDON HILL

BREDON HILL FORT. The fort occupies the N spur of the hill, and excavation has shown it to have two main periods of construction. The first, marked by the inner rampart, which encloses 11 acres, belongs to the C2 B.C. The rampart is of dump construction and is broken by a single entrance. In the C1 B.C. the outer rampart was added, doubling the defended area. The new rampart was provided with an outer stone revetment with two inturned entrances set at each end of the line of defences. The entrance of the earlier fort was also remodelled at this time. In the early C1 A.D. occupation of the fort came to a sudden and violent end. The bodies of over fifty of the defenders, many of them brutally hacked, were found in the ditch adjacent to the inner entrance. This attack is probably to be associated with the NW expansion of Belgic peoples into the area.

Inside the fort PARSON'S FOLLY, a tower of the late C18 built by Mr Parson of Kemerton Court. It is square and not high.

9030

BREDON'S NORTON

ST GILES. A long, low church with an unbuttressed W tower. In the porch entrance and the S doorway fragments of Norman work: trumpet scallop, zigzag, lobed hood-mould.* The chan-

* For the furrowed zigzag Mr Stratford refers to Malvern Priory. As for the dating, Mr Stratford suggests *c.*1150–75 for the outer entrance, *c.*1175–1200 for the inner. Both entrances were probably re-set in the C19 rebuilding.

cel arch is early C13. Moulded arch, including fillets. Capitals with stiff-leaf growing perversely horizontally. The nave is early C13 too – see the W lancet which was shortly after covered by the tower. Much else is rebuilding by *F. Preedy*, 1883. – PLATE. Cup and Salver Paten of 1708. – MONUMENT. Large tablet to William Hancocke † 1719 and his wife 1685. The date is probably nearer her death than his. Two columns, open segmental pediment.

MANOR HOUSE, ¼ m. SE. Stone. Long, with gables and two-storeyed dormers. Some original mullioned windows. An archway leads to the front garden. This is dated 1585 and has a round arch and a gable on pilasters starting in an unstructural manner half-way up from a kind of trefoils (cf. Woollas Hall, Eckington). Fluted frieze below the gable.

NORTON PARK. Large, Victorian-looking Tudor house formerly carrying the surprisingly early date 1830. There is nothing pre-Victorian in the handling of the stylistic material.

BRETFORTON 0040

ST LEONARD. The earliest parts of the church are the arcades. Both are late C12 to very early C13, and both have pointed arches. The S arcade is probably ten or twenty years earlier than the N arcade. Both have round piers with round abaci, but the S capitals are excessively high trumpet scallops, and the S arches have one step only. The N arches have a step and a chamfer, and the capitals are flatter, with decorated trumpets and heads, and one even has a lively dragon devouring a human being. The tail sprouts out into leaves (cf. the font at Elmley Castle). The style and the choice of subject point to inspiration from the S transept and the nave of Wells Cathedral, i.e. work of *c*.1210–15.* Also, there is nailhead decoration in one respond. The roof pitch of the original N aisle is still visible. At the W end is a puzzle. The W pier of the S arcade was originally a respond. The W half and the half-arch were only done to connect it with the Perp tower. But on the N side the arcade is complete. Where then was the W wall? It must have been in agreement with the N side, which means that on the S side a piece of the S wall of the preceding aisleless building was left standing, and the SW respond followed only a little further E. Late C13 chancel (cf. Church Honeybourne) with

*Mr Stratford stresses the links with Wells. He points to similarity even in the round abaci.

cusped lancets, in the E wall a stepped group of three lancet lights under an arch. Also a window with cusped Y-tracery. The same motifs repeat in the S transept. Dec N transept. Short Perp nave. – WOODWORK. In the S transept panels of mixed sources, e.g. blank arches separated by atlantes. Also Jacobean leaf patterns. One panel is dated 1615. – STAINED GLASS. Bits in the N transept N and one N aisle window. – PLATE. Cup *c.*1680 and Paten Cover *c.*1686, by *T. C.*

By the church the MANOR HOUSE, a three-bay stone house with three gables and the dates 1605–1877.

BRETFORTON HALL is a charming three-bay neo-Gothic house, stuccoed, with ogee-headed windows and an embattled tower. Convex porch with Roman Doric wooden columns. The MHLG gives 1830 as its date – it certainly looks earlier. (In the garden the original E window of the church has been re-erected.)

GRANGE FARM HOUSE. This is a medieval house. It is L-shaped, and in the projecting gabled wing there is, besides Elizabethan windows, one two-light, straight-headed Perp window. The room below was a store-room. It has a tunnel-vault with three single-chamfered round transverse arches. (Chimneypiece with the three Magi; Elizabethan.) – Good timber-framed C15 BARN.

BRICKLEHAMPTON

9040

ST MICHAEL. Built in 1876. Witness of this is chiefly the poor embraced W tower with its saddleback roof. But much of the masonry of the church is old, and it includes a late C12 S doorway with one order of colonnettes and zigzag in the arch set both diagonally and at r. angles to the wall. The trumpet-scallop capitals are decorated with small flowers (cf. Bredon). Old also a small and a larger trefoil-cusped lancet. – FONT. Norman, round, with tapering sides. On it two crosses and two rosettes (cf. South Littleton and Bishampton).* – SEDILIA. One original C12 or C13 stone arm. – STAINED GLASS. By *Kempe* W window and chancel side windows; all before 1900. – PLATE. Cup and Cover Paten by *H. W.*, 1571; Paten by *Robert Timbrell*, 1698.

A nice timber-framed COTTAGE of *c.*1600 SW of the church.

BRICKLEHAMPTON HALL. 1848. A good example of the spacious Italianate villa. The asymmetrically placed tower open

*Observation of Mr Stratford.

in its top stage is particularly characteristic. The house, when built, had fifteen bedrooms. It was built for the Woodward family.

BROADHEATH

8050

CHRIST CHURCH. 1903–4 by *C. Ford Whitcombe*. Quite large, but of no special architectural interest. – PLATE. Salver Paten by *R. I.*, 1780; Chalice by *T. H.*, 1796; Chalice, 1805.

CHAPEL OF THE COUNTESS OF HUNTINGDON'S CONNEXION, SE of the church. Built in 1825. Red brick, of three bays, with arched windows.

BROADWAS

7050

ST MARY MAGDALENE. Nave and chancel and timber bell-turret. The church is mostly of *c.*1200. To that time belong the small lancets in nave and chancel – especially handsome the row of three in the N wall – and also the S doorway with its waterleaf capital and lively mouldings of the pointed arch. In 1344 a chantry chapel was founded, and that must be the present S chapel with its separate roof and arcade of two bays and a quatrefoil pier and Dec arch mouldings. The windows are renewed, but apparently correctly (VCH). The cusped E lancets with nicely moulded rere-arches and the mouchette wheel above are specially attractive. The bell-turret space is divided from the nave by timbering and has a Jacobean balcony railing. – PULPIT. Dated 1632. It has rather bold scroll patterns. – BENCHES. Plain, C17 (NW corner of nave). – TILES. Some in the chancel. – PLATE. Cover Paten by *A.K.*, 1571. – MONUMENT. Henry Roberts † 1761. By *W. Stephens*. Aedicule of pilasters and broken pediment. Draped urn in it.

BROADWAY

0030

Broadway is the show village of England. Visit it on a fine Saturday afternoon in the summer, and the cars and coaches and their milling-round inmates will have smothered all its delights. But come on a breezy spring or autumn weekday morning, and you will agree that Broadway deserves its fame. There is only one thing to be said against it. Everybody over the years has been so full of good will, so tactful, so conformist to its beauties that the result has become almost too good to be true. Broadway is by no means lacking in variety. Not only are Tudor, Stuart, and

Georgian happily mixed, but the early C20 also has contributed, not in the modern idiom, but by the efforts of architects of sensibility and some individuality. A walk through Broadway should be taken seriously and done at leisure.

ST EADBURGA. Externally the church is mostly Perp, but the interior reaches back to about 1200. The three-bay arcades have round piers, scallop, trumpet, and moulded capitals, round abaci, and arches of one step or one chamfer – all pointed. Of this Norman building, once one watches for it, the two W buttresses and the stump of the middle E buttress still tell. So the church was Norman to its whole present length. The crossing is a confused sight. First of all, the crossing tower was built into the nave. The piers of a fourth bay have been preserved, and so have the E responds, though their capitals have been crowned with battlements. The W and E arches of the tower are C14, and not too late, with their beautifully sheer continuous double chamfers. But the plain imposts of the chancel arch of 1200 seem also still to be there. The N and S arches die into their imposts. There is a vault of eight radiating ribs in the tower (cf. Hampton), and its upper parts are Perp. Perp also the more conspicuous chancel fenestration, especially one S window with odd tracery, but there is also evidence of two C13 lancet windows. The PISCINA is pointed-trefoiled and has a continuous roll moulding. The S transept must be of the C13 too, though of its end – see the S window with its three stepped pointed-trefoiled lights. The nave roof stands on a pretty wall-plate with fleurons. – FONT. Stem of a former hexagonal font (?) with slender shafts and moulded capitals. Probably of the late C13. – PULPIT. The Perp traceried panels come from the chapel which stood on the site of St Michael (*see* below). – SCREEN. Minor, Perp, with one-light divisions. Made up from bench ends. – BENCHES. In the chancel. Also made up of old parts. – COMMUNION RAIL. Jacobean, with knobs. – SCULPTURE. Wood panel with eight small saints. It looks Flemish and may be the front of a chest. – TILES. C15; by the font. – STAINED GLASS. Fragments in the W window and small bits in other windows. – PLATE. All of 1729. – MONUMENTS. Two parts of the effigy of a priest, late C13? (S transept). – Antony Daston † 1572. Brass. This is a palimpsest. At the back part of a Flemish brass plate; the other part of it is at Westerham in Kent. – Walter Savage † 1641. Small tablet, still entirely Jacobean. Columns and strapwork. – William Taylor † 1741. By *Samuel Chandler*. Large tablet with columns and an open segmental pediment. In the frieze two cherubs and a crown.*

ST MICHAEL. 1839 by *H. Eginton*. Of that date the exterior. Well and solidly built of yellow ashlar. W tower with W doorway. Lancets and buttresses along the sides. Are the two-light aisle windows with their bar tracery also of 1839? For the rib-vaults inside with the stiff-leaf capitals of their shafts must belong to the restoration of 1890. The chancel also has been lengthened, as the former N and S windows of the original chancel show. The porches at the E end of the aisles are a surprise. – PULPIT. From St Eadburga. A very sumptuous Elizabethan piece.

ST SAVIOUR'S MONASTERY, Willersey Road. The Passionist Fathers in 1850 enlarged premises built *c.*1828. Of that date the church with its arched windows (but not the façade) and the house behind. Of 1850 the church façade in neo-Norman and the bigger house on the l. with tall mullioned windows and a doorway rather E.E. than Norman.

PERAMBULATION. A perambulation is most likely to start at the Green, at the W end of the High Street, and by the Lygon Arms. But before embarking on the High Street, it may be just as well to look at Church Street between the old church and the green and at the few interesting buildings W of the green.

CHURCH STREET, from the old church N: COURT HOUSE is the fragment of a larger mansion, made large again in 1898 by *Guy Dawber*. Elizabethan chiefly the gateway arch, little decorated. Then follows a three-bayhouse, C17 at the back, early C19 at the front, but with cross-windows of the 1920s by *Bateman*. By St Michael's church the houses join up more closely. S of St Michael a good five-bay house of *c.*1700, with gatepiers. Opposite an early C20 pair with straight-sided bays and gables projected to be flush with the fronts of the bays. Opposite a house with a delightful open curly pediment with a thick garland, all *ex situ*. Then the archeologically most important house in Broadway.

ABBOT'S GRANGE was indeed a grange of the abbots of Evesham. The house is of the C14, with Elizabethan alterations and two very good C20 wings to the W. The house is L-shaped, with an extension S beyond the L to where one jamb of the original gateway survives. The long arm of the L is the

* The Broadway VICARAGE is in the Leamington road. In its garden the bell-cupola of 1608 of the church has been re-erected.

hall, the short arm the solar, i.e. the abbot's study and his chapel projecting E from the angle between hall and solar. The hall has to the W two different two-light windows with transoms and ogee-headed lights. To the E is one hall window and a second in a skew position to admit light in spite of the chapel wing. On the W front the most prominent window is that of the solar, also of two lights with a transom, but with a two-centred arch. To the E the solar has a simpler two-light window, so as not to compete with the fine chapel E window, of two lights with a reticulation unit in the head and no transom. S of the solar much was tudorized, but the S wall still shows C14 work. The hall is entered near its N end. The main entrance was from the W. The three service doorways from the former screens passage are fully preserved, two of them ogee-headed, the other arched with a flat top. At the high-table end is another ogee-headed doorway, this one leading to the (renewed) staircase. From the chapel to the hall opens a circular window, originally apparently quatrefoiled. The hall roof has arched braces to collar-beams, and one tier of wind-braces. The solar roof has wind-braces too. The SCREEN in the solar is not *in situ*. One-light divisions.

The next houses face the GREEN, first a Georgian one of five bays, but not too formal, and then FARNHAM HOUSE, late C17, symmetrical, with two dormers with blank ovals, horizontally placed, in the gables, but still a cambered doorhead.

From here to the W as far as the branching off of the Cheltenham road. First LIFFORD HALL of 1915–17 by *A. N. Prentice*.* Neo-Cotswold, but in a well considered rhythm. Then the TELEPHONE EXCHANGE, neo-Cotswold too, and as late as 1950. After that RUSSELL HOUSE, a Georgian stone house of four bays, but with three of them meant to be read symmetrically. Long r. attachment, once F. D. Millet's studio, quite original with its paired slit windows and oval windows over and the big curving-out bay in the middle. To the l. of this a charming Gothick pavilion with ogee doorway and shaped gable, probably of *c*.1800. Behind a small castellated tower of the same vintage.

So now past the Green and into the HIGH STREET. It is an exceptionally long street, longer than the main street of many a small town (say Evesham or Pershore), and its appearance changes all the time. There are grass verges all the way along

* The attribution is not certain.

and prettily kept front gardens. Trees are only near the green. We start with the BROADWAY HOTEL, the only major building with prominent black and white work, and therefore appropriately more of the Green than of the High Street. The r. wing is timber-framed, the l. wing stone. Then on the other side two buildings of GORDON RUSSELL'S (whose modern factory front by *Russell, Hodgson & Leigh* is behind in the Back Lane). The High Street front is of two parts. The first has a date-stone 1588 on the chimney, probably *ex situ*, and looks *c.*1700, but the square closed-in porch is by *Bateman* (*see* below), *c.*1916. It has oval windows, the house cross-windows. The adjoining house is Georgian, of beautiful simplicity and heightened in its effect by the exemplarily chosen and applied lettering which takes the place of a fascia. The Cotswold wing to the r., with gable and mullioned windows, bears the surprisingly late date 1687. Round the corner it has a timber-framed overhanging upper floor and gable. Opposite are the POST OFFICE, by *Guy Dawber*, 1899, nice and subdued, and ST PATRICK'S TEA ROOMS, stone, with gables, much re-done. Opposite again is the LYGON ARMS, formerly the White Hart, and yet earlier a private house. Lord Torrington in 1787 saw in the White Hart still 'all the marks of having been a manor house', and so can we. It is by far the best house of the Cotswold type in the village, even if less monumental than Tudor House. Recessed centre and two projecting wings. They have their gables, the centre two two-storeyed dormers. The windows in the l. wing are mullioned and transomed; in the centre they are all of the cross-type. Door surround with tapering pilasters, a strapwork top, and the date 1620. Inside, the small doorway between centre and l. wing is C16 and was once an outer doorway. The place where it probably was is still visible in the outer wall of the room in which it now is, looking towards the main entrance. The chimneypiece in the room into which it leads must be as early as the time of Henry VIII. Is it *ex situ*? It has a leaf and an animal in the spandrels. A monumental late C17 fireplace in another of the ground-floor rooms comes from a house at Winchcombe. To the r. *C. E. Bateman* of Birmingham in 1910 added a new large dining room for the hotel. It fits in outstandingly well, with its scale and its display of two different motifs. At the back facing the yard with its chestnut tree a gabled wing was added by *Bateman* in 1911, another longer one opposite (with garages) by *Bateman* (and later *Leslie Mansfield*) in 1913–26, and then in 1960–1 a perfectly

C20 extension just to show that such a thing can be done and should be done. It is by *Russell, Hodgson & Leigh* and has a stone ground floor and then two projecting brick storeys with wood slatting to stress the verticals of the window bays. One upstairs room of the old part has an ornamental plaster frieze and ceiling and a large Jacobean chimneypiece.

LLOYDS BANK across the road, by *G. H. Hunt*, 1915, is well done, conforming yet not effacing its function. No. 32 opposite is a good small gabled house. The shop is a shocker. Again opposite a one-gabled three-storeyed C17 bit. Then, again on the N side, BARN CLOSE, C17, with two gabled wings not projecting the same distance. The MIDLAND BANK opposite is much less satisfactory than Lloyds Bank. Once more on the N side, PICTON HOUSE is a plain, dignified Georgian stone house of eight bays with a stone wall and big gatepiers to the street. BROAD CLOSE a little farther up is much more elaborate. It is late C18. The ground floor has two shallow bows and a doorway with pediment on Tuscan columns, and the first floor tripartite windows. The lower l. wing has the same windows. In the centre of the main block at the top a rather starved broken pediment.

Back to the S side for TUDOR HOUSE, a splendidly monumental building of 1660. The façade is symmetrical and has three storeys, the top one reaching into the gables. Canted projecting centre bay of two storeys ending with a parapet. The doorway is at one end, not in the middle, and still has a cambered head. Mullioned windows no longer with individual hood-moulds. Continuous drip-courses instead.

Then ST MICHAEL'S SCHOOL, 1869, Gothic, with a turret. Perhaps in such a street you need an occasional *gaffe* to reduce the pitch of perfection. The METHODIST CHURCH opposite is two bays wide, with arched windows and a steep gable instead of the usual pediment. It dates from *c.*1811. Back to the S side for LITTLE GATES, late C17, with a drip-course and no hood-moulds. The doorway has a hood-mould on big lozenge stops – a Late Perp motif. Opposite PRIOR'S MANSE, medieval, L-shaped, and with an early C14 doorway. Sunk-quadrant moulding, keeled hood-mould. The OLD HOUSE on the S side, in its garden, is a fine large late C17 house. Small gables with vertically placed blocked ovals and a large gable in the projecting r. wing. Next to it the CONGREGATIONAL CHURCH (1842–3, but remodelled recently by *Peter W. J. Neale*). The front is set back and treated very modestly – an excellent attitude for such a job in such a place. No. 70 opposite is of the C18. Ashlar, five bays, the door-hood on pretty iron brackets. No. 74, also ashlar, is early C19 and has a doorcase with Tuscan demi-columns and a broken pediment. After that an attractive stretch of uneventful houses, e.g., on the S side, LEEDS HOUSE of three bays and two and a half storeys with two bow windows and a pretty porch, and another house on the same side, ashlar-faced, Georgian, of three bays with a doorway with broken pediment. Opposite is a deplorable piece of bad new (builder's ?) Cotswold imitation and the equally deplorable POLICE, of 1911. On the same side, after a while, BARN HOUSE, a strange house lying back at an angle to the street. It seems to have a three-bay Queen Anne centre and early C20 Cotswoldy attachments. Also at the r. end the barn was converted in the early C20 and given oval windows and a large two-transomed window under a half-hipped gable. The C20 work was done by *Prentice* *c.*1908. Opposite HAWSTED HOUSE with an early C18 front with two-light mullioned windows. Then ORCHARD FARM COTTAGE, dated 1722. This is symmetrical, except for the placing of the doorway, but still has two-light mullioned and not sashed windows and even hood-moulds. Then on the N side TOP FARMHOUSE, C17, with a part added *c.*1908 by *George Hunt* of Evesham in collaboration with *Bateman*. It is connected with the old house by an archway, an attractive idea. Back to the S side and ORCHARD FARMHOUSE, much rebuilt (by *Prentice*), but with a doorway with four-centred head and a hood-mould on large lozenge stops. The door spandrels have leaves. No. 153 is dated 1718 and almost a mirror image of the cottage of 1722. Finally COURT FARM HOUSE, C17, but very much enlarged (also by *Prentice*).*

Broadway Hill leads up in long curves to the FISH INN, originally a summer house of Sir John Cotterell's estate. It is a curiously barbaric piece of architecture, with a rusticated Venetian window and a triglyph frieze whose metopes are simply rubble. Lord Torrington called it 'the most extraordinary gaze-about house in the world'.

(Off the Broadway–Willersey road is BIBSWORTH, *c.*1904 by *Guy Dawber*.)

(In WEST END LANE, the lane connecting the road to the old church with the Cheltenham road, is WEST END, a C17 house rebuilt correctly *c.*1906 by *Bateman*.)

* The house includes part of the timbers of a late C14 hall.

Also off the road to the church, but $\frac{1}{2}$ m. past it and to the E, is KITE'S NEST, an interesting house. It has two fronts of two different phases of the C17. To the N symmetrical, of three bays and three storeys with mullioned windows with hood-moulds. The only break in the symmetry is that on the ground floor the hall window is stressed by having five instead of four lights. To the S the windows have all become cross-windows, and between the two gables is an incongruous segmental pediment. The dates could be *c.*1660–70 and *c.*1700 (yet it is the S side which has rainwater heads with the date 1666; VCH).

90 BROADWAY TOWER was built as a folly by the Earl of Coventry in 1800. Three round turrets and three canted sides, i.e. a total of nine corners. Norman details, i.e. round arches. The balcony railings on the second floor are intersecting arches. The uppermost windows are horizontal ovals. Top battlements.

MIDDLE HILL is of *c.*1725, enlarged *c.*1780, but in appearance rather early C19. Ashlar-faced. Five bays, spaced 2–1–2. The three-bay, two-arch porch is Victorian. Round the corner a big bow window.

DOR KNAP, $\frac{3}{8}$ m. NW of the former. Just three cottages, but a nice early C20 addition with an oval window. The architect seems unknown.

SPRINGHILL HOUSE, 3 m. SE. This was Lord Coventry's house, and *Capability Brown* worked for it in 1763. In 1830 it was bought by General Lygon, who added in front of the two wings. The house is of ashlar stone and quite plain. Stables with cupola. The planting has been much altered.

BROCKAMIN *see* LEIGH

BROCKENCOTE *see* CHADDESLEY CORBETT

9070

BROMSGROVE

'A large but dirty place, full of shops and manufacturers of nails, needles and some . . . coarse linens' (*Beauties of England and Wales*). Today Bromsgrove is neither large nor dirty.

ST JOHN BAPTIST. The town lies below the hill on which St John is built. One reaches it by a long, informal flight of steps. It is a large church of red sandstone, and its spire dominates views from quite far away. Of the Norman church hardly anything remains: the re-used arch of the S doorway and parts of the E respond of the N arcade and a respond of the N arcade one bay farther W. In the later C13 the chancel of this Norman church was rebuilt – see the Priest's Doorway, the side windows of two lights, the E window of five stepped lancet lights, and the chancel arch. In its responds is a little nailhead. At about the same time a S transept was built. Of this the only evidence is the present S aisle E window and the PISCINA close to it. Again of the same time is the N arcade of three bays linked by *Scott* (at the restoration of 1858) to the Norman responds. The C13 piers are quatrefoil, the arches double-chamfered. A doorway into this part of the aisle (with a depressed two-centred arch) is flanked by windows of stepped lancet lights. It looks as though the W tower was begun about 1300 too. The doorway has that appearance, and the C19 N and S windows may represent what had been there. But the splendid upper parts of the tower are of course Perp. Big W window, above it three niches with original figures, bell-openings of two lights continued by blank arcading richly appointed, and a panelled parapet behind which rises the spire. Perp also most of the aisle windows and the aisle battlements and pinnacles, and also the embattled clerestory. The N aisle windows are simple, those of the S aisle more interesting. To the E two with pointed arches (one blocked) flanking a most curious square-sided bay window made no doubt for a funerary monument. Farther W very tall straight-headed three-light windows. Perp also are the S arcade of four bays with a fine section of the piers, the high and wide tower arch, and the splendid arch from the chancel to the N chapel, deeply panelled with a kind of Gothic coffering. – STAINED GLASS. The large W window is by *S. B. Capronnier*, 1870. – E window by *Lavers & Barraud*. – MONUMENTS. Sir Humphrey Stafford † 1450 and wife. Alabaster of excellent quality. – Sir John Talbot of Albrighton † 1501 and two wives. Made *c.*1550. Also alabaster and also excellent. Against the tomb-chest richly cusped panels. – Defaced effigy of a man praying. – Totally defaced effigy of a woman. All these are in the N chapel. – In the churchyard is an even more hopelessly defaced effigy, probably C17. – In the chancel fine alabaster effigy of Lady Talbot of Grafton Manor † 1517. Against the tomb-chest minimum Gothic panelling and standing deacons holding shields. – Are the quatrefoil panels of the seat in the chancel S wall also re-used tomb-chest material? – George Lyttelton † 1600. Semi-reclining on his elbow in a stiff position. He wears robes. Flat back arch with strapwork cartouche. Two columns. – Bishop Hall of Bristol † 1710. Architectural tablet, but near the top putto heads. – In the churchyard headstones to Thomas Scaife and Joseph Rutherford. They are called 'engineers', meaning here apparently engine-drivers. They died in 1840 when the boiler of their engine, a Birmingham and Gloucester Railway engine, blew up. The poem on the gravestone of Thomas Scaife reads thus:

My engine now is cold and still
No water does my boiler fill;
My coke affords its flame no more,
My days of usefulness are o'er.
My wheels deny their wonted speed,
No more my guiding hands they heed;
My whistle too, has lost its tune,
Its shrill and thrilling sounds are gone;
My valves are now thrown open wide,
My flanges all refuse to guide.
My clacks, also, tho' once so strong,
Refuse to aid the busy throng.
No more I feel each urging breath,
My steam is now condensed in death.
Life's railway o'er, each station past,
In death I'm stopped and rest at last.
Farewell, dear friends, and cease to weep,
In Christ I'm SAFE, in Him I sleep.

ALL SAINTS, Birmingham Road. 1872–4 by *John Cotton*, the tower of 1888. Quite a big church. Well detailed NW tower with lancets. The tracery of most of the windows of the church is geometrical. Aisles and a polygonal apse. Yellow brick interior with polychrome patterns. W of the chancel arch another such arch to single out the pulpit bay and draw attention to the transepts which the arcades themselves do not reveal. The end windows of the transepts differ, a hint at a long C13 building history which of course does not exist.

ST PETER (R.C.), Worcester Road. 1858 by *Gilbert Blount*. Aisleless, with a wide apse and a big bellcote. The whole W front is quite ornate and boldly handled. The tracery is geometrical to ogee.

NONCONFORMIST CHAPELS. The CONGREGATIONAL CHAPEL in Chapel Street just off the High Street to the E is of 1833 and looks in the clumsiness of its motifs a little later. Stuccoed. Three bays with over-long windows, a Greek Doric porch, and a window which reaches up into the roof. – The HEPHZIBAH CHAPEL (Methodist) in Birmingham Road is of 1861, red and yellow brick, with arched windows and a big pediment. – But the BAPTIST CHAPEL in New Road of only six years later is Gothic with an asymmetrically placed turret.

Red brick, lancet windows. – All this is characteristically flatter, i.e. more Early Victorian, than the motifs of the METHODIST CHAPEL in New Road of 1883, also red brick, also Gothic, also with an asymmetrical turret. W window with plate tracery.

URBAN DISTRICT OFFICES, St John Street. Brick. The core is a building with shaped gables. This was built in 1848 by *Henry Day* as the vicarage of St John's. Many later additions.

SHENSTONE TRAINING COLLEGE, opposite All Saints Church. 1962–4 by the County Architect, *L. C. Lomas*.

BROMSGROVE SCHOOL, Worcester Road. By the road the oldest building, a late C17 five-bay house of two storeys with a doorway whose segmental pediment rests on carved brackets. The school extends much wider to the E than the road frontage would make one expect. The Victorian buildings are of little interest. Former Chapel, stone, with lancet windows, small, of 1850. Enlarged by *Hopkins* in 1869. Hall 1883 by *John Cotton*. Houses 1890s by *Lewis Sheppard & Son* of Worcester. New Chapel by *Sir Giles G. Scott*, 1928–39, completed to the W in 1958. Pale brick, with prominent buttresses, but nothing like as bold as Scott's Charterhouse Chapel. Conventional Gothic windows.

Former SCHOOL by the Congregational Chapel. Red brick, one-storeyed, with two projecting wings. Arched windows. The date is 1852, and it is a nice building.

Former WORKHOUSE, Birmingham Road. 1838, and still just a utilitarian Late Georgian range of brick. Not cruciform in plan. Nine bays, two and a half storeys, with a thin three-bay pediment and a humble doorway.

PERAMBULATION. S of the church in the KIDDERMINSTER ROAD is PERRY HALL, the home of A. E. and Laurence Housman. C18, brick, with pretty Gothic glazing bars. To its S the picturesque ruinous wall of a C17 house with mullioned windows. A foray W to the end of the road to see, off to the S, along Monsieur Lane, MONSIEUR HALL, stone, C17, much restored. Mullioned windows and a high brick chimney with frieze of blank arches just below the top. Now from Perry Hall E, through ST JOHN'S STREET with one nice five-bay red brick house with a segmental pediment over the doorway, and so to the High Street.

First down to the S along WORCESTER ROAD to see the GOLDEN LION, No. 7, a charming later C18 three-bay house with a broken door pediment and Venetian windows, their arches of Gothick ogee form (cf. Chaddesley Corbett). Then to the N along the HIGH STREET. No. 1 is timber-framed and of the late C16. (Originally it had four gables to the street. Two of them and part of a third were destroyed for the Victorian building to the N. FWBC.) The façade has concave-sided lozenges and some fleur-de-lis motifs. Then some plain Georgian houses on both sides. After that, on the E side, Nos 22–4, six bays, four giant pilasters, two storeys and a separate attic storey above the cornice. The ground floor is altered. Now turn into NEW ROAD, just for No. 1. This was originally the HOP POLE INN and stood in the High Street, where New Road now starts. In re-erecting it it was much restored and also altered, but the three-gable composition, small–large–small, is original, and so are the concave lozenges and fleurs-de-lis. The date 1572 is also original. So this is a remarkably early case of such lavish decoration. (Far out in NEW ROAD, No. 52 is FORDHOUSE FARM, brick, of three bays with a parapet sweeping up to a pediment in the middle. Below the pediment a lunette window. The other windows have moulded surrounds. NMR)* On in the High Street to the RED LION (No. 73) on the W side, brick, three widely spaced bays, segmental door pediment. On the E side follows Nos 108–10, a much restored C16 timber building with close-set studding and two gables. No. 112 next to it is Late Georgian, of six bays and three storeys, with segment-headed windows and a shallow Tuscan porch. After that the lane to the Congregational Chapel (*see* above). Then No. 120, mid-C18, of five bays and two storeys with giant fluted angle pilasters alternately blocked. Middle window with pilasters widening in a curve at the bottom. The ground floor is altered. Continue along the BIRMINGHAM ROAD to look at No. 28, which has five bays and three storeys and a doorway with Doric pilasters set against the rusticated door surround. Finally at the N end, by All Saints church, the CRAB MILL INN, very similar to No. 7 Worcester Road, but with normal un-ogeed Venetian windows.

BROOME

9070

ST PETER. This must once have been an uncommonly charming C18 church. Red brick, quite small. Little W tower with pyramid roof. Nave of only two bays length. But the E end of 1861, though quite well in keeping, is too long. – FONT. Norman,

*Recently pulled down.

small and round, with arcading of which it is difficult to say whether it is meant to be intersecting or normal. The arches are beaded. Small band of scrolls at the top. At the top of the shaft grotesque heads. – MONUMENT. Anne Hill † 1804. By *Flaxman*. Young woman seated in profile on the ground. Beautifully spaced and lettered inscription.

BROOME HOUSE. A stone house with two worth-while façades. The older has three widely spaced bays and a lively skyline: the outer bays square with battlements, the centre bay with a big ogee gable with a quatrefoil in it. Below is the porch with an ogee arch and battlements. The ground-floor windows are arched. Round the corner a slightly later front, towards the lake. Five bays, two and a half storeys, semicircular porch with columns carrying capitals already reeded in the Adam way. But the Venetian window and tripartite lunette window above the porch are still mid-C18 custom. Three-bay pediment. So the relative dating is not easy. The semi-Gothick side can hardly be earlier than 1760. Is the other side then *c.*1770?

BROUGHTON *see* DRAKE'S BROUGHTON

BROUGHTON COURT *see* HANBURY

BROUGHTON HACKETT 9050

ST LEONARD. Nave and chancel in one. Weatherboarded bell-turret with pyramid roof. Dec W window. – PLATE. Cup and Cover Paten by *H. W.*, 1571.

(CHURCHILL MILL. The blue lias stone walls and exceptionally large size of this mill, built *c.*1620, probably saved it from demolition in the late C18. Most of Worcestershire's water mills were rebuilt at this time. This one was altered internally, but the main structure with its great brick-shafted chimney-stack survived. FWBC)

BUSHLEY 8030

ST PETER. Of grey chalk. 1843 by *Blore*, the chancel with a demonstratively higher high-pitched roof by *Scott*, 1856. To him Blore's early C19 Gothic must have been distasteful. Blore here still works in the Commissioners' conventions. W tower, aisleless nave, transept, and (before Scott) a short chancel. The details are all Perp, whereas Scott's are of course Middle Pointed, i.e. of *c.*1300. His chancel has a pierced quatrefoil parapet and pinnacles. – PLATE. Flagon by *Thos. Farrer*, 1723. – MONUMENTS. Brass to Thomas Payne † 1500 and wife. 25 in. figures. – Also Dowdeswells (*see* below): Roger † 1633, already post-Jacobean, classical with an open pediment. – Judith † 1666 and William † 1683 – each just an urn on a column. – Richard † 1673 with twisted columns. – Finally William † 1775. This is by *John Hickey*. Relief of a seated woman leaning against the plinth of a wreathed urn.

SE of the church by the crossroads a timber-framed house with brick infilling and a cruck truss. ¼ m. farther is PAYNE'S PLACE, of *c.*1500, timber-framed with brick infilling. All closely set studding.

PULL COURT (Bredon School). Built for Canon Dowdeswell in 1836–46 by *Blore*, a large, competent, highly monumental mansion in the Jacobean style. Centre and two far-projecting wings, partly of the height of the house, partly lower. They are connected by a rather low screen of square piers and arches. In the middle a large gateway. The entrance to the house is flanked on either side by a high three-transomed three-light window. Shaped gables everywhere, also on the equally sym-
96 metrical garden side. Here the centre is treated with two Tudor turrets as if it were a gatehouse. The high entrance hall has two pillars on the l. to screen the grand staircase and two on the r. as well. Several more richly appointed rooms. On the clock tower is the date 1847. The grounds are attributed to *Capability Brown*. (In the grounds an artificial RUIN, dated 1843. This includes two C14 windows from the old church.)

SEVERN BRIDGE, 1 m. SE. By *Telford*, a single iron arch (cf. Holt).

CALLOW END *see* POWICK

CALLOW HILL *see* FECKENHAM

CASTLE BOURNE *see* BELBROUGHTON

7030

CASTLEMORTON

ST GREGORY. A Norman church. This is demonstrated by the two chancel N windows, and the N and S nave doorways with scallop capitals, and furrowed zigzag at r. angles to the wall (cf. Earls Croome). In the N doorway a tympanum with the lamb.* Inside the nave S windows still exist, above the badly

* Cf. the tympanum of Preston-by-Ledbury in Gloucestershire, only a few miles away (N. Stratford).

treated arcade. Its elements were probably re-assembled, jumbled up, and partly replaced in the C17. In 1647 the church was apparently in very bad repair. The S transept is late C13 work, see the intersecting tracery of the S window and the pair of trefoil-pointed E lancets with a joint but two-arched hood-mould on head stops. In the nave N wall a one-light Dec window with transom and a three-light Perp window nicely enriched by canopied niches inside. Perp W tower with recessed spire. Perp timber N porch. – FONTS. One a half-broken Perp piece, the other an C18 baluster with foliage (nave). – COMMUNION RAIL. With flat openwork balusters, a very late occurrence of this motif, considering the inscribed dates 1683 and 1684. – STAINED GLASS. Bits in the chancel S window. – PLATE. Chalice and Cover by *I. C. F.*, 1821. – MONUMENT. Tablet († 1821) by *Sydney Gregg*. Mourning woman with torch by an urn.

ROUGH FARM, W of the church. A three-bay brick house, but attached to it a timber-framed wing with exposed crucks.

THE ALMSHOUSE. Now 'period' restored as private house. Formerly a victorianized group of tiny rooms with a forest of chimneystacks. Before that it had been elizabethanized from a cruck house with a relatively large two-bay hall, spere truss, and smaller cross-wing. All its periods of reconstruction can still be recognized (FWBC).

BANNUT FARM HOUSE. *Voysey*'s first country-house job. Dated 1890 and built for R. H. Cazalet. Already pebbledashed and already with great emphasis on horizontals, mullioned windows, and big roofs. This is especially noticeable at the back. The front has four even gables and a picturesquely detailed chimney to their l. The gables are timber-framed, a motif Voysey later more or less discarded. The upper floor of the house below the gable juts and is supported by Voysey's typical sloping buttresses without set-offs. Nice solution of the r. corner, where the ground floor is canted, the upper floor a right angle coming forward beyond the canting below. The cost was £1,120.

CATSHILL

9070

CHRIST CHURCH. 1838 by *H. Eginton*; chancel 1887. Red ashlar. The W part is as characteristic of its date as the E part. W typically 'Commissioners', the tower with clumsy pinnacles, the sides with long lancets and thin buttresses. On the E parts plate tracery. The only a little uncommon feature is that the chancel side chapels have their entrance arches at an angle. – Miniature FONT, a small white earthenware receptacle with Perp detail. One finds them in a number of churches.

CATTESPOOLE *see* TARDEBIGGE

8070

CHADDESLEY CORBETT

ST CASSIAN. The church is dominated by a large C18 W tower with recessed spire. The spire has bands of quatrefoils, and a large blank quatrefoil faces W, as typical an C18 Gothic motif as the Y-tracery of the window below. As one examines the church more closely, attention will, however, be focused on the brilliant chancel, the most spectacular piece of the Dec style in any Worcestershire parish church. The E window is of
32 five lights. They are of course ogee-headed, and above them are reticulation units, reversed ogee-sided spherical triangles and at the top a large roundel with four triangles in Kentish tracery. This latter motif appears in a S window as well, in another is a bold mouchette wheel, in the third cusped and subcusped trefoils. To the N there are no windows, because the chancel was built – rebuilt, as we shall see – against a N chapel of *c.*1280. The date is indicated by the Y-tracery of the N windows and the three stepped lancets under one blank arch in the E window. The S aisle has a Dec W window, but Late Perp S windows and an ogee-headed outer tomb recess. The windows of the N aisle are Victorian, but the doorway prepares for the interior. It is Norman and probably re-set. One order of colonnettes with scalloped capitals. Zigzag arch, also with incised zigzags. And so inside. There the arcades are Norman and both impressive and teasing; the chancel is of course Dec. Ogee-headed SEDILIA and PISCINA, the arches on heads. Opposite an AUMBRY, also ogee-headed, with crockets and finial, also on heads. L. and r. of the E window two image niches. The interior of the N chapel and its two-bay arcade and W arch tell of a late C13 date. The arcade arches have two hollow chamfers. The Norman N aisle arcade is obviously of two periods. The three E bays are convincingly mid-Norman in every respect. Strong and relatively high round piers, round multi-scalloped capitals, with bits of decoration, square abaci, single-step arches. The W pier of this lot was the W respond. Then a W bay was added and at the same time the S arcade built which covers the same E–W distance by only three bays. Yet the capitals and other details – as far as they are not renewed – are

identical. What happened, then? To venture an explanation, one must first look at tower arch and chancel arch. The tower arch is double, in the sense that the C18 arch stands behind an earlier one, with thin chamfers. This means that there was a previous tower here. The arch is hard to date. The VCH makes it C14; but it might just as well be C15, and the C17 cannot be excluded. The chancel arch tallies more or less in the details, and is clearly a makeshift affair. Might it not be then that, when the church received its earlier W tower, the S arcade piers and responds were re-spaced to the new length required and a new, Norman-looking W bay provided by using the chancel-arch responds? The explanation of the VCH that the S arcade and the W bay of the N arcade followed the rest of the N arcade before the end of the C12 must in any case be excluded. Such widely spaced single-step arches are out of the question. –
FONT. The Chaddesley Corbett font is an outlier of the Here- 16
fordshire school of Norman carvers and must be of *c.*1160–70. It is of goblet shape with a short stem and a tapering base, and it is decorated all over. On the base is interlace, on the stem plaiting, and on the bowl a main band of four dragons, their tails wildly but not tightly twisted. Why is this motif on a font? Had the carvers any good reason, or were they just enjoying themselves? At the top another band of interlace. – (SCULPTURE. In the W wall of the porch is a fragment of a mid-C12 tympanum with Christ in Majesty holding a book. The drapery and the ornamental detail are both very close to the Pedmore tympanum.)* – PLATE. Chalice of 1570 and Paten of 1724. – MONUMENTS. Effigy of a Knight, late C13, cross-legged and wearing a hood of mail. Frieze of flowers along the border. Limestone. – Effigy of a priest, C15 (?). Sandstone. – Brasses of Thomas Forest † 1511, wife and children. 37 in.
figures. – Humfrey Pakington † 1631. Already classical. Black 63
and white marble. No effigies. Side columns and pediment, but many still somewhat restless details. A fine piece of its date. – The contrast to the neighbouring tablet († 1696) is telling.

The village street is one of the most attractive in the county. At the foot, opposite the church, is the CHARITY HOUSE, dated 1812, three symmetrical brick cottages. Then, opposite, next to the churchyard, LYCHGATE HOUSE, Early Georgian, of three bays, with lively details. Odd parapet starting l. and r. gable-wise. Fluted keystones. Again opposite the TALBOT INN,

*Information given me by Mr Stratford.

with a long, impressive timber-framed frontage. The ground floor has close studs, but what is original of the porches? Higher up, on the same side, TUDOR HOUSE, wrongly so called, as its main features are two canted bays with Venetian windows broken round them and two big ogee gables. The doorway in the middle has a classical pediment, but the blank doorways and windows in the end bays are ogee-headed again. So the date is probably about 1750. The Golden Lion at Bromsgrove is very similar. N of Tudor House a two-bay brick cottage dated 1785.

The best timber-framed houses are at the far end (N) on the r. The farthest was a typical yeoman house with cross-wing. The house became three cottages, probably in the C19, but the hall bays are now re-united as one house. The row of cottages S of the cross-wing contains a cruck, quite unsuspected from outside the building. FOLD FARM opposite the church (E) once had a six-bay cruck barn dated C14 (FWBC).

BROCKENCOTE HALL, ¼ m. W. Symmetrical, quite grand neo-William-and-Mary house with a high hipped roof, early C20 presumably. The doorcase must be of *c*.1760, re-used. Fluted columns and a pediment.

CHADWICH MANOR *see* RUBERY

CHARLTON

0040

ST JOHN EVANGELIST. 1872–83. Goodhart-Rendel writes: 'Old Barn bedevilled by a Mr *Workman*, Esquire, with Mr *Forsyth* of Worcester as his aid'. Henry Workman was indeed the squire. Forsyth of course was a sculptor (*see* Worcester Cathedral etc.). Nave and chancel in one.

CURSUS, 1 m. NW. Aerial photography has revealed a long, ditched, rectangular enclosure orientated N–S in close association with a circle symmetrically placed over its S end.

CHÂTEAU IMPNEY *see* DROITWICH

CHILDSWICKHAM

0030

ST MARY. W doorway of *c*.1130–40 hidden by the W tower. One order of columns, single-scallop capitals, one roll in the arch. Above the former W window. Of the early C13 the chancel with a shafting arrangement clearly devised for rib-vaulting. The shafts are triple, the middle ones keeled. Close trumpet-scallop capitals and the two against the E wall sprouting small leaves.* Arch into a former Perp N chapel. E.E. N transept with a two-light window with plate tracery. The W tower starts Dec (see the doorway and the S window) and carries a later recessed spire with lucarnes at the bottom. Much of the church is Victorian. – FONT. The oddly elementary patterns suggest a date in the early 1660s. – STAINED GLASS. In the S chancel window original fragments. – PLATE. Chalice and Paten Cover, undated.

CROSS. In the centre of the village. Instead of the head an C18 urn. By the cross a cottage dated 1711. This is no longer in the Tudor and Stuart tradition. It has five symmetrically set sash-windows. But may they not be a replacement? The date is early for a Worcestershire village.

CHILDSWICKHAM HOUSE. Here the date is 1698, and here the windows still have mullion and transom crosses. But the front is also entirely symmetrical, and there is one string course instead of individual hood-moulds.

CHURCH HONEYBOURNE 1040

ST ECGWIN. The church was dedicated in 1295, and of that date may indeed be the chancel, the nave, and the former S aisle. The chancel windows are cusped lancets, and the E window is a stepped group of three of them under one blank arch. The nave instead has Y-tracery, as had the S aisle. But the aisle is demolished and the arcade filled in, with the aisle windows re-set. The W tower has a Dec spire. The tower pinnacles and the octagonal spire start in the main directions flush with the tower, in the diagonals behind the pinnacles. There are three tiers of lucarnes, the lowest right at the foot. They are large, of two lights, and have Dec tracery. It is all quite a personal job. The chancel is internally of very satisfying proportions. Perp S porch with a stone roof on four transverse stone arches. Entrance with pierced tracery spandrels. Hood-mould on very large round stops. The window W of the porch has the same. – PLATE. Cup of 1703 (or 5?).

CHURCHILL 8070

½ m. N of Blakedown

ST JAMES. By *W. J. Hopkins*, 1868. Nave and chancel and NE tower. Hopkins's typical flat geometrical tracery. Inside E

*Mr Stratford compares these leaves with some on capitals at Abbey Dore in Herefordshire, and the triple shafts and their capitals with those in the Pershore chancel.

of the chancel arch on either side a recessed seat with a canopy.

(PARK HALL, 1½ m. SW. Brick, of various periods, with a very good C18 staircase and two-storey bow windows. MHLG)

9050

CHURCHILL

½ m. S of Broughton Hackett

ST MICHAEL. Nave and chancel and bell-turret. Externally all of the restoration of *c.*1910 etc. – PULPIT. A simple C17 piece. – Chancel PANELLING also C17. – COMMUNION RAIL. Jacobean, with vertically symmetrical balusters. – SCULPTURE. Fine lion *couchant*, in two pieces, from the bottom corner of a gable. What date is it? – STAINED GLASS. In the E window one original shield. – PLATE. Cup and Cover Paten by *H. W.*, 1571. – MONUMENT. Fine cartouche to Thomas Barker † 1688. Skull with bats' wings at the foot.

CHURCHILL FARM. Brick, with a shaped gable. Also a timber-framed part.

CHURCHILL MILL, *see* Broughton Hackett, p. 113.

0050

CHURCH LENCH

ALL SAINTS. W tower and nave and chancel. Late Norman S doorway with one order of colonnettes and a moulded arch. The N doorway is of the same time but plainer. Two-bay C14 S arcade of broad continuous hollows. The E bay with its four-centred arch is later. In the E respond an image niche. The church is of 1852–3 (by *Preedy*), and in 1887–8 much restoration took place. – PAINTING. Over the chancel arch Christ in Glory and angels. High Victorian in style but probably done under a bequest of 1886. – STAINED GLASS. Fragments in the tympanum of the N doorway. – EMBROIDERY. Early C16 Cope of blue velvet, the orphreys with saints split vertically and used as a border. – CANDLESTICKS. Heavy, imitation Limoges–Romanesque.

SCHOOL, opposite the church. Brick, with long bands of edifying stone inscriptions. Built in 1864.

CLAINES *see* NORTH CLAINES

0040

CLEEVE PRIOR

ST ANDREW. W tower, nave and chancel, and a low C18 transept victorianized at the restoration of *c.*1863, when the chancel was redone too. However, it kept some of its early

C14 windows. The nave is Norman; see the simple N doorway. The S doorway is E.E., as are nave N and S windows. The windows are plain lancets; so they might just be coeval with the S transept arch on its elementary imposts. The W tower is probably mid to late C14. The arch to the nave has a sunk quadrant and a broad hollow moulding, the bell-openings have Dec tracery and a transom. – PLATE. Cup by *T. F.*, 1728. – Several enjoyable HEADSTONES in the churchyard.

MANOR HOUSE, NE. A very fine late C16 house, on an asymmetrical plan. The porch has a round arch and l. and r. of it medallions with frontal busts. The porch and the other elements, especially the mullioned and transomed windows, are finely detailed. Five-light windows on the ground floor beneath the large gable of the projecting r. wing.* – DOVECOTE of the manor house. Round.

A group of fine stone COTTAGES in THE GREEN.

(At the W end, on the N side of the road, is a stone house dated 1619. It has a gable and mullioned windows and was called derelict by the VCH in 1913.)

CLENT 9070

The Clent Hills are one of the chief Birmingham hiking areas. Houses in gardens are scattered over the parish, and roads are happily intricate and confusing. The hills rise to 1035 ft, and on them is an EARTHWORK.

ST LEONARD. Perp W tower, including the arch towards the nave with its characteristic respond capitals. Perp also the chancel. E window with transom at the arch springing. S doorway with ogee arch and the inscription: Juxta hunc lapidem jacet corpus Johannis Cleye. Wagon roof inside. The S arcade, though it is much renewed, is late C12, see the trumpet-scallop capitals of the round piers and the single-stepped arches. The N arcade is of 1864–5, by *Kirk & Parry*. – PLATE. Mid-C16 Cup; Salver of 1693. – MONUMENTS. Several tablets, including one of † 1650 with twisted columns and an open segmental pediment.

Of CLENT HOUSE only the STABLES remain. They date from 1709. Brick. Eleven bays, with a three-bay centre stressed by a steep pediment and a cupola.

* Granville Squiers reports a PRIEST HOLE under the floor of a first-floor room.

FIELD HOUSE, Field Lane, 1⅛ m. W. A fine three-bay two-and-a-half-storey brick house of *c.*1750, enlarged by *Forbes & Tait* in 1921. Most of the windows are of the Venetian type. There are also giant pilasters, on one side four, on the other side only two, at the angles. The former side has a one-bay pediment.

7060

CLIFTON-ON-TEME

ST KENELM. C13 W tower (lancet windows) with a later shingled broach spire. The arch to the nave has two continuous chamfers. Nave and chancel. In the chancel also a lancet. The nave N windows with their entertaining tracery are of the restoration by *Cranston* (1847–53). S aisle of short octagonal piers with double-chamfered arches. This is probably early C14. – STAINED GLASS. Some early C14 fragments in the S aisle E window. – PLATE. Cup 1570; Flagon by *I. B.*, 1634; Almsdish by *T. H.*, 1681. – MONUMENTS. (Effigy of a cross-legged Knight; C14.) – For the tablet to Henry Jefferys † 1688 the contract with *Grinling Gibbons* exists. Yet it is really nothing special, nor would it be even if the top and bottom were in their original state. The neighbouring tablet to Lady Winnington née Jefferys † 1718 is no doubt also by him. Both have hanging draperies l. and r. of the inscription plate, cherubs' heads at the top, and flowers and leaves at the foot.

WOODMANTON FARM, ¾ m. SE. To this farm belongs a former CHAPEL, now a farm building. The chapel has a remarkable roof and a timber window of two lights with ogee-trefoiled heads. Licence to crenellate Woodmanton was given in 1332. The chapel is timber-framed. The ground floor at some stage was converted into the farm kitchen, with a big fireplace and chimneystack built right through the upper part of the chapel. The first floor is a C17 insertion. The roof is more or less complete over two bays and is a wagon vault. It is one of the few examples of a rafter roof with curved ashlar pieces, originally supported by a wholly timber-framed substructure. This has necessitated an enormously broad wall-plate, made up of two sections, both heavily moulded (FWBC).

HAM CASTLE FARMHOUSE, 1¼ m. E. Where Ham Castle has been there is now only a C17 or C18 basement preserved. It is tunnel-vaulted in brick and has the amazing length of about 100 ft.

Rectangular EARTHWORK of Roman date showing three periods of occupation. Whether civil or military is uncertain.

COFTON HACKETT

0070

ST MICHAEL. Much of 1861 by *Henry Day*, but the W mid-buttress and double bellcote with its pinnacles are old – C16 probably, and so is the timber porch. The chancel decoration is typical of the sixties. – STAINED GLASS. One-light window in the chancel by *Kempe*, 1881. – PLATE. Paten with the Vernicle, early C16; Cup of 1661; Paten of 1827. – MONUMENTS. Incised slab to William Leycester † 1508, his first wife † 1514, and his second wife whose date of death remained blank. An unusually good piece. – Tablets to Joliffes of Cofton Hall † 1651, † 1692, † 1719, † 1758 – quite illuminating as a sequence.

COFTON HALL. To the l. of the quite plain and ordinary six-bay, three-storeyed early C19 house is an ashlar-faced part. The ashlaring seems C17, but it hides one of the finest late medieval halls in Worcestershire, *c.* 38 by 21 ft high, with nine hammerbeam trusses up to collars and thin queen-posts over. The arched braces are gently cusped, with one shallow and two less shallow curves between the cusps. It is said that the two end bays are C17 work. It is also known that much excavating has been done on the site, with very interesting but entirely unpublished results regarding earlier stone structures on the site. The STABLES are of the C18, with two projecting wings. Centre with pilasters and pediment.

CONDERTON *see* BECKFORD

COOKHILL

0050

ST PAUL. 1876; not small. Nave with bellcote and chancel. Small lancets and pairs of lancets.

COOKHILL PRIORY, 1 m. S. This was a Cistercian nunnery, in existence in the late C12 and refounded in the C13 by the wife of William Beauchamp, Earl of Warwick. It was never well-off. Of the church parts of the E and N walls of the chancel exist, notably the very large blocked surround of the E window. The N wall contains the E jamb of a N arcade, probably towards a chapel. The details, including a broad wave moulding, are C14 or early C15. This fragment in 1783 became the chapel of a brick house built in 1763 by one of the Fortescues who had been granted the site in 1542. The house stands on part of the nuns' quarters. It is oddly irregular, as if it had been meant to be of seven bays with a middle doorway. Instead of the l. three there is a wide canted bay window. The doorway has Doric pilasters and a segmental pediment. The chapel is stuccoed and crenellated. The N windows with their Y-tracery and the quatrefoiled roundel are very characteristic of late C18 Gothicism.

8080 COOKLEY

ST PETER. 1849 by *E. Smith*, enlarged 1872 by *J. T. Meredith*. The mixed red and blue brick walling is no doubt of 1849; so is the W tower. – BOX PEWS with poppy-heads. That is Georgian trying to become archeologically correct. – STAINED GLASS. The E window must be of *c.*1850.

LODGES to LEA CASTLE, ½ m. SE. The house of the Knight family exists no longer. The lodges are castellated and flank a tripartite entrance, the centre part larger and also castellated. All this looks *c.*1850.

Ironworks were founded at Cookley in the late C17 and flourished for over a hundred years.

COOKS HILL *see* SALWARPE

7050 COTHERIDGE

ST LEONARD. White all over, except for the upper parts of the remarkable timber S tower. Only the lowest stage of its timbering is exposed, the rest is weatherboarded and modern. The solid timbering of this lowest stage, however, consisting of wide oak planks 4 in. thick, tongued and grooved into each other, is reminiscent of Greenstead Church, Essex, and suggests a very early date. So do the S door and W window. They may be of *c.*1300. The church itself is Norman. Buttresses survive in both nave and chancel. The chancel arch is narrow and has one order of columns with a beaded spiral band. Decorated scallop capitals, treated like folded material. Zigzag arch. One Perp S window was inserted to give more light to the rood. The N chapel is probably Jacobean, see the E window, straight-headed with round-arched lights. – PULPIT. A fine mid-C17 piece with its tester. – COMMUNION RAIL. C18. – BOX PEWS. – TILES. C15. Chancel floor. – PLATE. Flagon by *A. M.*. 1662; Paten, 1662; Chalice and Paten Cover, *c.*1680.

COTHERIDGE COURT. The side and part of the back is C16 timber-framing with close studs. The front was added in 1770.

The centre looks in its fenestration earlier, but the short projecting wings have Venetian and tripartite windows so coarsely detailed that they must be post-Georgian. (The principal staircase is Elizabethan, with square balusters. VCH)

COW HONEYBOURNE

1040

CHURCH. 1861–3 by *W. J. Hopkins*. The Perp W tower is original. The three-light Perp N window is an oddity in Hopkins's *œuvre*. – PULPIT. Elizabethan and quite lavishly decorated. It is said to have come to the church at the time of rebuilding.

E of the church a good C17 Cotswold farmhouse. To the N, the THATCHED TAVERN has a thin exposed cruck-truss. MANOR FARM HOUSE, another typical Cotswold house, has a date 1627.

CRADLEY *see* BIRMINGHAM OUTER WESTERN SUBURBS

CRAYCOMBE HOUSE *see* FLADBURY

CROOME D'ABITOT

8040

After various changes of hand the d'Abitot estate was bought in 1592 by Thomas (later Sir Thomas) Coventry. His son became Lord Keeper of the Great Seal and, in 1628, Lord Coventry. The earldom started in 1697. The sixth earl began the house, laid out the grounds, built the church, and placed the Coventry monuments in it, thereby nearly choking it.

ST MARY MAGDALENE. Built on a new site in 1763; we don't quite know by whom. It is most probable that *Lancelot Brown* (Capability Brown) was responsible for the carcase (*see* Croome Court), *Robert Adam* for the interior and the furnishings. Adam had begun work for Croome in 1760. The church, when first planned, was intended to be classical. As built, it is medievalizing, and both externally and internally of the highest merit. It is in fact one of the most serious of the Early Gothic Revival outside, one of the most elegant inside. With its W tower and its large E window it must have looked archeologically perfectly convincing from the house as well as the road. The tracery used is Y-cusped and intersecting-cusped. We can of course recognize the high W porch inside the tower with its vault of twelve radiating ribs and the

quatrefoil motif higher up the tower as Gothick; and the interior is pure Georgian Gothic. Slender piers carrying flat ceilings for the aisles, a coved ceiling like a flattened tunnel-vault for the nave. Delightfully dainty stucco centres and borders. Ogee-headed Commandment and Creed boards on the chancel arch imposts. The chancel is long for an age that did its chancels short and would have satisfied the Ecclesiologists, if it were not for the monuments. – FONT. Of wood,
86 exquisite in shape and exquisite in detail. – PULPIT. Playfully Gothic, but also done with the greatest daintiness, especially the brackets for the tester. – COMMUNION RAIL. Pretty, in the Chippendale way. – BENCHES. Altered, but the panelling of the ends probably original (see the pulpit). – PLATE. Two silver-gilt Almsdishes, 1627; silver-gilt Cup and Paten Cover and silver-gilt Flagon, all 1635. – MONUMENTS. Thomas,
64 first Lord Coventry, † 1639. Large standing monument of white and black marble. He is seen semi-reclining. In front cushion and mace, on the l. and r. standing figures of Justice (holding the Great Seal of England) and Virtue. Big arched reredos with two more allegorical figures reclining on the top. Excellent quality and iconographically very progressive. Attributed by Dr Whinney to the workshop of *Nicholas Stone*. – Second Lord Coventry † 1661 and Lady Coventry. Two identical monuments, both poorly done. Standing monuments, black and white. Semi-reclining effigy, twisted columns, open segmental pediments. She holds a baby, and two tiny figures kneel behind the l. column. – Sir Henry † 1686, convincingly attributed to *William Kidwell*. Very large tablet with white allegorical caryatids l. and r. Open curly pediment. – Fourth Lord Coventry † 1687. By *Grinling Gibbons* (contract 1690). The top garlands are worthy of him; the figure carving is dull. Standing monument of white marble, semi-reclining figure, but the upper part of the body turning round so that he looks to the E, where his view is blocked by one of the assistant figures. They are Hope and Mercy. Wide reredos back wall with exquisite Corinthian pilasters. – Sixth Earl † 1809. By *Bacon Jun.* Kneeling woman bent over the pedestal of an urn. In the style of Bacon's father.

CROOME COURT. The house was begun in 1751, the architect being apparently *Lancelot Brown* – a curious choice, considering that he had until then been a landscape gardener exclusively. He was thirty-five in 1751. However, it should not be forgotten that the sixth Earl of Coventry, for whom Brown worked, wrote in 1752 to *Sanderson Miller* of his house: 'Whatever merits it may in future time boast, it will be ungrateful not to acknowledge you as the primary author'. Was this flattery, and really only meant to refer to siting? Or did Miller indeed do the initial design? Miller's Hagley is remarkably similar. The Earl when still Lord Deerhurst had begun the gardens already in 1748. This date we also know from a letter to Sanderson Miller. As regards the interior of the house, *Robert Adam* was largely responsible for it. He made the first drawings in 1760 and the last as late as 1791. The house is of a warm-coloured Bath stone, but a cool composition, deliberately correctly Palladian or Jonesian. Eleven-bay entrance (N) side, of basement, *piano nobile*, and upper floor with low square angle eminences carrying pyramid roofs – Jones's Wilton motif (and of course the motif of Hagley). Top balustrade otherwise, and the only ornamental enrichments the spacious two-armed open staircase (cf. e.g. Lord Burlington's Palladian Chiswick), the doorway with two Tuscan columns and a pediment, and the window pediments of the *piano nobile* under the eminences. The garden (S) side is grander, with its tetrastyle portico of unfluted Ionic columns to which a broad open staircase leads up. Venetian windows on the *piano nobile* under the eminences. The W side is quite short, just the two eminences and a canted bay window: that is all. The interior is no longer what it was. It had to be adapted to a new use, and much of the decoration has disappeared, including one room which is now in the Metropolitan Museum in New York. Entrance hall on the *piano nobile* with a screen of four Roman Doric columns. The space behind is part of a cross-corridor. This room is pre-Adam. So is the Saloon with its sumptuous pedimented back doorway, its broad frieze, its coving, and its three ceiling panels. The style is Kent's here. In the SE corner is the library, with a Venetian window and fine bookcases designed by Adam *c.*1761–3. On the W side is the long gallery. The chimneypiece has white frontal caryatids holding a garland. This room also is Adam's and of the early 60s. The staircase is cantilevered, runs up two storeys, and has an iron balustrade.

To the W of the house is a brick service wing and then the STABLES quadrangle, also brick, with pedimented entrance arches.

The GROUNDS were landscaped by *Capability Brown* and

contain more park furnishings than most in England. Some of them are at the time of writing in a desperate state of neglect. The lawn to the N of the house is given interest by the church appearing slightly to the E quite near by, *Robert Adam*'s TEMPLE or GREENHOUSE of 1760 appearing to the NE. It is really a temple façade with very little space behind. Six Tuscan columns, triglyph frieze and pediment. Just one closed bay l. and r., screened by columns inside. So there were the Classical and Gothic motifs introduced at once. The other garden furnishings cannot be taken in the strict order of any perambulation. Not far from the Temple is the DRY ARCH BRIDGE, an arch over an underpass, of vermiculated rustication with a keystone mask. The rusticated blocks are of *Coade* stone. They are dated 1797. Then the PUNCH-BOWL GATES, a gateway with two elegant, low, and flat urns. Further W, at the top of the lake the GROTTO, a curved rocky front with several roughly arched openings. In the lake on the island the SUMMER HOUSE, with Corinthian columns *in antis* and a finely carved frieze. Plaques inside, two purely ornamental, the middle one representing the Aldobrandine Wedding. – To the ESE of the house, apart from urns and termini busts the ROTUNDA. It has pedimented openings and garland plaques above them. The dome is coffered inside, and the walls have stucco decoration, more mid-C18 than classical. The PERSHORE LODGE has a thin arch with paired Ionic columns, the WORCESTER LODGE just gatepiers and a separate lodge.

Outside the present grounds towards Severn Stoke is the PANORAMA TOWER, by *Adam*, 1766, though probably altered later. It is round, with four groups of two Tuscan columns *in antis*, the solid walls between lightened by niches, a recessed drum, and a dome. (Also towards Severn Stoke the GOTHIC RUIN, a 'Norman' tower and a piece of wall, and the PARK SEAT, at the S end of the lake, an archway with Tuscan columns *in antis*. Giant Corinthian columns and, inside, plaster apses. MHLG)

For DUNSTALL CASTLE *see* Earls Croome.

9040

CROPTHORNE

ST MICHAEL. Unbuttressed Norman W tower with small windows, one in each of the N, S, and W mid-buttresses.* Arch

*Cf. Fladbury and Shrawley.

to the nave pointed and with two slight chamfers and a hood-mould of nailhead. That is C13 and must be a later heightening and widening. The tower top is Perp. It has tall transomed two-light bell-openings with panel tracery in the heads and small tracery below the transoms. Norman also the two four-bay arcades with round piers, very flat capitals, square abaci, and single-step arches. Again Norman the chancel arch, or at least its scallop capitals. The pointed arch with two slight chamfers would belong to the time of the alteration of the tower arch and also probably to the rebuilding of the chancel: for the chancel has a N lancet and a N doorway of one continuous chamfer. The S nave doorway incidentally has the same moulding. Also early C13 the S porch entrance. The porch was originally two-storeyed. Divers Perp windows. – BENCHES. The ends are traceried. – CROSS HEAD. The best 6
piece of Anglo-Saxon art in the county. The arms are double-cusped or lobed. On front and back are animated birds and beasts in bold trails, and on the sides is, surprisingly enough, all close Greek key. The head is supposed to be of *c.*825–50. – PLATE. Cup and Cover Paten by *H. W.*, 1571. – MONUMENTS. In the N aisle early C14 ogee-headed tomb recess with ballflower decoration. Inside is the coffin-lid or the tomb-slab of a priest. – Francis Dineley and his wife who died in 1624. Two recumbent effigies with the children kneeling small against the tomb-chest. Back wall with inscription. It is a poor job. – Edward Dineley and wife; 1646. Big tablet with two kneeling figures facing one another across a prayer desk. Two columns l., two r. Straight top and achievement. The children kneel small below the kneelers. No names recorded. – In the churchyard CROSS with the shaft whole.

Cropthorne has a specially pretty village street, but one with scattered houses in gardens, not one of real street character. Much of the nicest work is black and white. The street runs down parallel with the Avon.

CROWLE 9050

ST JOHN BAPTIST. Nearly all by *Preedy*, 1881–5. However, the high Late Perp tower arch with big hollow mouldings and bands of capital following the same mouldings is original. So is the heavy timber porch, a C14 piece. The roof of the porch is C14 too. – FONT. Octagonal, Perp, with traceried panels on the stem, fleurons on the underside, and on the bowl cusped panels. – LECTERN. A mystery-piece, if ever there was one. It had been lying in the churchyard for some time, when *c.*1845 the vicar restored it. It was first described in 1851. The material is a limestone similar to Purbeck. The stem seems entirely of 1845, and the foliage is certainly also drastically re-cut. The plain top surface, however, is old, but what else is? Certainly not the capitals. The central figure is most trustworthy.* It is as tellingly Romanesque as it is Italian, and yet it is most probably of *c.*1200 and English. It represents a kneeling man, kneeling dead-frontally on nothing. He holds two symmetrical vine tendrils. For the motifs one ought to compare e.g. the ambo of S. Ambrogio in Milan, which is of *c.*1100.‡ Yet can it be an Italian piece? What makes this specially improbable is the fact that a companion piece is at Norton and a third very similar piece, though without a seated figure, at Much Wenlock. The date of those two is most likely also *c.*1200 or a little later. – PLATE. Chalice and Cover Paten 1571; Flagon 1783.

59 CROWLE COURT FARM. The farm has a barn with stone walls and 30 ft span trusses. Two bays are now ruined. There are also the neglected remains of a small stone building said to have been the kitchen of the medieval manor house.

CRUISE HILL *see* FECKENHAM

DANES CAMP *see* BECKFORD

9040

DEFFORD

ST JAMES. The architectural interest of the church is the timber-framed upper part of the W tower, the sculptural interest a small female head used as the keystone of the S doorway. It is a queen of the lineage of the *Portail Royal* of Chartres. There are few successors of that type in England, the Rochester W portal chiefly. So the little head, probably a label-stop, assumes importance. – WEST GALLERY. Late Georgian. – PLATE. Cup and Paten Cover, 1571.

NOKES COURT. Three-bay cruck house with single-bay hall, one of the best looking externally, as the pair of crucks, almost straight, stand out beyond the plaster of the lower

*But the chin has been patched.

‡And Mr Stratford adds that the foliage is much like that of the Trivulzio Candlestick in Milan Cathedral, which in its turn has been claimed as English work of *c.*1200. The foliage is indeed reminiscent also of that of the Wells S transept, which again points to a date *c.*1200.

gable wall. As usual a fireplace and first floor have been inserted.

Cruck trusses are also recorded by the NMR at BUXTON COTTAGES. These were probably BOX TREE COTTAGES on the way N out of the village. They were a complete little history of domestic architecture – cruck hall C13 or C14, C16 close-timbered solar wing, C17 two-storey and attic, brick-nogged, service range with original fireplaces, doors and windows with ovolo mouldings. The village still has a comparable cruck hall and cross-wing. This is WHITE HOUSE opposite the church (S), now mostly brick and grey rough-cast, and very dilapidated (FWBC).

DODDENHAM 7050

ST MARY. 1856 by *A. E. Perkins*. Nave and chancel in one. Polygonal stone bell-turret. 'Middle-Pointed'.

DODDERHILL 9060

ST AUGUSTINE. A very interesting church, and surprising outside and inside. The exterior is dominated by the mighty S tower built in 1708. The tooling betrays the date, but the windows, from tall lancets to Perp bell-openings, are either Victorian – and they don't seem to be that – or original. If so, they must come from the former crossing tower which the church had and which was taken down after the Civil War. There are objections to that explanation too, as we shall see. The crossing has late C12 or early C13 responds to all sides, with keeled shafts and trumpet-scallop capitals, the scallops a little decorated, and also one early stiff-leaf capital (cf. St Andrew Droitwich). The arches are already pointed – the age knew that pointing was advisable when a heavy weight had to be carried – and there is indeed a consecration date 1220 recorded. The nave has completely disappeared. The tower takes the place of the S transept, and the long lancets may belong to that and thus also to the C13. But how is the quadruple-chamfered arch to be explained, immediately S of the S crossing arch? It really can't be of 1708. The long N transept is of brick, early C19, but has one re-set window of four lights with flowing tracery. This goes well with the ambitious five-light chancel E window and the chancel side windows. They are shafted inside. They represent the date 1322, when new altars in the church were dedicated. The N wall of the chancel is all early C19 brick. In the S wall PISCINA and SEDILIA, low–high–low (an unusual composition), with ogee arches, and a blocked shafted low-side window. – PULPIT. Victorian, round, of openwork wrought iron. – PLATE. Cup and Cover Paten 1571; two Flagons and a Plate 1797. – MONUMENTS. Fragment of a monument to members of the Dannet family. Four kneeling children with the initials of their Christian names.

CHÂTEAU IMPNEY *see* Droitwich.

HILL COURT. Early C19, stuccoed, of five bays. Greek Doric porch. Round-arched middle window.

(ASTWOOD FARM. H-shaped, of the early C17. It is timber-framed, but was refronted in brick *c.*1700. VCH)

ROMAN REMAINS *see* Droitwich.

9070

DODFORD

HOLY TRINITY AND ST MARY. The best church of its date in the county. The date is 1907–8, and the architect was *Arthur Bartlett*. The composition first of all is excellent, an aisleless building with a two-bay-long transept and a bold tower rising on the outer bay. It is finished in a small saddleback roof. Church and tower are connected by a dog-leg wooden passageway in such a way that a little paved courtyard is formed. In the tower wall is an outer PULPIT towards that courtyard. The architectural details in and out are Arts and Crafts Gothic, and they culminate in the fanciful rose window at the end of the transept, i.e. in the tower, with a centre medallion in flowing tracery. Inside, the nave is crossed by diaphragm arches with square Gothic fleurons. Such also decorate the ROOD BEAM. – STAINED GLASS in a mild Art Nouveau. – Off the chancel a two-bay S chapel which is rib-vaulted.

VICARAGE. Also 1907–8, and so no doubt by *Bartlett* too. Higher up than the church. Varied in outline and surfaces. Pebbledashed, but with a tower whose brickwork is exposed.

DODFORD PRIORY, $\frac{3}{8}$ m. N. Founded *c.*1184 for Premonstratensian canons. All that remains is one wall with buttresses and a doorway. The windows are, needless to say, not ancient.

9050

DORMSTON

ST NICHOLAS. The thing one will remember is the timber-
48 framed W tower with its heavy bracing inside. It is of the Shropshire type of Clun. Mr Charles dates it *c.*1450. Of heavy timbers also and perhaps a century earlier the S porch. Dec

nave and mostly Victorian chancel. – SCULPTURE. Part of a Crucifixion, probably from a churchyard cross. – Near by also architectural fragments. – STAINED GLASS. Bits in a S window. – PLATE. Cup and Cover Paten by *H. W.*, 1571.

DORMSTON MANOR, formerly Bag End Farm, ¼ m. SE. Partly timber-framed, with brick infilling. Probably of *c.*1600. Very picturesque with its two dovecotes. One of these has gables facing in all four directions. The house has close studding on the ground floor, but square panelling above. Inside several good chimneypieces, one with panels of two broken shapes, another with columns, and a staircase with very imposing newel-posts.

MOAT FARMHOUSE, ⅜ m. SW. A remarkable timber-framed house, dated 1663, high, with three gables along the front and one to each short side. (Of a type clearly evolved from medieval solar wings. The hall has become a single-storey projection at the back, in other words, the kitchen. The house is one of the few which have retained their tile weatherings, bracketed from the wall framing at first-floor level. There is also a dovecote of the same date as the house. FWBC)

DOVERDALE

8060

ST MARY. Nave and chancel and a bell-turret with spire by *Preedy*, 1860. The exterior of the church looks that date, but there are some C17 windows. – PANELLING of the nave walls C17. – STAINED GLASS. C15 Virgin, much restored (nave N). – PLATE. Cup and Cover Paten of 1571.

DOVERDALE MANOR, ¾ m. NNE. A five-bay early C18 brick house of two and a half storeys. Windows with keystones. The tripartite porch with segmental pediment is probably later. Fine staircase with three balusters to the tread: twisted–columnar–twisted. Carved tread-ends (cf. Ombersley Court). – (In the grounds an ICEHOUSE, derelict.)

DOWLES

7070

ST ANDREW. The church has recently been pulled down.

MANOR HOUSE. A small but exceptionally complete Elizabethan manor house, timber-framed, with central hall and living room wing and kitchen wing, both with cross gables. Stone ground floor and timber-framed upper floor with close studding. Inside much of the timber framing must have been exposed; for the amazingly fully preserved decorative wall paintings take the posts into consideration. The hall, the room above it, and the drawing room and the room above that all have their paintings, grey and red, and very boldly done, largely arabesques, but also in one upper room a gentleman and a lady. In the former kitchen a wooden Elizabethan overmantel from a house at Bewdley. Between the kitchen and the hall there is still a hatch. The house lies in perfect seclusion in a dip surrounded by wood.

DRAKELOW *see* WOLVERLEY

9040

DRAKE'S BROUGHTON

ST BARNABAS. 1857 by *W. J. Hopkins*. Nave and chancel and a thin SW tower with weatherboarded spire. The details are E.E. to Dec. The interior is brick-faced. The chancel is given prominence by leaf capitals. – PLATE. Paten by *Jos. Clare*, 1719.

DRAYTON *see* BELBROUGHTON

8060

DROITWICH

Salt was the centre of interest of Droitwich already before the Conquest. The *salinae* appear in Domesday Book, and when King John gave Droitwich to the burgesses, he gave them the *vill cum salsis et salinis*. But the town remained small, and Leland (*c.*1535), Torrington (1781), and *The Beauties of England and Wales* (early C19) are unanimous in calling Droitwich dirty. In 1826 the town still consisted only of the High Street, St Andrew's Street, and the street to the bridge. The great change came with the discovery of the possibilities of Droitwich as a spa. The ensuing development is almost entirely due to John Corbett. His Stoke Prior Salt Works were erected in 1828, and at Droitwich he built the Salters' Hall and the St Andrew's Baths, acquired the older Royal Baths, and started or remodelled the Raven Hotel, the Worcestershire Hotel, the Royal Hotel, and others. The Corbett style is brick with half-timbered upper parts.

ST ANDREW, St Andrew's Street. The finest parts belong to the
25 early C13, namely the chancel arch and the N tower with its S arch at r. angles to the chancel arch and its E and W arches. The tower has two shafted lancets to the N. The arches have crocketed capitals with uncommonly many heads and moulded arches with keels and fillets. Only the S respond of the chancel arch still has trumpet scallops (cf. St Augustine, Dodderhill,

and Stoke Prior). Of the C13 also are the nave W buttresses and the W part of the chancel (with lancets). The E wall of the chancel is not medieval.* Otherwise, the aisle arcades and S chapel arcade are all early C14. Octagonal piers, double-chamfered arches, but differing details. The arch between S aisle and S chapel rests on two busts, a king and the mason (?). The short N chapel is Perp, the nave W window typical of *c.*1800 (three wide, stepped lancet lights). The N aisle dates from *c.*1910. – FONT. Probably Jacobean. Square stem, goblet bowl. Elementary geometrical motifs (cf. St Peter). – Sweet little FONT COVER with turned balusters. – STAINED GLASS. Bits in the S chapel window. – MONUMENT. Coningesby Norbury † 1734 (nave E). Large tablet with trophies l. and r.

ST AUGUSTINE. *See* Dodderhill.

ST NICHOLAS, Ombersley Street. 1869 by *John Smith* of Droitwich. Red sandstone, with a SW tower. The tracery goes from plate to Dec. French Early Gothic capitals, but most of the capitals uncarved. – MONUMENT. G. E. Penrice McConnel † 1886. By *F. J. Williamson* of Esher. Free-standing white angel by a white rock.

ST PETER, St Peter's Lane, 1 m. S of the old town and once quite separate from it. Norman chancel with three small windows. The chancel arch is Norman too. Coupled columns as responds with decorated scallop capitals.‡ Of the early C13 the S aisle and S transept. The S aisle however has been demolished, and only traces of the arcade remain. The capitals are of early stiff-leaf type and the one preserved of the aisle arcade has heads as well (cf. St Andrew). The S transept E window is of three stepped lancet lights, i.e. of the late C13. Dec N transept, see the N window with reticulated tracery. Perp W tower, Late Perp timber-framed clerestory. Of the same time the handsome low-pitch roof. A riddle is the two blocked arches in the S transept W wall. One would connect them with the S aisle, but the aisle cannot have had the width of both. Was there then in addition a chapel S of the S aisle? – FONT. Jacobean, with square stem and goblet bowl. Elementary geometrical motifs, inspired no doubt by Norman motifs (cf. St Andrew). – STAINED GLASS. In the S transept E window figures and decoration of the early C14, with the characteristic yellow and dark green, e.g. a Crucifixus. – E window by *F. Preedy*, 1853. – TILES. In the vestry and by the

* Good Perp chancel roof.

‡ The triple arch above is C19.

font C15 tiles. – PLATE. Cup 1571; Paten 1696; Flagon 1781. – MONUMENTS. George Wylde, Serjeant-at-law, † 1616. In robes, lying on his side. Flat arch and two columns. – Richard Nash † 1690. Tablet, naïve and engaging, with two allegorical girls and two trumpet-blowing cherubs.

ST PETER'S MANOR, W of the church. With a modern but convincing date 1618. Three-storeyed, with three by two even gables. The front has all close studding. The house is 'much modernized, but not without interest' (F. B. Andrews). Inside are two chimneypieces with stucco overmantels. They have strapwork and excessively tapering pilasters (NMR).

BAPTIST CHURCH, Ombersley Street. 1905–6 by *F. B. Andrews*. Brick and stone dressings. Fancy Perp with a small louvre-like turret.

TOWN HALL, St Andrew's Street. Stuccoed brick. Humble, not detached. Placed on a curve. The part on the l. is the original town hall. It was built in 1826, has columns on the ground floor, and was originally open. The windows were at that time different. – CORPORATION PLATE. Maces dated 1646 and 1660.

OLD BRINE BATHS, on the hill N of Queen Street. Demolished in 1959. They were a relic of the time before John Corbett. Their date of building was *c.*1836. They formed one composition with the ROYAL HOTEL, a three-storeyed, stuccoed building of five bays with giant pilasters which was replaced *c.*1900 by the ST GEORGE'S BUILDING. This was built for John Corbett, still as the Royal Hotel too, and is now County Council offices. Brick with shaped gables.

ST ANDREW'S BRINE BATHS, Victoria Square. First built by John Corbett in 1887. Rebuilt in 1909 and 1933–5. Brick and half-timbering.

HOTELS. The RAVEN, St Andrew's Street, has a C16 centre which was originally St Andrew's House. It was bought by John Corbett *c.*1887 and converted into a hotel. Considerable additions to l. and r. The whole is timber-framed. (In the hall STAINED GLASS from Huddington, with dates 1501 and 1580. Also cast-iron PANELLING in the bar etc., painted to simulate wood.) The WORCESTERSHIRE HOTEL in Corbett Road is yet bigger and was built by *J. R. Nichols* for John Corbett at one go in 1891. It cost £15,000. Steep roofs and thin timber strips. The ROYAL HOTEL in Queen Street is smaller and simpler. Stuccoed brick with upper timber bits. Arched ground floor. For CHÂTEAU IMPNEY *see* below.

PERAMBULATION. We start at Victoria Square with the SALTERS' HALL at the corner of St Andrew's and Ombersley Streets, a half-timbered Corbett building of 1881. Down St Andrew's Street one enters the old town. Minor small buildings l. and r. By the town hall and St Andrew's church turn W into FRIAR STREET with the more interesting houses. First opposite the large, dull, semi-between-the-wars-modern NORBURY HOUSE, built as another hotel in 1936, Nos 79–81, a timber-framed house with overhang, and then the OLD FOLK INN, licensed in 1712 but incorporating a window from the destroyed former St Nicholas' church: four lights, the tracery dating it to *c.*1300. Also two medieval heads. On the opposite side minor Georgian houses, e.g. the HOP POLE, which is C17 at the back. Next to this PRIORY HOUSE, the largest timber-framed building in Friar Street after the destruction of the more valuable Chorley House (see p. 57). The street range of Priory House is of *c.*1650, with decorative timbered front, badly restored in the last century. One of the gable chimneystacks at either end still has its original rectangular shaft with ornamental brickwork. The two rear side wings are of much earlier date, the original solar wing still having a fine collar truss of *c.*1500.

In the HIGH STREET the STAR AND GARTER has nice early C19 lettering. Nos. 21–3 are timber-framed. Opposite more simple Georgian houses and No. 38 (STEPHENS), which is the three-bay solar wing of a house of *c.*1400. The hall part is of stone and of later date. The solar is uniquely rich in its timber moulding with heavy first-floor beams and an open collar-truss dividing the two bays of the original great chamber. There is an ante-chamber comprising the third bay. The wall-framing has large curved braces in the upper storey and the roof is heavily framed with cusped wind-braces between two tiers of purlins. The roof, unfortunately now obscured by the first-floor ceiling, is a perfect example of medieval carpentry. The fireplaces in the flank wall at each floor level are probably not contemporary, though it is difficult to be certain of this (FWBC).

Turn l. along Queen Street, r. into Hanbury Road, and r. up HOLLOWAY to see the COVENTRY HOSPITAL, almshouses, founded in 1686 and built of brick. Three-bay centre with plaque and pediment. Low l. wing. The r. wing has been replaced, and the original parts much modernized.

CHÂTEAU IMPNEY, N of the Salwarpe and the Canal, i.e. really

at Dodderhill. In ample grounds. This was John Corbett's palace, but it is now a hotel. How self-assured he must have been to build thus. Compact, towering, brick and stone château in the highest-pitched Louis XIII that his architect, *Tronquois* of Paris (local architect *Richard Phené Spiers*), could dream up.* The building was begun in 1869 and carries a date 1875. Entrance side with a deep porte-cochère. Façade to the garden
100 nearly but not quite symmetrical. Steep pavilion roofs with small, large, and very large dormers. Spacious staircase. At the back the former conservatory with iron roof and an iron apse.

There existed at Droitwich Roman SALINAE, so named because of the near-by salt springs. At Dodderhill the remains of a FORT were found, occupied first in the period 47–70 and again in the early C2. Other traces of Roman occupation are known: in Bays Meadow the laying of the railway in 1847 uncovered part of a building with two mosaic pavements, and close by a winged corridor house 130 ft long has recently been excavated, dated to the C3 to C4. More Roman material is known from the area S of the river Salwarpe.

DUNSTALL CASTLE *see* EARLS CROOME

8040

EARLS CROOME

ST NICHOLAS. A Norman church, with a neo-Norman W tower, probably of the 1840s. A drawing records the richly decorated former W front with blind arcading. The two nave doorways have one order of columns, the columns decorated with flat incised all-over zigzag (cf. Pershore e.g.), the capitals scalloped with a little decoration, the arches with a roll moulding and zigzag at r. angles to the wall.‡ The chancel arch evidently belongs. It has the same columns, but one leaf capital and one with entwined trails and a remarkably classical leaf trail in the abacus. The arch is like the S doorway arch. The chancel has one Norman N window and one small Norman window in the gable.§ The late C13 E window still has its

* John Corbett's wife was French.

‡ For the furrowed chevron – the term is Mr Stratford's – cf. Malvern Priory.

§ Mr Stratford notes that the foliage of a capital of the N door wanders from the capital on to the adjacent wall, cf. the much later Leigh. The arrangement of carved panels flanking the chancel arch capitals is found at Ribbesford, Rock, etc., and in the Herefordshire School. Interlace similar to that at Earls Croome occurs at Beckford and Halesowen. In the foliage of the abacus on the S side of the chancel arch a lion ought to be noted.

Norman form inside. So has the earlier C13 chancel S lancet. – PLATE. Cup and Paten Cover, 1571. By *T. E°.*

EARLS CROOME COURT. Timber-framed; C16 to C17. Centre and two cross-gabled wings. Five-light transomed windows. Mostly closely-set studs, but in the centre also concave-sided lozenges. On another side three identical gables and closely set studs exclusively.

BAUGHTON COURT, ¼ m. E. Timber-framed; C16. Front with two gables. Close studding as well as square panels.

On BAUGHTON HILL, 1 m. E of Baughton hamlet, is a polygonal house with pointed windows, probably one of the Croome d'Abitot follies, as is the following.

DUNSTALL CASTLE, 1¼ m. ENE of Earls Croome church. Ascribed to *Sanderson Miller*. A sham Norman castle ruin. Two round towers with an (unrealistically) high archway between them, and at an angle from the r. tower a continuation by a trefoil-cusped archway and a thin square tower.

EASTHAM

6060

ST PETER AND ST PAUL. A Norman church, built of tufa. The S doorway and the four intersecting blank arches above are slightly projected in front of the wall (cf. the Introduction, p. 15). One order of columns with block capitals. One roll moulding and one order of thin saltire crosses. All this is very similar to Martley, Knighton, and Stockton. Stockton also has another motif of Eastham: small panels with figures. At Eastham these are, probably re-set, in the wall E of the S doorway (Sagittarius and another) and in the nave E wall (Agnus Dei, a monster). The N doorway is of *c.*1200 with a continuous keeled roll. But Norman again are the flat buttresses of nave and chancel. The chancel E wall is now completely windowless. This is likely to be due to a restoration. But is the round window in the gable correct at least in shape? Norman also one nave N window. Other windows are of the late C13. These have two lights. The W tower is of 1825: brick, with a large W lancet opening. – FONT. Large, Norman, of cauldron shape, with just a rope moulding at the foot of the bowl. – PULPIT. Made up of C17 panels. – CHANCEL PANELLING. Also made up of such pieces, including perhaps an overmantel or a bed-head. Also one roundel of *c.*1535. – SCULPTURE. There are four small Norman panels, two outside, two inside. They are a small Centaur and an unrecognizable animal, and a roundel with the Lamb and Cross and two affronted beasts with one head. – PLATE. Set of 1739.

EASTHAM GRANGE, 1¼ m. SE. By *Tapper*, 1910. A good, if not a highly personal design. Brick, free Tudor in the Hampstead-Garden-Suburb way. One big gable is straight, the balancing one half-hipped.

LOWERHOUSE FARMHOUSE, 1⅜ m. ESE. A nice early C18 composition. Brick, seven bays, the middle three with a big shaped gable into which rises a round-headed window. Below, the three windows consist in the Queen Anne way of one of normal shape and two very narrow ones.

PUDDLEFORD FARMHOUSE, 1½ m. ESE. Timber-framed with brick infilling. Porch with overhang on shaped brackets.

EASTHAM BRIDGE. 1793, of three brick arches, with roundels in the spandrels.

TALBOT HOTEL, Newnham. At the sharp angle of two main roads. Gothic, with the two chamfered angles emphasized by high, tight windows with a detached shaft to halve them. Small, half-hipped dormers.

EASTINGTON HALL *see* LONGDON

9040

ECKINGTON

HOLY TRINITY. The nave is Latest Norman, as is proved by the W wall and W portal. One order of colonnettes with early stiff-leaf capitals, the arch with the motif of crenellation with triangular merlons interlocked with the same the other way round. Also lozenges broken round an angle.* The W wall also had lancet windows – of the same date? Their traces are interrupted by the Perp W window. Inside, the S arcade is of three bays, also Latest Norman. Round piers, typical capitals, base spurs, single-step arches. The W part of the N wall is of course Norman too. The N arcade is of 1887, but the aisle wall (of brick) dates from *c*.1830. The Perp SW tower was built into the S aisle. Its arches to N and E are recognizably Perp. The S aisle has a late C13 E window which shows that the aisle was formerly narrower than now. Early C14 chancel. – STAINED GLASS. In the chancel N window bits. – PLATE. Cup by *I. F.* and Cover Paten 1571.‡ – MONUMENTS. John Hanford † 1616. Elaborate stone monument

*Mr Stratford observes: zigzag with flowers occurs also at Bredon, Netherton, and Shrawley. Netherton may be by the same hand as Eckington.

‡The paten is the only one in the Archdeaconry of Worcester which has the 'veronical' pattern.

with two large kneeling figures facing one another across a prayer desk. Flat arch, two columns, achievement. The children kneel against the base. The carving, especially of the children, is reminiscent of *Epiphanius Evesham*. The Bigg Monument († 1613) at Norton is very similar. – Tablet by *Squire* of Worcester, the architect († 1746).

BRIDGE, ½ m. N. C15 or C16, narrow, with cutwaters on both sides.

WOOLLAS HALL. High, gabled stone house of 1611 with an irregular façade. In the middle a three-storeyed porch. The pilasters l. and r. of the arched entrance start half-way up out of flat trefoil shapes (cf. Bredon's Norton Manor House). To the r. the two hall windows, of four lights with two transoms and two little gables. To the l. a bigger and higher gable, and below it completely different floor heights. The whole façade is framed by screen walls shaped like the two sides of a shaped gable. Inside a screen with Ionic pilasters, and in the room to the l. of the screens passage a chimney-piece with long thin columns and an overmantel with the usual blank arches. The STABLES have a symmetrical front with three dormers, and mullioned and transomed windows below, mullioned windows in the gables.

NAFFORD CIRCLES AND ENCLOSURE. Aerial photography has revealed three rectangular ditched enclosures and a large, double-ditched circle.

200 yds N of the village a ROMAN VILLA was found when the railway was built.

ELDERSFIELD

7030

ST JOHN BAPTIST. Above the S doorway are remains of the Norman doorway with one column and some part of the zigzag arch. Norman also but excessively restored the chancel arch. Shafts in the respond corners. Plain abacus with flat incised decoration.* Late C13 chancel, early C14 N arcade, very renewed. Quatrefoil piers and double-chamfered arches. Perp S transept and W tower. The tower carries a recessed spire and has to W, N, and S a little niche flanked by small quatrefoils. – FONT. Perp, entirely re-cut. – PULPIT. Simple Jacobean. – BENCHES. Some of the C16 with linenfold panels. – SCREEN.

*Mr Stratford's comment: The capital (like folded material) is very close to Beckford. For the furrowed zigzag cf. Malvern Priory. The date is probably *c.*1160–75.

A few re-used bits in the pulpit and lectern. – STAINED GLASS. Some good C17 coats of arms, one of them dated 1629. – PLATE. Chalice by *Richard Green*, 1716.

8060 ELMBRIDGE

ST MARY. Drastically restored and mostly rebuilt in 1872. Nave and chancel in one, and bellcote. Late Norman S doorway with two orders of colonnettes. Shapeless capitals. In the arch zigzag at r. angles to the wall and lozenges, also broken round a step in the moulding.* Early C13 N arcade with round piers and very simple moulded capitals. They may even be contemporary with the doorway. The arches are of 1872. – COMMUNION RAIL. Jacobean with flat, cut-out balusters. – PLATE. Cup and Cover Paten, 1571. – MONUMENT. Tablet to Edmund Purshull † 1650 with garlands at the top and a skull with bat's wings at the bottom.

PURSHULL HALL, $1\frac{3}{4}$ m. N. Large brick-built house of several periods, but the original four-bay cruck house is still discernible within. One of the crucks survives, buried in a later partition. Most of the house is Early Jacobean brick with characteristic porch and porch room above. On the opposite front a mid C18 projection with tall narrow windows. The C17 timber-frame of the hall and cross-wing is pretty complete. The house is said to have been, like Harvington Hall a few miles away, a recusant-priests' hide-out.

BADGE COURT, $1\frac{1}{2}$ m. NNE. A Talbot house, timber-framed, probably of the early C16. All close studding, and some big diagonal struts. At the back two gables and in the recessed centre, placed asymmetrically, the hall chimneybreast with three fine long, diagonally set stacks. In the late C16 the house went to the Wintours and was yet another Catholic stronghold.

9040 ELMLEY CASTLE

Elmley Castle derives its name from the CASTLE which stood S of the village. It was built by Robert le Despenser in the late C11 and became for a time the principal seat of the Beauchamps. It then decayed, was re-fortified in the C14 and once more in decay in the early C16. Leland saw only 'one Tower and that partly broken'. (Some masonry fragments still remain on the site.)

*The outermost order has a kind of trapeze ornament, according to Mr Stratford unique in Worcestershire.

ST MARY. The main street of the village runs straight towards the middle of the N side of the church, and the treatment of the church shows that this must always have been so. Transept, N aisle, and N porch are all embattled, and the windows l. and r. of the porch (but also the W window of the aisle) are given specially pretty tracery. The transept had a five-light window to the E. The porch entrance has a (re-set ?) arch with two continuous rolls which is likely to be C13. The W tower is not high. It is unbuttressed and dates from the C13. But the chancel is the oldest part of the church. With its herringbone masonry it is most probably of before 1100. This being so, the interior poses a problem. The N arcade is a straightforward, plain job of the C15, except that the E arch – i.e. the transept arch – points to a somewhat earlier date. But the S arcade consists of two E bays separated by an octagonal C14 pier and then no piers at all but just C14 arches connecting square chunks of wall. Such an arrangement always indicates the use of the earlier walling of an aisleless church. If this is so here, we would have to assume a church of Saxon proportions, long nave, long chancel, and made yet longer by the C13 tower. The VCH's dating of the square piers to the C14 does not satisfy in any case. Or can the piers be connected with rebuilding in 1629 (date on the S wall outside) ? – FONT.
Octagonal, with shields, Perp, but on an existing base which is 18
most probably early C13. It consists of fully carved, very menacing dragons, their tails showing a tendency to develop stiff-leaf tips.* – SCULPTURE. Apart from Norman architectural bits worked into the walls, there are in the porch a small stone with a pig and a small stone with a rabbit. – BENCH ENDS. Plain, straight-topped. – STAINED GLASS. In the S aisle E window original bits. – The E window has good glass of *c.*1875. It is presumably by *Powell*. – PLATE. Set, by *John Parker* and *Edward Wakelin*, 1769. – MONUMENTS. Only two need be mentioned, but both among the best of their dates in the county. William Savage and Giles Savage † 1631
and the latter's wife. Three recumbent effigies, she holding 62
her baby in her arms. By their feet supporters, including a stag's head, the neck pierced by an arrow, and beyond them small kneeling children. No large superstructure, just two back plates. – First Earl of Coventry † 1699. Intended for Croome d'Abitot church, but refused admission by the second

*Mr Stratford suggests for comparisons a dragon capital at Bretforton and also the font base of East Penard in Somerset.

earl. The first earl's wife married after her husband's death
Thomas Savage of Elmley Castle. The monument is by
William Stanton and dates from shortly after 1700. White and
65 black marble. Semi-reclining effigy with wig. Two columns
carrying a depressed rounded arch above which, above the
curves of a vestigial pediment, are two small allegorical
figures. Two large figures outside the columns, the l. winged.
– SUNDIAL in the churchyard. C17, with very odd geometrical decoration, of a kind of gross Chippendale-fretwork character. Probably from the garden of the mansion, which was pulled down a few years ago.*

The MAIN STREET has no highlights but is attractive with its unbroken row of houses on the W side, its row of trees on the E side. The first house on the E side is the VILLAGE HALL, with a stone ground floor connected with the existence here in the C14 of some collegiate establishment; the upper floor is timber-framed and has (re-made) slightly projecting windows. At the far end of the street the VILLAGE CROSS, C15 probably and fairly well preserved. HILL LANE, running W from the church end of the main street, has a number of nice houses.

8060

ELMLEY LOVETT

ST MICHAEL. 1839–40 by *John Mills*, except for the C14 W tower with its recessed spire and much of the walling material. The spire has roll-mouldings up the angles. Nave and chancel with lancets and battlements. The E window is of three stepped lancets. – CROSS in the churchyard. The base with big angle spurs.

Close to the church a COTTAGE with mullioned windows.

OLD RECTORY, in the village. Five-bay brick house of the early C18. Doorway with apsed hood on carved brackets. On the upper floor instead of the middle window a pedimented tablet.

(STONE HOUSE. An unusual farm building. Originally it was of three bays and two storeys with an attic, all beneath one roof. The walls are red sandstone. Some original mullioned and transomed windows have survived, and the most impressive room, at least until recent restoration, was the ground-floor kitchen with an 8 ft wide lateral fireplace. The date is *c.*1640. FWBC)

*The Rev. R. H. Lloyd tells me that it bore a series of dials, cylindrical, concave, equinoctial, etc., to indicate the time in any part of the Old World.

EVESHAM

Evesham is a small town of many attractions. It has the river Avon, and the town has wisely made the most of it by tree-planted walks and lawn along the stretch that matters most. It has the abbey precinct, entirely unexpected in what it does not present and in what it does present. And it has its streets with good houses, a few of them of a high order, though on weekdays the roaring traffic of the A44 makes it impossible to look at them.

THE ABBEY PRECINCT

Evesham Abbey was founded in 714 by Bishop Egwin of Worcester. The church collapsed in 960 and was rebuilt thereafter. Whether this is the same building as that said to have been entirely built from *c.*1045 to the consecration in 1054, we do not know. In any case another rebuilding took place after the Conquest under Abbots Walter of Cerisy (1077–1104) and Reginald of Gloucester (1122–49). Of the early phase was the E, of the later the W part. Excavations undertaken in the early C19 have shown the Early Norman crossing and transepts (with E apses) and the Late Norman nave with rounded piers. The chancel with crypt, aisles, and square end was of the time of Thomas of Marlborough (1207–36), the narrow Lady Chapel of the late C13 or early C14. The *Chronicle of Evesham* furnishes a good many more dates, but the visible remains are scarce. All that can be seen is this.

Of the CHURCH a lump of the N transept with the base of the N respond of the arch to the N aisle. Of the CHAPTER HOUSE the very fine entrance arch with twin niches l. and r., each with a little vault, and in the arch orders one set of standing and one set of seated figures. Their style allows one to date the arch *c.*1285–90. The chapter house itself was a decagon. Much more substantial is Abbot Lichfield's
TOWER, a free-standing campanile or clocher such as many 39
medieval English cathedrals used to possess, although the Evesham one is exceptionally late. Clement Lichfield became abbot in 1513. It is a most lavish piece, 110 ft high and pierced by an archway. The outer and inner sides are panelled all over, and the gate arch, the main four-light windows, and the paired two-light bell-openings all have ogee gables. At the top are openwork battlements and pinnacles. The N and S sides in contrast are absolutely closed up to the bell-stage. It is astonishing how unaware England's abbots were of the

gathering storm. If they had not been, how could they indulge in such conspicuous display? Nothing else belongs to the claustral part.

Farther away were two gatehouses and buildings adjoining one of them.

The NORMAN GATEWAY or CEMETERY GATE connected the abbey cemetery with the town. The upper parts are timber-framed and gabled with close-set studding, probably C15 work, and this goes on in the adjoining VICARAGE (which has inside some painted decoration). But the lower part of the gateway is of stone and forms part of the gatehouse built by Abbot Reginald. The details in fact look even earlier than 1120. Single order of columns with block capitals. Inside, blank arcading on thin triple shafts. This gateway is N of the abbey nave. It is continued to the E by a length of Abbot Reginald's wall. W of the church and a good deal farther on are the remains of the GREAT GATE. This forms part of a beautiful L-shaped house of 1711 which faces Merstow Green (*see* below). It has two storeys, simple windows without special surrounds, and a hipped roof. The two doorways are Late Georgian. The Tuscan porch to the E looks mid-C18. Excellent iron gates and railings towards the Green. Visible only inside is one jamb of Abbot Cheriton's gateway. Cheriton's dates are 1316–44. To the E the blocked arch can be seen. To the N in the projecting part towards the Green is a small doorway into the gateway passage. Adjoining the gatehouse on the S are the remains of a vaulted passage or room of the early C14. Thin vaulting-shafts and springers of the vault. Beyond this are the so-called stables, again with a medieval doorway and window. Finally W of the gatehouse the so-called ALMONRY, a C14 or C15 house, the l. part of which is stone, the r. part timber-framed. In the l. part a high C17 four-light mullioned window. The timber-framed part has close studs and a gabled overhang with an oriel window. One bracket of the overhang has leaf decoration. (Inside, a chimneypiece with five big quatrefoils in the lintel and a stone lamp-niche with ogee arches and a spirelet.)

THE CHURCHES

The most curious thing about the abbey precinct is the presence of two parish churches. This has never been fully explained. Both churches lay within Abbot Reginald's wall. One was the church of the parochial cemetery, an unusual function, the other the parish church. Abbeys liked a parish church in their immediate neighbourhood so as to get rid of parish duties. An example is St Margaret Westminster.

ALL SAINTS. The church appears Perp throughout but is in fact Norman. The W doorway of a towerless nave of *c.*1200 is preserved. Round arch with one slight chamfer. Imposts not of the most elementary shape. Dec are the chancel arch, the N transept arch, and, later, a three-light S aisle window. The rest is Perp. The W tower carries a recessed spire and is preceded by a lavish W porch with the entrance from the N, i.e. the Norman gate. The front is panelled, the entrance arch four-centred. To the W is only a five-light window and again panelling. Openwork battlements and pinnacles. The arcades are of the same design, but the S arcade is higher. The piers have four flat canted projections separated by hollows. The arches re-echo that arrangement. The E arch of the N arcade, being the transept arch, is of course different (*see* above). But the climax of the Perp work is the Lichfield Chapel, built for his own burial by Abbot Lichfield when he was still prior, i.e. shortly before 1513. It is of two bays and has a fleuron frieze, openwork battlements and pinnacles, and inside a fan-vault. Below the windows inside all quatrefoils with big flowers. The S transept must have been built before the chapel, as its formerly external W window shows. – FONT. Octagonal, Perp, with fleurons in quatrefoils. – CHANCEL GATES. Low, good Arts and Crafts; 1910. – SCULPTURE. Several bosses from the abbey church, and also a fine small late C13 or C14 seated figure of Moses – STAINED 30
GLASS. In a N window a seated Christ; C14. – The N transept N window typical *Capronnier*. It is dated 1882. – PLATE. Cup 1624; Alms Plate 1683, by *T. R.*; Salver Paten 1728, by *Richard Bayley*. – (CROSS. A C14 cross was discovered in 1910 and serves as a processional cross.) – MONUMENT. Elizabeth Baylies † 1754. Wreathed urn in front of an obelisk. The inscription panel is curved in plan. At the foot a putto with an anchor.

ST LAWRENCE. Perp W tower with a short, not at all happy spire of 1836, when *H. Eginton* did a great deal to the church. At the foot of the tower a defaced small relief of the Crucifixion. The W doorway has traceried spandrels. Perp also the spectacular E side. The aisles have their separate roofs and not much in the way of features, but the chancel has a six-light window all surrounded by panelling which even extends

to the diagonal buttresses. They have battlements where they jump back. The window has instead of a transom a most odd tracery arrangement. Equally tall, narrow two-light N and S windows, one each side. The S aisle windows and openwork battlements are Perp, the N aisle is entirely of 1836. On the S side projects a chapel, probably the Chantry of St Clement, built *c.*1520. Abbot Lichfield's Christian name was Clement. It has a transomed five-light window and battlements above a fleuron frieze. Inside, the arcades are Perp in style and identical. They are of four bays plus three lower chancel-chapel bays separated by the stretch of wall where the rood screen stood. In fact only the S arcade is original. The N arcade was copied by Eginton. But the completeness of the scheme, especially with the roof of 1836, is an asset. The piers have four thin shafts and in the diagonals hollows set between raised ledges. Panelling above and two small two-light clerestory windows per bay. The S chapel, singled out by its large window externally, is rich inside with its panelled arch
40 and its fan-vault with a central pendant. Elaborate niches l. and r. of the E window, whose sill is higher than that of the S window because a reredos was originally there. Panelling below the S window. The tower arch of the church is also panelled, and there is a tierceron star vault in the tower. – STAINED GLASS. In the E window glass by *Willement*, two large pictorial scenes. – PLATE. Paten on foot, 1694.

ST MARY (R.C.), High Street. 1912 by *Pugin & Pugin*. Large and rockfaced, with a SW tower. Dec and Perp details. Aisles, transepts, and a polygonal apse.

METHODIST CHURCH, Bridge Street. 1906 by *Fredric Foster*. Brick and stone dressings. Large, in a free Gothic typical of Nonconformist architecture of that date.

MILL STREET MEETING ROOM. 1788. Four bays with a two-bay pediment and arched windows.

UNITARIAN CHAPEL, Oat Street. 1737. Ashlar-built, of four bays, with a hipped roof. Pedimented porch. Two giant pilasters between windows one and two and three and four.

PERAMBULATION*

As one leaves the abbey precinct through the Norman Gate one has on one's l. immediately a fine timber-framed house with an overhang, closely set studs, an oriel window on the ground floor, and a doorway with leaf spandrels. This may be the

* PUBLIC BUILDINGS are included.

BEDEHOUSES erected by Abbot Zattoni (1379–1418). So one reaches the MARKET PLACE. The most prominent building is the LIBRARY, 1908–9 by *G. H. Hunt* of Evesham in a dignified neo-Georgian with a big porch. Brick and stone dressings. However, the most remarkable building is the BOOTH HALL, 52
or Round House. It is late C15 and has recently been restored practically as it was before restoration, except that it is no longer black-and-white, nor leaning precariously to the W. An exceptional building in scale and all-round completeness, with each upper storey jettied and the attic storey gabled on all four sides. The walls are close timbered. The windows are reproductions of C19 replacements. It was originally an inn and never a booth (or market) hall. The TOWN HALL is of little interest in its C16 to early C19 (1833–4) parts, but gains conspicuousness by the remodelling of 1884–5, also by *G. H. Hunt*, and the addition of the cupola.* From here three ways are open. Bridge Street to the E is a normal street, but the High Street to the N and Vine Street to the S both have informal trees down the middle, and Vine Street continues in Merstow Green, a true green, also with trees. This is an asset Evesham must retain and cultivate. Car parking has already reduced its amenity considerably.

First BRIDGE STREET. No. 8 is early C18, of three bays with segment-headed windows and a top balustrade with urns. Then, opposite, Nos 55 and 56 with very shallow upper bows, opposite the MIDLAND BANK of *c.*1780, five bays with two doorways with segmental pediments, the first-floor windows with alternating segmental and triangular pediments all entirely without bases and with excellent rainwater heads and pipes. Then, again on the S side, the CROWN HOTEL. The side to the street does not exist any longer, so that the inner courtyard, the 'inn', is now exposed. The two wings to the street have gables with big brackets. Finally, on the same side, at the very end of the street, a length of buttressed medieval wall.

The HIGH STREET is more attractive as a whole than rich in individual houses. Yet the best house in Evesham is there, DRESDEN HOUSE (No. 51), dated 1692 (on a rainwater head, itself an outstanding piece of lead-work). It is of five bays and three storeys with plain windows, except for the middle one, which has an open pediment, and with a doorway with

*CORPORATION PLATE. Two Maces of 1620; Rose Water Basin and Loving Cup of 1660.

gloriously big iron brackets l. and r. The staircase has twisted balusters. (In the garden is a large re-set Elizabethan stone chimneypiece with uncommonly elegant foliage decoration and a three-storeyed SUMMER HOUSE of *c.*1750 with an elaborate stucco ceiling. VCH) Another good house is No. 88, early C19, of four bays, stuccoed, with fluted Ionic giant pilasters and porch pillars with incised ornament. The ELECTRICITY SERVICE, in spite of its Venetian windows, is probably of *c.*1840. Otherwise ANCHOR HOUSE, Victorian, with an upper floor nearly all plate glass, and a number of Georgian houses with decorated keystones and some nice doorcases.

In VINE STREET the KING CHARLES II INN, C18, with a carved modillion frieze, the FALCON HOTEL, four-bay, stuccoed, with giant Ionic pilasters, the ROYAL OAK INN, with mostly recent black and white work, and the OLD RED HORSE INN, with close studding. The view is closed to the S by the abbey precinct buildings, i.e. the gatehouse and the almonry, already described. Turn r. into MERSTOW GREEN. In front of the Gatehouse the STOCKS. Facing the Green itself the OLD GRAMMAR SCHOOL, or mainly the stone porch to it with inscription: Orate pro anima Clementis Abbatis. The date must therefore be after Lichfield had died in 1546.

ABBEY MANOR, 1¼ m. NW. The house seems to be of *c.*1840. Flat front of five widely spaced bays with slight projections for the first and fifth bay. The front is castellated, and on the projections are corner pinnacles. Deep, asymmetrically set porch. (In the grounds an OBELISK to commemorate the battle of Evesham, the LEICESTER TOWER, a folly, and an ICEHOUSE of 1852.)

9070 FAIRFIELD

ST MARY. 1854 by *B. Ferrey*. Nave and chancel in one. Bellcote. Lancet windows and windows with plate tracery. Nice treatment of the chancel N and S windows. Two lancets, and between them a shaft well detached from the wall.

FAIRFIELD HOUSE, N of the church. Timber-framed, of typical Tudor appearance and chiefly remarkable because of its late date: 1669.

FAIRFIELD COURT, ½ m. N. C17 stone house of three bays with mullioned windows, the middle projecting as a porch. Star chimneys. To the l. C16 timber-framed part with close studding.

FAR FOREST

7070

HOLY TRINITY. 1844 by *A. E. Perkins.* Nave and transepts and lower chancel. W bellcote and W porch. Lancet windows.

FECKENHAM

0060

ST JOHN BAPTIST. Square W tower; wide nave. The chancel was rebuilt by *Butterfield* in 1853, but the two Norman W windows and two C13 S windows represent probably what had been there. The nave S wall is by *Day* of Worcester, of 1866–7. Perp N aisle, but E.E. N arcade. Four bays, round piers and octagonal abaci. One capital has wind-blown stiff-leaves. So the date is probably *c.*1240–50. The double-chamfered arches have heavy PAINTING with geometrical motifs including perspective effects. They are based on original patterns in the easternmost arch. – MONUMENT. Robert Boulton Walden † 1823. Large, with a young woman with a child on her arm standing by a pedestal.

FECKENHAM FOREST was a large royal forest and in it, at Feckenham, was a royal manor much used in the C12 and C13. The house was bought by the abbots of Evesham in 1356, taken down, and presumably rebuilt there, though nothing has survived.

In the HIGH STREET are timber-framed houses of most periods on unusually high stone plinths and several C18 brick houses, especially a Late Georgian one of three bays, with the centre doorway and upper window surrounded by a giant arch.

(MANOR FARM. T-shaped, of *c.*1500. The house is an example of the type with a lower-end cross-wing, originally entered from the screens passage. The hall part is of two bays and was originally open to the roof. At the upper end is a very small ground-floor parlour with a jettied first-floor chamber. The wall framing was originally close-timbered throughout, but the ground-floor framing of the cross-wing is now brick-cased. FWBC)

SHURNOCK COURT FARMHOUSE, 1¼ m. ESE. Timber-framed and partly C16 (S wing with close studding). Two stacks of star-shaped brick chimneys. One of the larger yeoman farmhouses, clearly rebuilt from a medieval predecessor. An interesting house.

(BRICK HOUSE FARM, Ham Green, 1¼ m. N. A typical farmhouse of *c.*1600 with a two-and-a-half-bay hall range and a two-bay cross-wing. The cross-wing has been extended in brick, and a date-stone reads 1601. This probably came from an earlier part of the building. There is a fine timber-framed barn of the same date, also a timber-framed latrine, and until recently there was an octagonal cider mill. FWBC)

(CROSS LANES FARMHOUSE, $\frac{5}{8}$ m. N of Ham Green. A farmhouse of *c.*1620 consisting of two bays in the hall range and an ornately timbered two-bay cross-wing. The fireplaces of the cross-wing are placed centrally, and there is a kitchen fireplace at the end of the hall range. The wall-frames were close-studded on the lower storey and square-panelled with straight diagonal braces above. FWBC)

(LOWER GRINSTY FARM, $1\frac{1}{2}$ m. NE of Ham Green. A farm group of *c.*1600 described in an inventory of 1617 as consisting of a 'hall-house' and a number of rooms in 'a fore-chamber of the house'. This fore-chamber is a separate building of T-shaped plan with three equal-sized rooms on each floor. FWBC)

(WHITE HOUSE, Callow Hill, $\frac{3}{4}$ m. NNE of Ham Green. Timber-framed Jacobean farmhouse of *c.*1640, originally conforming to the standard T-plan. The hall part, however, has been extended on both sides. On the N side is a single very large gable, but on the S side a gabled staircase structure, probably of the same date as the hall part, and a second gable sandwiched between the stair and cross-wing. The framing is of small square panelling throughout, but the solar wing has a shallow jetty at the first-floor level of all three external walls. The fireplace of the N flank wall of the hall range is nearly 10 ft broad. FWBC)

(LANE FARMHOUSE, next to White House, Callow Hill. A timber-framed farmhouse of *c.*1600 with more original features than any other of the period in Worcestershire. Splendidly built three-bay 'solar' with an original large dormer window complete with its mullions and part of its glazing. Other original windows with heavy mullions built in with the structure also survive. There are two staircases, the earlier one a spiral stair of solid oak constructed exactly like a masonry stair. The later stair is contemporary with a brick extension, which appears to be of *c.*1700. This extension also has original mullioned and transomed windows and fixed glazing in rectangular caimes. This is one of the very few houses in which the timbers remain in their original untreated condition. The solar wing is jettied at the gables, the wall framing is close studded throughout with intermediate rail and tiled weatherings at storey height. FWBC)

(LOWER BERROW FARMHOUSE, 1 m. NW, CRUISE HILL FARMHOUSE, West Ham Green, and two others at Cruise Hill are also splendid timber-framed farmhouses. FWBC)

FIELD HOUSE *see* CLENT

FINSTALL

9070

OLD CHURCH. Just E of the railway bridge. Dated 1773. Red sandstone. Small, with a hipped roof. Only three bays long. Pointed windows, a triplet in the E wall.

ST GODWALD. 1883–4 by *John Cotton*. Nave, chancel, and S transept, the latter two bays deep from W to E. The N transept has not been built. The style is that of about 1300, and the details are poor. The interior is faced with yellow brick.

(FINSTALL HOUSE. Of *c*.1830. Irregular, with a fine, heavy Grecian porch and a long cast-iron veranda. An outbuilding has Gothick windows and is presumably C18. NMR)

ARCHWAY, just W of the railway bridge. This must be of *c*.1700 and is probably connected with Rigby Hall near by.

THE FIRS *see* NORTH CLAINES

FLADBURY

9040

ST JOHN BAPTIST. The W tower is Norman below (see the W window set in the mid-buttress*). When its heightening was begun, the Norman walls were strengthened by adding a new inner facing. This is represented by the pointed rere-arches of the Norman window embrasures. The arch towards the nave shows that this heightening and thickening was done already in the C13. The arch has three slight chamfers. The bell-openings have cusped Y-tracery and may well be of *c*.1300. The panelled Perp-looking battlements are according to the VCH of 1752. If so, they must be renewed. The rest of the church is not of special interest, except for the splendid porch, which is rib-vaulted, because it had originally an upper floor. The ribs are single-chamfered and stand on capitals looking early C14. The entry arch however has a wide wave moulding more usually Perp than Dec. The arcades of four bays are Dec and have the routine octagonal piers and double-chamfered arches. The

*For this motif cf. Cropthorne and Shrawley.

coved nave ceiling is clearly Georgian. The chancel is essentially by *Preedy*, 1865 etc. – STAINED GLASS. In a chancel N window excellent C14 shields. – In the vestry window an even more excellent early C14 Virgin and Child. – TILES. C15, usual patterns and many with letters. – PLATE. Tudor Chalice and Cover; Chalice, *c.*1640; Flagon by *Ed. Vincent*, 1739. – MONUMENTS. Under the tower exceptionally large tomb-chest with two excellent brasses 4 ft long. They represent John Throckmorton † 1445 and his wife. The tomb-chest has cusped quatrefoils in panels. – Thomas Morden, priest, † 1458. Demi-figure, 19 in. long (chancel). – William Plewme † 1504, 12 in. long (chancel).* – Bishop Lloyd † 1717 (contract with *James Withenbury* 1718). Standing monument with elaborate flowers and foliage l. and r. and at the top frontal demi-figure. The arrangement is not as it originally was. – Many tablets, e.g. Elizabeth Charlett † 1746, by *John Ricketts Jun.*, with bust on top. – George Perrott † 1806. Big, dignified tablet with straight-sided sarcophagus.

ST THOMAS, Lower Moor, 1½ m. NW. 1869 by *Preedy*. Close to St John's the following:

RECTORY, to the S. Built in 1710; centre and projecting two-bay wings. Hipped roof. The recessed centre filled in, probably early in the C19, in a somewhat Soanian manner – see the odd stepped or reeded angles with urns.

HOUSE, W of the church. Early C18, brick, of four bays, with segment-headed windows. The top frieze must be Victorian.

SCHOOL, N of the church. 1864–5 by *Preedy*.

WHITE HOUSE, also N, on the opposite side of the road. Early C19, stuccoed, with giant pilasters. The first-floor windows have blank arches filled with shells.

MANOR HOUSE, N of the former. Red brick, *c.*1700, of five bays with a one-bay centre with steep pediment. Giant angle pilasters with urns. Urns also on the pediment.

FLADBURY MILL, by the lock. Picturesque. Much of the machinery is still there.

CRAYCOMBE HOUSE, ¾ m. NE. Built *c.*1791 for George Perrott of the East India Company. By *George Byfield*. Ashlar-faced and only five by three bays in size. The detail extremely reticent, e.g. no window mouldings at all. The ground-floor windows are set in blank arches, and in the spandrels are paterae. Three urns at the top, the middle one larger. The only ornamented piece is the doorway. It is tripartite, with Corinthian

*Also Edward Peytoo †1488, 2ft 3in. long.

Fladbury church, brasses to John Throckmorton †1445 and wife

pilasters, garlands in the frieze, and a lunette with fan glazing above. The motif was taken up later round the corner for a subsidiary doorway and a bay window. Between them an original large urn, in a niche, with the inscription: Solus vivat que jucunde. The rooms inside have hardly more decoration than friezes. Staircase with thin iron balustrade and round skylight. – To the NE, in the wood, a five-bay ORANGERY, with arched openings.

9050

FLYFORD FLAVELL

ST PETER. W tower, nave and chancel, and N transept. Mostly by *Hopkins*, 1883. Old parts were re-used or heeded, e.g. for the Norman N doorway. – FONT. Perp, octagonal, with three small motifs against the underside. – BENCHES. Two nice plain Jacobean ones. – TILES. Some of the C15 under the tower. – STAINED GLASS. Bits in one S window. – PLATE. Cup and Cover Paten, *c*.1571.

8070

FRANCHE

1 m. NNW of Kidderminster church

ST BARNABAS. 1871 by *Chamberlain & Martin*. Red brick also inside. Geometrical tracery. The little square tower behind the S porch originally carried a spire.

BROOMFIELD HALL has been demolished.

9080

FRANKLEY

ST LEONARD. View to the N over the reservoirs for the Birmingham water supply and over high Birmingham blocks of flats. The church has medieval masonry but hardly any features. The short tower was built into the nave in 1751, but the nice tripartite arrangement of the supports is of 1931 (after a fire) and by *Bateman*. The wagon roof is Perp. – PLATE. Chalice, Cup, and Cover Paten 1708. – In the churchyard an Anglo-Saxon CROSS SHAFT with interlace and traces of scrolls, but all very badly weathered.

GARMSLEY CAMP *see* STOKE BLISS

GLASSHAMPTON MONASTERY *see* ASTLEY

9050

GRAFTON FLYFORD

ST JOHN BAPTIST. W tower of the C14 with recessed pyramid roof or low spire. The church itself is almost entirely of 1875.

Architect *W. J. Hopkins*. Old e.g. the C14 window-head in the N wall. – PULPIT. Simple, Perp, with arched panels. – PAINTINGS. Signs of St John and St Mark; on square boards; probably Elizabethan or a little earlier. – STAINED GLASS. Some in the top of the E window. Also bits in the W window. – PLATE. Cup by *H. W.* of 1571 and Cover Paten of 1577; Plate 1679. – MONUMENT. A fine, completely unornamented inscription tablet to Roger Stonehall † 1645.

(RECTORY FARM. Originally a base-cruck hall of *c.*1300, but little more than the central truss, still with crown-post and vestiges of the original rafter roof, has survived. The hall part of the house is completely unrecognizable from the outside. It was radically altered and cased in brick in the C18. The detached three-bay solar wing is medieval but later than the hall. It has heavily moulded timbers and four-centred doorhead. The black barn is of cruck construction, possibly contemporary with the hall (FWBC).

HILL COURT, 1 m. N. Timber-framing and brick infill. Of *c.*1600. Big stone chimneybreast with brick star-shaped stacks.

GRAFTON MANOR

9060

1½ m. SW of Bromsgrove

The house is of the early C16, with stepped gables, but the whole range projecting S from the W end of the main range and most of that main range are of the 1860s (by *David Brandon*). Only the N side has at its W end a stone-faced originally straight-gabled front which may be yet older. Then, in 1567, John Talbot modernized the house and in the process gave it its porch and the S window of the Upper Parlour. They are nationally memorable examples of their date. The porch entrance is flanked by coupled Roman Doric columns carrying *55*
a triglyph frieze. On the upper floor three pilasters framing two tall, slender cross windows and carrying a pediment with a roundel in. The parlour window is of five lights with roll-moulded mullions and a fluted band as the transom. Frieze and pediment over. The inscription in the frieze reads: Plenti and grase bi in this plase whyle everi man is plesed in his degre there is both pease and uniti Salaman saith there is none acorde when everi man would be a lorde.

CHAPEL. To the W of, and connected with, the house. Perp, but over-restored. Nave with bellcote and chancel. Pretty WEST GALLERY on three ogee arches, *c.*1800.

9040 GREAT COMBERTON

ST MICHAEL. There is one mystery about this church. The W tower is Perp and embraced by narrow side attachments which make it as wide as the nave. The base moulding of the tower goes round them and yet inside they are represented by shallow compartments open in shapeless arches which stand on imposts which look Early Norman. The arch to the nave is higher, equally shapeless, and also has such an impost. Is all this accident, and all it means is that the tower was built into the nave and the inner buttressing never tidied up? The solution does not satisfy. – STALLS. With Jacobean panels. – BENCHES. C16, with absolutely plain, straight-topped ends. – PLATE, Paten by *R. S.*, 1658; Salver Paten by *Thos. Wallis*, 1785.

GREAT DODFORD *see* DODFORD

GREAT HOUSE *see* KNIGHTON-ON-TEME

7040 GREAT MALVERN

The following account includes Malvern Link.

Malvern began as a settlement outside the priory. The first parish church, now long gone, stood in the NW corner of the churchyard. Its function ceased when, after the Dissolution, the parishioners purchased the priory church. Yet as late as 1562–3 Malvern had only 105 families. A more promising development set in only in the late C18, long after the discovery of the medicinal waters of Malvern Wells in the C17. Prosperity followed as an effect of Dr Wall's publication in 1756 on the properties of the waters. In 1796 the first guide for visitors was brought out. At the beginning of the C19 there were several hotels (which still exist), and the Pump Room and Baths were built in 1819–23. In 1830 Princess Victoria spent some time at Malvern. In 1842 Dr Jas. Wilson created a sensation with his introduction of the German type of hydropathic treatment. In 1858 the railway reached Malvern, and the time from *c.*1845 to the sixties marked the greatest expansion. Abbey Road, Priory Road, College Road were laid out, and the buildings on the N side of Church Street erected. Malvern College was founded in 1862. The population grew from 2,800 in 1841 to 7,600 in 1871. But C20 Malvern is less a spa than a desirable town for retired people and more and more for Birmingham and Worcester commuters.

MALVERN PRIORY

MALVERN PRIORY was Benedictine. It may have been begun before the Conquest, but 1085 is more probable. The Norman parts were built after that. For the Perp parts, 1460 is the dedication date of the second bay of the presbytery. So *c.*1420 may be the date of the start, *c.*1460 the date of the completion. The Perp work is specially valuable historically, as monastic churches in the late Middle Ages rarely built so sweepingly. The church was saved from destruction at the time of the Reformation by being purchased by the town. When Pugin saw the church in 1833 it was, he wrote, 'in dreadful repair'. *Scott* restored it in 1860–1. Of the monastic buildings nothing but the gatehouse remains.

EXTERIOR. The exterior as we see it now is entirely of the 37
most ornate Perp. Only the most inquisitive student will discover anything earlier. Yet Norman evidence is not wholly absent. It consists of two trumpet-scallop, i.e. Late Norman, capitals in the former crypt, now exposed at the E end, mysteriously not at the same level and one carrying a heavy single-chamfered rib; the doorway from the S aisle into the former cloister, with two orders of columns, all detail much decayed; and, in the stump of the former S transept, which was destroyed at the time of the Reformation, part of the arch which once led into an apse or chapel E of the transept. The Perp building reads as follows. Relatively short nave with N aisle and a two-storeyed N porch (rebuilt in 1894). The nave and aisles have three-light windows, those of the clerestory with transoms, and panelled battlements. The nave battlements are openwork. The W window is of staggering size, nine lights in a three–plus–three–plus–three arrangement. The whole porch façade is panelled, above more busily than below. Image niche above the entrance. Panelled battlements. A lierne star vault inside. The N transept is lower than nave and chancel. The height is probably the Norman one. One three-light transomed W window, no E window, but a six-light N window, divided three plus three. The chancel, as it was an entirely new structure, has wider bays than the nave. The battlements here are humbler. The aisle windows are of four lights (two plus two), the clerestory windows have the same arrangement, but transoms. The giant E window is of eight lights (four plus four), inspired of course by what Gloucester had done a hundred years before. At the foot of the E window is the rough

junction with the former Lady Chapel, a low, wide depressed arch, probably (again as at Gloucester) only to a passage. The S side of the chancel is the same as the N side. But the S side of the nave of course had the cloister standing against it. The rough masonry indicates this, and the three Perp windows were only put in in 1841. The crossing tower dominates the whole building impressively. It is of three stages, the two lower panelled, the top one with two two-light bell-openings under steep ogee gables and again panelling around. Open-work battlements and square pinnacles on the Gloucester pattern.

8 INTERIOR. The nave, as one enters, reveals its Norman date at once. It is only six bays long, with short round piers of about 4 ft 6 in. diameter and round, very heavily and bulgily detailed capitals, inspired probably by the Tewkesbury nave. The style of the nave speaks for a date about 1120. Double-step arches. The high Perp clerestory is very effective above this massive substructure. The wall has a rebate at the arch height of the clerestory windows, and that indicates perhaps an intention to vault. For Norman vaulting in nave or aisles there is no evidence. Minor Norman details are the doorway to the cloister already mentioned – a small Perp doorway went from the aisle W bay into the cloister – a blocked window above it, and the arch from the aisle into the S transept. This has a little decoration with saltire-crosses and an arch with furrowed zigzag, that is, it seems to be later than the nave.* Round the crossing also there is Norman evidence in the thin shafts set against sheer wall which still exist to W, N, S, and E and must be connected with the Norman tower, although the shallow convex curve in the middle of the group is surprising. For the Perp tower the space of the crossing was reduced and the transept arches given tracery tops as a bracing device. The Perp style appears in the crossing also by the panelling of the responds and the lierne-vault. The chancel is the only com-
38 pletely Perp part of the building. Three bays, piers of many fine shafts, all carrying little capitals, those to the aisle arches low, those towards the nave high up. Springers up there indicate that the chancel was to be vaulted – like those of Gloucester, Tewkesbury, and Pershore. Panelling above the arcade. Panelling around the clerestory windows. The vaulting

* Mr Stratford compares this with the furrowed zigzag at Beckford, Bredon's Norton, Castlemorton, Earls Croome, Eldersfield, Pendock, and Queenhill, which he regards as third quarter of the C12.

of the aisles with plain diagonal and ridge ribs is original. At the E ends of the chancel aisles panelled imposts. Where the entry to the Lady Chapel was, the mid-mullion of the eight-light window is carried on a big ogee arch – another Gloucester motif.

FURNISHINGS. The most important by far is the STAINED GLASS, more complete than anywhere in C15 England. One can still get the impression at Malvern of what the total effect was like. It was certainly light, not obscuring as C13 glass had been. Of darker colours only blue is fully represented, but not in large areas, and red very little. Instead there is much yellow and brown. The E and W windows, the N transept N window, and several aisle and clerestory windows are in a relatively good state, and most of the older windows contain at least fragments. As regards dating, everything is of the sixty-odd years between *c.*1440 and *c.*1506. In detail the following need be said.*

EAST WINDOW. This window is of *c.*1440. It is very similar to the St William Window in York Minster. The lowest tier has benefactors, originally at the bottom of the clerestory windows. Among the names are Besford, Harewell, Lygon, and Lyttelton. The three tiers above have the Passion, from the Entry into Jerusalem to Doubting Thomas. In the very centre are the Nailing to the Cross and Christ Crucified. The latter is very fragmentary. In the tracery lights are the twelve Apostles, and above them the Annunciation and the Coronation of the Virgin; also many small figures and fragments.

SOUTH CHANCEL AISLE. Old Testament stories, originally nave S clerestory. There were seventy-two scenes. First window from E: scenes from Genesis, from the Creation to the Expulsion and Adam delving and Eve spinning. – Second window: story of Noah and the Ark; the Tower of Babel; scenes from the story of Abraham and Isaac. – Third window: the continuation of the preceding, i.e. the Journey to Mount Moriah, then the Sacrifice of Isaac and two Isaac scenes, then two Joseph scenes, the Finding of Moses, the Manna, the Golden Calf, the Exposing of the Worshippers of the Golden Calf. – In all three windows fragments from other scenes are used.

NORTH CHANCEL AISLE. First window from E: little

*The following details are based on L. A. Hamand: *The Ancient Windows of Great Malvern Priory Church* (St Albans, 1947), which in its turn is based on G. McN. Rushforth: *Mediaeval Christian Imagery as illustrated by the Painted Windows of Great Malvern Priory Church* (Oxford, 1936).

preserved. The main figures were the four Latin Doctors of the Church and Sir William de Bracy as the donor. – Second window: also little preserved. This was the Seven Sacraments window. – Third window: fragments from many windows, including the Baptism of Christ, the Mass of St Giles, St Nicholas and the Sailors.

NORTH CHANCEL CLERESTORY. First window from E: story of the Virgin. Below the transom, from the Annunciation to Joachim to the Birth of the Virgin. Above, Annunciation and Presentation in the Temple. – Second window: six saintly Bishops, Virgin and Child, St Anne teaching the Virgin to read. – Third window: the Founders' Window. Legend of St Werstan, i.e. his Vision, his second Vision, Grant of a Charter to Malvern by Edward the Confessor, Martyrdom of St Werstan. Then, below the transom: the Saint, William the Conqueror grants a charter, Osbert Fitzpons makes a donation, the Earls of Gloucester and Hereford make donations. Heads in the spandrels.

SOUTH CHANCEL CLERESTORY. First window from E: St Peter, St Andrew, and small figures from the nave tracery lights, e.g. Cherubim, Virtues, Angels, Seraphim, Instruments of Christ's Passion, Fathers of the Church, two Evangelists. – Second window: St Katherine, still in its original place, two Sts James the Greater, an abbot, and below the transom Crucifixion and angels. – Third window: an archangel, an archbishop, an apostle, and, below the transom, Orders of Angels.

TRANSEPT NORTH WINDOW. Given in 1501 or 1502 by Henry VII. In the four centre lights the Joys of Mary, i.e. eleven scenes representing the Magnificat. Well preserved the Visitation, the Nativity, Jesus in the Temple, the Wedding Feast at Cana, the Ascension, and the Coronation of the Virgin in a round halo. In the outer light were the four Archangels. Only Michael and Uriel are preserved. Saints and
46 Angels in the tracery. At the bottom of the window Henry VII, the Queen, Arthur Prince of Wales (who died in 1502), Sir Reginald Bray.

TRANSEPT WEST WINDOW. St Paul, St John Evangelist, and St John Baptist come from the N nave clerestory. The Last Supper, below the transom, is *in situ* and almost complete.

NORTH AISLE. One window was enough to collect what remained of the glass of the five. The Annunciation is nearly perfect. The others are Visitation, Nativity, Adoration of the

Magi, Presentation in the Temple, Temptation, Pool of Bethesda, Healing the Sick, Healing the Deaf and Dumb Man, Healing the Centurion's Servant and Cleansing the Leper, Marriage of Anne, Annunciation to Anne; Saints in the tracery.

WEST WINDOW. Originally this had the Last Judgement, and below the Virgin and six Virgin Martyrs. Now there are below five Bishops, the Virgin and Child, and Mary Salome; second tier Joachim, a Bishop, Angels, St Katherine, St Anne teaching the Virgin to read; top tier St Anne and the Virgin, St Katherine, St Laurence, St George, St Christopher, St Margaret, the Virgin. In this window were originally the arms of Richard III when still Duke of Gloucester. That gives a date between 1461 and 1483.

REREDOS. 1884 by *Blomfield*, made by *Powell's*. Mosaic. – STALLS. The two tiers of six N and six S stalls are original. The superstructure is missing, but the MISERICORDS are very complete. They comprise representatives of the Labours of the Months, and also (N) four rats hanging a cat and divers monsters and (S) the bust of a man, a sick man and his doctor, an angel with a zither, a mermaid, and more monsters. – SCREENS. Behind the stalls are screens of one-light divisions, very restored. – TILES. The screen walls of the chancel are faced with tiles of the C15, the only wall tiles in England. We are told that there are about twelve hundred of them, in ninety different patterns. Malvern must have been a centre for tile-making: the parish churches of Worcestershire are full of them. The colours – pink, golden-brown, and lavender – are delightful. – MONUMENTS. Effigy of a Knight (chancel), *c.*1240. He seems lying to attention. His head is on a square pillow. His legs and feet lie rigidly parallel. The slab is very flatly carved. – John Knottesford † 1589 and wife (chancel). Alabaster. Tomb-chest with two excellently carved effigies. Their daughter kneels – the same size – to the N, facing the altar. No superstructure. – John Dandridge † 1785 and members of the family to 1836 (N transept). By *Sir R. Westmacott*, when? Gunnis says 1830. At the foot of the tablet the beautiful figure of a resting pilgrim. – Thomas Woodyatt † 1811 (S chancel aisle). By *Hollins*. White marble. Seated woman in profile and draped urn with profile medallion. – Sophia Thompson † 1836. Also by *Hollins*. White marble. Semi-reclining woman on a couch of which only the head part is portrayed. – Sir H. E. F. Lambert † 1872 (nave W end). Designed by *Sir G. G. Scott*. Large Perp arch and small inscription tablet.

Great Malvern, Malvern Priory, wall tiles, fifteenth century

MONASTIC BUILDINGS. Of all the monastic buildings only the gatehouse remains. It is a great pity that the REFECTORY was not spared. It was timber-framed and stood until 1841. The GATEHOUSE has a town façade all elaborately panelled (and rebuilt in 1891). Bigger motifs below, daintier above – just as in the N porch. An oriel above and decorated battlements. Towards the monastery the upper floor is of brick.

OTHER CHURCHES

ALL SAINTS, The Wyche, Malvern Common. 1903 by *Nevinson & Newton.** Against the hillside. With an E apse and no tower. Lancet windows. Brick-faced interior.

ST ANDREW, off Poolbrook Road. 1885 by *Blomfield.* – (FONT. Inscribed 1724. VCH) – PLATE. Flagon by *H. P.*, 1736.

ASCENSION, Leigh Sinton Road, Malvern Link. By *Sir Walter Tapper*, 1903. Unassuming exterior and interesting interior. Yellow stone and stuccoed brick. Minor W tower, bellcote on the E end of the nave, all windows lancets and all quite high up. Inside a wall-passage with detached shafts runs along the windows. The chancel is rib-vaulted in brick, the nave has a pointed tunnel-vault. – High metal SCREEN, attractively designed by *G. Bainbridge Reynolds*, 1903.

CHRIST CHURCH, Avenue Road. 1875–6 by *T. D. Barry & Sons*. Grey, large, rockfaced, with a W steeple and a turret near the E end. The W spire has broaches. Dec features. The one unexpected detail is the cross-gable behind and above the S porch.

GOOD SHEPHERD, Upper Colwall, The Wyche.‡ 1910. Small, pebbledashed, with a half-timbered gable. Voysey buttresses.

CHAPEL OF THE CONVENT OF THE HOLY NAME, Ranelagh Road, Malvern Link. 1893 by *Comper*. Simple, tall brick building with late C13 windows high up. Intersecting (E) and Y-tracery. The high interior is white, with much gilding of the furnishings. The wagon roof has a decorated celure over the presbytery. The windows are set in deep arches on wall-shafts. – The STAINED GLASS is by *Comper* too, in his pale style, but dates from 1924–8. – REREDOS, much gilt, with seven figures and ogee-headed doorways l. and r. – WEST SCREEN. Prettily Perp. A low, narrow cloister runs along the chapel.

ST JOSEPH (R.C.), Newtown Road. 1876 by *T. R. Donnelly*.

* Another attribution is *Troyte Griffith*.

‡ Administratively in Herefordshire.

ST MATTHIAS, Church Road, Malvern Link. Originally built in 1844–6 by *G. G. Scott*, but enlarged and quite changed in 1880–1 by *F. W. Hunt*. The tower is of 1899. A large church of red granite with a broad SW tower. Lancets and tracery of *c.*1300. The clerestory windows alternate between two and three lights. – SCREEN. The dado painted with figures of saints in the East Anglian way. Done by a sister of the Community of the Holy Name, *c.*1918. – STAINED GLASS. E window by *Kempe*.

OUR LADY AND ST EDMUND (R.C.), College Road. 1905 by *P. P. Pugin*. Stone, Dec to Perp, with a wide, almost nave-like N aisle.

ST PETER, St Peter's Road. 1863–6 by *Street*. Malvern granite in 'crazy paving'. Nave and chancel, N bellcote. Plate tracery and odd clerestory windows. They are half quatrefoils under round arches. The interior is far more remarkable. The arcades have round piers with most boldly simplified, deliberately primeval capitals. The arches have only a slight chamfer and above the buff ashlar changes into a slightly rougher blue stone. – The PULPIT is typical Street: a semicircular railing of columns of various coloured marbles.

HOLY TRINITY, Worcester Road, Link Top. 1850–1 by *S. Dawkes*, enlarged 1872 by the *Haddon* brothers. Quite large, with an E turret and cross-gabled clerestory windows. Plate tracery. – STAINED GLASS. The E window by *Kempe*, *c.*1902. – PLATE. Chalice by *T. R.*, 1664.

CONGREGATIONAL CHURCH, Queens Drive. 1875 by *J. Tait* of Leicester. With a high, badly detailed 'NW' steeple. The features geometrical to Dec.

EMMANUEL, Countess of Huntingdon's Connexion. 1874 by the *Haddon* brothers. Neo-Romanesque with a NW tower. Along the side windows with Venetian tracery. It is all architecturally poor stuff.

PUBLIC BUILDINGS

PUBLIC LIBRARY, Graham Road. By *Henry Crouch*, 1906. Single-storeyed, symmetrical, in a free William-and-Mary.

MALVERN COLLEGE. Malvern College was founded in 1862. It was a good time for founding public schools, and Malvern started ambitiously in scale and architectural worth. The designs of *Charles F. Hansom* of Clifton were accepted in 1863. The main building is large and impressive, even if not distinguished in the details. Gatehouse range and two wings far-projecting to the E, Early Tudor in style. To the W the ranges l. and r. of the high turreted gatehouse are low and gabled and followed by again higher gabled end bays. These are continued as the wings on the E side and end there with square turrets. The E view is entirely symmetrical too. *Hansom* also built the first boarding houses. First School House, 1864, N of the main building, of stone and Gothic like the main building, and then Houses 3 and 4, 1867–8, at the southern perimeter along Thirlstane Road. They are of brick and decidedly forbidding. So are, also by *Hansom*, Houses 1 and 2, close to Woodshears Road. They date from 1870–1 and have blue brick ornament. House No. 6, E of Nos 3 and 4, is of 1871, by *Haddon*. House No. 5, E of Nos 1 and 2, by *Perkins*, Tudor in style, of 1894, is one of the best.

The CHAPEL is by *Blomfield*, 1897–9. Large and externally in a rather fussy Gothic. The interior is more original, with the low (ritually) S aisle and an addition of 1908 with its four-centred arcade arches. – STAINED GLASS. All by *Kempe*, a big job.

102 The best building of Malvern College is the MEMORIAL LIBRARY. This is by *Sir Aston Webb*, 1924, i.e. later than it looks. It goes with early Aston Webb rather than his Buckingham Palace façade. Front with a chamfered giant arch. The segmental arch with three big fleurons dies into the chamfers. Pretty portal and three-light window above with two transoms and also with a segmental arch. The long sides have three five-light windows with two transoms and round-arched lights. Interior with a white tunnel-vaulted ceiling and wooden pillars setting apart the entry and the far end with its fireplace. The Gothic is handled lightly and imaginatively, and the library mood is established from the very first.

Of later buildings The Grub is by (Sir) *Howard Robertson*, 1927, the Preston Science School by *Hubbard*, 1938, the New Science Schools by *Hammett & Norton*, 1957–65.

GIRLS' COLLEGE, Avenue Road. The college is a C20 foundation. As a sign of its coming into its own it bought up the IMPERIAL HOTEL, a large hotel close to Great Malvern Station. This was built by *E. W. Elmslie* in 1861–2, for £18,000. It is eminently Gothic, towards the entrance surprisingly so for a hotel, but then goes on in a more utilitarian way. It is a very large building – four storeys and dormers, segment-headed windows, big, somewhat French roofs. A new boarding house called Hatfield is by *Maurice W. Jones* of Worcester, 1964–6, a workmanlike modern job with many polygonal shapes perhaps inspired by the new range of St John's College Oxford.

HOSPITAL, Lansdowne Crescent. 1868 by *Henman* of Birmingham. Tudor style.

WINTER GARDEN, Grange Road. 1884 by *John Johnson*. Of no architectural value. Italian Gothic porch but flimsy Mixed Renaissance behind and above.

GREAT MALVERN STATION. 1860–1 by *Elmslie* (see above). Long and low, gabled. The tower has unfortunately been demolished. Platform with nice cast-iron tracery and bold floral capitals.

MALVERN LINK STATION. 1861. Also long, low, and Gothic.

PERAMBULATION

The town climbs up the superb hills. Walking and driving is 1
much as in the small towns on the banks of North Italian lakes.

A true perambulation can hardly be done, but the elements can be indicated sufficiently to be plotted on a map. When Malvern was smaller, there were of course villages and hamlets around, and they had their timber-framed houses like other Worcestershire villages. One such survival is PICKERSLEIGH COURT, Pickersleigh Road, of *c.*1500.

Of Central Malvern the earliest group and a fine one, all stuccoed, is at the S end of WORCESTER ROAD. The middle piece is the former PUMP ROOM by *Samuel* and *John Deykes* of 1819–23. Three-bay centre with Greek Doric columns and two entrance bays l. and r. Wreathed frieze. The middle gable ill fits this classical composition. To the l. a two-storeyed extension. To the S of this BARCLAYS BANK, with a S bow with columns à la Regents Park or the Charing Cross group, originally the ROYAL LIBRARY, also by *Deykes*. To the N the FOLEY ARMS HOTEL, built in 1810, by *Deykes* as well. The wings are of 1812 and 1817. The attractive inscription is cast iron. A little SW and a little above this group in BELLEVUE TERRACE is the MOUNT PLEASANT HOTEL, red brick, with a tripartite doorway with pediment and a Venetian window. This dates from just before 1817. Next to it a dignified Italianate house of nine bays and three storeys, probably of *c.*1840. Is it a remodelling of the Crown Hotel when it was bought by James Wilson *c.*1842 ? And how much of it was rebuilt in 1930 ? The classical mood still held in 1845, when PARK VIEW was built in ABBEY ROAD, as James Wilson's hydropathic establishment, rightly called Priessnitz House. Long three-storeyed range with a centre emphasized by giant pilasters and a Greek Doric porch *in antis*. Giant pilasters occur in other places as well, e.g. farther out in CROWN LEA HOUSE, Barnards Green, of 1855, to which a chapel was added in 1936, but with windows from Blackmore House, Hanley Swan.

Round this centre after 1840 or so Malvern grew apace. One can follow the development from the standard so-called Regency house of *c.*1830, e.g. in GRAHAM ROAD or HOLLAND HOUSE in CHURCH STREET (with a Greek Doric porch), to the Italianate stuccoed villas of *c.*1840–50 (e.g. GROSVENOR HOUSE and its neighbour, next to Holland House, with the typical round-arched window lights of the forties, or the ALDWYN TOWER HOTEL in Foley Terrace with its unmistakable tower (built before 1855) or, simpler, the long terraces of LANSDOWNE CRESCENT), and the barge-boarded Tudor villas and then the Jacobean brick ones with shaped gables. Telling examples of these two types are in WELLS ROAD at the N end and in PRIORY ROAD. Jacobean also MALVERN HOUSE in ABBEY ROAD and of course the ABBEY HOTEL next to the priory. This dates from 1848–9. Thoroughly debased Italian are the SEVERN WATER BOARD, formerly a hotel, and the former MUNICIPAL OFFICES (by *Rowe*, 1861) in Church Street.* Finally there are the more ambitious mid-century Tudor and Gothic mansions. Of these a number must be picked out. Gothic comes of course in all sizes. The shop next to the priory gatehouse shows it small and stuccoed, a charming pair of houses in COLLEGE ROAD in stone. The shop itself is much earlier – before the thirties. Now the large buildings. First and foremost *Elmslie*'s Imperial Hotel of 1860 (*see* Girls' College) and his former MALVERN LINK HOTEL in Somers Road of 1860–1. Red and black brick, with an informally placed tower with higher circular stair-turret and an aura of gloom. It cost nearly £6,000.‡ In ABBEY ROAD is SOUTH BANK, red brick with blue diapers and a high turret. At the N end of GRAHAM ROAD is DAVENHAM HOUSE, stone, by *Elmslie*, 1880, enlarged for C. W. Dyson Perrins by *Henman* in 1900, a much more extensive and elaborate job. In AVENUE ROAD is

* Since demolished.

‡ And has recently been pulled down.

PRIORY PARK MANSION, asymmetrical and Perp. This is of 1874. In GRANGE ROAD, PRIORS CROFT is picturesque, gabled, and provided with a tower.*

GREAT WITLEY 7060

ST MICHAEL, on the A-road. 1882 by *Perkins*; enlarged 1895. Brick. Nave and chancel, apse and bellcote. Cusped lancet windows. – FONT. An C18 baluster and bowl.

ST MICHAEL AND WITLEY COURT. Church and house form an unforgettable whole, the church stately, self-assured, and unshowy, the house enormous and ruinated. The church was planned by the first Lord Foley and built by his widow. It was consecrated in 1735. Witley Court owes its present appearance to the eleventh Lord Ward, first Earl of Dudley, who bought the estate in 1835 and *c.*1859–61 converted the Foleys' house into a palace, regal in size and grandeur, and to a fire which took place in 1937. The Foley mansion went back to a Jacobean brick house which was bought by Thomas Foley, son of a Stourbridge industrialist, in 1655. It was made use of when another Thomas Foley rebuilt in 1683. He was created Lord Foley in 1712 and died in 1732. The chapel, being his conception in the first place, must be looked at first.

ST MICHAEL, to repeat it, was consecrated in 1735. Its architect is not known. He may have been *Gibbs*; or he may have been a local man. The building is a plain rectangle of cream-coloured stone, except for the two shallow projections N and S of the E end. The W tower does not project. The rectangle is of three by five bays with a very shallow chancel and is topped by a balustrade. The windows are arched, have pilasters with sunk panels, and are set in blank arches. The W end has a porch of two Tuscan columns with a pediment and above a square bell-stage and an open, though quite substantial cupola. All this in the C18 was of brick exposed and with stone dressings. It was faced with ashlar by *Dawkes* when he built Witley Court.
Enter and you are transported into a different climate. Here is 78
the most Italian ecclesiastic space in the whole of England. This came about in the following improbable way. The Duke of Chandos had built himself at Canons near Edgware a large mansion. He began it in 1713 and had the chapel dedicated in 1720. The estate was broken up and the house demolished in

*At the corner of St Andrew's Road and Peachfield Road is a LETTER BOX in the form of a Doric pillar.

1747. It was then that the second Lord Foley bought the ceiling paintings and the painted glass of the windows and had mouldings made of the stucco work. How the pieces can have fitted his chapel so perfectly remains a mystery. *Gibbs* was the architect responsible for the fitting. The chapel is all white and gold. The walls have panels, in their style just pre-Rococo. The ceiling has a coving with penetrations above the windows – one place where one senses an irregularity. The other is above the organ case. A specially interesting feature of the ceiling is that what seems to be stucco is in fact papier-mâché. It was the use of this material which made the copying of the Canons stucco work possible but allowed for modifications. Papier-mâché had been invented a short time before by Henry Clay of Birmingham. The Duke of Chandos's *stuccadore* was *Pietro Martire Bagutti*, who appears also as Burgooty and Pargotti. The three large and the twenty small PAINTINGS on the ceiling are by *Antonio Bellucci*. The main scenes represent
79 the Nativity, the Ascension, and the Deposition. There are in addition twenty medallions. Bellucci was born in 1654. He was thus nearly thirty years older than Piazzetta, over twenty years older than Pellegrini, and five years older even than Sebastiano Ricci. Pellegrini painted at Castle Howard and Kimbolton in 1708–13, Sebastiano Ricci in various places in England *c.*1709–*c.*1716, Bellucci arrived in 1716. Though the oldest of the Italian invaders of England, his style already approaches that of Piazzetta. His colouring is still sombre – not as blissfully light as Pellegrini's and sometimes Ricci's – but his figures already have Rococo proportions, and his compositions are bold in their precipitous recession. – The STAINED GLASS was all designed by *Francisco Slater*, who painted at Canons and in other places. It was done by the leading glazier of the time, *Joshua Price*, and has dates from 1719 to 1721. It is carried out purely pictorially, i.e. without any consideration of the natural prerequisites of stained glass. It is the extreme contrast to what was demanded of stained glass in the Middle Ages and what we insist on now as well. – WOODWORK. This is largely by *Dawkes* and interesting as an attempt to marry the Italian Baroque with certain English church traditions. Thus e.g. the BENCHES have poppy-heads, though poppy-heads of acanthus foliage, and the LECTERN has more than a touch of the Norman. But the PULPIT is Baroque in style, and here Dawkes indeed made use of the C18 stair railing of wrought iron and apparently of some

woodwork as well. The reliefs of course are Victorian.* – The FONT is by *James Forsyth*, white marble, and very chaste with its four kneeling angels. – The ORGAN CASE is that of the Canons chapel. – PLATE. Paten with the Vernicle engraved, *c*.1500; Elizabethan Chalice; Cup and Cover Paten of 1676; Flagon of 1713. – MONUMENTS. Thomas Foley † 1677 (N transept). Tablet of black and white marble with two columns and a curly open pediment in front of a segmental one. – First Lord Foley, by *Rysbrack*, completed before 1743. This must be one of the largest funerary monuments of the C18 in England. Its base alone stands up 6 ft. Grey sarcophagus and grey obelisk, the rest white. On the sarcophagus the semi-reclining figure of the deceased. He turns with a telling gesture to the onlooker. By him his seated widow with a child. L. and r. two standing allegorical figures. Above large damask drapery are the base of an urn and high up the two standing figures of younger Foleys (?).

WITLEY COURT was burnt out in 1937 and remains as a supremely splendid shell. It all looks mid-C19 at first, but much earlier parts were kept when rebuilding took place. The towers to the N belong to the Jacobean house of the Russell family, the long wings projecting to the N to the house of 1683 built by Thomas Foley.‡ But what one gasps at is not what was taken over by Lord Ward, but what *Samuel Dawkes* made of it about 1860. The entrance side has a three-storeyed centre with a five-bay giant portico of two storeys with unfluted Ionic columns. This portico incidentally was an early C19 addition, prior to the time of Dawkes. It is without a pediment. Beyond are the two four-storeyed towers and the two-and-a-half-storeyed wings projecting six bays and given canted bay windows at their ends. To the E is a plainer façade of one plus five bays with two canted bay windows. To the garden is a giant portico 98
of seven bays, again unfluted Ionic columns and also of early C19 date, and three plain bays l. and r. The centre is again raised. Top balustrade throughout. Dawkes's details are very remarkable. He evidently intended to keep in harmony with the chapel. Hence, though the scale is colossal and the principal features are grand, the rest is very restrained. The motif of the main windows – round arches and surrounding blank arches – e.g. is inspired directly by the chapel. This is Early Victorian,

* The pulpit does not come from Canons. The Canons pulpit is at Fawley in Bucks.

‡ The NMR has a photograph of a rib-vaulted cellar.

handled with great assurance, and not at all High Victorian. Only the bold curved seven-bay wing on the l. of the garden façade is an exception; for this ends in a pavilion whose giant pilasters and columns set into the ground-floor openings are derived from Michelangelo and Bernini. Or is that also an allusion to the chapel, though to its interior? The curved wing led to the (now roofless) ORANGERY, a thirteen-bay Italian-villa structure with columns rather Quattrocento than C16 or C17. The terraces and gardens were laid out by *W. H. Nesfield*, who had worked so much for Barry. Below the garden
99 façade is the PERSEUS FOUNTAIN by *James Forsyth*, with its prancing horse 26 ft high above the water and displaying all the Baroque abandon which Dawkes kept away from. In front of the E façade is the TRITON FOUNTAIN, with four tritons blowing their shells – the famous Bernini motif – and a small figure now fragmentary at the top.*

LODGES, on the A-road, in a much livelier Italianate, each with two quadrant porches.

(HILLHAMPTON HOUSE, ½ m. NE. See VCH II, 291.)

WOODBURY HILL CAMP, 1½ m. SW. This univallate hillfort is roughly kidney-shaped in plan and encloses some 26 acres. The best preserved portion of the rampart is on the NW. Entrance gaps occur on the NW and NE, the latter inturned.

GREEN FARMHOUSE *see* QUEENHILL

8060

GRIMLEY

ST BARTHOLOMEW. This is a Norman to E.E. church, but the evidence takes some finding. In the S wall of the nave is the stump of a Norman buttress, though there are also Dec windows, and the S doorway is Norman. One order of colonnettes with (renewed) trumpet-scallop capitals. Heavy roll moulding in the arch. The doorway is set in a piece of projecting wall (cf. Stoulton and other places). The chancel has small lancets and had flat E buttresses. That will be *c.*1200. But the E window is Perp. So is the W tower. The rest, and much restoration of what has already been mentioned, is of 1886. – STAINED GLASS. Old parts in one N and one S window. – PLATE. Cup

* Captain M. J. Gibbon in *Country Life*, vol. 98, p. 120, draws attention to the PUMPING MACHINERY for the fountains, 'a ramshackle building deep in a steep-sided dell'. It reminds him of Piranesi's *Carceri* with its 'huge wheels, larger than one can take in at a view, ropes, chains, hooks, bars, spikes, crumbling walls and shafts of light amid darkness'.

by *W. S.*, 1635; Flagon by *Peter & Wm. Bateman*, 1812. – MONUMENT. Martha Farmer † 1781. By *Stephens & Bott*. Urn and thin palm frond.

THORNGROVE. A curious design, perhaps early C19. Ashlar, of seven bays. Porch of pairs of unfluted Ionic columns. The giant angle pilasters are oddly thin, and the one-bay pediment is underdeveloped too. Round the corner two canted bay windows and one bow, the latter with an ogee-headed opening. In the grounds a three-arch bridge with a pretty cast-iron parapet. The centre is a kind of a ship's helm, and above it are lamp-holders. For several years Lucien Bonaparte, Napoleon's brother, lived at Thorngrove.

The ditches belonging to a ROMAN FORT have been partly excavated.

THE GROVE *see* STOKE BLISS

GUARLFORD

8040

ST MARY. 1843 by *Thomas Bellamy*. The crazy-paving walling is a surprise. Otherwise the church still represents the Commissioners' type. Nave and chancel, W porch, lancet windows. In the E wall a group of three lancets.

RHYDD COURT, 1½ m. E. The house is partly of *c.*1800, but largely by *D. Brandon*, of 1863. It is of no architectural interest. Attached to it is the CHAPEL, designed by *Hansom* in 1864 and completed by *Norman Shaw*. This is an apsed Gothic building with geometrical tracery, quite conventional, in spite of Norman Shaw. – Mosaic REREDOS. – The STAINED GLASS apparently by *Hardman*.

HADEN HILL *see* BIRMINGHAM OUTER WESTERN SUBURBS

HADLEY *see* OMBERSLEY

HADZOR

9060

ST JOHN BAPTIST. Nave and chancel and a tight little W tower with details a little funny. The church is Dec, but was so much restored in 1835 and again in 1866 (*Street*?) that it appears of that date. Original the base courses of masonry, some parts of the windows, and some parts of the pretty frieze of square fleurons under the eaves. – Inside a MONUMENT with an enormous canopy, very Gothic, to John Howard Galton

† 1862 in Rome. The VCH considers the monument partly C14. – Next to it sweet little brass kneelers praying for a recumbent gentleman. This is to Robert Cameron Galton † 1876. – Several tablets. – STAINED GLASS. A little is of the C14. It has to be searched out. – Several windows evidently by *Hardman*. – PLATE. Cup and Salver Paten of 1812.

ST RICHARD AND ST HUBERT (R.C.), W of the former, on the road. Small, of brick, all in one. By *C. A. Buckler*, 1878.*

HADZOR HOUSE. The core is of 1779, but the appearance now is what *Matthew Habershon* made it in 1827. Seven bays, two and a half storeys, with a three-bay pediment and a porch of four Greek Doric columns. To the S pediment on giant upper pilasters. Staircase with a handsome iron railing. Close to the house the former CONSERVATORY. The glass was unfortunately replaced by walls when the little building was converted into a chapel. Very pretty cast-iron columns or baluster shafts and acroteria.

HAGLEY

9080

ST JOHN BAPTIST. The typical estate church, close to the Hall, away from the (present) village, and generous in dimensions and smooth in architecture, the latter although it is essentially by *Street*, 1858–65, who could at the same time be so much more forceful and blunt (*see* St John Stourbridge). In fact the church is medieval, see some S aisle masonry, and parts of the octagonal arcade piers. Also the N arcade and aisle were built already before Street, by *Rickman* in 1826. Street lengthened the church by one bay to the W. The tower has a broach spire. The details of the church are all Middle Pointed, i.e. late C13. – The PULPIT, round and of stone, and the iron screen are probably also *Street*'s. – STAINED GLASS. By *Henry Holiday* and much influenced by Morris & Co. a S aisle window. The S aisle E window is also by him and more monumental, but also a little showier. Both were made by *Powell*'s, the former in 1876, the latter in 1907–8. – PLATE. Silver-gilt Set given by Sir Thomas Lyttelton in 1746. – MONUMENTS. A coffin lid with a specially rich foliated cross, C13, in the N aisle. The ogee-arched recess in which it is displayed is only very partially medieval. – 'Luciae' it says on the urn to the wife of the first Lord Lyttelton, † 1747. There is a delicate relief on the urn and a sturdy putto sits next to it. The carving is by *Roubiliac*, but

* So Mr Denis Evinson tells me.

the design by *Sir Charles Frederick*. – First Lord Lyttelton, erected by the second Lord. Designed by *Soane*; 1808.

HAGLEY HALL. Hagley Hall was built for the first Lord Lyttelton in 1754–60 by *Sanderson Miller*, a gentleman architect, better known as a pioneer of Rococo Gothic than as a classicist. The gardens and garden ornaments however were begun already in 1747 or a little earlier. The house is in the Palladio–Inigo-Jones tradition and very probably immediately inspired by Croome Park, which had been begun by Capability Brown in 1751, though Sanderson Miller seems to have had something to do with that house as well (*see* p. 126). On Hagley Hall several other amateurs were also consulted: John Chute of The Vyne, Thomas Lennard Barrett of Belhus, and Thomas Prowse of Axbridge and of Wicken. Hagley Hall lies brown and neat on its spacious lawn. It is of the type with four corner turrets or square eminences with low pyramid roofs, a type initiated by Inigo Jones at Wilton. The W front is of eleven bays with a large open staircase in two arms leading to 87
the main doorway. Below the landing in front of the doorway is a recess with a rusticated arch. In fact the whole basement is of smooth rustication. Above are the *piano nobile* and a half storey. In the eminences is one more storey. The doorway has unfluted Ionic columns and a pediment. The centre of the whole front has a three-bay pediment. To the S are five bays, to the E again eleven. There is also a three-bay pediment, and in place of a pedimented doorway is a pedimented window.

The interior was seriously damaged by a fire in 1925 but skilfully restored in 1926. The entrance hall or White Hall has niches with statues and very pretty stucco decoration. The chimneypiece by *James Lovell* has atlantes, a lintel with a lion, and a rustic relief of a satyr and a cupid above. The relief is signed by the stuccoist *F. Vassali*. In the back wall is a lower tunnel-vaulted recess which receives cross corridors from N to S. The vault is coffered. Big Rococo cartouche on the ceiling. The Dining Room (former Saloon) behind the entrance hall has 88
a splendid Rococo ceiling* and garlands and trophies on the walls. The trophies represent music, painting, acting, hunting, and war. The library, to the l. of the entrance hall, has small busts on top of the pedimented bookcases. In the Old Dining Room is a chimneypiece with frontal termini. The Gallery runs all along the S side. It has column screens in front of both ends and a Rococo ceiling. In the ceiling of the Tapestry Room are

* Reinstated from photographs after the fire.

medallions by *James Stuart*, Athenian Stuart, the architect, on whom *see* below. The chimneypiece is more intimate, white and brown with a Rococo overmantel. The staircase is not in its initial state.

The STABLES are of nine bays with a three-bay pediment.

Hagley is exceptionally rich in garden ornaments. Foremost among them is the TEMPLE OF THESEUS, N of the main road from Birmingham. It is by Athenian *Stuart*, who with Nicholas Revett had petitioned the Society of Dilettanti in 1748 to finance them to go to Athens and measure the ancient buildings there. The two had indeed gone in 1751 and returned in 1755. The first volume of their *Antiquities of Athens* only came out in 1762 and did not contain the so-called Theseion. But they had measured it and, here at Hagley, as early as 1758 they copied it *en miniature*. The building is the earliest example of the Doric, i.e. Grecian, Revival anywhere and thus vastly memorable, although the majesty of the order of course does not lend itself to the smallness of the copy and the picturesque setting. The temple has six fluted Doric columns in front but is sadly lacking in depth.

Also N of the Birmingham road is an uncommonly slender OBELISK.

NE of the church is the PRINCE OF WALES'S COLUMN, round, with a free composite capital and a statue of the prince in Roman garb.

89 The largest of the garden ornaments is the CASTLE, oblong in plan, with four corner turrets. Only one of them and a three-bay stretch of building to its r. (with pointed windows) is complete. The rest is deliberately ruinous. It is a typical *Sanderson Miller* piece and was begun already in 1747. Horace Walpole saw in it 'the true rust of the Barons' Wars'. At the same time, across the valley, an Ionic ROTUNDA was built. This is mentioned as to be built in a letter by Shenstone in 1747. Shenstone was something of a neighbour, building similar garden attractions at The Leasowes near Halesowen. The Rotunda is in a sad state now. Other garden furnishings have disappeared.

ROCKINGHAM HALL, Birmingham Road. White, apparently Later or Late Georgian, with a Gothic porch, gables, and a castellated tower. (Inside two Jacobean plaster ceilings.)

(HARBERROW HALL. Inside a room with a thin-ribbed Jacobean ceiling. NMR)

WYCHBURY HILL CAMP, ¾ m. NE. This strategically situated

site commands a fine view of the Stour valley. The fort is roughly heart-shaped in plan and is univallate except on the S, where a more gentle approach to the hilltop necessitated the construction of a second bank and ditch. Trial excavations in the C19 produced a bronze terret.

HALESOWEN

9080

ST JOHN BAPTIST. This is indeed an impressive church, large, in a prominent position and with a slender Perp crossing tower crowned by a fine recessed spire. The spire is grey, the rest red. To understand the highly confusing exterior and interior it may be said, to begin with, that the C12 church was as large as is the present church, that it had a crossing tower a good deal farther E than is the tower now, and that that tower must have collapsed towards the W in the C15 taking with it the whole E part of the nave, which was then rebuilt quite differently. This explains why so much Norman work remains and yet the church is not at all Norman in its character. The W wall is Norman with a doorway with zigzag arch and one order of colonnettes. The nave buttresses l. and r. are Norman too, and so is a buttress base farther l. This marks the W end of the Norman N aisle. The lancet above the doorway is of course E.E. The S doorway is Norman too, with two orders of colonnettes. The arch has zigzag again. The capitals are of the scallop type except for one which has poor thin trails. Enter for a moment and you will see what the Norman nave was like. Composite piers, sturdy, with big scallop capitals. Four big demi-shafts and four thin ones in the diagonals. The arches have a single step. Of this nave two W bays survive. No gallery, but a doorway leading probably to a wooden W balcony. Norman also the present chancel arch, thin and with not quite accurately preserved detail. In the arch a rope moulding and a band of pellets. This must have been the E arch of the Norman crossing. Before the C19 it was much lower. To its N, into the aisle, is some rough upper masonry indicating the Norman N transept E wall. In the chancel there is one small Norman N window, now inside, and there is a change from smooth to rough masonry on the N and S walls and a blank arch in the E wall suggesting that there had originally been a tunnel-vault here, which would make Halesowen a great exception in England. Outside the chancel above a big Victorian window is a length of Norman interlaced blank arcading.

Having taken in these Norman parts,* we can now look at the rest, first outside then inside. The crossing tower, as has already been said, is Perp. The spire has lucarnes in three tiers. The S aisle windows are of *c.*1300, the outer S aisle (with its arcade) dates from 1883 and is by *John Oldrid Scott.* The S chapel E end and the vestry corresponding to it are Victorian too. The N chapel with its N gable is Perp, and the N aisle also. The chapel window is of four lights with a transom. Inside, the major confusing fact is that in the C15, when the Norman tower had fallen, the nave was rebuilt in two wide bays, with arcades much higher than the Norman ones, and that a new crossing tower was built much farther W, in fact following immediately E of the two remaining Norman bays. The tower has a tierceron star vault. The details of the responds and the nave arches are rather flimsy. The two-bay arcade to the S chapel is C14. Octagonal pier, double-chamfered arches.

FURNISHINGS. FONT. Big, Norman, but round the round bowl very broad snaky interlace of a decidedly Viking style. In the corners four small figures, obviously not earlier than Norman.‡ – SCULPTURE. Cross-head from a churchyard Cross (nave W). On one side the Crucifixion, on the other the Virgin. – STAINED GLASS. The E window is of 1873, clearly by *Hardman.* – TILES. Many displayed by the S entrance. – PLATE. Two Chalices 1682; Almdish 1730; small Paten 1799; large Paten undated. – MONUMENTS. Coffin of a Priest, C14, with recumbent effigy in outline, badly preserved (SW corner). – William Shenstone of The Leasowes (*see* below), the poet, † 1763. Plain free-standing urn on a pedestal. – John Halliday. By *Thomas Banks,* 1797. Large and somewhat heavy-handed. Big obelisk with a very high pedestal in front on which stands a Grecian urn with a fine relief of a seated young woman and a
91 naked boy. To the l. of the pedestal an over-life-size man in a large mantle. His gesture expresses grief. To the r. of the pedestal a kneeling young woman, holding the small dog to save which Halliday was drowned. – In the churchyard a CROSS crowned by a ball probably of the C17. It originally stood in Great Cornbow.

ST MARGARET, Hagley Road, Hasbury. By the *Cutts* brothers, 1907. Brick, reactionary.

* Mr Stratford dates them all *c.*1150–60.

‡ This, says Mr Stratford, is not a Worcestershire type of font, but it is similar to Devon and Cornwall fonts. The drapery of the figure seems to have been ribbed like that at Romsley. The date may be *c.*1150–60.

HALESOWEN ABBEY. The remaining fragments are mixed up with the farm buildings of MANOR FARM, S of Manor Lane. The abbey was Premonstratensian. It was founded by Peter de Roche, Bishop of Winchester, in 1218, and what still stands dates, with one exception, from the years round about 1220–30. The fragments are as follows: some high walling of the chancel N wall with one lancet window and the springers of rib-vaulting; the W wall of the S transept with two lancets and the springers of the vault; also the upper doorway into the former dormitory. A doorway below led no doubt into the vestry. This W wall is continued to the N by the S jamb of the arch from the former S aisle into the transept. The aisle S wall remains for quite a stretch. Round the cloister, the CHAPTER HOUSE in the E range was excavated in 1938. Of the S range, there is one piece up. It belongs to the S wall of the REFECTORY and has small windows below and fine high windows above with deep rere-arches. To the outside are buttresses. A good deal farther E is an oblong building of the late C13. It was two-storeyed and still has some of its transomed two-light upper windows. It is supposed to represent the abbot's house, or it may have been the guest-house. Inside, set in the S wall, two MONUMENTS: miniature figure of a C14 Knight with crossed legs, probably made for a heart burial, and coffin lid of the C13 with a kneeling figure in profile below a Crucifixion.

Little else has to be visited at Halesowen. N of the church in CHURCH STREET are some acceptable houses, especially IVY HOUSE, whose doorway has a shell pediment, and the stone-built LOCK-UP behind Nos 18–20. In the commercial centre S of the church nothing of note except perhaps in GREAT CORNBOW a few nice Georgian doorways – especially that of No. 25. Looking down into it from the W is some good new HOUSING E of HALES ROAD. It is of 1962–4, by *R. & M. Granelli* and *M. Rhys Davies*. It consists of two heavy ten-storey blocks and smaller blocks of three to five storeys in lively grouping. Their detail has the restlessness of the 1960s, but the effect is cheerful here, even if the corner balconies are perhaps a little assertive. The site is nicely turfed. W of Hales Road was HIGHFIELD PARK, a pretty Gothick brick house of the late C18 of which only one bay window with ogee-headed windows remains. The house ought to have been preserved amid the new.

(Factory and Offices for SANDVIK Ltd, by *I.D.C.* of Stratford-on-Avon, 1965–6.)

THE GRANGE, Grange Road, just S of the by-pass. Early Georgian, brick, with stone dressings. Five bays and two storeys. Angle giant pilasters. Doorway with demi-columns, a bulgy frieze, and a segmental pediment. The upper middle window is flanked by pilasters. The whole S front is later C18.

THE LEASOWES. William Shenstone was born at Halesowen in 1714. He went to Oxford, but took no degree, and from 1745 lived peaceably at the Leasowes, wrote essays and letters and poetry, but published hardly anything. He was of sweet but vulnerable temper and wore his own hair and no wig. 'Water-gruel bard' is Horace Walpole's description. Shenstone's passion was the beautifying of his estate, and his ambition to be admired for it. The house as it now is dates probably from the early C19. It is pebbledashed, of three bays only, with a semicircular Ionic porch, and has attached side pavilions. Shenstone's Gothic STABLES have alas been pulled down recently. Of his furnishings of the grounds only a fragment of the PRIORY RUIN has remained.

8050 HALLOW

ST PHILIP AND ST JAMES. 1867–9 by *W. J. Hopkins*, and his most interesting work. It is a large townish church with a W tower (of 1879) crowned by a broach spire. The style is that of *c.*1300, but the tracery patterns in the round clerestory windows, as Hopkins liked them, are fanciful. The chief interest is the impressive stone diaphragm arches inside, resting on long shafts which in their turn stand on corbels. The weight of the arches is also carried by outer flying buttresses and by arches across the aisles which in the spandrels towards the nave are traceried. Four-bay arcades. Chancel arch impressively high and with some pierced cusping. – FONT. By *Forsyth*, *c.*1870. With two small figure reliefs and small strips of ornamented tiling. – REREDOS. By *R. Boulton* of Cheltenham. Crucifixus with the Virgin, St John, the Magdalen, and the other Mary in detached figures. Gothic shrine. – PLATE. Cup and Cover Paten, early C17; Paten on foot, C17; Flagon by *P. & W. Bateman* of 1807. – MONUMENTS. Several tablets, the best John Pardoe † 1680, a cartouche with a fruit and flower surround and a putto head at the top, and Richard Harrison † 1795, by *W. Stephens*, with a plain urn on which a coat of arms.

HAM CASTLE FARMHOUSE *see* CLIFTON-ON-TEME

HAM GREEN *see* FECKENHAM

HAMPTON

0040

ST ANDREW. Perp. Aisleless nave, central tower, with a vault of eight radiating ribs and a large circle for the bell ropes. The imposts of the tower have large spurs. S porch with a stone roof on three chamfered transverse arches (cf. Church Honeybourne). Doorway with leaf spandrels. – ARCHITECTURAL FRAGMENTS. Norman; in the nave walls. – PLATE. Cup and Cover Paten by *I. F., c.*1571. – In the churchyard CROSS base with quatrefoils and fleurons and MONUMENT to John Martin † 1717, a sarcophagus with jolly carving.

HAMPTON LOVETT

8060

ST MARY. The church is basically Norman, see the N doorway with one order of columns and a roll moulding, the flat buttresses l. and r. of it, a Norman buttress stump on the W side, and a Norman chancel buttress. The S tower is Dec, see the entrance with two continuous chamfers and the bell-openings. The nave also has Dec features. Perp chancel details and Perp N (Pakington) chapel, built *c.*1414. – BENCHES. Some with traceried panels, probably from the screen. – SCULPTURE. White Pietà, no doubt Italian, C19. – STAINED GLASS. (In a nave N window heraldic glass of 1561.) – Chancel E window by *Hardman*, 1859. – PLATE. Cup of 1755. – MONUMENTS. John Pakington † 1551. Still entirely Perp, with a tomb-chest, a recess with panelled wall, a depressed arch and top cresting, but nearly entirely of the restoration of 1858–9. – Dean Hammond † 1660. Signed by *Joshua Marshall*. Large tablet with a demonstratively learned inscription, mixing Latin and Greek and characterizing the Dean as *errorum malleus, veritatis hyperaspistes* etc. – Sir John Packington † 1727. Signed by *Joseph Rose* Senior. Good semi-reclining effigy against a good reredos background. – In the churchyard high CROSS to the memory of Augusta Anne Lady Packington † 1841.

HANBURY

9060

ST MARY. In an elevated position with views to the S, including the Malvern Hills. Late C18 exterior of red sandstone. The W tower was built in 1793. The doorway has an ogee arch, the window over Y-tracery. There are also circular windows. The body of the church has wide pointed windows. The E parts

were rebuilt in 1860–1 by *Street*, but they are not of his best. Externally and internally the E.E. details are gross and tend to be over-dimensioned. On the outside MONUMENT to Thomas Bowater Vernon † 1859. In the C18 parts some features make one suspect that medieval evidence was there, e.g. the window surrounds and the S doorway with a sunk quadrant moulding. Even so, the interior comes as a complete surprise. The arcades are fully medieval. The S arcade is no later than, say, 1210. Round piers, round capitals, double-chamfered arches, but one capital still trumpet-scalloped. The N arcade is Perp and no good. Of Street's additions the internally most prominent one is the Vernon Chapel. – FONT. Probably by *Street*. Given on the occasion of the restoration, in 1860. – The WEST GALLERY, pretty, on thin shafts, and the BOX PEWS belong no doubt to *c*.1795. – CHANDELIER. Brass. Given in 1795. Of the Baroque shape. – SCULPTURE. German early C16 relief of the Adoration of the Magi, *c*.3 ft high. – PLATE. Large set of 1721. – MONUMENTS. All Vernons. In the chancel Richard V. † 1627 and wife. He kneels in front of her, both facing E. Recess with pilasters and straight top. – Thomas V. † 1722.
83 By *Edward Stanton* and *Christopher Horsnaile*. Large, white and grey standing monument. Semi-reclining effigy in contemporary clothes with a wig. To the l. seated Justice, to the r. seated Learning. The 'reredos' has Corinthian columns, looped-up curtains to reveal the inscription, and a broken pediment. – Bowater V. † 1735. By *Roubiliac*, but not one of his best. Also a standing monument. The deceased stands pensively with one elbow on a pedestal and a book in the other hand. The posture is taken from Guelfi's Craggs in Westminster Abbey. In front of the figure a putto holds a medallion with the portrait of Bowater's wife. – Thomas V. † 1771. Tablet. Exquisite lettering. Above a female figure by an urn. – Thomas Taylor V. By *Chantrey*, 1837. White marble. Kneeling woman in profile with two children. The sentiment is quite convincing. – Nice Georgian iron RAILINGS and GATES.

HANBURY HALL. As you approach the house through its grounds and the most welcome Victorian forecourt with its two pavilions (even if their roofs are a little fanciful), you will be struck by the perfect Englishness of the picture which offers itself. It is a substantial house, thirteen bays wide and two storeys high, of brick with stone dressings and a central cupola. It could be in no other country. The (E) façade is handsomely
70 articulated by somewhat projecting three-bay wings and by a

pedimented three-bay centre flanked by rather tightly placed giant columns on high pedestals. The inscribed date 1701 is no surprise. This is clearly the Wren Age, and the carved decoration with volutes round the middle window is as clearly *circa* 1700. It even suggests the name of an architect, *Talman*. This is a guess (enforced by Mr John Harris's opinion). The similarities are with Talman's Thoresby in the first place, and also Chatsworth, both Talman's E front, and the W front begun in 1700, and with Talman's work at Drayton (Northants) of 1702. Actually a name is recorded for Hanbury Hall: *William Rudhall* of Henley-in-Arden, who signed the drawings of the house which are still kept there and have different details (the columned centre only one bay wide, the pediment segmental, and more decoration), but it is unlikely that he was more than the builder. The house was built for Thomas Vernon, who was a barrister. Of further features of the façade the elegantly framed windows and the porch with Corinthian columns are all that needs a mention. The sides of the house are as composed as the front; only the back is haphazard. To the N the rhythm is 3–recessed 4–2. The l. bay of the recessed centre was formerly a subsidiary doorway. It has an open segmental pediment and pretty decoration. The S is quite different in character, long and even, with a 2–7–2 punctuation.

The entrance hall is spacious and opens on the l. direct without any intermediate screen to the large, square, open-well staircase. This has prettily decorated thin balusters and carved tread-ends, and the walls and ceiling are – according to the fashion of about 1700 – painted all over with large figure scenes. Comparable staircases are at Hampton Court, Burghley, Drayton, Boughton, and Burley-on-the-Hill (Rutland). The Hanbury staircase is by *Thornhill* and must according to topical allusion date from *c*.1710. The scenes are flanked by painted fluted pillars in perspective, and the walls and ceiling are connected in the Baroque way by a feigned flying figure also painted. Baroque the staircase no doubt is, but of course nothing like as exuberant as it would be in Italy or Germany. The quality of the painting is quite high, although this also cannot compare with the brio of most Italian and some German work. But it is as high and perhaps a little higher than the best of Verrio, one of Thornhill's preferred foreign competitors. The scenes represent Thetis in
Vulcan's Forge, Achilles choosing a spear, Ajax and Ulysses 72
contending for the arms of Achilles, and on the ceiling the

Assembly of the Gods with Mercury holding (or rather a cherub next to him holding) a portrait of Dr Sacheverell which is to be torn by furies. The Sacheverell trial took place in 1710. Thornhill had suddenly risen into fame when, in 1708, he was commissioned to paint the great hall of Greenwich Hospital. At Hanbury Hall he also painted in the large Long Room or Dining Room two ceiling panels: Apollo and Leukothea and the Rape of Orithyia. The panels are surrounded by good plaster foliage of a variety of species. The chimney decoration with overmantel is exquisite Rococo wood carving of *c.*1750. In
58 another ground-floor room is a wooden Jacobean overmantel from Tickenhill Manor at Bewdley, brought to Hanbury probably already when part of that house was demolished about 1700. It has coarse caryatids and deeply moulded panels. On the first floor two doorways are singled out by open segmental pediments.

In the grounds is the ORANGERY, all on its own, i.e. forming its own picture. It is nine bays long and has a three-bay pediment with beautiful fruit and foliage carving: a basket and two garlands. Nearer the house is the LONG GALLERY, perhaps intended for ball games. This is seven bays long and has a chimneypiece made up of C17 and C18 bits. A little farther distant than the orangery is the ICE HOUSE, an uncommonly well preserved specimen among the ever-decreasing numbers.

BROUGHTON COURT, 1¾ m. SSW. Timber-framed with square panels. The date is late C16 or early C17.

MERE HALL, 1¾ m. S. The front faces a pretty Georgian forecourt of brick walls with two corner pavilions with ogee roofs. (Fine early C18 iron GATES. VCH) The house is timber-framed
54 and dates from *c.*1560. The date 1337 on a bracket is not ancient and not justified by anything about the house except perhaps the general plan of central hall and two wings.* The hall has a porch of the late C17 and a square bay. Above the centre are five delightful little gables with finials. The wings each have a large gable. Decorative motifs comprise close studding, herringbone struts, and concave-sided lozenges. Pretty Gothick glazing bars, probably by *M. Habershon*, *c.*1830–40, and a pretty central lantern. (Fine carved chimneypiece in the W

*Mr Charles tells me that the wings were considerably altered, probably by *M. Habershon*, *c.*1830-40 (see text below); also that the house is interesting as one of several in which an attempt was made in Elizabethan times to reproduce the appearance of a long gallery in the attic.

wing. VCH) Central chimneystack of four star-topped chimneys.

RECTORY, E of the church. By *David Brandon*, 1862. Big SCHOOL, opposite the church turn. By *Street*, 1860, but nothing at all special.

HANLEY CASTLE 8040

The CASTLE lay S of the village and was built in 1206–13 by King John. It was the seat of the Earls of Gloucester and Warwick. Towards the end of the Middle Ages it fell into decay. Now only the moat remains.

ST MARY. Of the plain Norman S doorway only the length of roll-moulding is original. The N aisle is of *c*.1300. It has windows with cusped Y-tracery, a doorway whose moulding matches that, and a four-bay arcade with round and octagonal piers and double-chamfered arches. Then, in 1674, the central tower, the chancel (its windows are Victorian), and the N chapel were built – all of brick. The chapel windows are interesting, as a posthumous essay in the Gothic. The E window has (incorrect) ogee arches to its three lights and panel tracery over. The side windows are straight-headed and more original. – FONT. Perp, octagonal, with small-scale decoration. – COMMUNION RAIL, N chapel. Early C18; the balusters alternatingly columnar and twisted. – MONUMENTS. Mrs W. Lechmere, undated, with a small kneeling frontal figure. – Rev. A. B. Lechmere † 1878. Alabaster tablet with the deceased kneeling before Christ. The scene is rendered in sgraffito.

The setting of the church is very attractive. To the N is a cedar tree, and overlooking the churchyard from that side are the ALMSHOUSES, timber-framed, of *c*.1600, and the original building of the GRAMMAR SCHOOL, also timber-framed and perhaps a little later. The school was founded in 1544. The Victorian part is of 1868. More additions since.

SEVERN END, ¾ m. NE. Much of the Lechmere mansion was consumed by fire in 1896. However, the centre of the entrance side with its lively timber-framing represents what had been there before except that the N bay had been of brick and was re-done in timber-framing. The decoration includes concave-sided lozenges, and keyed-in ovals both horizontal and vertical. Might not even they have belonged to the decade 1660–70, when Sir Nicholas Lechmere built so much? Only the chimneystacks with star tops must be original. Of Sir Nicholas's activity the two wings of the house tell most. They date from 1673 and are of brick, with Dutch gables crowned alternatingly by triangular and segmental pediments and with small doorways with steep triangular pediments. In the N wing is the only original plaster ceiling, conservative for its date, i.e. still entirely untouched by the Inigo Jones innovations. Broad bands and foliage bits. – In the house is the LECHMERE STONE, a small part of a tombstone with a cross on one side and a small figure with big coiffure. Rounded top. The style is similar to that of the mysterious figures at Newburgh in the North Riding. But what is the date? The C9, as Kendrick suggests, or the mid C11, as seems right for Newburgh? – Timber-framed BARN, dated 1658. – Square brick DOVECOTE of 1677. – SUMMER HOUSE in the garden, square, of two storeys, the upper partly standing on two stone arches. The date of this is 1661.

The parish is especially rich in enjoyable houses. The MHLG has listed thirteen as Grade II apart from those mentioned here.

6060 HANLEY CHILD

ST MICHAEL. Nave and chancel and stump of the former W tower. The church was built in 1807; the tower fell in 1864. Pointed windows and E window with Y-tracery. – COMMUNION RAIL. Contemporary. – PLATE. Cup and Paten, probably C18.

8040 HANLEY SWAN

ST GABRIEL. By *Sir George Gilbert Scott*, 1872–4. Rockfaced, with a NE tower with broach spire. The details are late C13. Circular clerestory windows. The best feature is the E window with five steeply stepped lancet lights. Dull interior. It might be by anybody. – REREDOS. Designed by *Clayton & Bell* and made by *Powell's*. Given by Sir E. Lechmere of Rhydd Court, Guarlford. To the l. and r. TILING; much more enjoyable, with geometrical patterns and flower scrolls.

OUR LADY AND ST ALPHONSUS (R.C.), ¼ m. NNE. The church lay by the entrance to the grounds of Blackmore Park, which does not exist any longer. It was by *David Brandon*, of 1862. The church is by *Charles Hansom* and was built in 1846.* The church is remarkably stately.‡ One feels nowhere the pinch of

* The VCH says *Pugin*, but both Mrs Stanton and Mr Evinson confirm the attribution here given. Pugin only did furnishings.

‡ Thanks to the generosity of the Hornyold and Gandolfi families.

poverty which mars so much of Catholic architecture in England before 1850. Rubble walling, nave and chancel, bell-cote on the E gable of the nave. Big roof. Lavish S porch and S doorway. The nave is all E.E., the chancel all Dec, and the junction is treated in such a way that it should look real history – an early example of this aspect of historicism. The nave has Dec rather than E.E. arcade piers to the aisles and rib-vaulting with stone ribs and plaster cells. The chancel also is rib-vaulted. The best window detail is the very long single W lancet which lights the nave. – Rich REREDOS with ogee arcading and angel busts in the spandrels.

The PRESBYTERY is connected with the church by a roofed covered way. Its steep gables and dormers look very much like Pugin's work.

HANLEY WILLIAM

6060

ALL SAINTS. Nave and chancel and a timber bell-turret with a shingled spire. The materials of the church are red sandstone and tufa. Norman chancel arch, unmoulded, on the plainest imposts. One Norman N window. – PULPIT. Really a three-sided screen only, but cut out of a single piece of oak. Imitation Elizabethan decoration. – LECTERN. With Jacobean panels, perhaps from the former pulpit. – STAINED GLASS. The E window fairly certainly by *Hardman*. – PLATE. Cup of 1640. – MONUMENT. Tablet with sarcophagus in relief to James Wakeman Newport Charlett † 1838. By *J. Stephens*.

(HANLEY COURT, ½ m. NE. C18, brick. Pediment over the centre and below it a tripartite lunette and below that a tripartite window. All this is the back part of a mansion otherwise now demolished. MHLG)

HARTLEBURY

8070

ST JAMES. 1836–7 by *Rickman*, except for the tower, which was built for Bishop Sandys in 1587, the chancel N chapel, *c*.1300, and the chancel, by *Rickman*, 1825. The arcade between chancel and chapel has a quatrefoil pier with thin shafts in the diagonals. Rickman's church is large and competent, similar in many ways to his church at Ombersley. High W porch, long three-light N and S windows, the tracery alternating (also across) between geometrical and reticulated. Thin Perp piers, 94
plaster vaults with ridge-ribs. Lightly detailed GALLERIES recessed behind the piers. The chancel and the S chapel are of

course Victorian (1877). – FONT. A little of the lower part of the bowl is C12 work. – PLATE. Set of 1713, all silver-gilt. – CROSS in the churchyard. The base with quatrefoils and angle spurs (cf. Ombersley).

In the churchyard THE GABLES, the former school. Doorway with Doric pilasters, triglyph frieze, and pediment.

ST MARY, Bishop's Wood. 1882. – PLATE. Cup, said to be of 1571.

69 HARTLEBURY CASTLE. Hartlebury Castle is a deliciously peaceful sight. Of its military past hardly anything remains visible. Bishop Walter de Cantelupe began a castle about 1255, and Bishop Giffard obtained licence in 1268 to complete it. The moat is a reminder of it, and the lowest parts of a round NW tower. Much was done in the C15, but in 1646 the castle was almost destroyed. Rebuilding began in the late C17 and continued into the late C18. The result is a comfortably stretching-out red-sandstone building with a central hall and higher projecting wings. The hall part is embattled and has a pretty lantern of *c.*1750–60, the wings have hipped roofs. There is a spacious turfed forecourt with two outbuildings with cupolas and two castellated entrance lodges. The centre is in fact the C15 GREAT HALL, but externally its date is not recognizable. What one sees is the large pointed windows with Gothic glazing bars of the later C18 and the porch of Bishop Fleetwood of *c.*1680. It has a heavily moulded door surround with lugs top and bottom and a big semicircular pediment. The medieval entrance to the hall was near its N end. The big arches W and E at the S end led into bay windows and have broad hollow mouldings. The hall roof has thin timbers, wall-posts, and elementary arched braces to collar-beams. Recently, on the upper floor, the head of a blocked C15 two-light window to the W has been found and the jambs of a second. The double staircase at the N end is probably of the late C18 (Bishop Hurd) and leads nowhere of any consequence. The chimneypiece is typical of *c.*1680, with its bolection moulding, the volutes of foliage l. and r. of the overmantel, and the top shell with angel wings.

The wings are of *c.*1680 too, and their hipped roofs are characteristic of the date. So are the windows, except of course those which go with the C18 remodelling of the hall. The place of the S wing is taken by the C14(?) CHAPEL, but its windows with Y-tracery must be again of the C18. The extremely pretty fan-vault is by *Keene* and was done for

Bishop Maddox (1743–59). So the windows probably date from the same years. The STAINED GLASS in the heads of the windows is by *J. Rowell*. The N side of the house is of brick without stone-facing. The W side is irregular. The buttresses and the canted bay window are mid-C18, the ample bow window yet somewhat later. It was introduced by Bishop Hurd (of the *Letters of Chivalry and Romance*), when in 1782 he installed the new library.

The INTERIOR of the ground floor has been much adjusted recently by *Marshall Sisson*. As for the principal rooms, the SALOON, S of the hall, has three windows, light Rococo wall decoration, and an elegant white Rococo ceiling. This dates from *c.*1760. The STAIRCASE with its heavy balusters is typical of the Fleetwood time, i.e. *c.*1680. Bishop Hurd's LIBRARY on the first floor, facing W, has already been mentioned. It is tripartite and has its original, very fine bookcases. The parts are divided by column-screens. The design for the library, by *James Smith* of Shifnal, is preserved. It is dated 1782.

Red brick LODGE, castellated and with pointed windows.

RECTORY. Built by James Stillingfleet, son of Bishop Stillingfleet (1689–99). Seven bays with a three-bay projection. Doorway with a ribbed hood. Stone window surrounds. Flat quoins.

HARVINGTON 0040

near Evesham

ST JAMES. Norman W tower with a spire of 1855. The tower has an arch to the nave which is pointed and has two slight chamfers. That would make the small, typically Norman W window post-1200. In the nave windows of *c.*1300 (cusped Y-tracery), in the chancel very odd early C14 single-light windows with short straight tops on ogee curves (or truncated ogee arches). – PLATE. Chalice by *I. W.* (?), *c.*1620. – MONUMENTS. Thomas Ferryman, rector, † 1619, tablet with corpulent side columns. The strapwork 'predella' seems to have been continued below by the handsome tablet to Thomas Jun., also rector, who died in 1622 or 1623. Plain strapwork surround.

RECTORY. In the garden the re-erected former E window of the church. The present E window is of *Preedy*'s restoration of 1855.

MANOR HOUSE. To the E a cruck truss, the exposed bottom of which is cut off.

The village has a number of attractive black and white houses along the main street, ending NW of the church in one with a cruck truss to the E.

8070

HARVINGTON

near Kidderminster

BLESSED VIRGIN (R.C.). 1825. With windows with Y-tracery and a castellated W porch. The E window, the outer porch, and the vestry are of 1854–5. – STAINED GLASS. E window by *Hardman*.

HARVINGTON HALL. Harvington Hall appears now as a picturesque, entirely irregular Elizabethan brick house. But the brick is in large parts only a covering of a late medieval building of timber-framing on a sandstone base. In 1529 this house came to Humphrey Pakington, a lawyer, and his son, John Pakington, seems to have done the refacing and much adding about 1560–75.* Much thought has gone into elucidating what is medieval, but visually the medieval work hardly counts. Visual interest is wholly Elizabethan. The house is approached from the E, and the lower part of that range is probably the oldest. The tower-like N end of the range has brick laid Flemish bond and must therefore in its present form be mid-C17 at the earliest. The one oval window to the E confirms such a date. The principal range is the S range. Its centre is the hall, placed on the upper floor and probably already there in the C15. The porch and the two rectangular bay windows facing N and S at the high-table end confirm this, and the oldest part of the E range would then have been Great Chamber and Solar.‡ The gabled S front is as varied as can be pictured. The windows are mullioned; only the hall bay has a transom as well. To the N the hall range has the curious and unexpected feature of a giant basket arch carrying the gables. It lies flush with the N hall-bay and the porch bay. This, including the gables and the attic rooms in them, is an alteration of 1701 (rainwater head). Inside, the staircase is a replica of the original one which the Throckmortons who owned Harvington Hall in the C18 and C19 took to Coughton Court in Warwickshire.

The principal items of interest are the priest-holes and the

*A date 1576 was scratched on a window pane.

‡Mr Charles suggests that the solar timbers may have been brought from elsewhere. The whole wing seems medieval, yet must be a later addition to the hall.

1. *Landscape:* Great Malvern, Malvern Hills

2. *Villagescape:* Abbots Morton
3. (above right) *Townscape:* Bewdley, Load Street (*Copyright Country Life*)
4. (right) *Townscape:* Worcester Cathedral, air view

5. *Caves:* Stourport, Redstone Rock Hermitage

6. Cropthorne church, cross head, *c.* 825–50

7. (left) Worcester Cathedral, crypt, 1080s

8. (below left) Great Malvern, Malvern Priory, nave after *c.* 1085, chancel *c.* 1420–60

9. (left) Pershore Abbey, south transept, *c.* 1100

10. (below left) Worcester Cathedral, chapter house, *c.* 1120–5

11. (above) Astley church, *c.* 1160
12. (right) Worcester Cathedral, west end of nave, *c.* 1185

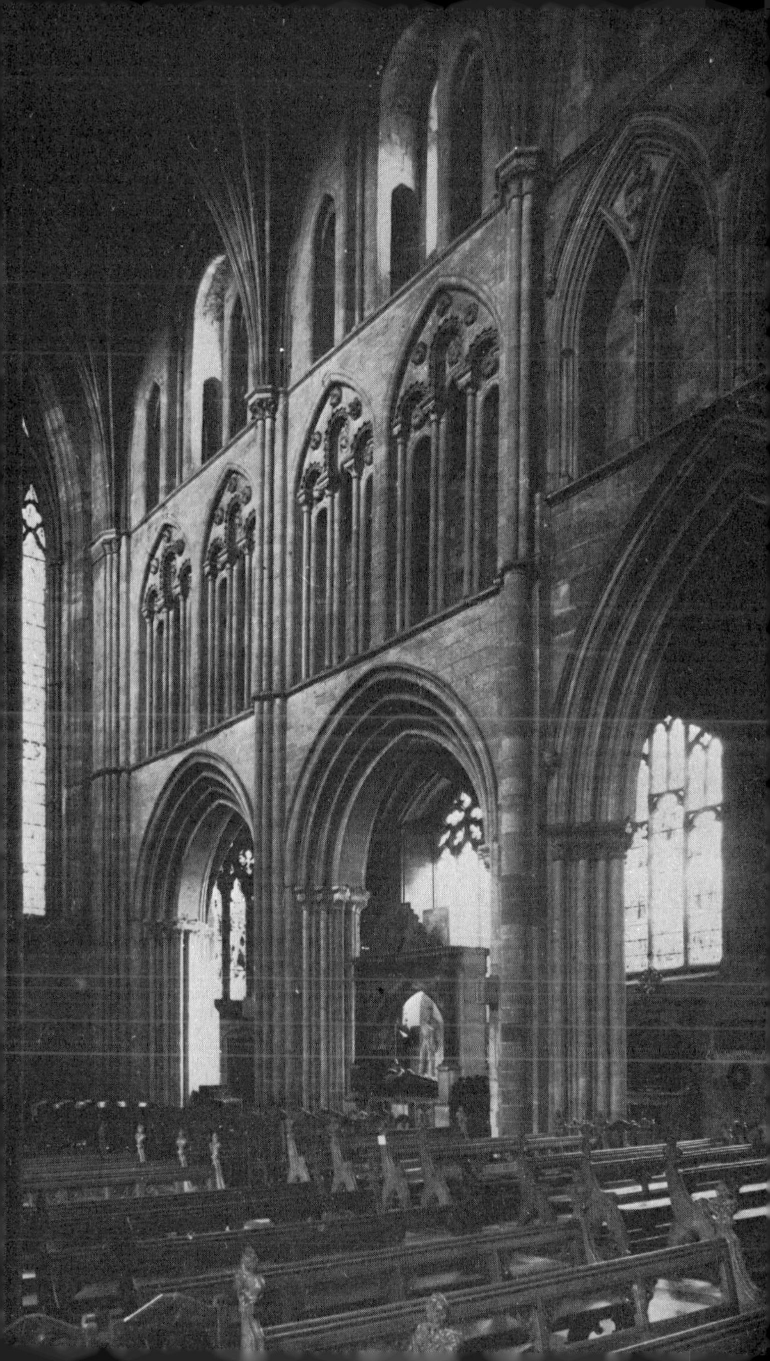

13. (left) Beckford church, tympanum of south doorway, Norman

14. (below left) Pirton church, Pirton Stone, Early Norman?

15. (right) Rous Lench church, Christ, above the south doorway, *c.* 1140–50

16. (below right) Chaddesley Corbett church, font, *c.* 1160–70

17. (left) Norton church, lectern, *c.* 1190

18. (below left) Elmley Castle church, font, base early thirteenth century, bowl Perpendicular

19. (right) Leigh church, standing figure, *c.* 1220

20. (left) Worcester Cathedral, refectory, Christ in Majesty, *c.* 1220–30

21. (below left) Worcester Cathedral, monument to King John, *c.* 1230

22. (right) Worcester Cathedral, chancel, begun 1224

23. (below right) Worcester Cathedral, chancel, begun 1224, triforium

24. (above) Worcester Cathedral, south-east transept, begun 1224, arcading
25. (above right) Droitwich, St Andrew, north tower and chancel arch, *c.* 1200 etc.
26. (right) Pershore Abbey, boss, late thirteenth century

27. (right) Pershore Abbey, chancel, consecrated 1239

28. (below right) Pershore Abbey, chancel, vault, c. 1290–1300

29. (right) Pershore Abbey, monument to a knight, *c.* 1280

30. (below right) Evesham, All Saints, Moses, late thirteenth or early fourteenth century

31. (left) Bredon church, coffin lid, early or mid fourteenth century
32. (above) Chaddesley Corbett church, east window, Decorated

33. (right) Worcester Cathedral, nave, begun *c.* 1320

34. (below right) Worcester Cathedral, cloister, east walk, fourteenth century

35. (right) Bredon church, stained glass, early fourteenth century

36. (below right) Birtsmorton church, stained glass, late fourteenth century

37. (left) Great Malvern, Malvern Priory, *c.* 1420–60

38. (below left) Great Malvern, Malvern Priory, chancel, *c.* 1420–60

39. (right)
Evesham, bell
tower, after 1513

40. (below right)
Evesham, St
Lawrence, south
chapel, *c.* 1520

41. (above) Romsley church, tower, Perpendicular
42. (above right) Stanford-on-Teme church, monument to Sir Humphrey Salway †1493
43. (right) Kidderminster church, monument to a lady, late fifteenth century

4. (left) Worcester Cathedral, Prince Arthur's Chantry, begun 1504
5. (above) Worcester Cathedral, canopy with a fortified city, fifteenth
entury or 1642

46. (left) Great Malvern, Malvern Priory, Henry VII in the transept north window, 1501/2

47. (below left) Ripple church, misericord, fifteenth century

48. (right) Dormston church, west tower, *c.* 1450

49. (below right) Huddington church, north porch, Late Perpendicular

50. (above) Worcester, Holy Trinity, roof of the Guesten House, 1326
51. (above right) Worcester, Commandery, great hall, late fifteenth century, oriel window
52. (right) Evesham, Booth Hall, fifteenth century

53. (left) Huddington Court, early sixteenth century and *c.* 1584

54. (below left) Hanbury, Mere Hall, *c.* 1560

55. (right) Grafton Manor, porch, 1567

56. (below right) Bengeworth church, monument to Thomas Watson †1561

57. (left) Astley church, monument to Walter Blount †1561
58. (below left) Hanbury Hall, overmantel from Tickenhill Manor, Bewdley, *c.* 1600
59. (below) Crowle church, chalice and cover paten, 1571

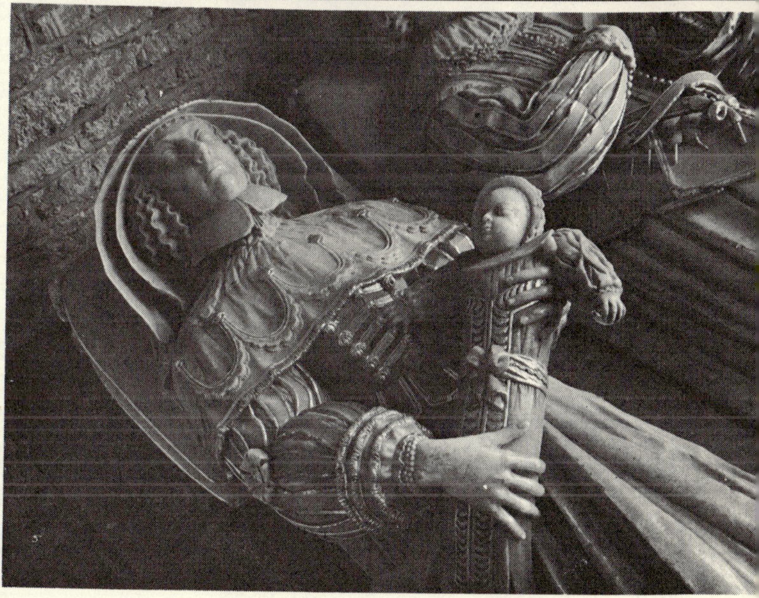

60. (left) Norton church, monument to Sir Thomas Bigg †1613
61. (above) Wickhamford church, monument to Sir Samuel and Sir Edward Sandys †1626
62. (below) Elmley Castle church, monument to William Savage and Giles Savage †1631 and the latter's wife

63. (left) Chaddesley Corbett church, monument to Humfrey Pakington †1631

64. (below left) Croome d'Abitot church, monument to the first Lord Coventry †1639

65. (right) Elmley Castle church, monument to the first Lord Coventry, by William Stanton, shortly after 1700

66. (below right) Salwarpe church, monument to Olave and Elizabeth Talbot †1689

CONSTANTIAM

Woman was full of
works; Alms-deeds
the did. And it
came to passe
that she was sicke
and all the Widdows stood
weeping Acts 9 v 36
37 39

67. (left) Westwood Park, *c.* 1600 and *c.* 1660–70 (*Copyright Country Life*)
68. (below left) Old Swinford Hospital, founded 1670
69. (below) Hartlebury Castle, *c.* 1680–later eighteenth century
70. (bottom) Hanbury Hall, 1701 (*Copyright Country Life*)

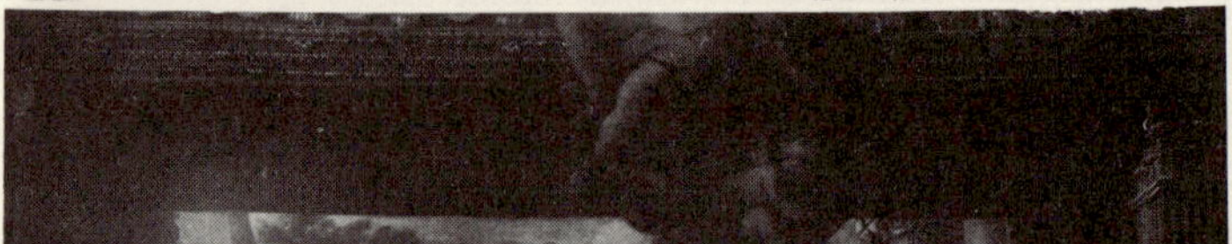

71. (above) Westwood Park, Great Chamber, ceiling, *c.* 1675
72. (below) Hanbury Hall, staircase, painting by Sir James Thornhill, *c.* 1710

73. (above) Worcester, Guildhall, by Thomas White (?), 1721–3
74. (below) Worcester, Britannia House, by Thomas White (?), *c.* 1725

75. (left) Worcester, St Swithun, by the Woodwards (?), 1734–6

76. (below left) Stourbridge, St Thomas, 1728–36

77. Worcester, All Saints, by Richard Squire (?), 1739–42

78. (left) Great Witley church, consecrated 1735

79. (below left) Great Witley church, Nativity, by Antonio Bellucci, *c.* 1720

80. (right) Upton-on-Severn, old church, tower, base *c.* 1300, cupola by Anthony Keck, 1769–70

81. (below right) Bewdley church, by Thomas Woodward, 1745–8

82. (left) Worcester, All Saints, sword rest, eighteenth century

83. (right) Hanbury church, monument to Thomas Vernon †1722, by Edward Stanton and Christopher Horsnaile

84. (below right) Worcester Cathedral, monument to Bishop Hough, by L. F. Roubiliac, 1746

85. (above) Powick church, monument to Mrs Russell †1786, by Thomas Scheemakers
86. (right) Croome d'Abitot church, font, *c.* 1763

87. (left) Hagley Hall, by Sanderson Miller, 1754–60
88. (below left) Hagley Hall, 1754–60, Dining Room
89. (below) Hagley Hall, Castle, by Sanderson Miller, begun 1747
90. (bottom) Broadway Tower, 1800

91. (above) Halesowen church, monument to John Halliday, by Thomas Banks, 1797
92. (below) Spetchley Park, by John Tasker, begun 1811

93. (above) Wolverley, Sebright School, 1829
94. (below) Hartlebury church, by Thomas Rickman, 1825 and 1836–7

95. (above) Powick, new bridge, 1837
96. (above right) Bushley, Pull Court, by Edward Blore, 1836–46
97. (below right) Tardebigge, Hewell Grange, by Bodley & Garner, 1884–91

8. (above left) Great Witley, Witley Court, by Samuel Dawkes, . 1859–61

9. (left) Great Witley, Witley Court, Perseus Fountain, by James Forsyth, *c.* 1860

00. (above) Droitwich, Château Impney, by Tronquois, 1869–75

101. (left) Wythall church, tower, by W. H. Bidlake, 1903
102. (above) Great Malvern, Malvern College, library, by Sir Aston Webb, 1924

103. Besford Court, staircase, by Randall Wells, 1912

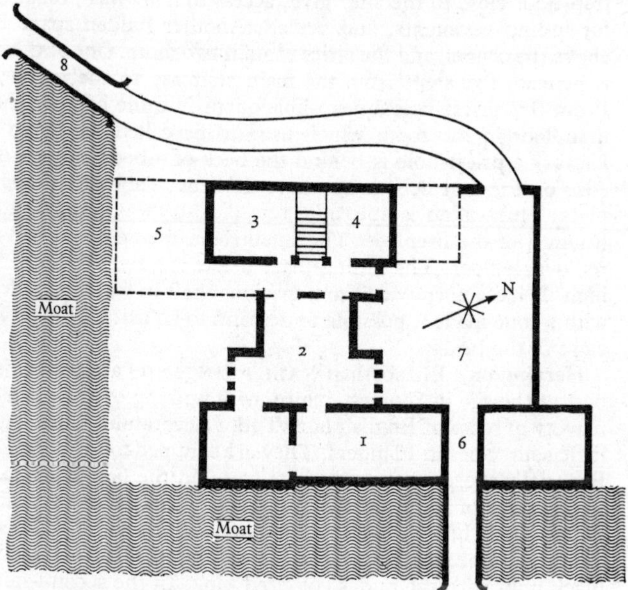

Suggested outline of the medieval house

1. Solar
2. Hall
3. Kitchen
4. Buttery
5. Sixteenth-century kitchen added
6. Gate-house and east bridge
7. Court
8. South-west bridge

Harvington Hall, plan

wall paintings. The house is riddled with PRIEST-HOLES. There cannot be many houses with so many hiding-places and such ingenious ones. Granville Squiers called it 'the most remarkable collection ... under one roof'. The house came into Catholic hands only about 1630, so the priest-holes cannot be earlier than that. There is one immediately by the main entrance, inside the gateway, a shallow hole 7 in. in diameter in a timber in the l. wall. At its back is a slot for passing food into the space in the angle of the wall between gateway and courtyard. Entry is from a room above. The room has the two doors l. and r. of the fireplace. They lead into a passage whose floor can be lifted up. The space itself is 10 ft below, and only 4½ by 2 ft in size. Another hiding-place is below the chapel. A trap-door close to the altar gives access to it. It was probably for hiding vestments, and vessels. Another hidden space is above the chapel, and the attics contain two more. One of them is beneath five steps from the main staircase to the garrets. From this priest-hole a peep-hole opens into the hall. On the first floor in the room which used to be called Dr Dodd's Library a priest-hole is behind the back of a book cupboard. Also on the first floor is access to the most elaborate hiding-place. This was an escape route as well. Entry was in the South Room l. of the fireplace. The small room thus entered had a removable floor. The hiding-place below is 3 by 5 ft and 6 ft high. It has a narrow exit to a spacious shaft in which a pulley with a rope made it possible to descend to an exit by the moat close to the bridge.

Harvington's Elizabethan WALL PAINTINGS are by far the best of the age in Worcestershire, with nothing of the clumsy naïvety of most of English later Tudor decoration. Their stylistic source lies in Flanders. They are confined to the W range. Especially those on the newel staircase, in the first-floor passage, and in a room on the second floor are exquisite arabesques with lush foliage and elegant nudes, some of them children, some women with leaf tails. The painting is done in black lines with the nudes coloured pink. In the second-floor passage are considerable remains of a series of the Nine Worthies. There again at least some of the figures are of a remarkable ease and delicacy, especially young David slaying Goliath. The panels of the door in the Great Hall are prettily decorated too, and one upper room, used evidently as a chapel, has on the walls vertical chains of drops of blood.

BELLINGTON FARMHOUSE. C16–C17. Timber-framed, gabled house with close studding.

HASBURY *see* HALESOWEN

HAWFORD *see* NORTH CLAINES

0060

HEADLESS CROSS

ST LUKE. 1867–8 by *F. Preedy*. Broad, fancy-Norman façade with bellcote. The arcades on the other hand a rather early Early English, i.e. with capitals of the Canterbury–Oakham kind and pointed arches. E apse.

METHODIST CHURCH. 1897. Red brick, Gothic, with an open-work spire.

HEIGHTINGTON 7070

St Giles. Nave and chancel in one and timber bell-turret. Remains of one N lancet. Roof with tie-beams.

HERMITAGE *see* ARELEY KINGS

HEWELL GRANGE *see* TARDEBIGGE

HIGHTREES FARMHOUSE *see* UPPER ARLEY

HILL COURT *see* GRAFTON FLYFORD

HILL CROOME 8040

St Mary. On a hill. Blunt W tower, unbuttressed, with a W lancet and a saddleback roof. The chancel is late C13, see the E window and the PISCINA. Why is this set diagonally? Was there the intention of an apse? – PULPIT, with tester. Nice and simple. – FONT COVER. Humble Jacobean. – COMMUNION RAIL. Jacobean. – PLATE. Cup and Cover Paten, 1571; Paten by *B. O.* (?), 1716.

The farm W of the church has a DOVECOTE of cruck construction.

HILLHAMPTON HOUSE *see* GREAT WITLEY

HILL SCHOOL *see* UPTON-ON-SEVERN

HIMBLETON 9050

St Mary Magdalene. Small Late Norman S doorway. One capital has waterleaf. Mid-C13 chancel with three closely spaced stepped E lancets. Dec S transept with two-light S window. C14 also the timber S porch. The largely weatherboarded bell-turret is assigned to the C15. Latest medieval N arcade with octagonal piers. The N windows go with such a date, but the several other windows which are just mullioned, of two lights, must be yet later. Nice Perp wagon roofs over chancel and nave. – FONT. C12. Of table-top type. The only decoration is one small medallion with the lamb and cross.* – STAINED GLASS. In the E window a female figure of the C13 and some contemporary leaf quarries. The rest of the window is an outstanding imitation of the style of *c.*1300. – In a chancel

*An C18 font is now in the Shell Chapel; so the Rev. R. Stockley tells me.

N window C15 fragments. – More fragments in the aisle NE window, including a C15 female saint, and in the S chapel E window. – The aisle E window is by *Kempe*, *c*.1900. – PLATE. Cup and Paten by *S. R.*, dated 1656; Paten inscribed 1688.

(SHELL MANOR FARM, 1 m. N. A hall and cross-wing house of *c*.1450 with classic medieval solar wing. It has a ground-floor parlour or cellar with heavy flat joists grooved for a wattle ceiling, and a splendid open roof over the two-bay upper chamber and single-bay antechamber. There are shaped doorheads, and the stone fireplaces and stack with huge diagonal brick shafts added in the C17 are remarkable. The hall and service wing are both of the late C16, but conform with the medieval cross-passage plan. There are two stone stacks each crowned with three star-shaped brick shafts, though they serve only two fireplaces. FWBC)

(SHELL COTTAGE. Just across the brook from the manor house is a thatched cottage. It is in fact a diminutive hall-house of the C15 with later inserted fireplace and first floor. Just discernible are shallow triangular doorheads marking the screens passage. Both solar and service bays are in the form of outshuts, but again the doorheads survive. The central roof-truss, purlins, and rafters are heavily smoke-blackened. FWBC)

PACKHORSE BRIDGE, by the ford near Shell Manor. Two round arches and a 6 ft width between parapets.

8050

HINDLIP

ST JAMES. Nave and chancel originally Dec, but almost entirely rebuilt by *Hopkins* in 1864 and given a S aisle in 1887. The W tower has Perp responds but C17 bell-openings. – FONT. Neo-Norman, with carved figures, tightly set in arcading. – TILES. Many of the C15, now on the tower walls. – STAINED GLASS. E window, evidently by *Hardman*.

HINDLIP HALL. Early C19. Of five bays and two and a half storeys. Three-bay pediment. Porch of four unfluted Ionic columns. Three-bay, two-storey wings in line with the house and two three-bay, one-and-a-half-storey outer wings.

CUMMIN'S FARMHOUSE. The house has a plaster ceiling and a staircase with dumb-bell balusters, both of *c*.1660. The ceiling has as its centre an oval wreath. The beams are stuccoed too, and there is a decorated frieze. (On the upper floor is a plaster panel with the date 1615, but that cannot apply to the ceiling below.)

HINTON-ON-THE-GREEN 0040

ST PETER. Norman N and S doorways. One order of colonnettes. Capitals with decoration as if it were folded material (cf. Beckford, Eldersfield, etc.).* Roll-moulding in the arches. The N doorway has a tympanum with an incised trellis. The W tower is Perp – see the broad hollow mouldings of the arch to the nave. The chancel is by *Sedding*, 1895. The five-light E window shows a personal interpretation of Perp. The windows of the nave are of 1865. The nave battlements and the gargoyles are Perp. – FONT. Octagonal, Perp, with fleurons in quatrefoils. – MONUMENT. Incised slab to a young Priest dated 149?.

HOLDFAST MANOR HOUSE *see* QUEENHILL

HOLIDAY FARM *see* BERROW

HOLLYBUSH 7030

ALL SAINTS. 1869 by *Preedy*. The finest thing about the church is its position, on its own against the Malvern Hills. Nave and chancel in one; plate tracery.

(MANOR HOUSE. Early or mid C18. Brick, three bays, with a Venetian window in the middle. MHLG)

HOLT 8060

ST MARTIN. One of the most impressive Norman village churches in the county. The re-set Norman entrance to the lychgate serves as an introduction. The colonnettes have odd capitals, with a kind of convex scallop somewhat reminiscent of beakhead. Norman then is the S doorway, with two orders of colonnetttes carrying fantastic capitals – a monster biting its tail, a man with foliage coming out of his mouth and held by his hands, a toothy monster-head – and zigzag arches. The N doorway is simpler, but also has figured capitals – one is the fable of the fox and the crane, both drinking from a barrel – and zigzag arches too. One order is at r. angles to the wall.‡ The N nave windows are again Norman; one of them is shafted and quite magnificent. It links up with a frieze of twisted rope

* Observation of Mr Stratford.

‡ Mr Stratford points to this as perhaps the earliest example of undercut zigzag in the county.

once no doubt longer. The chancel, which is also Norman, had instead a frieze of crenellation. The windows are long and round-arched, but this is a lengthening of a little later. Altogether, except for Rock, Holt is the most profusely decorated Norman parish church in Worcestershire. The chancel E window is Dec. So is the S chapel. The W tower with its slightly projecting bell-stage is Perp. Inside, the original chancel arch is preserved. The capitals have scallops with heads over, plainer scallops, and trails. In the arch is zigzag and a sort of crenellation with sparse triangular merlons. The hood-mould has chain-links and a blob in each link. At the apex of the arch is a beast's head.* The S arcade consists of two bays plus a wider one into a S chancel chapel. Their details are all the same, coarse, with round arches. The one free-standing pier has a round capital. This and the roundness of the arches may at first suggest the C13, but the time of the Reformation is more likely. – FONT. Norman, drum-shaped, on a short, thick, round stem with spiral fluting like that of the piers of Durham. On the bowl big monster-heads with symmetrical trails, the whole forming a chain. – PULPIT and LECTERN are neo-Norman, and the *Building News* in 1858 says: 'We refuse to criticize [them], as they are the work of a lady and it is pleasing to find them taking an interest in these matters.'‡ – MOSAIC, over the chancel arch. 1859. Copied from the Mausoleum of Galla Placidia at Ravenna. – STAINED GLASS. In the S chapel C15 Annunciation; fragmentary. Also bits in another window. – In the chancel E window glass by *Kempe*, 1892. – PLATE. Chalice and Flagon by *Jno. Bodington*, 1698; Paten, *c.*1698. – MONUMENTS. Effigy of a lady on a tomb-chest. C15. – On the S aisle W wall tablet to Mercy Bromley † 1704. Twisted columns; rays and putto-heads. Rich details.

HOLT CASTLE. A C14 tower of four stages with small Dec windows and a two-bay rib-vaulted entrance (with ridge-ribs as well as diagonal ribs) stands in front of a C15 hall with early C18 panelling. The rib-vaulting is probably C15 too. To the r. of the entrance in the tower is a chamber with three slit windows, to the l. a straight staircase in the thickness of the wall. The C15 hall range was L-shaped with a solar wing projecting to the E. The part between the hall and the wing was

* For the date of the Norman work Mr Stratford proposes *c.*1160–75, and compares with Herefordshire (e.g. Bromyard, Upper Sapey), but not the so-called Herefordshire School.

‡ I owe this quotation to Peter Ferriday.

filled in early in the C18, and a spacious staircase built. This has some floral ceiling stucco and an elegant wooden handrail. On the first floor the solar roof remains, but (VCH) 'few other details of interest'. (On the garden side an early C19 porch of two pairs of Greek Doric columns. NMR)*

BRIDGE. By *Telford*, 1828. One iron arch, rather crudely handled. The simple parapet is of iron too.

HONEYBOURNE *see* CHURCH HONEYBOURNE *and* COW HONEYBOURNE

HOOK COMMON *see* UPTON-ON-SEVERN

HOPTON COURT *see* LEIGH

HUDDINGTON *9050*

ST JAMES. Close to the Court. Norman nave with an original N window and a plain S doorway. The nave has also got a N window of *c.*1300. There is a short S aisle. The two-bay arcade has piers of a handsome section, cruciform with hollowed re-entrant angles and demi-shafts attached to the ends. Moulded capitals and moulded arches. Late Perp timber N porch and 49
stately Late Perp chancel E window of three stepped lights with stepped panel tracery above stepped transoms. To the l. and r. of the window, inside, image niches. – SCREEN. Jacobean, with widely spaced balusters. – STALLS. The fronts are linenfold panels of about 1520.‡ – COMMUNION RAIL. Mid-C17, with vertically symmetrical balusters. – BENCHES. Some entirely plain old ones. – STAINED GLASS. In one S aisle window a jumble of old fragments. – In the E window much restored Crucifixus with the Virgin and St John, early C16. Said to come from Cornwall. – TILES. In the S aisle, a good many, of the C15. – PLATE. Cup, undated but signed *S. R.* – MONUMENTS. Brass inscription tablet to Adrian Fortescue † 1653. The wooden surround is a C20 imitation. – Sir George Wintour † 1658. White and black marble. Of very good quality.

HUDDINGTON COURT.§ An early C16 timber-framed house

* The owner of Holt Castle, Mr Harper, would not allow me to see the first floor. I had written two letters to ask for permission which, he told me, he had thrown straightaway into the waste-paper basket.

‡ Mr Brian S. Smith comments: S side *in situ*, N side *ex situ*, only the latter true linenfold.

§ More on the house is in Mr Charles's Introduction to timber-framed buildings, on p. 61.

with many alterations of *c.*1584. It was originally larger than it is now. An inventory in 1650 speaks of ten rooms below, twelve above. The owners were the Wintours till 1658. Seen
53 from the E, it is the most picturesque house in Worcestershire. It is L-shaped from here, and in the angle is a deliciously fanciful chimney of the kind familiar from Hampton Court and the houses of the time of Henry VIII. The entrance is on the N side. It has thin Ionic columns of *c.*1584. The windows are mostly of that time too, slightly projecting oriel-wise as was the tradition. Only the E window of the projecting wing on the E side is a C20 addition. The timbering is all with close studs. Inside, the most interesting features are the staircase of *c.*1584, a proper, fully convincing, really safe priest-hole on the second floor – the Wintours were involved in the Gunpowder Plot – and a spectacular early C14 stone frieze of four quatrefoils with suspended shields. The quatrefoils are studded with ballflower in the West Country fashion, and big ballflowers are also inside the quatrefoils. The shields are held by a bird, a dog, a hooded man, and a hare. The frieze probably comes from the preceding house, to which also no doubt the moat belongs. – In the garden are two timber-framed C17 DOVECOTES, both said to come from elsewhere, a simple SUMMER HOUSE from Strensham Court, and ornate C18 iron GATES from an estate in Yorkshire.

COTTAGE, N of the gates to Court and church. Of cruck construction.

HUNNINGTON *see* ROMSLEY

HUNT END *see* REDDITCH

HYDE FARM *see* STOKE BLISS

0050

INKBERROW

ST PETER. What is easily visible is Perp or Georgian or Victorian rebuilding (S transept 1784; chancel 1887, the latter by *Ewan Christian*). The best side is the N, with battlements and pinnacles and quite an ornate porch displaying large gargoyles. W tower with four-light window. Heavy Late Perp N arcade of octagonal piers. The N chapel is suggested to be yet a little later. – FONT. Square, of *c.*1200. On the underside a kind of elaborate dogtooth, on the sides medallions with the lamb and cross, and various rosettes. – PULPIT. Of *c.*1800, with thin

Gothick panelling. – STAINED GLASS. In the N aisle W window saints and angels; in the N chapel E window more bits; all C15. – PLATE. Cup with baluster stem and Cover, by *Robert Signall* (?), 1592; Cup and Paten on foot, by *R. A.*, 1629; Salver Paten, by *G. S.*, 1658. – MONUMENTS. John Savage † 1631. Alabaster. Recumbent effigy, damaged kneeling family against the tomb-chest. Columns carry a canopy whose underside has, instead of Renaissance coffering, Gothic quatrefoiled panels with sub-cusping – an interesting case of early Gothic Revival (cf. Wickhamford, 1626). – Also a retardaire tablet to Francis Sheldon † 1690. Both monuments are in the S transept.

OLD VICARAGE. Brick. Rebuilt in 1762, enlarged and altered in 1837 (VCH). The appearance now is all Tudor, with straight-headed windows and bargeboarded gables.

Pretty village GREEN with timber-framed as well as brick houses and cottages.

MORTON HALL, 1½ m. N. Brick; Georgian. Five bays, two and a half storeys. Porch of pairs of Tuscan columns. Lower l. wing; no r. wing.

IPSLEY

0060

ST PETER. Nave and chancel and Perp W tower with high, narrow arch to the nave. The church had two aisles. Both were demolished in 1785. The S aisle, to judge from the decoration of the W respond (with the head of a lady), dated from the late C13 or thereabouts, the N aisle was later. The window details are all renewed or new. – FONT. Big, seven-sided, early C14, with ballflower up the edges and crenellation. – PULPIT. A very fine, ornate Elizabethan piece from Easton in Herefordshire. – SCULPTURE. Sacrifice of Isaac; small Netherlandish wood relief, probably early C17. – PLATE. Small Porringer of 1682. – MONUMENTS. Two incised alabaster slabs, each showing one couple. They represent Nicholas Huband † 1553 and his wife † 1558 and Sir John † 1583 and his wife † 1557. So they probably date from *c.*1560.

IPSLEY COURT. The house of the Huband family. Interesting, though only fragmentarily preserved. What remains is two long parallel ranges; the connecting centre has disappeared. Instead there is a brick wall with a small Tudor doorway, no doubt *ex situ*. The wings are substantial, with hipped roofs and wide eaves, and cross windows, as far as they are original. All this looks late C17, though the only date available is 1724 for the demolition of the centre.

RECTORY. A pretty, though cemented, Late Georgian front with arched windows and vases on the top corners. Stables with cupola. The MHLG dates the house 1812.

9030

KEMERTON

ST NICHOLAS. By *R. C. Carpenter*, 1847, except for the W tower, originally unbuttressed and of the early C13. Tower arch with two slight chamfers. The tracery patterns of the S aisle are surprisingly wilful for Carpenter. The N aisle is quieter. Interior in the early C14 style, as is the tracery. – STAINED GLASS. All the chancel glass by *Willement*. His initials T. W. occur. – CORONA in the nave, quite ornate. By *Hardman*. – PLATE. All of 1843 and 1848. – MONUMENT. Portrait slab of marble inlay to Thomas Thorp † 1877.

RECTORY FARM, SW of the church. Early C18, of five bays, roughcast, with a handsome shell hood on carved brackets.

SCHOOL. Also by *Carpenter*. Nothing special.

8040

KEMPSEY

ST MARY. The earliest evidence is the W lancet of the S aisle, a flat buttress next to it, and a broader, similar buttress in the E wall of the N transept. So the church was quite large already about 1200. Then, about 1250–60, the grand chancel was built, with its beautiful five stepped lights of the E window gathered together under a blank arch and shafted inside, and its three pairs of N lancets, also under blank arches. The chancel arch is Victorian. The SEDILIA have cusped arches, the PISCINA a trefoiled arch. The S transept has just such a PISCINA too, although its large transomed five-bay window is of course Perp. The N transept N window is identical, but the PISCINA here has an ogee arch, i.e. is Dec. The three-bay arcades are both Dec or of *c.*1300. They are very similar but differ in two ways. The piers are quatrefoil, with a convex rounded shape in the diagonals in the S piers, a projecting diagonal spur in the N piers. The S arches have two hollow chamfers, the N arches two normal chamfers. The arcades clearly take the existing transepts into account. Perp W tower with deeply recessed W window and panelled arch to the nave. Perp S aisle windows. – STAINED GLASS. Eight very good C14 figures in chancel side windows. – PLATE. Cup of 1571; Paten by *S. R.*, 1639; Flagon by *Charles Martin*, 1732; two silver-gilt Almsdishes, by *Jas. Hobbs*, 1823. – MONUMENTS. Sir Edmund Wylde † 1620. Recumbent effigy against a shallow arch. Columns l. and r.

and at the top an achievement and the unusual motif of balustrading. – Mrs Eaton † 1790. By *William Stephens* of Worcester, and remarkably good. Standing monument with sarcophagus and urn before obelisk. On the sarcophagus a fine relief. – Thomas Foley † 1821. By *J. Stephens*. With a bust at the top. – Sir Richard Temple, G.C.S.I., C.I.E., P.C., LL.D., D.C.L., F.R.S., † 1902. Bronze bust with moustaches and a goatee.

The village has a number of pleasant houses, both timber-framed and Georgian, especially along the Worcester Road.

THE NASH, $1\frac{3}{8}$ m. SE. An interesting brick house with stepped gables, much pulled about *c*.1900. The oldest part seems – externally probably *temp*. Henry VIII – the corner where the Parlour is. There is here brickwork with blue brick diapers, there is close studding exposed inside, and the fireplace appears to be early too. The other best features may be of *c*.1600, i.e. the delightful plaster ceilings of the Dining Room and the room above it, with bands of generally ogee-shaped forms arranged so that they are almost like reticulation units. In the upper room the overmantel has columns decorated with strapwork. Another overmantel, very rich, with caryatids and architectural inlay patterns, was found in the house. The main staircase must be of *c*.1700–10, with its slim balusters, twisted and columnar, and its carved tread-ends. In the cellar is one part with octagonal brick piers supporting brick vaults.

A ROMAN MILESTONE was found here, erected during the reign of Constantine (early C4).

KENSWICK 7050

(KENSWICK MANOR. In the house panelling and an elaborate Jacobean overmantel from Wichenford Court.)

KIDDERMINSTER 8070

Kidderminster appears as a cloth-weaving town already in the C13. Carpet-weaving was introduced in 1735 and soon became the staple trade. In 1772 there were eleven master carpet-weavers, in 1784 300 carpet looms. Power-looms replaced hand-looms only after the middle of the C19, and up to nearly the present day the carpet industry was an industry of relatively small family businesses. The result is a town uncommonly devoid of visual pleasure and architectural interest. The only exception is Church Street, rising to the open space in front of the splendid church. This being so, the authorities have decided to absorb that very open space in the new ring road, cutting off Church Street from the church. It is a crying-out crime against the town.

ST MARY. A large and very varied building of red sandstone. Much of it is Victorian, and what is older seems all to belong to the first third of the C16. Mighty SW tower, richly appointed and refaced in 1895. S doorway with traceried spandrels, five-light S window, higher up three stepped image niches. Bell-openings of two lights with transom, and the same repeated blank l. and r. Panelled parapet; pinnacles. The lierne-vault inside the tower was reinstated in 1895. At the same time the grand clerestory was refaced. Essentially, however, it is C16. Two slender straight-topped two-light windows to each bay. Panelled parapet and battlements. Rood-stair turret. The interior looks as Victorian as the exterior. The S chancel aisle indeed is of 1850, and the cloister which connects the church with the vestry of about 1790 is of 1888. From the vestry a door leads to the Lady Chapel. The Lady Chapel is a separate C16 building (like that of Long Melford, though less subtly handled). The chapel has three bays and no direct C16 connexion with the chancel. There is a separate S doorway (as at Long Melford) with traceried spandrels. The nave is dominated inside by its enormous eight-light W window, which is again Victorian. The arcades are of *c.*1500. They are of four bays with concave-sided octagonal piers and capitals, and four-centred arches. Perp also the three-bay N chapel. Finely moulded responds and cross-arches. The chancel is in all its Dec features Victorian. – STAINED GLASS. In the chancel by *O'Connor*, *c.*1855. – PLATE. (An Elizabethan Loving Cup, nearly 24 in. in height); two Patens, one presented in 1623. – MONUMENTS. Brass to Sir John Phelip † 1415, Walter Cookesey † 1407, and their wife. 5 ft figures* under concave-sided gables (in front of the communion rail). Good. – Lady,
43 late C15 (S aisle E). Tomb-chest, high, with four frontal angels. The effigy behind close-set buttresses rising from the chest and carrying a big canopy with four headless statuettes under little canopies. The underside of the main canopy is a panelled vault. – Sir Hugh Cokesey † 1445 and wife (chancel N). Recumbent alabaster effigies in a projecting recess with four-centred arch and big top cresting. – Thomas Blount † 1568 and wife (chancel N). Recumbent alabaster effigies, he below her. Back wall with small figures of the children in a row. –

* The Rev. W. F. Cox told me the measurements.

Kidderminster, St Mary, brass to Sir John Phelip †1415, Walter Cookesey †1407, and their wife

Sir Edward Blount † 1630 and two wives (S chapel). Alabaster effigies, he stiffly on his side.

ST AMBROSE (R.C.), Coventry Street. 1857-8 by *G. Blount*. Brick with SW steeple. Poor interior. – STAINED GLASS. The S aisle E window by *Hardman*.

ST GEORGE, Coventry Street. Kidderminster's second parish church. 1821–4 by *Francis Goodwin*. A fine, stately church of the Commissioners' type. Ashlar. W tower high with transparent top and W doorway remarkably high. Perp side windows of three lights between buttresses. Five bays. Tall thin Perp piers. Entrances in the W bays of the aisles. Short, low polygonal chancel. Rose window high up in the E wall (with cast-iron tracery, according to Marcus Whiffen). (The interior of the church was burnt out in 1924 and reconstructed by *Sir Giles G. Scott*.)

ST JAMES, Jerusalem Walk, Horsefair. Brick, small. 1872 by *Davis*, a local man.

ST JOHN, Bewdley Road. 1843 by *G. Alexander*. To him goes the responsibility for the blue-brick SW, former W, tower with the atrocious detailing of the top and spire. His church had a S aisle and a S transept and apse which remain, but *J. A. Chatwin* in 1890–4 built a new nave to the N, made the S transept into a porch, and gave the new chancel a wide polygonal apse. Very red sandstone outside, yellow brick with red-brick patterns inside. Lancet windows and windows with geometrical tracery.

BAPTIST CHAPEL, Church Street. 1867. Coarse Gothick, of red and black brick. Two outer staircases lead to porches.

BAXTER CONGREGATIONAL CHURCH, Bull Ring. 1884 by *F. D. Tarring*. Large, of brick with stone dressings, with a commanding NW steeple. Geometrical tracery. The old, simple, red-brick building of 1821 is still behind.

METHODIST CHAPEL, Mill Street. 1803, enlarged 1821. Stuccoed. Three bays with one-bay pedimental gable. Arched windows. Porch of pairs of columns with a bargeboarded pediment!

METHODIST CHURCH, Birmingham Road. Of *c.*1911. Brick and terracotta, no tower. Geometrical tracery.

MORMON CHURCH (formerly Countess of Huntingdon's Connexion), Park Street. 1895, brick, with Gothic details. By *H. E. Lavender*.

SALVATION ARMY CITADEL (formerly Countess of Huntingdon's Connexion), Dudley Street. 1820, with lancet windows and a porch of 1865.

UNITARIAN CHURCH, Church Street. 1883 by *Payne & Talbot*. Rockfaced with fancy Gothic detail, quite different from anything Anglican. (Inside Baxter's PULPIT. Very rich Jacobean work with tester, dated 1621.)

CEMETERY. The chapel of 1840 has a portico *in antis* of Tuscan columns and a pediment across.

TOWN HALL. 1876–7 by *J. T. Meredith*. Four bays with a Frenchy tower over the r. bay. The whole is really indescribably debased.

CORN EXCHANGE, next to the town hall. 1853 by *Bidlake & Lovall*, a much more controlled piece of work in spite of curious details. Giant pilasters and a mid-gable.

LIBRARY and MUSEUM and former School of Art, Exchange Street. 1878–92 by *J. M. Gething*. White brick, Italianate, quite a composition, with its high centre. The three buildings almost create a Civic Centre. A pity no more was made of them.

GRAMMAR SCHOOL, Bewdley Road. The one-storeyed Gothic buildings along the road are of 1848. The house between the school and the church is said to be of *c*.1784.

SION HALL SECONDARY SCHOOL. By *Sir F. Gibberd*, 1958–9. Good.

PERAMBULATION. The only worthwhile street is CHURCH STREET. It has handsome or at least acceptable Georgian houses on both sides, some (especially No. 30) with pretty doorcases, and also a timber-framed house of *c*.1600 with overhang and two upper oriels. Off to the E ARCH HILL SQUARE, a small, neglected square whose best house, with an ogee window and an ogee gable, is derelict. At the S end of Church Street the Italianate MIDLAND BANK, probably of *c*.1880. Church Street ends in or starts from the BULL RING. The statue of Baxter with raised arm is by *Thomas Brock*, 1875. Off the Bull Ring in SWAN STREET No. 13 has a tunnel-vaulted basement with a small two-light brick window to connect the two apartments. At its end the MARKET HALL of 1822 with two giant pilasters, a four-centred arch, and a pediment, and more or less opposite it, in WORCESTER STREET, the NATIONAL PROVINCIAL BANK, brick, with a Tuscan porch. Then along VICAR STREET, where properties have a more cityish scale than elsewhere. On the E side LLOYDS BANK, of grey brick, in a good Italianate, probably of 1857. On the W side a range of eleven bays and an Italian Gothic one of nine bays and four storeys. So to the town hall square with the

STATUE of Rowland Hill, of 1881, by *Brock*. Messrs Brinton's factory right in the centre demonstrates what the old-fashioned factory offices of the leading manufacturers were like.

So much for the centre. Now, fanning out, at the foot of Worcester and Oxford Streets a Gothic canopied FOUNTAIN of 1876 by *Meredith*. Farther S, in CASTLE ROAD, off New Road, the octagonal tower of CALDWELL HALL, *c.*1500, red sandstone, with embattled parapet. (Inside, the room on the lower ground floor has sixteen radial ribs, alternately single-chamfered and single-hollow-chamfered. NMR) To the E in BIRMINGHAM ROAD one or two nice early C19 houses, notably MORTIMER HALL, with giant pilasters and a veranda, and the DRILL HALL, with a porch of pairs of Ionic columns. To the N, a little farther out, two square, castellated brick early C19 LODGES of the former Lea Hall.*

New high HOUSING has recently gone up at the S end of Kidderminster between the Worcester and Chester Roads and W of the long HOO BROOK VIADUCT. The viaduct is of stone and blue brick, has twenty arches, and dates from 1883.

S of the town on the road to Stone is a SCHOOL for Dr Barnardo's Homes. It is by *D. R. Surti*, 1964–6. It shows the architectural fashion of the sixties at its most *outré*. Dagger-shaped pre-cast concrete members produce a restlessness made even less acceptable by the crude contrast of black and white.

KINGTON

9050

ST JAMES. Nave and chancel and timber-framed bell-turret. The ground-stage is of stone and was built to carry the turret. The windows of the base are C14. The style of timbering (close studding) would generally be ascribed to the C15, or even the C16. Mr Charles suggests, however, that it may be contemporary with the stone base, particularly since the top stage has curved braces. The structure rests on big beams across the stonework. The nave was widened to the S in the C16. The chancel is mostly of 1881 (by *Hopkins*). – SCREEN. Parts of the former screen now on the S wall. – In addition there is some decayed wooden tracery on a window sill. It is not known where this comes from. – PLATE. Salver Paten by *Thomas Bolton*, 1703; Cup of 1784.

* Two more at Cookley.

KNIGHTON-ON-TEME

6060

ST MICHAEL. A C12 church. The nave was lengthened to the W in the C13 (see the two W lancets), and part of that extension now carries a very nicely simplified shingled bell-turret. This is by *Godwin & Greenway*, 1959. Norman are the flat buttresses, and Norman is the S doorway with the plain blank four-bay arcading above, the whole projecting a little (cf. Stoulton and other places for this motif). The doorway has one order of columns with decorated shafts and block capitals with a thin roll down the angle (cf. Stockton). The arch has a roll and thin saltire crosses. In the chancel are small lancets of the ending C12. The nave was made lighter by two late C13 two-light windows for the benefit of the rood. The chancel arch is of the same date and has similar details to the doorway. Unmoulded arch. To its l. and r. with their sill at the height of the springing of the chancel arch are two-light Norman openings, probably blank from the start. They have block capitals too. What can their function have been? The Norman work at Knighton was done, so Mr Stratford suggests, by the same masons who worked at Eastham, Martley, and Stockton. The W part of the nave is divided from the rest by a timber-framed wall with square panels, its purpose being the support of the bell-turret. Good nave roof with moulded tie-beams and painted ceilure. – STAINED GLASS. Bits in a N window. – PLATE. Cup and Cover Paten, the latter dated 1577.

GREAT HOUSE, 7/8 m. NE. Symmetrical brick front of the later C17 with two projecting wings. The wings have shaped gables and under the r. one are still its wooden cross windows. The outer side of the l. wing shows its (older) timber-framing with brick infilling.

KNIGHTWICK

7050

CHAPEL. 1879. Two-bay nave and chancel in one; bell-turret – really a minimum job. – FONT. Round, with some zigzag; Norman. – PLATE. Cup and Cover Paten of 1676.

OLD RECTORY, by the church. Five-bay, two-storeyed Georgian house. Arched middle window.

MANOR HOUSE. Early C18, of seven bays in a rhythm of two–three–two. Hipped roof.

KYREWOOD HOUSE *see* TENBURY WELLS

6060

KYRE WYARD

ST MARY. One Norman nave N window. The Norman chancel arch was cut away in 1833. Dec S chapel with windows with Y-tracery and reticulation. The chancel E window is reticulated too. To the chancel the chapels open in one very broad arch with two continuous chamfers. Over the nave W end is a bell-turret with broach spire. This may be C17, as the beam carrying it looks of such a date. The roofs of church and chapel are all single-framed and may well be Dec too. – COMMUNION RAIL. C18. – A C17 BIER is in the S chapel. – PAINTING. In the W jamb of the chapel SW window is a female saint, beautifully done, and certainly early C14. – PLATE. Cup of 1571; C17 Flagon; Paten of 1644. – MONUMENTS. Edward Pytts (cf. Kyre Park) † 1672. Black and white marble with an oval inscription plate surrounded by a wreath. Columns l. and r., garlands at the foot, a segmental pediment at the top. – Mrs Catherine Pytts † 1702. Also black and white, but with twisted columns and an open segmental pediment. – Jonathan Pytts † 1807. With a straight-sided sarcophagus.

ALMSHOUSES, SW of the church. Founded by Anne Pytts in 1715. Range with projecting wings and a steep pediment. Wooden cross windows. It might all be 1675.

KYRE PARK. The house of the Pytts family, now a home for spastics. The house consists of a medieval W wing projecting to the S and has its main frontages to N and S. Of medieval work there is only the stone walling visible now. The main S front is of brick, two and a half storeys high, with the half-storey above the cornice. There are seven bays plus a C20 r. addition. In the centre is a doorcase of the late C17 with pilasters, a bolection frieze, and a segmental pediment. In the S wall of the medieval wing in *c.*1754 a canted bay window was added and next to it two Venetian windows, one above the other, and a tripartite lunette. The W front of the medieval wing is faced with brick and has five bays with the three middle ones slightly projecting and pedimented. The N front has in the centre a C20 freely Georgian porch and in the medieval wing another canted C18 bay window and next to it other Venetian windows. Of the interiors of the C14 to C18 hardly anything remains, just the grand staircase of *c.*1754 (three balusters to the tread and carved tread-ends) and a subsidiary staircase with flat cut-out balusters which may be Elizabethan. The house indeed is basically an Elizabethan and Jacobean addition to the medieval wing. The work of *c.*1754 is probably by *William Hiorn* (Colvin).

Close by is a fine group of a large Jacobean brick BARN with stepped gable-ends and a circular medieval DOVECOTE, re-erected in its present position in 1756. Four lakes in the grounds. The grounds are by tradition ascribed to *Capability Brown.*

(OLD RECTORY. The VCH in 1924 illustrated this house with a cruck-truss showing under one end-gable.)

LANGLEY *see* BIRMINGHAM OUTER WESTERN SUBURBS

LAUGHERN HOUSE *see* MARTLEY

LEA CASTLE *see* COOKLEY

THE LEASOWES *see* HALESOWEN

LEIGH

7050

ST EADBURGA.* The church of Leigh (pronounced Lye) is one of the most interesting churches in its district. The story starts with a Norman nave and chancel. The buttresses are unmistakable, although – quite exceptionally – they are stepped in section. The N window, high up as at Rock, may be original or a device to house the figure on which anon. At Rock there are both windows and blank windows in this position. The capitals are of the block type. Similarly elementary are the capitals of the chancel arch. They represent the one-scallop type. The S arcade is later Norman than the rest. Round piers, decorated scallop capitals and one trumpet-scallop capital, single-step pointed arches, i.e. end of the C12. The E and W responds indeed already have crocket capitals. The E wall of the aisle has two lancets. Later alterations are the late C13 long cusped lancets in the chancel and the W wall of the S aisle, the two-light nave windows of *c.*1300, the Dec W tower (the arch to the nave partly dies into the imposts), the re-erected Perp W porch, and the Victorian S wall of the aisle. – FONT. Norman, round, with scallops and a zigzag band.‡ – COMMUNION RAIL. Probably mid-C17. – SCREEN. In the S aisle. Perp, of

* Of Pershore.

‡ Mr Stratford is not convinced that this is a genuine piece.

one-light divisions. But how much is of 1855? – STAINED GLASS. Bits in the S aisle. – TILES. Some of the C15 inside the S door. – PLATE. Cup and Cover Paten by *H. W.*, 1571; Salver Paten, by *K. E.*, 1700; Flagon, by *Gabriel Sleath*, 1719. – MONUMENTS. In the blank Norman window is a statue of
19 Christ, about 4 ft high and dated by the VCH *c.*1100. In fact it is a re-set coffin lid of *c.*1220 with the head of a recumbent effigy missing, the arms not correctly re-adjusted, but the very French drapery in good order. It must have been a very fine piece. – Edmund Colles † 1606 (chancel S). Recumbent effigy of a man of bad character. Till the C19 he wore a real leather skull cap. Tomb-chest overcrowded with atlantes, caryatids, close strapwork, and shields. Back panel also with strapwork. The quality is not good. – William Colles † 1615 (chancel N – as are the following). Two kneeling figures facing E. The children against the tomb-chest. Pillars carry a segmental arch. – Essex Devereux † 1639. Two kneeling figures face one another. A child sits precariously on the ledge. Columns l. and r. and achievement. – Walter Devereux, *c.*1640. Alabaster. Two recumbent effigies. Canopy on four front columns. Tomb-chest with kneeling children.

LEIGH COURT. A badly restored late C16 or early C17 brick house. More interesting the two narrowly spaced LODGES with their big shaped gables and especially the great BARN with tremendous timbers. (This is not only the largest cruck building in the county, it is also the longest medieval barn. It is over 150 ft long, 34 ft wide and about the same height. There are eleven cruck trusses standing practically as first built, the gable trusses reaching only to collar-beam level, so that the roof is half-hipped. The two wagon porches are also of cruck construction. Dating must await carbon-14 analysis, but by comparison with other buildings of this order one would be entitled to guess a date not later than the early C14. FWBC)

GREAT HOUSE FARMHOUSE, Brockamin, ⅞ m. W. An exceptionally good early C18 brick house. Five bays, two storeys, with a parapet rising in the middle in a curve. The windows are segment-headed, and so are the blank panels of the parapet. Angle quoins and quoins for the centre, but the latter of even length. Round-arched mid-window. The doorway unfortunately is not original.

HOPTON COURT, 2 m. WSW. The long Late Georgian front is of little interest. Five-bay, three-storeyed centre and five-bay, two-storeyed wings. Giant pilasters, two for each wing, four for the centre. All this would not require description if it were not for the fact that *Nash* is known to have made alterations to the house after 1803 (*see* Colvin).

A ROMAN TILE KILN was found at Leigh Sinton, 1½ m. S, datable to the C2. It made roof tiles, bricks, and flue tiles.

LICKEY

9070

The Lickey Hills are the nearest hill-walking one can get, if one lives at Birmingham. The highest elevation is Beacon Hill (987 ft). From 1899 they have gradually become communal property, though much of the area had by then already been developed as gardens of well-to-do villas.

HOLY TRINITY. 1856 by *Henry Day*. Nave and chancel in one; aisles. Dull interior, whitened. E.E. style.

OBELISK, Monument Lane, E of the church. A high ashlar obelisk erected in 1834 by *John Hanson* to commemorate Henry Windsor, eighth Earl of Plymouth.

LICKHILL MANOR *see* STOURPORT

LINDRIDGE

6060

ST LAWRENCE. 1861 by *T. Nicholson* of Hereford. A large church with a proud SW steeple. The details are geometrical to ogee. The S aisle has two cross-gables, perhaps to answer the spire. – PLATE. Cup and Cover Paten 1698; Flagon and two Credence Patens 1771. – MONUMENT. Arthur Onslow, Dean of Worcester, † 1817. For its date very fanciful in the details, e.g. in the Empire forms of the sarcophagus. Above against the fancy obelisk are rays and an angel on a cloud.

EARDISTON HOUSE. A large house, stuccoed and probably of *c*.1830. Tuscan porch in the middle. The four-bay parts of the façade l. and r. of the middle have a pediment each.

LITTLE COMBERTON

9040

ST PETER. Stately, ashlar-faced Perp W tower, the arch towards the nave four-centred. In the nave three Norman windows, one with a rope motif in the head, all, according to the VCH, not *in situ*. The N doorway has a very strange tympanum with a cross and bulgy whorls, four l. and four r. The chancel and the S attachments are by *William White*, 1886. – STAINED GLASS. Original bits in the SW window. – TILES. C15 tiles in the chancel. – PLATE. Chalice and Salver Paten by *J. P.*, 1772.

NASH'S FARMHOUSE, N of the church. A large C17 timber-framed farmhouse and by its side a circular DOVECOTE of stone. Is this medieval?

LITTLE DODFORD *see* DODFORD

7040 LITTLE MALVERN

ST GILES. This was the church of a Benedictine priory founded in 1171.* Of the church chancel, central tower, and transept alone remain. The view from the plain towards chancel and tower is impressive. The chancel was accompanied by two-bay C15 chapels, which are in ruins. Beyond them it projects with a six-light E window and a three-light N and a three-light S window in both of which the reticulated head must be re-used material. The tower is Dec below – see the W and E arches – and Perp in its outside view, with panelled walls round the large bell-openings. Perp also the broad arches from the chancel into the chapels. The capitals are decorated by scrolls with writing, no doubt once painted. The Perp work dates from 1480–2, i.e. the time of Bishop Alcock. Farther W hardly anything exists. The Late Norman respond by the present entrance, W of the N transept, must be re-set. There is a small Norman doorway from the nave S side to the cloister, and that is all. – PILLAR PISCINA. The bowl has handles. – SCREEN. Of broad one-light divisions; Perp. The two foliage bands above are part of the ROOD BEAM. – STALLS. The misericords have been chopped off, but the decoration on the arms remains, heads, an angel, two pigs, etc. – SCULPTURE. Wood-carved figure of a man; where from? – Many ARCHITECTURAL FRAGMENTS. – TILES. C15, in the chancel. – STAINED GLASS. In the E and one chancel N window glass of some interest. It dates from Alcock's time, and the kneeling figures in the E window as well as the seated God the Father in the N window are well preserved. – PLATE. Cup and Cover, by *Hy. Boswell*, 1571. – MONUMENT. Front of a late C14 tomb-chest with four elegant little figures in panels. The separate head of a Knight may well have belonged to it.

LITTLE MALVERN COURT. The house stands to the W of the original priory cloisters, the refectory or prior's hall representing their W range. This is the only surviving medieval building which now forms part of the house. The N range, which may incorporate some of the stone of the original S aisle of the

* Some hazier evidence indicates a date before 1150.

church, is timber-framed at first-floor level, of very wide span and with richly moulded floor beams. Its date could be close to the Dissolution, but it was restored in the C19, very badly, and is now being restored again. The W side of the house is by *Charles Hansom*, 1860. This is attached to a round tower on the S side which contained a spiral staircase to the Elizabethan three-storey block. A second stair is in the diagonally opposite corner of this block which still retains a large untouched mullioned and transomed window uncovered during the present alterations. The E range is the refectory or prior's hall. A floor has been inserted, and there are signs in its later additions and repairs that it suffered considerable violence, probably during the Civil War.* The contrived planning of concealed stairs and small rooms shows – as indeed we know – that the house was a recusant hide-out. But the entire medieval roof is perfect. It is a five-bay double-purlin roof with cusped wind-braces to each purlin and has open collar trusses with cusping in the upper triangle. There is a spere truss with quatrefoil and dagger tracery in the spandrels between tie-beam, knee-braces, and posts. The date of the roof is early C14 and until present restoration had never been touched since the day it was ceiled when the house was secularized in the C16. It will be a remarkable piece of restoration if its smoke-blackened timbers can retain their venerable character. In this restoration, going on at the time of writing, interesting earlier evidence has been found, especially the shafted jamb of a W window of the hall, which seems C13 if not even C12. Other masonry detail has also come out, and many small finds. It is to be hoped that the results will be made known.‡

ST WULSTAN (R.C.), Wells Road. 1862 by *B. Bucknall*. The chancel is missing. Aisleless nave with windows with geometrical tracery. W portal and very big rose window over.

LITTLE WITLEY

7060

ST MICHAEL. 1867 by *Perkins*. In the early E.E. style. Nave and chancel and round apse. Bell-turret square, but set diagonally. The W corner is propped by a far-projecting bracket, rather like a bit of machicolation. The N doorway is a re-set early C13 piece, quite simple, pointed, with a continuous

*Mr Brian S. Smith emphasizes that in the archives there is no evidence of such violence.

‡Again, Mr Smith reminds me that there is documentary evidence of much work in the later C18. But is anything left of it?

roll moulding. The stone carving in 1867 was done by *Mrs Sale*, the rector's wife. Does that include the remarkably lush and free capitals of the chancel arch ? The chancel altogether is more richly adorned than the nave. – PLATE. Cup and Cover Paten, 1571.

8030

LONGDON

ST MARY. W tower of *c*.1300. The arch to the nave has three chamfers dying into the imposts. The bell-openings are tall, of two lights, with Y–tracery and a transom (cf. Upton-on-Severn). The body of the church is of *c*.1786. The S aisle has two large arched windows flanking a Venetian one. The chancel and apse are of 1868. The design is said to have been the vicar's. That he chose Norman is interesting. He must have felt that the existing church tied him to the round arch, and that un-medieval round arches would not do. – PULPIT. A charming late C18 piece with a little inlay, a thin back wall, and a small concave-sided tester. – CHANDELIER. Of brass, dated 1789, of the Baroque type. – PLATE. Chalice and Cover Paten inscribed 1627; Set by *John Wakelin & Wm. Taylor*, 1791. – MONUMENTS. Brasses to William Bridges † 1523 and wife; 3 ft ½ in. figures. – Thomas Parker † 1794. By *W. Stephens*. With a straight-sided sarcophagus before an obelisk; quite an elegant piece.

MANOR FARM HOUSE, W of the church. Brick, of three bays, with four Venetian windows.

MOAT HOUSE, S of the church. A lively half-timber front of *c*.1600, with diagonal struts and double-curved struts.

EASTINGTON HALL, 1½ m. WNW. A splendid piece of timber-framed architecture, probably built for William Bridges *c*.1500. Three sides of a square, nearly all with close-set studs. (Fine star chimneystack. The E range has elaborately carved barge-boards with vine trails to a gable, and an oriel below it. There are rich oak and rose carving, and even little figures around here. The spandrels of the doorway are fully carved too. The hall has heavy moulded beams. VCH)

LOWER GRINSTY FARM *see* FECKENHAM

LOWERHOUSE FARMHOUSE *see* EASTHAM

LOWER MOOR *see* FLADBURY

LOWER SAPEY 6060

OLD CHURCH, 1 m. SE of the new church. Norman the S doorway with scallop capitals, and in the W wall one small window.

ST BARTHOLOMEW. 1877 by *Frederick R. Kempson*. Nave and chancel with lancet windows arranged in a nicely different rhythm N from S. The chancel is a little more elaborate than the nave. Broad twin bellcote on a flat projection. The little church is quite thoughtfully designed and not at all run-of-the-mill. – PLATE. Cup 1571; Cover Paten by *S. R.*, *c.*1650.

LOWER STRENSHAM *see* STRENSHAM

LOWER TUNDRIDGE FARMHOUSE *see* SUCKLEY

LOWER WICK *see* WORCESTER, p. 318

LOWER WOLVERTON HALL *see* STOULTON

LULSLEY 7050

ST GILES. 1892–3 by *H. Rowe & Son*. Red ashlar, with an open bell-turret. The features are geometrical to Dec. – FONT. Is this C17? It is a strange shape, heavily moulded. – PULPIT. One loose Jacobean panel with one of the usual blank arches may have come from the pulpit. – COMMUNION RAIL. Jacobean, heavy, with big, elongated knobs. – SCULPTURE. Relief of a man, W wall. *c.*18 in. high. Assigned to the C12. – PLATE. Cup and Paten Cover by *H.W.*, 1571; Paten by *T.S.*, 1681; Flagon by *S.R.*, *c.*1693.

LULSLEY COURT, ¼ m. N. C16, the two r. gables of the façade with close studding, the l. one with square panels. The bargeboards and finials Elizabethan or Jacobean.

LYDIATE *see* BELBROUGHTON

THE LYE *see* STOURBRIDGE

MADRESFIELD 8040

ST MARY. 1866–7 by *F. Preedy*. Aisleless, with windows in the late C13 to early C14 style. NW tower with elaborate recessed spire. Buff stone with red stone bands. – MONUMENTS. The tablets to Earls Beauchamp are exemplarily unassuming. – Against the W wall memorial to the Hon. Edward Lygon and the Hon. Richard Somerset. By Countess *Gleichen*, *c.*1900. Three figures and Arts and Crafts decoration.

The OLD CHURCH stood close to the house.

MADRESFIELD COURT. The mansion stands in a perfect moat. The masonry of the moat walling indicates a C15 house. But of features now visible nothing is earlier than the Elizabethan age, and most is Victorian. A panel over the entrance, not *in situ*, gives the dates 1546 and 1593. Building was for the Lygons, who later became Earls Beauchamp. 1546–93 may mean the build now represented by the l. half of the S front with its stepped gables. Nearly all the rest is by *P. C. Hardwick*, who began work in 1863, completed the chapel in 1867, set up the bell-turret in 1875, and added a storey to the (old) l. half of the S wing in 1885. The house is very large, of brick, and extremely varied. Heights nowhere tally, symmetry is shunned throughout, and projections and recessions follow each other all the way round. Where this variety leads to the happiest results is in the inner courtyard. Here timber-work, the red ornamental patterns of the infilling, and the contrast of the façade of the great hall with its vast Perp windows and the less high and formal parts are in wholly successful interplay. That is not so everywhere outside. The younger Hardwick was not an exemplar of architectural discipline. The high bell-turret, however, is again an excellently calculated vertical accent. The major rooms are on the grand scale. In the GREAT HALL the minstrels' gallery is said to be structurally a C15 relic. In several rooms are chimneypieces, Elizabethan and Jacobean, which have been brought in from Kempsey and Newland. Behind the great hall is a second HALL, made in 1913, with three circular skylights and a staircase and balcony with crystal balusters. The CHAPEL is particularly interesting. It is an exceptionally complete piece of Arts and Crafts decoration of 1902. The furnishing was done by Birmingham craftsmen for Countess Beauchamp, as a wedding present to the seventh earl. Work went on till 1923. The PAINTINGS – latest Pre-Raphaelite, one might say – are by *A. Payne*. The STAINED GLASS is by him and others. – The TRIPTYCH is by *Charles Gere*. The small CRUCIFIX and the CANDLESTICKS are by *A. J. Gaskin*. – The ornamental GLASS quarries of the screen, especially pretty, are by *M. Lamplough*. – *C. R. Ashbee*'s guild also did woodwork.

TEMPLE, with four Tuscan columns and a pediment, at the end of the poplar avenue.

DOVECOTE. Brick, circular. Restored in 1867 by *Norman Shaw*. His is the curious stone inset, with a two-light window, the flight-holes, and the château dormer.

WEST and NORTH LODGES. Also by *Norman Shaw*. Picturesquely half-timbered jobs, the North Lodge with a high star chimney.

LODGE COTTAGES. By *Voysey*, 1901. A symmetrical pair with an archway between. The completely flush surrounds of the horizontal windows of several lights are unmistakable.

MALVERN *see* GREAT MALVERN

MALVERN LINK *see* GREAT MALVERN

MALVERN WELLS *7040*

The prosperity of Malvern began at Malvern Wells. The medicinal waters were discovered in the C17. However, they did not catch on at once. Neither Celia Fiennes nor Defoe mentions Malvern. The story of the effects of Dr Wall's publication of 1756 is told under Great Malvern on p. 158.

ST PETER. 1836 by *Jearrad*. Nave, transepts, and short chancel. Lancet windows, cambered ceilings. – FONT. Grossly neo-Norman. – STAINED GLASS. In the S transept clearly of *c*.1836. – In one S window *Morris* glass of 1885. – The E window with its lively composition and strong warm colours is by *Heaton, Butler & Bayne*, of 1865. – PLATE. Set by *B. P.*, 1835. – WAR MEMORIAL. By *Voysey*, 1919. On a concave-sided polygonal base a shaft, and a pediment on top. Typical Voysey lettering.

MAMBLE *6070*

ST JOHN BAPTIST. Nearly entirely of *c*.1200, i.e. the W end with a small lancet, the N wall of the nave with another small lancet, the S arcade with round piers, very plainly moulded capitals, and arches of one step and one chamfer, the chancel with renewed lancets, and the chancel arch with capitals of broad flat leaves, but already fillets down the demi-columns. The arch is moulded with much variety. So this may have been the last piece. In the S aisle a C14 tomb recess with an ogee arch. The bell-turret of timber behind the W wall is placed on a splendid system of scissor-braced members and divided from the nave by a timber-framed wall. The N (Blount) chapel is of red brick, the lower courses with blue-brick diapers of *c*.1560, the upper of *c*.1800. – STAINED GLASS. In the E window a very fine panel of the early C14 representing Christ crucified. –

PLATE. Paten 1698; Chalice probably of the same time. – MONUMENTS. Effigy of a Knight, late C13, a slender figure, wearing his helmet. Crossed legs. Both hands lie along his body, which is unusual, and he has no shield. – Brasses to John Blount and his wife, who died in 1510. The figures are 3 ft long. – Thomas Blount † 1561 and several members of the family. Tomb-chest with strapwork panels and on it not the effigy one expects but a recumbent skeleton on the customary half-rolled-up mat. Back wall with inscriptions, shields, and more strapwork.

8060

MARTIN HUSSINGTREE

ST MICHAEL. Nave and chancel in one; bell-turret. The S aisle is of 1883. The masonry of the church is Norman, and one chancel window is still recognizable inside as Norman. Perp chancel window, but the E window called *c.*1625 by the VCH on the strength of a date stone in the E gable. – MONUMENTS. Several tablets, especially one † 1775 with a very conservative foliage border of a cartouche.

COURT FARM, W of the church, is of brick, C17, with mullioned and transomed windows and a massive chimneybreast.

The RECTORY, N of the church, is C18, brick, with very fine joints. Five bays, two storeys, hipped roof.

7050

MARTLEY

ST PETER. A large building with a very red Perp W tower with large three-light W window. But the church itself is much earlier. Both nave and chancel are Norman, as the flat buttresses and stumps of buttresses prove. Norman also of course the slightly projecting N portal. One order of columns, decayed. The arch with a roll between two square mouldings; an order with small saltire crosses and another with small lozenges. The S doorway has almost exactly the same motifs. The date is probably before 1150. The capitals are scalloped. The chancel doorway has just one continuous roll. But that is more likely to belong to *c.*1200, as the small lancet windows certainly do. About the year 1315 a chantry was started in a chapel S of the chancel. This does not survive, but of that time more or less will be the chancel E window with cusped intersecting tracery, the chancel side windows, and the damaged PISCINA with its head stops. The single-framed roofs are assigned to the C14 too. The only division between nave and chancel is a timber-framed C17 tympanum. – BENCHES. Two Jacobean forms without arms or back in the chancel. – PAINTING. C13 masonry patterns and ornamental borders in the chancel. – C15 scenes in the nave on the N side: St Martin and the Beggar and a small Adoration of the Magi. – TILES. Some old ones in the chancel floor. – PLATE. Bowl of an Incense Boat of the C13; pair of undated (early C17 ?) Dishes with fleur-de-lis handles; Cups of 1571 and 1829; Salver Paten of 1715. – MONUMENTS. Alabaster Knight of *c.*1460. Good. For the front of the tomb-chest *see* Rectory; below. – George Nash † 1840. Plain Grecian sarcophagus by *J. Stephens*.

RECTORY. An attractive but quite informal and unassuming house. It contains as its centre a C14 hall whose roof timbers survive in considerable part.* In the hall over the fireplace the front slab of the alabaster TOMB of *c.*1460 in the church. Six frontally placed angels holding shields. They stand under crocketed ogee arches. The alabaster is coated with a sand-stone-looking film. To this centre were added Elizabethan wings, perhaps replacing earlier ones. The main staircase is Elizabethan too. Infilling was done *c.*1675 and *c.*1800, and the bargeboarded gables look *c.*1840. Of *c.*1675 also the two porches at entry and exit of the screens passage. Of *c.*1800 the ample bow of the N wing.

LAUGHERN HOUSE, ¾ m. ESE. Mid-Georgian with an ashlar-faced centre and two-bay brick wings continuing in the same line. In the centre tripartite, pedimented doorway, a tripartite window with two thin Ionic columns over, and a top pediment. The house is of two and a half storeys.

THE NOAK, ½ m. NW. Partly Victorian and partly C17; brick with mullioned windows.

WORKHOUSE, ¼ m. W. 1838. Brick with a plain, still Georgian seven-bay front.

(PUDFORD FARMHOUSE, 1½ m. NW. Stone house of the C17 with mullioned windows. MHLG)

*Mr Charles writes: This is probably of *c.*1300 and thus the earliest post-and-truss frame of a domestic building in Worcestershire. The front door is still the entrance to the original screens passage with a spere-truss and gallery. The hall is of the usual two bays, but with a most remarkable formation of timbers in the roof trusses. The tie-beams and knee-braces both of the spere and central truss are enormous. The principal rafters and purlins are extremely light by contrast, and the roof pitch is nearly 60 degrees. The present roof has been built over the original trusses without destroying them. The form of the struts is vaguely reminiscent of cruck construction. Both cross-wings are contemporary, though very much altered. The solar cross-wing of three bays stands some 5 ft away from the gable of the hall. The Elizabethan staircase has been built into the gap.

MERE HALL *see* HANBURY

0040

MIDDLE LITTLETON

ST NICHOLAS. A mixed church. E.E. the tower below (Perp above) and the lancets in the chancel and the nave (S). N transept of *c.*1300, but no doubt lengthened later, and the ambitious S chapel with its battlements and straight-headed three-light windows of the early C16 (built by Thomas Smith, who mentions it in his will of 1532. His brass is lost). The tower arch is a re-set doorway. It has huge leaf spandrels (cf. Offenham). *Preedy*, who restored the church in 1871, must have shifted it. – FONT. Norman, round, with tapering sides. One band of thin lozenges (cf. Suckley). – PULPIT. With Perp panels. – BENCH ENDS. Straight-topped and traceried. – PLATE. Cup and Paten Cover of 1571.

MANOR HOUSE. A beautiful and reposeful mid-C17 stone building with short gabled wings. In the centre the doorway and the two flanking three-light windows connected by a string course instead of hood-moulds. Above four-light windows.

Behind the house the great TITHE BARN of the Abbey of Evesham, built according to documentary evidence between 1367 and 1379, but according to carbon-14 analysis *c.*1260. The structure would confirm the earlier date. Stone built, buttressed, of ten bays with two S wagon porches of which one has now gone. The length is 136 ft internally, the width 32 ft. The framing consists of an aisled bay at either end and eight base-cruck trusses dividing the nine intermediate bays. One of these trusses has been replaced, and the others are now supported by inserted aisle posts and cross-beams which destroy the barn's scale and appearance. There are wind-braces throughout the length of the roof springing from the cruck-blades and rising to the roof-plate and, at the higher level, from the upper principal rafters to the top purlins (FWBC).

MILDENHAM MILL *see* NORTH CLAINES

MITTON FARMHOUSE *see* BREDON

MORTON HALL *see* INKBERROW

NAFFORD *see* ECKINGTON

THE NASH *see* KEMPSEY

NAUNTON BEAUCHAMP 9050

ST BARTHOLOMEW. W tower C14. The rest 1897 by *Hopkins*. Nave and chancel in one. – PULPIT. Of wood, and probably of *c*.1550, see the combination of linenfold panels with angle balusters and the loose leaf motifs of the top row of panels. – COMMUNION RAIL. Jacobean, with vertically symmetrical balusters. – PLATE. Chalice and Paten, by *I.N.*, 1663. – MONUMENT. Tablet with pretty surround. Long rhymed inscription to Humphrey Lyttelton † 1624.

NAUNTON COURT. Timber-framed, but the W wing of stone with an ambitious two-storeyed, canted bay window to the E. The lower floor has a transom, the upper has not. In the room on the lower floor beams with stucco vine-leaf decoration. The rooms in this wing were probably great chamber and solar to a hall on its N side. The S wing may well represent the beginning of a projected total rebuilding.

NETHERTON 9040

RUINED CHAPEL by Netherton Farmhouse, ¾ m. NE of Elmley Castle. The N doorway is Late Norman, the shafts are keeled, and the arch has typically late complicated motifs: deeply undercut zigzag with flowers (cf. Bredon etc.), two chains of crenellation with triangular merlons, the one upside down and interlocked with the other, and elongated hexagons broken round an angle.* The S doorway has an earlier Norman tympanum (probably not *in situ*) with a splendid winged dragon.‡ There are also two windows with a continuous roll, one of them in an outbuilding. The chancel seems of *c*.1200, see the one small lancet. Later C13 E window of one light. The bellcote on the broad W buttress still existed fifty years ago.

NEWLAND 7040

ST LEONARD. An unexpected group with the BEAUCHAMP ALMSHOUSES. Church and almshouses are by *P. C. Hardwick*, 1862-4. He began work at Madresfield Court in 1863. The almshouses are brick, the church is stone. The church consists

*Mr Stratford suggests that the same workman may have done the W doorway at Eckington.

‡Mr Stratford suggests the second quarter of the C12 for this tympanum and refers to tympana with fantastic animals at Egloskerry (Cornwall) and Wynford Eagle (Dorset).

of nave and chancel and has a rather thin NE steeple, turning octagonal above the ground stage. Behind it the almshouses go on. W of the church nave also the almshouses extend, and here the two jobs don't get on at all with each other. The gate tower of the almshouses with its steep French pavilion roof is too high and too broad for the church, although, seen as part of the almshouses only, its scale is right; for to the N they extend generously round two more sides of a turfed quadrangle. In axis with the gatehouse at the far end are iron GATES bought in 1871 for Madresfield Court and said to be part of the choir gates of Cologne Cathedral. They are C18. The interior of the church is remarkable for the paired marble columns in the French Early Gothic style which separate the seats in the chapel from the church and for having its walls almost completely covered with PAINTINGS in red outline with some green. – SCREEN. Stone below, iron above. – FONT. E.E., drum-shaped, with just one band of dogtooth. – In the W wall of the church is a romantic oriel, gabled as if it were part of a castle. This connected the infirmary with the chapel.*

NEWNHAM *see* EASTHAM

THE NOAK *see* MARTLEY

NORCHARD HOUSE *see* PEOPLETON

NORGROVE COURT *see* WEBHEATH

NORTHAMPTON *see* OMBERSLEY

8050

NORTH CLAINES

ST JOHN BAPTIST. Late Perp throughout, characterized by straight-topped windows, their lights with ogee heads. The S chapel is more ornate than the rest, with quatrefoiled parapet and pinnacles. The two-bay arcade has a pier which is octagonal with two small hollows in the diagonals and arches in accordance with that. Arcades of tall octagonal piers with coarse capitals and single-chamfered arches. Single-chamfered also the chancel arch and the tower arch. That is almost as if it were post-Reformation Gothic. So the architecturally best part of the church is the outer N aisle, and especially the N porch. They are a free paraphrase on Gothic by *Aston Webb*, 1886–7. –

* Mr B. S. Smith tells me that part of the C14 timber-framed chapel was re-erected as the almshouse mortuary.

TILES. C15, in the N porch. – PLATE. Cup, *c.*1571, and Paten Cover by *Henry Sutton*, 1577. – MONUMENTS. John Porter † 1577. Recumbent stone effigy on a tomb-chest with pilasters separating panels of a surprisingly Gothic shape with shell-arches. – Mary Porter † 1668. Nice tablet with pediment and an angel head at the foot. – Also two wooden tablets with cartouches and lively surrounds, † 1693 and † 1709. – Sir Harry Wakeman † 1831. By *Hollins* of Birmingham. White marble. Bust on top of a draped sarcophagus.

The nearness to Worcester betrays itself by the number of well-to-do C18 brick houses, all of five bays, and nearly all plain, except for the doorway – a standard English product for the prosperous middle class, if ever there was one. The examples are HAWFORD HOUSE and HAWFORD LODGE, 1 m. N of the church, THE FIRS (COMMON HILL HOUSE), and BEVERE MANOR, 1 m. W, on the former island of Bevere. Hawford House has segment-headed windows, Hawford Lodge a door pediment on carved brackets, Bevere Manor two shallow curved bow windows. Only BEVERE HOUSE, by *Anthony Keck*, *c.*1750, is something special. It has a porch of four Ionic columns, a Venetian window over, a tripartite lunette window above that, moulded window surrounds, and a three-bay pediment. Nash, the county historian, lived here. (In the grounds is a bridge with a pretty C18 railing. NMR)

Adjacent to HAWFORD GRANGE is a square timber-framed DOVECOTE of the late C16. Closely set studs.

PORTERSHILL, 1¼ m. NNE, is timber-framed and has star-topped chimneys, a plaster ceiling with a large uncomplicated knot, Elizabethan or Jacobean, and a late C17 staircase with twisted balusters.

(MILDENHAM MILL, ¼ m. SW of Portershill, is of brick, with the machinery still *in situ*.)

NORTH PIDDLE

9050

ST MICHAEL. 1876 by *Henry Rowe* of Worcester. Nave and chancel. The features Middle Pointed, i.e. *c.*1300. The S vestry was added in 1893. Brick-faced interior. – The chancel PISCINA is a re-used C13 bust corbel. – TILES. In the outer vestry. – PLATE. Cup and Cover Paten by *H.W.*, 1571.

NORTON

0040

ST EGWIN. W tower, nave and chancel and N transept. The church is largely of 1844, but what there is of original work is

Perp. Very large lozenge-shaped or round hood-mould stops characterize it. Perp chiefly the W tower. The four-light window in the nave on the N side is imported from Bengeworth. The entrance to the churchyard is a Perp arch, re-set, on two heads. – FONT. Octagonal, Perp, with quatrefoils. – LECTERN.
17 A splendid and mysterious piece. It was dug up in 1813 in the churchyard of Evesham Abbey, described in *Archaeologia* the year after, and finally installed at Norton in 1865. It is of a limestone similar to Purbeck, and in this as in the whole programme of carving and the details the companion piece of the Crowle lectern. It has a seated, caryatid-like figure of a cleric as its centre and rich leaf scrolls l. and r. The figure and its function are decidedly Italian, reminiscent of ambones, such as that of S. Ambrogio in Milan of *c.*1100, but the foliage is English. It may well be the *lectricium capituli* made for Abbot Adam, who ruled the abbey in 1160–91, and if so must belong to his last years. – PANELLING in the chancel, early C16, linenfold. – A separate panel with a low, broad, blank arch is Jacobean and may come from a pulpit. – The PULPIT in the church is Jacobean too, but different. Its back wall with bold reticulation is mostly probably Early Gothic Revival. – PLATE. Cup and Paten Cover by *R.C.*, 1570; Plate by *T.S.*, 1686. – MONUMENTS. Thomas Bigg † 1581 and his wife, sister of Sir Philip Hoby of Bisham. Recumbent effigies. Tomb-chest with kneeling children in profile and frontal and strapwork piers.
60 Finely detailed. – Sir Thomas Bigg † 1613. Large kneeling effigies facing one another across a prayer-desk. The children below against the base. The style is reminiscent of *Epiphanius Evesham*. Two columns. The Hanford Monument † 1616 at Eckington should be compared. – Sir Thomas Bigg † 1621. Alabaster. Recumbent effigy. Four black columns, straight top with shield. – In the church two inscription tablets to members of the Boulter family, by *Eric Gill*, † 1908 and † 1912 (the latter must be by him for stylistic reasons). – Also by *Gill* in the churchyard two Boulter gravestones, one low with a crucifix in his early Expressionist style, the other high and slender and more sentimental.*

Many black and white houses in the village.

WOODNORTON. The seat of the Duc d'Aumale and then his great-nephew the Duc d'Orléans. The earlier work is externally insignificant, the later must have extended over quite a

* The Rev. L. Guest tells me that there is a third Boulter gravestone which looks like *Gill*'s work as well.

period. A chapel was built in 1865, a gable has the date 1897. The house looks Victorian and nothing special, and the upper parts are gutted. The entrance GATES were moved to Woodnorton from Orleans House, Twickenham by the Duc d'Aumale in 1872. They are said to come from Versailles, but have lost their finest ornamental parts.

CURSUS. This site, visible only from the air, lies ¾ m. SW of Harrington railway station, in a field adjacent to the railway line.

NORTON-BY-KEMPSEY

8050

ST JAMES. Quite a large church. The first impression is that of a Victorian building, the result of the restoration by *Hopkins* and *Ewan Christian* in 1874–5. In fact the (minor) S doorway is Norman, and in the N wall is a small Norman window and a blocked doorway. Also the chancel masonry may be Norman – see the quoins. The W tower is Perp. It has one small W window. Inside the Victorian style – or rather *a* Victorian style – comes out characteristically in the gargantuan moulded capitals of the S arcade. – PLATE. Chalice and Cover by *G.S.*, 1675; Paten by *T.F.*, *c.*1677. – MONUMENTS. Thomas Brewer † 1810. A mourning woman kneeling by a pedestal. – Hooke family to 1848. Draped inscription on a sarcophagus in flat relief.

VICARAGE, W of the church. By *Hopkins*, 1875. Red brick with a big roof on steep gables.

NORTON BARRACKS. 1876. Red brick with battlements and stepped gables. A long, symmetrical façade. The stop-chamfered undersides of the window lintels ought to be observed.

ODDINGLEY

9050

ST JAMES. Almost wholly of 1851, by *R. C. Hussey*, built for J. H. Galton of Hadzor. However, the church was initially Perp, and the tower is of the C17 – see the bell-openings. The only noteworthy feature in the interior – the walls have been ruthlessly stripped – is the wooden arch to the S transept with the start of a small opening for the rood-loft stairs. – FONT. Perp ? Against the underside alternatingly a flower and an odd stirrup shape. Why ? – Jacobean COMMUNION RAIL. – Plain, but old BENCH ENDS. – Also an HOURGLASS STAND of iron, now on a front bench. – STAINED GLASS. Much of *c.*1500, both in the E and the chancel N window. In the E window a St Martin, a St Katherine, an *Orate* inscription, and several kneeling donors, including one Dns Johnes Haryes. – PLATE. Salver Paten, 1754; Cup, gilt inside, 1802.

(ROSE COTTAGE. With two late C15 spiral-fluted and octagon-topped chimneys.)

0040 OFFENHAM

ST MARY AND ST MILBURGA. 1861–2 by *F. Preedy*. E window with crude and fanciful plate tracery. Only the tower is medieval. It is of the C15, but the delightful arch to the nave must be a re-set doorway. Oversized leaf spandrels. Frieze with fleurons. – FONT. Octagonal, Perp, with fleurons in quatrefoils. – PULPIT. Open parapet with columns of various marbles, i.e. *c.*1860–70. – PLATE. Cup, *c.*1650.

OLDBURY *see* BIRMINGHAM OUTER WESTERN SUBURBS

9080 OLD SWINFORD

ST MARY. 1842–3 by *Robert Ebbles*. The recessed spire is of 1888. The church itself is of the Commissioners' type. Red sandstone. Long sides with closely set buttresses and tall windows. The geometrical tracery looks High Victorian. An odd feature of the church of 1842 is the polygonal SW projection, used as the vestry. The chancel is by *J. A. Chatwin*, 1898. Wide interior, no galleries. The thin roof timbers have tracery. – BOX PEWS. – MONUMENT to James Foster † 1853. By *P. Hollins*. Tablet with sarcophagus and a bust on top.

Close to the church the RECTORY, red brick, five bays, broken door pediment. The house was built *c.*1700.*

Nearly as close SWINFORD OLD HALL, with a rather overcrowded exterior, mid-C18, also brick. This is seven bays wide and two and a half storeys high. Giant pilasters shut off the two end bays. Venetian middle window and tripartite lunette window over. Three-bay pediment. Most of the windows have open broken curly pediments and keystones. In CHURCH ROAD also THE CASTLE, early C19, partly castellated, but lately rather spoiled by the introduction of too-antique-looking half-timbering. The row of cottages Nos 6–16 all have pointed windows, Late Georgian no doubt.

OLD SWINFORD HOSPITAL (now FOLEY COLLEGE), Hagley Road, N of the old village nucleus. The hospital was founded in 1670 by Thomas Foley. The proud original building now

* Canon Leatherbarrow refers to the petition and a letter of that year.

stands most dramatically at the back of a spacious lawn.* It is 68 of exceptional height and compactness for C17 almshouses. Brick. Three storeys, the top one in the gables. There are three of them, and behind the middle one is a turret and a (new) cupola. The turret rises segmentally to make space for the clock. The fenestration of this front is nearly symmetrical and all of small two-light windows. Only in the gables are they of three lights – stepped, in the North Country fashion. On the roof also two lines of eight chimneys each, emphatically part of the composition. The doorway must be taken last. It takes some time to digest. There is a round arch on pilasters, and the pilasters stand in front of rustication, but outside that are monstrous volutes and there are smaller volutes at the top of the doorway and l. and r. of the top. The DOOR is original. Front garden with original gatepiers. Also at the back a smaller contemporary range with slightly projecting wings. Small mullioned windows.

OMBERSLEY

8060

ST ANDREW. The typical estate church, large, well-built, and in the grounds of the Court, though in this case easy of access from the village too. The architect was *Thomas Rickman*, and the work took from 1825 to 1829. The style Rickman chose is the Dec, with flowing tracery. The aisle windows are of three lights, the E window has four. The stately W tower carries a recessed spire connected by thin flying buttresses with the pinnacles of the parapet (the Louth type). To the l. and r. of the tower side entrance lobbies. The chancel is short and preceded by transepts. Spacious, high interior, but rather dull and thin arcades of Perp type. Wooden galleries kept inside the aisles. Plaster rib-vaults throughout. – BOX PEWS. – Original STAINED GLASS. – STOVE. High Gothic iron stove.‡ – PLATE. Cup and Cover Paten of 1573; Cup of 1630; two Flagons and Almsdish by *R. C.*, 1684; Paten on foot by *Stephen Coleman*, 1697. – In the churchyard a CROSS of the C15. Quatrefoils on the base, a C17 or C18 ball at the top.

OLD ST ANDREW, S of the church. Only part of the chancel was allowed to remain, and this is now the Sandys Mausoleum. New W and E walls were provided *c.*1830. The side walls are late C13, with small cusped lancets of deep mouldings shafted

*To the l. *Sir Frederick Gibberd*'s new building for the college, a rather featureless curtain-walling job of 1956–7.

‡So Mr R. J. Collins tells me.

inside. SEDILIA with pointed trefoiled arches. Two head-stops help to support the arches. – MONUMENTS. For example Edwin Lord Sandys † 1797 by *Nollekens*, with a bust on top, and Samuel Sandys † 1685 by *William Bird*, a cartouche with ugly putti.

OMBERSLEY COURT. Built in 1723–6 by *Francis Smith* of Warwick for the first Lord Sandys. The house was then brick with stone dressings. It was refaced in 1812–14 by *J. Webb*, after *Nash* had made plans for sweeping alterations to the façades in 1808. Seven-bay entrance side (E) of two and a half storeys. Porch by Webb of four unfluted Ionic columns. The other sides have hardly any pronounced emphases. A lower wing to the N. A second one originally extended to the S. The STABLES quadrangle with a high arched entrance under a pediment is entirely *Webb*'s. The glory of the house is its INTERIOR. The entrance hall runs through two storeys. A balcony passage at the back connects the upper rooms. The lower part has pilasters and blank niches. Noble ceiling, probably mostly of 1814, with simply distributed panels. Of the Smith period entirely the three principal rooms to the W, all three with dark wood panelling punctuated by pilasters of different orders and details. Fine door surrounds and overdoors. In the Saloon marble chimneypiece, the lintel with a young head and garlands l. and r. The staircase is also of *c.*1725. Each step has three balusters: twisted – columnar – twisted. The tread-ends are carved, and the underside is wonderfully wavy. Plaster ceiling of *c.*1725 too. The service staircase with small skylit dome and a simple handrail is of the Webb time. The two rooms l. and r. of the entrance hall are probably Webb's in their details. On the first floor a room with painted Chinese silk panels and drapes over the doors, rather in the Brighton-Pavilion taste. On the second floor a room with a *Dufour* wallpaper of Constantinople, datable to *c.*1816. – LODGE on the Worcester road. No doubt again of *c.*1815. Modest segmental arches with paterae and only one dwelling.

Ombersley is a specially rewarding village. The MAIN STREET runs S–N with a roundabout two-thirds down. Starting from the S there are the CROWN INN, late C17 or early C18, brick, whitewashed, with five even gables, then the KING'S ARMS, partly pre-Reformation, timber-framed with a nice early C17 plaster ceiling inside, some estate cottages of perhaps *c.*1840–50, a castellated four-bay brick house, and then, lying back, the VICARAGE, late C18, of five bays, the doorway with a broken pediment. Opposite this series some more timber-framed houses and the churchyard. By the roundabout turn W for the DOWER HOUSE, early C17, timber-framed, with square panels. Inside a modest but pretty plaster ceiling with stray motifs and two stone chimneypieces. Back to the main street and now N to the POST OFFICE, brick, of three bays, the middle one up to full height treated as a giant blank arch.

At the N end of the village are also two CRUCK HOUSES. (The first has decorated Victorian timberwork on the gable facing the roundabout in which the upper part of the cruck blades are, with difficulty, discernible. The front framing is also restored, in square panelling which bears little resemblance to the original wall-frame. The crucks are wholly visible at the other gable and also inside the house. The house has been floored throughout and subdivided into small rooms, but it was an open-roofed, two-bay hall with solar and service bay at each end – the typical four-bay cruck house to which any date pre-1450 could be given. The other house, farther N on the opposite side of the road, now consists of the two-bay hall and service cross-wing of two bays. The solar bay was demolished over fifty years ago: at least the present owner, who has been there that length of time, does not remember it. As in the former house, the great central cruck arch dividing upper from lower bay of the hall still survives but is concealed by plaster and wallpaper. Only one bay of the cross-wing is floored, and this, being at the service end, may be as originally built for keeping livestock in the unfloored bay. FWBC)

At HADLEY, E of Ombersley, HADLEY CROSS FARMHOUSE, timber-framed, early C17 with square panels and gables. (Also a cruck cottage. NMR)

(At NORTHAMPTON, 1¼ m. NW, EDEN FARMHOUSE, late C17, brick, whitewashed, with a two-storeyed porch. MHLG)

ORLETON

6060

ST JOHN BAPTIST. Brick; of 1816. Small W tower. Slightly pointed-arched nave S windows, chancel E window with intersecting cast-iron tracery.

ORLETON COURT. H-shaped, of brick. One short side has a five-bay front with one-bay pediment.

OVERBURY

9030

ST FAITH. The church is dominated by its Perp central tower. But the nave is Norman. The arcades have round piers, many-scalloped capitals, square abaci, and single-stepped arches. Capitals and bases are a little later N than S. S has decorated hood-moulds. The Norman windows stand above the spandrels, not the apexes, of the arches. S doorway with tall scallop and volute capitals.* Shafts with fillets, round, much-moulded arch. i.e. a date later than the arcades. The finest piece of architecture in the church is, however, the E.E. chancel. Pairs of lancets, shafted outside and inside and with nicely moulded surrounds. The E window of course is Perp. Internally the chancel is rib-vaulted in two bays. The ribs and the vaulting-shafts have fillets and the bays figured bosses. Stiff-leaf capitals. The arches of the crossing tower have been severely interfered with. What for instance are the imposts standing on? The tower vault is of 1880. The bell-openings must be post-Perp and may be C17. Dec aisle windows. – FONT. Of a steep goblet shape. Norman, with two standing figures (one holding a church) and a large symmetrical scroll panel. Nearly half the upper half is a re-doing of the C18 (?). This obscures the issue. The original parts may be of *c.*1150–60.‡ – PULPIT. With parts of the C15 SCREEN. – BENCH ENDS. With traceried panels. – PLATE. Cup and Paten, the latter dated 1571. By *M* on a heart. – The LYCHGATE of heavy timbers and with the stone memorial block inside is by *Sir Herbert Baker*.

OVERBURY COURT. A large, early C18 stone house. The façade is of seven bays with a three-bay centre projection and rusticated quoins of even length. Doorway with unfluted Ionic columns and pediment. The windows with moulded surrounds, that in the middle just a little emphasized. The attic storey above the cornice is more typically early C18 than the rest of this façade. Short, segment-headed windows in the three middle bays, which also carry a pediment. Round the corner to the l. a five-bay side with a pedimented doorway with Gibbs surround and a similar attic. Round the corner to the r. a five-bay front with porch-like centre projection. This rises to a proper third floor with one large round-arched window. Little is left of *Norman Shaw*'s work of 1895, and recent work was done by *Victor Heal* (1959). The OFFICES are a little more

*Mr Stratford notes the colonnettes of the inner order, which have no necking. That is a West Country peculiarity (Wells, St Davids) and suggests the end of the C12.

‡Mr Stratford compares the foliage with the Gloucestershire lead fonts and the stone font at Coleshill (Warwickshire), which latter also has a similar figure.

rustic, but all the more lovable for that. Five bays, mid-gable, slender wooden cross-windows. Doorway with surround of stones of alternating sizes. Hipped roof and lantern.

Overbury is one of the most attractive villages in Worcestershire. Houses of stone with gables and timber-framed houses are thrown together, and houses Stuart and Georgian and houses Late Victorian. Of the latter some timber-framed ones are at once recognizable (e.g. the STORES). But the best is *Norman Shaw*'s VILLAGE HALL of 1895–6, ashlar, with a neo-Tudor end and a heavy English Baroque porch with an arch of alternating rustication. Big dormers in the roof to give lantern lighting to the hall. The best C17 house is a three-gabled stone house dated 1639. The best Georgian house is just N of the village hall: RED HOUSE, of brick, three bays and three storeys and six Venetian windows. *Shaw* did improvements of cottages as well as the Village Hall.

SCHOOL. 1876. Ashlar, Tudor with a high bellcote.

BREDON HILL FORT *see* Bredon Hill.

PARK HALL *see* CHURCHILL

PEBWORTH

1040

ST PETER. Mostly Perp. Only the attractive four dormers in the nave roof are a C19 innovation. In the chancel a late C13 single-light window. The W tower had a very large W window and still has a high arch to the nave. S arcade with piers of a typical Perp section: octagonal with small hollows in the middles of the diagonals. The arch corresponds. Niche with canopy in the S wall. The S aisle is called the 'new Ile' in the will of Edmund Marten in 1528. – FONT. Perp, octagonal, with fleurons in quatrefoils. – PULPIT. Jacobean, with blank arches and arabesque top panels. – COMMUNION RAIL. Late C17, deprived of half its balusters. – STAINED GLASS. Bits in the E window. – MONUMENTS. The effigy of a priest of 1380 (*Little Guide*) in the chancel floor is at present all but invisible. – Defaced effigy of a priest in the churchyard. – Robert Martin † 1620. Tablet with columns and some strapwork. – Robert Martin † 1720. By *Edward Woodward* of Chipping Campden. Stone tablet with pilasters, a segmental pediment, and an urn on top. Two putto heads below the inscription. – Elizabeth Shekell † 1825 and others. By *Lewis* of Cheltenham. The usual mourning female by the pedestal of an urn.

BROAD MARSTON PRIORY. Mostly early C17, also the detached former chapel.

9080

PEDMORE

ST PETER. Crude, but impressive Norman tympanum with Christ and the Signs of the Evangelists, close in style to the Herefordshire School. Christ has a Mongol moustache, blesses with a huge hand, and wears a crown. He is placed in an almond-shaped glory, and this – very English, i.e. of Anglo-Saxon descent, and very barbaric – ends in two monster-heads.* The angel, bird, and beasts all look towards Christ, the ox throwing its head up. Only the angel holds on to the almond-glory. Also Norman the two-stepped arch to the organ chamber, once the chancel arch of the Norman church. The present church is by *Preedy*, 1871. W tower, nave and aisles; C13 tracery, plate and bar. – FONT. Octagonal, with panels with figures of eight. Is that Jacobean? – PLATE. Cup of 1571.

(PEDMORE HALL. Five-bay centre of three storeys with upper giant pilasters and two projecting, low wings. But there are also C17 windows, and the staircase with its openwork panels looks mid-C17. NMR)

8030

PENDOCK

CHURCH. Built *c*.1170, see the N doorway with one order of colonnettes, decorated scroll capitals, a zigzag arch, and hood-mould with pellets, and the chancel arch, no doubt widened later. Also one order of colonnettes, and also scallop capitals.‡ The W tower is Perp and has a two-light W window with pretty tracery and a pyramid roof. – SCREEN. The dado with blank tracery panels remains. – COMMUNION RAIL. Jacobean. The top rail may not belong to the balusters. – BENCHES. Some are C16 and have linenfold panelling. – PLATE. Plate and Flagon of 1748; Bread Knife of 1750; Cup of 1766.

PRIOR'S COURT, to the NE. Late C17, brick, H-shaped with end-gables. Good chimneystacks with arched panels.

7060

PENSAX

ST JAMES. 1832–3 by *Thomas Jones*. This is an amazing job. The nave is wide, as was usual in the thirties, and the buttresses along the sides may also fit the thirties. But otherwise the

* Mr Stratford suggests that the carver may have misunderstood the type of representation of Christ where he sets his feet on two beasts.

‡ Mr Stratford compares the scallop capitals which are decorated with a cross with Pirton, the zigzag on the abaci with Beckford and Eldersfield, the pellets with Ashton and Queenhill, the furrowed zigzag with Malvern Priory.

degree of exactitude in the Perp detailing is far beyond what one would expect from anyone in 1832 except Rickman. The W tower is substantial, and its three-light W window as well as those of the nave N and S sides have surrounds no Late Victorian could have improved on. The chancel is a rebuilding of 1891. – PLATE. Chalice and Paten of 1719.

PENSAX COURT, E of the church. The house with its steep, gaily bargeboarded gables and its central cupola looks *c.*1840 and is a pretty sight.

PEOPLETON

9050

ST NICHOLAS. Nave and chancel and a low brick W tower built into the nave in the early C19 to encase a timber bell-turret. The beautifully carved beam is part of the former ROOD SCREEN. It has the most delicate leaf frieze. The nave W windows are Perp. A variety of other windows, including two in the chancel which one can hardly accept as pre-Reformation. The chancel arch is finely moulded Perp. – COMMUNION RAIL. Probably mid-C17. – MONUMENT. Tablet to Mark Dineley † 1682. Gristly cartouche; designed with gusto.

NORCHARD HOUSE, ½ m. NE. Brick. The centre of the house is Queen Anne, with five narrowly set bays. Later porch with capitals decorated with swags. Also Late Georgian lower one-bay additions l. and r.

WHITE HOUSE. Cruck-built hall, brick-cased during the last century but still containing more original timbers internally than any similar house in the county. Instead of the normal four bays under one roof with hipped gables at each end, this house has a solar cross-wing in place of the upper bay. The cruck part could be C14, the cross-wing C15 (FWBC).

PERSHORE

9040

THE ABBEY

It is assumed that Pershore Abbey was founded by King Oswald about 689. It was destroyed about 976, restored by Ethelwold in 983 and reformed by him. Nothing is known about the date of beginning of the Norman building. A re-entry of the monks is recorded for 1102. So perhaps one can assume that building at Pershore, as at Gloucester and Tewkesbury, started about 1090. Again no fixed date exists for the rebuilding of the chancel, but at the consecration of 1239 it was probably complete. A fire in 1288 did grave damage to the building, and the chancel vault is clearly after that date and very probably not much after. The abbey was dissolved in 1539. The nave and the Lady Chapel at the E end were then pulled down. The N transept collapsed, and in 1686 the crossing tower was shored up on that side. The E apse dates from 1847, the general restoration by *Scott* from 1862–5. The restorations of the early C20 are by *Sir Harold Brakspear*. The abbey is built of local limestone. It was originally *c*.325 ft long (Tewkesbury *c*.325, Norman Gloucester *c*.365). The nave arcades are laid out by young trees W of the remaining parts, and GATES mark the W wall. Of the monastic buildings which were S of the church nothing at all is preserved.

EXTERIOR. So what we have is a stump of the nave, the crossing, the transepts, the chancel, and the apse. Of this only the first three are Norman, and examination should start by the SOUTH TRANSEPT, because the work on major medieval buildings nearly always started at the E end, and as the chancel has disappeared, and so has the N transept, the S transept contains the earliest work. The S wall shows first of all at the very foot the bases of two shafts of the blank arcading of the former SLYPE, then the roughly blocked place where the night-stair inside the transept would, by a doorway, have led into the DORMITORY, then three widely spaced C13 lancets, and finally in the gable intersecting blank arcading with zigzag at r. angles to the wall. So that gable can hardly be older than the mid C12, which means very slow building, if the start dates back to before 1100, and if it can be taken for granted that the side where the monastic buildings were was treated with some priority. In the E wall is one shafted window and the blocked opening into a former transept E chapel. That chapel was replaced about 1300 by a new sacristy two bays from N to S and two bays from E to W. The details which remain, i.e. shafts and vaulting springers, are elegant and slender. There is also wall arcading with crockets. In the transept W wall is a Perp window. Of the Norman N transept nothing is preserved, except an arched opening in the tower towards its roof. The straight-headed five-light window in the new wall after the collapse of the transept is probably C17 Gothic.*

The NAVE can be reconstructed from what little survives as of the type of Tewkesbury and Gloucester. The E responds and the first piers, merging into buttresses of 1913, were high and round – 25 ft, as against Gloucester's and Tewkesbury's 30½.

*The VCH says guardedly 'late'.

That means that the gallery was very small. The naves at Gloucester and Tewkesbury were begun *c.*1120–30. One can assume a similar date for Pershore. The piers have bulgy, simply moulded capitals and round abaci (cf. Tewkesbury and Gloucester). Of these upper parts all that can be seen is the jamb-shaft of the E end of blind arcading which must have incorporated the clerestory windows. The aisles were of course very high, as the blocked arches into the transepts show. They have shafts with one-scallop capitals. The aisles were vaulted – see the E springers. The vaults were no doubt groin-vaults. The elegant doorway into the former cloister must be of *c.*1300. Above it is a jamb of a window of the same date.

Now the CHANCEL. This is characterized by the lancet windows in aisles and clerestory which fit a building period between *c.*1200 and the consecration in 1239. In the N aisle is one different window, three stepped lancet lights under one arch, perhaps a replacement made soon after (*see* the interior). In the S aisle are two Dec five-light windows. The E end is strange in that it had the former straight-headed Lady Chapel of three bays framed by two one-bay chapels and had in addition a N and a S chapel like a minor second transept. The English, ever since Canterbury, had liked that kind of plan, but at Pershore it clashes with the high chancel which ends in an apse of three sides of an octagon. The present low apse is a somewhat starved replacement. A corbel-table runs along the top of the clerestory. The two E chapels have the earliest details so far met in the chancel. They have flat buttresses with nook-shafts, and the nook-shafts have fillets and trumpet-scallop and crocket capitals. That is hardly later than 1200. The N and S chapels (the S chapel was rebuilt by *Scott*) have different buttresses of a proper C13 type, with set-offs.

The CROSSING TOWER is a beautiful piece of the early C14. It has plenty of ballflower decoration to confirm such a date. Polygonal buttresses with pinnacles (of 1870). Two two-light windows in each side with very curious tracery consisting of a broad top trefoil into which the pointed-trefoiled heads of the two lights stick up. No ogees yet. The bell-openings are also two of two lights, but there are blank two-lights l. and r. They have all tracery with reticulation units, and gables cover their tops.

INTERIOR. We must again start in the SOUTH TRANSEPT. What 9
is there at once evident is that, just as at Gloucester and Tewkesbury, the system of elevation differed in the chancel

from that in the nave. Whereas, as we have seen, the nave had high piers and high narrow aisles, the arches into the chancel aisle show a perfectly normal height, which in Norman terms means enough space for a gallery of normal height. The arches are simple, with just one roll moulding, and the capitals are simple, with just one scallop. The blocked opening to the E chapel or apse follows in the E wall. Here one capital is even more distinctly ancient, i.e. of *c.*1100 in type, the one with a vestigial volute. To the S of the blocked opening is the shafted window. Below it blank arcading begins which continues round the S wall. The shafts are all missing, but the arches are there and have thinly incised zigzag. Above the aisle arch is the blocked arch to the gallery, above the apse arch the blocked arch of an upper apse at gallery level (cf. Tewkesbury and Gloucester). Then a low wall passage which again runs on in the S wall. The shafts have block and scallop capitals. The upper part of the wall sets a problem. There is above the gallery a row of small single openings with short shafts and a wall passage. Were they the clerestory openings, i.e. open to the outside? The external wall shows nothing of that. Or were they an upper triforium followed by a clerestory yet higher up? The space for such a clerestory is there, and the fact that one can see no traces is not surprising, as the building of the vault involved a rebuilding of the top parts of the wall. If Pershore had a clerestory at that level, then the result was a four-tier elevation such as Clapham has postulated for Tewkesbury as well. Four-storey elevations are a very rare thing before the mid C12, when for a short time they become an accepted system in French Early Gothic cathedrals (Noyon etc.). On the Continent these French cathedrals are preceded by St Donatian at Bruges and Tournai Cathedral, but both are later than Tewkesbury and Pershore (*c.*1130–40). The wall passage at Pershore anyway continues in the S wall with a larger two-bay opening, and this has columns with zigzag. The E wall passage also has slightly lighter capitals than the stages below. That tallies with the zigzag arches in the gable outside and shows that it took a long time before the top levels of the S transept were reached. In the NORTH TRANSEPT what little survives fits this interpretation. The S transept vault has ridge-ribs, one pair of tiercerons in the E and W walls, and large bosses. One shield refers to a C15 abbot (Abbot Newnton 1413–57), but the vault is earlier. More of this will be said presently.

The CROSSING arches have responds of paired demi-shafts, once more as at Tewkesbury and Gloucester. Among the capitals is one with lively busts (SW pier). The arches are single-stepped. Above is the early C14 work, a glorious grille of window openings and blank panelling, with the window openings having double-tracery, one layer to the outside, one to the inside.

The CHANCEL is of four bays plus the canted bays which, 27
with the entrance arch to the former Lady Chapel, form the three-sided apse. The piers are almost as exuberantly subdivided as at Wells. There, in work begun *c.*1185, they have twenty-four shafts in eight groups, at Pershore sixteen in eight groups, with singles in the diagonals and triplets in the main directions. The arches are subdivided accordingly. The capitals are of the richest stiff-leaf, much richer than the shafts in the W bays of the chancel aisles, which are clearly early stiff-leaf and close to the preceding crocket type. So let the aisle walls be *c.*1210 and the chancel piers *c.*1230. Above the arches are hood-moulds on stiff-leaf sprays. In the spandrels the vaulting-shafts start. They end again in lush stiff-leaf, but they end very low compared with the upper system of openings. This is of a peculiar and very characteristic kind. The clerestory lancets are placed very high up, but a wall passage runs inside at a much lower level. From that level rises a stepped tripartite shafting of clusters of shafts with stiff-leaf capitals tying the lancets in with the passage. It is a pulling together of what used to be gallery or triforium with the clerestory, and the result is a two-tier instead of three-tier elevation. Pershore follows in this St David's and Llanthony (of *c.*1180 and *c.*1190 respectively). That far the chancel represents what was consecrated in 1239.

Whether the former Lady Chapel and the arrangements at the E end connected with it should be dated so early remains doubtful: for in the apse part and in the remaining W bay of the Lady Chapel Purbeck marble shafts appear in profusion. They also occur in the one three-light N window which seems an advance on normal lancets. Also the entry arch from the apse to the Lady Chapel is higher than the others, and a certain muddle appears in the shafts of the S entry pier. The confusion becomes worse when one looks up and sees what is happening in the tripartite arcading above, which is here of course blank. The shafts are gathered together by big round capitals and they are late trumpet scallops, almost as if pleated. Such capitals seem impossible after 1239, and also shortly before 1239. Are they then re-used from the earliest years of the new chancel, the years of the outer walls of the E chapels?* What is old in the first bay of the Lady Chapel is easily distinguished from what is competent E.E. of 1847. In the W bay of the S chancel aisle the former entry (of *c*.1300) to the sacristy is as evident as we found it outside.

The aisles have quadripartite rib-vaults and so have the chapels, except for the SE chapel, whose vault has ridge-ribs
28 and is perhaps a remodelling. The chancel vault is extremely beautiful and historically very important; for it must have been re-done entirely in the late C13 and probably shortly after the fire of 1288. This being so, it is remarkable that the early and the late C13 blend so perfectly in the chancel. The historic interest of the vault is this. It consists of transverse arches, diagonal ribs, ridge-ribs, one pair of tiercerons to N and S, but in addition lierne-ribs forming a kind of scissors movement: open–closed–open–closed, all along. Now these scissor liernes appear in the crypt of St Stephen's Chapel in the Palace of Westminster in 1291 etc., and at Bristol Cathedral in 1298 etc.
26 As at Pershore the beautiful large bosses are still naturalistic and not yet of the bossy C14 foliage type, Pershore must be as early as any place in this enrichment of rib-vaulting introduced with a view to creating pleasant confusion. It is indeed delightful to watch how the eye shifts from seeing what has just been described to seeing instead a system of stars. The S transept vault has bosses of the same kind and so was probably re-done at the same time. Perhaps the fire of 1288 brought down the Norman crossing tower and so called for a renewal of vaults. It must, however, be noted that no traces of a fire appear in the lower stonework.

FURNISHINGS. FONT. Norman, round, with tapering sides. Christ and the Apostles under beaded intersecting arches. Against the shaft trumpet-scallop capitals. The dating is not easy, for reasons set out below by Mr Stratford.‡ – REREDOS.

* Cf. the following note by Mr Stratford for his answer.

‡ Mr Neil Stratford comments on Pershore as follows. A number of capitals survive in crossing and transepts, and in a photograph taken in 1961 a pile of fragments is visible in the S transept, including two Norman capitals, one of the foliage type of the Lincoln façade frieze (of the 1140s), the other similar to the decoration of the font. Both these capitals have disappeared since. Capitals which remain *in situ* are generally of the simple volute, scallop, or block types. The scallop capitals (E crossing arch, S) have trefoil-leaf patterns like the font, and two heads. The capital of the arch from N transept into N

In the S transept, stone, Perp, blank traceried arcading, and a foliage frieze as in wood in rood screens. – SCREEN. N transept. Part of a screen inscribed: MC bis bino triplex et addere quarto/ Ann Willelmis d[ni] Newnton fect Abbas. Also a king's head with H.VI. a° XII and an abbots's head with W.N. a° XXII. All this makes it 1435. – PAINTING. Traces of a large figure against the N side of the SE crossing pier. – On the W wall memorial to Dr Williamson † 1865. – STAINED GLASS. SE chapel E by *Kempe* *c.*1885. – TILES. In the SE chapel; C15. – PLATE. Flagon by *William Fawdery*, 1707; Chalice by *John Payne*, 1752. – MONUMENTS. Knight, cross-legged, 29 *c.*1280. – Priest, probably early C15, much rubbed off. On a low tomb-chest with quatrefoils. – Thomas Haselwood; Late Elizabethan. Standing monument, long and low, with one recumbent effigy and two large kneeling figures l. and r. Three columns in front and a straight top. – Fulk Haselwood; Jacobean. The effigies are not preserved. Kneeling children against the tomb-chest.

ST ANDREW. In a typical position in relation to the abbey premises. The SW tower is Perp and was built into the very wide earlier Perp S aisle of a Norman church which received a N arcade about 1190 or 1200. The arcade is of five bays with round piers, round trumpet-scallop capitals, and single-chamfered arches. The nave W window is Dec (reticulated tracery). The S arcade has castellated capitals. – PAINTING. Moses and Aaron and Commandments and Creed all in one frame. Early C18. From the abbey. In a very bad state at the time of writing. – PLATE. Set by *Jos. Clare*, 1719.

---

chancel aisle has beaded interlace, and one of the triforium capitals has the same, but spreading indiscriminately round the angles. On the S crossing arch W is again beaded interlace, but with human busts. No similar capitals survive in Worcestershire, but their style indicates the second quarter of the C12, which fits the general similarities with Tewkesbury and Gloucester. However, the E crossing arch S capital raises a problem. The same leaves, as has been said, occur on the font. But the font has trumpet-scallop capitals on the stem, and that makes a date before 1170 seem unlikely. Perhaps the capitals, and hence the upper parts of the crossing, do not date from the original period? One thing is certain: they are *in situ*. A further complication are the capitals of the E triforium opening of the chancel. Their trumpet-scallop forms are of the very latest variety, the so-called cornucopia variety which occurs with stiff-leaf and moulded capitals e.g. at Bretforton, Slimbridge (Glos.), and Wells (nave, W end), i.e. well into the C13. They can therefore at Pershore be *in situ* too. So trumpet scallops at Pershore occur for nearly fifty years, from the font to the E end triforium.

THE TOWN

Pershore is a pleasant little town, mostly of brick houses, two storeys high. Three storeys is a distinction. Specifically Victorian display is absent.

BROAD STREET is really a market square. It stretches at r. angles to the abbey towards the main E–W street. The houses are not eventful. The BAPTIST CHAPEL, though free-Gothic, manages to fit in its façade of 1888 well.* Otherwise Nos 1–5 on the W side is late C18 of three storeys. It is of three bays and has two canted bay windows, Venetian windows over, and tripartite windows above them. On the S side several nice doorways and nice one-storeyed bay windows, and so to the ashlar-faced THREE TUNS HOTEL, which has a pretty upper veranda. The decorative E side of Broad Street belongs to High Street and Bridge Street.

We go first down BRIDGE STREET. The Three Tuns is at the NW corner. The porch is Victorian. Opposite, facing Broad Street, is BARCLAYS BANK, late C18, of seven bays, with an elaborate tripartite doorway with segmental fanlight (and a charming Gothick staircase; *C. L.*). Bedford House, No. 7, is Regency, stuccoed, with an iron upper veranda. Then the finest house in Pershore, PERROTT HOUSE, built *c.*1760 by Judge Perrott, a Baron of the Exchequer. Three bays, three storeys. Canted bay windows, Venetian (and bent round) on the ground floor. Venetian also the doorway and the middle window. The whole third floor has tripartite windows. One-bay pediment. All this is typical county motifs, but for the interior decoration the judge must have employed London designers (*Robert Adam*, who designed for Croome d'Abitot ?) and craftsmen. Extremely delicate stucco work with a reclining female figure in the centre of one room, wall panels of musical instruments and tyrsuses and grapevine in another. Delightful staircase to the top of the house with restrained panels and glazed skylight. After that WESTERN HOUSE with a broken pediment on Tuscan columns and further variations on the theme of Tuscan columns for doorways. Just compare Nos 27, 29, and 31. Then, on the other side of the street, No. 48 with a Victorian Gothic stone portal, Nos 56–8 with a double doorway of three Tuscan columns and parapet with three roundels, No. 60 with two canted bay windows and rusticated window lintel

*The chapel itself is of 1843.

(late C18), Nos 70–2 with two small doorways, their hoods curving backward in plan, No. 74 with a porch of columns with swag-capitals and a hood on carved brackets, and so to the MANOR HOUSE HOTEL, Early Victorian Tudor with barge-boarded gables and a castellated porch, the red brick MILL HOUSE and CORN MILL opposite, and finally PERSHORE BRIDGE, perhaps partly still medieval. It is in two parts, the first of three segmental arches with cutwaters, the second of one large middle arch and five smaller ones also with cut-waters.

Back now to the centre and down HIGH STREET, where there is much less of interest. The MIDLAND BANK is the best building here. It is Early Georgian, of five bays and three storeys, with segment-headed windows, decorated keystones, and quoins of even rustication. Next the ANGEL HOTEL, well re-fronted in 1920. (Inside an inlaid overmantel and a painted female figure dated 1575; *see W.A.S.*, II.) No. 19 has a nice doorway with fanlight, Nos 21–5 a double doorway with Adamish columns and in the cellars medieval tunnel-vaults. In one of them is a beautiful pointed-cinquefoiled C13 PISCINA, apparently *in situ* so that this must have been a chapel. The RURAL DISTRICT OFFICES are of three bays and three storeys, the same provincial type as met before. Canted bay windows, and on the top floor tripartite lunette windows instead. Doorway with broken pediment on unfluted Ionic columns.

INSTITUTE OF HORTICULTURE, 1 m. SE. AVONBANK, an ashlar house of *c.*1840, spacious, with an Ionic porch, is the nucleus. *Richard Sheppard & Partners* in 1955 added a straightforward curtain-wall range, and in 1964–6 one range of light engineering bricks between the former and the house and a higher smaller block behind. These two new jobs are in the idiom now fashionable, with a broken skyline, sudden mono-pitches, and an odd tubular feature cut off diagonally at the top – a Le Corbusier gimmick (cf. La Tourette). It contains a staircase.

PINVIN

9040

ST NICHOLAS. Nave and chancel and a funny bellcote (of 1884–5) triangular in plan. Plain Norman S doorway, just stepped, but the two steps rounded (cf. Worcester Cathedral). Over the porch entrance an E.E. stiff-leaf capital. – FONT. Late Norman, octagonal, each side with two very elongated round-arched blank panels. – PULPIT. Incorporating the legs of a Jacobean communion table. – WALL PAINTING. On the nave S wall, remains of a late C13 cycle in two tiers. Two at least of the scenes are well preserved and not blatantly restored. They show the Adoration of the Magi and the Crucifixion. Also, above, good drapery round the legs of a seated figure. – PLATE. Cup and Cover Paten by *H. W.*, 1571.

8040

PIRTON

ST PETER. The church has two treasures, one large, the other tiny. One is the timber-framed N tower, the only one in Worcestershire which has aisles like such Essex towers as Margaretting; the other is the Pirton Stone. The tower has narrowly spaced studs and big diagonal braces and internally between nave and aisles double scissor-braces of a formidable scantling. The VCH calls the tower early C16, but its timbering, with great cruck forms as braces, and its proportions would suggest a date in the C14 or even earlier. Norman nave, Dec chancel. S doorway with one order of colonettes with bulgy scallop capitals and an abacus decorated with angular Ses in relief. The arch has zigzag at r. angles to the wall. The doorway is set in a wall-projection, a motif not unusual in the county (cf. p. 15). The N side of the nave has the outline of a doorway and two windows. It is clear from the changing thickness of the walls and certain irregularities outside that the E part of the nave was once a central tower. The wide chancel arch also has one order of colonnettes. The arch is single-stepped. The top stone has a carved figure upside down. – SCULPTURE. One Norman corbel-head above the S doorway;
14 inside. – The PIRTON STONE is a mysterious object which would deserve a scholar's full investigation. It is only $4\frac{3}{4}$ by $3\frac{1}{2}$ in. in size, and is a die for casting. The material seems some sort of lithographic stone. It is roughly elliptical and shows, in a style probably Early Norman, Christ crucified with the Virgin and St John. But their figures are fragmented by parts of the stone which are raised and seem to have remained uncarved. There are four such raised areas, and their existence makes the rest a cross-shape. Also there is a frame round the raised part again lowered as much as the Crucifixion, and this again has simple Norman motifs. However, at the top of the cut part, i.e. the top of the cross-shape, is the figure of a bishop and the model of a church which is without any doubt Gothic and C13. What was the whole then? It has been suggested that

it was a die to cast pilgrims' badges and that the building represents Canterbury Cathedral. The style of the Crucifixion is most reminiscent of metal work and has plenty of C11 affinities. – The N and S DOORS have large original C12 hinges. – COMMUNION RAIL. C18. – Over the N doorway inside is an Anglo-Saxon MASS DIAL. – PLATE. Set of 1684–5, by *C. K.*

PIRTON COURT. A large timber-framed house of the late C16 with specially gay decoration, but much restored. Inside, in one room, is a big chimneypiece with a semicircular pediment filled by a shell. In the room behind this a Jacobean plaster ceiling with a few simple decorative motifs.

POOL HOUSE *see* ASTLEY

PORTERSHILL *see* NORTH CLAINES

POWICK

8050

ST PETER AND ST LAWRENCE. A large church, and large already in the C12 and early C13; for in the E walls of the two transepts are two long, Late Norman windows, and the S respond of the arch from S aisle to transept has a filleted shaft. So there were transepts and at least a S aisle already there. The transepts, or at any rate the S transept, seem to have had E chapels or apses. There is a mysterious arch inside the E wall which is most likely evidence of such a chapel, though the exterior shows nothing. The chancel was rebuilt or lengthened in the first half of the C13. The E wall has three widely spaced stepped lancets, shafted inside, and the S wall two single lancets near the E end. In the second half of the C13 the N transept received its rather uncouth E window of three pointed-trefoiled lancet lights with a barbed trefoil in plate tracery over. Dec N as well as S aisle windows. Perp transept end windows. The interior of the nave and transepts is dominated by Perp features, particularly by the piers and responds. Their profiles consist of four chamfered projections, with the chamfers replaced by waves. Double-chamfered arches. Perp also the W tower. Its arch to the nave is panelled. – FONT. Octagonal, Perp, with flowers in quatrefoils. – PLATE. Cup, Cover Paten, and Plate, by *T. R.*, inscribed 1674. – MONUMENTS. Sir Daniel Tyas † 1673. Tablet with two standing allegorical figures and two on the pediment. Rustic work. – Mrs Russell † 1786. By *Thomas Scheemakers*. Extremely good. Semi- 85
reclining female figure, one breast bare. On the sarcophagus a

delightful roundel with the young mother teaching her child music. Still lifes of musical instruments l. and r.

ST JAMES, Callow End, $1\frac{1}{4}$ m. S. 1888. The church is of brick, quite small, with a louvre-like bell-turret. But can the domestic S windows and the two small two-light W windows with their free treatment of the Gothic style really be of 1888?

STANBROOK ABBEY, 1 m. S. In 1838 the Benedictine nunnery for English ladies which had been founded at Cambrai in 1625, expelled from France in 1808, and settled at Salford Priors, moved to Stanbrook. The house with its Tuscan doorway they must have found on the site, and also the two octagonal lodges. The new monastery was begun in 1878; the large L-shaped domestic quarters with cloister and cells along corridors instead of a dormitory were completed in 1880, after the church had already been consecrated in 1871. The architect was *E. W. Pugin*. Red brick, with Gothic windows, a big, high block with the church at the S end. It is a large church, externally interesting because of the high square tower with higher stair-turret, striped in the Sienese–Ruskinian way. – STAINED GLASS. By *Hardman*.

POWICK HOSPITAL, $1\frac{1}{2}$ m. SW. The first buildings date from 1852. They are large and still in the Georgian tradition, brick, with the ground-floor windows arched and set in blank arches.

POWICK BRIDGES, $\frac{1}{2}$ m. N. The C15 bridge is of three skew segmental arches of sandstone with cutwaters. The new bridge
95 is of 1837 and has an iron arch of the *Telford* type (cf. Holt).

THE TERRACE. A substantial Late Georgian brick house in the centre of the village. Five bays, two storeys, with a three-bay pediment. The doorway is tripartite, and the square porch with its pillars may be original. The ground-floor windows are set in blank arches. Pretty iron veranda round the corner.

WHEATFIELD, $\frac{3}{4}$ m. S. A substantial Italianate villa, in style *c.*1850 and similar to *Dawkes*'s work.* Quite subdued, with a symmetrical five-bay façade and an asymmetrical side.

PUDDLEFORD FARMHOUSE *see* EASTHAM

PUDFORD FARMHOUSE *see* MARTLEY

PURSHULL HALL *see* ELMBRIDGE

* The house appears in a directory of 1855.

QUEENHILL

8030

ST NICHOLAS. Nave and chancel and W tower. The top of the tower with the saddleback roof is by *Scott*, 1855. Late Norman S doorway with one order of colonnettes, scallop capitals, zigzag arch, and pellet hood-mould.* C13 chancel with nicely chamfered lancets. Inside, in the N wall, an upside-down head of a Norman window with two rosettes. – PULPIT. C17, but with a top band which comes from the top of the SCREEN or the ROOD BEAM. – SCREEN. Perp, of one-light divisions with ogee tops. – STAINED GLASS. In the nave N window good C14 parts. The shield represents the arms of England before 1340. – The E window by *E. Franklin*, 1892–3, is ghastly. – PLATE. Paten by *H. N.*, *c.*1660; Chalice by *T. C.*, *c.*1670. – MONUMENT. Incised slab to Henry Field † 1584.

GREEN FARMHOUSE, ⅝ m. NW. Late C17, brick, of seven bays with a hipped roof and wooden cross windows. Over the porch an elementary shell hood.

HOLDFAST MANOR HOUSE, 1⅛ m. NW. Late C17. Brick. Of seven bays with a hipped roof and wooden cross windows.

THE WELLS COURT, or PULL COURT, *see* Bushley.

RADFORD

0050

1¼ m. N of Rous Lench

(Barbara Jones in her admirable book on *Follies* reports a LETTER BOX here like that at Rous Lench, blown up to the size of a small one-bay timber-framed house. The date must be about 1880.)

RAINBOW HILL *see* WORCESTER, p. 318

REDDITCH

0060

Redditch, a wide-reaching-out town of 34,000 inhabitants (1961) with little architectural character, is the centre of the English needle and fishing-hook industry. In 1782 400 were employed in it; now there are *c.*2,000. The principal factory is Herbert Terry's. Redditch is going to have large 'new-town' extensions, but it is too early to pronounce on the plans. The master plan is by *Wilson & Womersley*, and it is being carried out by the *Redditch Development Corporation*.

* The segmental head is not old. For the furrowed zigzag cf. Malvern Priory. Mr Stratford suggests a date before 1175, and points to similarities with Pendock.

In the Middle Ages, just N of Redditch was BORDESLEY ABBEY, a Cistercian house founded by the Empress Maud in 1138. It was quite a sizeable establishment, with thirty-three monks in 1332 and nineteen in 1381. The plan of the church was of a standard Cistercian type, with a square-ended chancel and three square-ended chapels E of either transept.*

ST STEPHEN, Church Green, the hub of the town. 1854–5 by *H. Woodyer*. Large, in the Dec style, with little of the radicalism often so eloquent in Woodyer's work. NW tower with spire. The octagonal piers of the arcades are weak. Much more convincing are the chancel arch and the chancel chapel arcades by *Temple Moore*, 1893–4. The chancel arch dies into the responds, and the chapel arches die into the round piers. Plaster vault with diagonal and ridge-ribs also by Temple Moore. – In the vestry TILES from Bordesley Abbey. – STAINED GLASS. In the S aisle two windows by *Kempe & Tower*.

ST GEORGE, St George's Road. 1876–7 by *Preedy*. In the C13 style. W window with dull plate tracery. The intended stiff-leaf capitals inside have remained uncarved.

OUR LADY OF MOUNT CARMEL (R.C.), Beoley Road. 1834 by *Thomas Rickman*. The church gives no indication of how archeologically convincing Rickman could be. It is entirely of the current Commissioners' type of the thirties. Red sandstone ashlar. W tower with ground-floor open porch. No aisles, but transepts, square-ended chancel. Thin-ribbed ceilings. – PROCESSIONAL CROSS. Of *c*.1500, 18 in. high, with roundels at the ends of the arms bearing the Symbols of the Evangelists. The roundels are mounted on blue enamel. The Virgin and St John standing at the foot of the cross apparently come from a different cross.

The PUBLIC BUILDINGS of Redditch are of no interest: brick, Gothic or round-arched, e.g. the LIBRARY of 1885 (by *G. H. Cox* of Birmingham).

Of PRIVATE HOUSES hardly anything deserves notice. The nicest Georgian houses are in PROSPECT HILL, starting with No. 7, almost still at Church Green. On the GREEN a funny but engaging cast-iron FOUNTAIN of 1883 with cranes, dock leaf, and at the top a maiden. No. 7 has its brickwork exposed, No. 29 is stuccoed and has giant pilasters of vaguely Soanian type. Lower down a factory and the owner's house, the latter with a Greek Doric porch.

* Excavations are proceeding at the time of going to press.

(HOLMWOOD, the offices of the Redditch Development Corporation, is by *Temple Moore* and was built in 1893.)

Several OUTLYING FARMHOUSES deserve to be listed.

CHAPEL HOUSE, formerly Lower Hunt End Farm, Hunt End, $1\frac{5}{8}$ m. SW of Headless Cross church. Inside the moat a small fragment of a Jacobean brick mansion.

BRICK HOUSE FARM, *see* Feckenham.

BEANHALL farmhouses, *see* Bradley.

REDSTONE ROCK HERMITAGE *see* STOURPORT

RHYDD COURT *see* GUARLFORD

RIBBESFORD 7070

ST LEONARD. Nave and aisles and timber bell-turret. The S aisle has Norman masonry. The doorway is badly mauled. One order of columns with poorly preserved capitals and panels flanking the capitals (*see* below). The N doorway has very involved capitals with beaded interlace. To the l. is a panel with a bird.* The abaci have chequer and zigzag patterns, the arch a roll moulding. Tympanum with an archer and two quadrupeds. N aisle, N arcade, and chancel were all built in 1877, after the church had been struck by lightning. Ruskin did not like the rebuilding and suggested instead letting 'the dear old ruin grow grey by Severn's side in peace'. The S arcade is C15 and of timber, the only case in the county. The arches are simply curved braces, the piers are octagonal. – SCULPTURE. Inside, on the S wall, Norman fragments including cylindrical pieces of a shaft with close plaiting (cf. Kilpeck, W window). Also, in a separate place, a length of zigzag. Could all this have belonged to the S doorway? Or does it represent the chancel arch? – SCREEN. The dado has tracery panels from the former screen. – LECTERN. With Jacobean parts. – STAINED GLASS. The W window by *Burne-Jones*, made by *Morris & Co.*, 1875. The glass was given by Alfred Baldwin of Wilden. – In the S aisle W window a St George and fragments; C15. – PLATE. Chalice and Cover Paten, 1636; Flagon, 1638; Paten 1759. – Also from Dowles church Cup of 1571 and Paten of 1796.‡ – MONUMENTS. In the N aisle three coffin lids with crosses. One has a

* For such panels see Earls Croome and other places. It is a Herefordshire motif (N. Stratford). The N porch is of timber and dated 1633.

‡ The Rev. W. G. Harward tells me that the cup is hallmarked 1571 and that the paten is by *Charles Aldridge*.

shield across the shaft. – John Solly and wife. She died in 1639. A typical 'modern' tablet of the thirties, i.e. already classical. – Francis Winnington Ingram † 1843. Brass in the revived C15 tradition. The effigy is under a canopy.

Opposite the church a long farm building. Near its N end two doorways with basket arches and horizontally placed oval windows l. and r. That makes them probably *c.*1650–75, but where did they lead, and what was the building's purpose?

RIBBESFORD HOUSE. This is a puzzling house, at first appearing in its cemented coat early C19 medieval but soon revealing older, though half-hidden features. Leland calls it a 'goodly manour place', and building about 1535 is indeed known. To this phase belongs the general plan including the two turrets facing S, though they were originally (or at least in the C18) circular, and though the corridor between them is early C19. To the N is a big porch and this leads into the hall, which retains its original moulded beams. A wing extending forward from the r. end of the N front still has diapered brickwork to the E. The building is badly in need of further research.

8030

RIPPLE

ST MARY. A large church, 137 ft long, with aisles, transepts, and a crossing tower. The church must have been begun in the late C12 and is still much in the state of the decades following the beginning. Only the chancel was replaced in the late C13. The new chancel has three-light red-sandstone windows with stepped pointed-trefoiled lights. The NE and SE windows, however, are of one light only with a trefoiled circle in the head. Perp E window. Shafts of the former E window or windows. The side windows have moulded rere-arches. Only the priest's doorway has a round arch, which is a curious thing for the late C13. Was it in deference to the earlier building, where the N doorway also had a round arch? So have the W windows of the transepts and the altar recesses inside the E walls of the transepts. Otherwise the arches are pointed. The oldest parts of the late C12 to early C13 building seem to be these transepts and the start of the crossing; for here the angle shafts indicating the intention to vault are distinguished from the other shafts of the crossing by not being keeled. The N and S arcades of the crossing are of one step only and were perhaps originally also round. But the W and E arches are of the new dispensation with steps and keeled rolls. The capitals of the crossing go from trumpet scallop to crockets and very early stiff leaf. They

correspond to capitals in the cathedral, i.e. the W bays of the nave and the transepts, which are work of *c*.1180–1210. The nave has three doorways of about 1230. The W doorway has three orders of shafts with mature stiff-leaf capitals. Only the hood-mould stops are re-used Norman, beasts' heads of the Malmesbury type, frequent in Gloucestershire and represented in Worcestershire by Bredon. Maybe they come from the original chancel. The W window is Perp. The stiff-leaf of the N and S doorways is specially attractively arranged. The leaf sprays of the middle shaft spread out to cover the l. and r. shafts, which therefore have no capitals at all. Once again, the N doorway has a round arch. The arcades are of six bays with quatrefoil piers and very odd capitals. They are of the most elementary trumpet-scallop shape, so much so that it seems most likely they are crocket capitals left uncarved. But the whole of the arcades has a suspiciously re-cut look. The clerestory has small lancet windows above the spandrels, not the arch apexes. Small lancets also in the aisles. The plain corbel-table is E.E. too. The upper part of the crossing tower is Perp and the very top with the balustrade of 1713 (re-done 1797). Originally the tower carried a spire. The N porch is Perp with a Georgian second storey. But the lower storey has springers for a vault, which implies the planning of an upper floor. The entrance to the porch has as its hood-mould a length of Norman billet, again perhaps from the original chancel. – FONT. Of *c*.1300, octagonal, of the Purbeck type, but the blank arches pointed-trefoiled. The font was re-tooled in 1851. – STALLS Of the C15, with sixteen MISERICORDS. Twelve represent the 47
Labours of the Months, in a delightfully lively manner. There are in addition Sun and Moon and Aquarius, the sign of January in the Zodiac. Also two highly traceried stall ends. – COMMUNION RAIL. Simple, Jacobean. – STAINED GLASS. In a chancel S window glass from the Perp E window. – The W window is by *Kempe*; 1885. – PLATE. Latten Censer, C15; Cup, 1571; Paten Cover, 1787; Set of 1793. – MONUMENT. Tablet to John Holt † 1734. By *White* of Worcester.

OLD RECTORY. 1726, with some C15 masonry. A very handsome brick house of five by six bays with a hipped roof. Decorated keystones. Small doorway with pediment.

ROCHFORD

6060

ST MICHAEL. Right by the Teme and its grassy banks. Nave and chancel and timber bell-turret with spire. Norman masonry, and Norman first of all the elaborate though very coarse N doorway set in a projecting piece of wall (cf. Stoulton and other places). Two orders of columns, summary volute capitals, abaci with plait, interlace, etc., an arch with zigzag at r. angles to the wall, and a tympanum with a flatly carved spread-out Tree of Life. It is the only example in Worcestershire of this familiar motif, but across the Shropshire border it appears twice in similar form, at High Ercall and Linley, and across the Gloucestershire border also twice, at Dymock and Kempley (N. Stratford). The tympanum has an arched border of rosettes. All much weathered. Norman windows in nave and chancel. The Norman building was lengthened to the W later on. The Norman chancel arch also has zigzag at r. angles to the wall. Zigzag at r. angles to the wall is a Late Norman motif, but it appears at Peterborough as early as *c.*1130–5 and at Shobdon in Herefordshire some time between 1131 and 1148.* Rochford probably dates from *c.*1150. – ORGAN. A very charming late C18 piece. – STAINED GLASS. In the E window very early *Morris* glass. It commemorates a death in 1863. Just one panel with an Adoration of the Child and two Angels, all this set in ample transparent patterned quarries. In the tracery three angel busts. The style is still unaffected by the conventions which chiefly Burne-Jones was to follow later. The work is fresh and naïve and infinitely superior to anything done at the time in England or abroad.

7070

ROCK

ST PETER. The largest Norman village church in the county, and singularly grandly detailed. The date is probably about 1170. One approaches the church from the N, and there is there a projecting portal with three orders of columns plus the zigzag band on the outer jambs (cf. Astley, Beckford). The capitals have decorated scallops and one is a complete mask (cf. Holt and several places in Herefordshire), the abaci are decorated, and the arch has zigzag at r. angles to the wall, crenellation, lobes, and thin rolls with a kind of radiating three-ray motif. Nave and chancel have flat buttresses of course. The eared corbels are decorated with heads. The windows are placed high up, above a string course, and they are consistently shafted throughout, outside as well as inside. Moreover, to the E of either of the two nave N windows is a blank window, apparently

* At Kempley the tympanum and similar capitals must be contemporary with the famous chancel frescoes, i.e. second quarter of the C12.

blank from the beginning. This is rhythmically not at all satisfactory. Why was it done? The capitals of all the shafts have plain blocks, scallops, or upright fluted leaves. The chancel arch is called by Mr Stratford 'by far the finest example of Norman decorative sculpture in the county'. It has responds with one major and three minor shafts, two to the W, one to the E. The capitals have entwined trails, except for one with a centaur, several with human heads, and one with a boat and a cross (?). Decorated abaci. Arches with zigzag set at r. angles to the wall and also diagonally.* Later than Norman are the following elements. The N vestry is C13. The chancel E window has reticulated tracery, i.e. is Dec. The chancel roof with tie-beams, collar-beams, and wind-braces may be Dec too. The W tower is Perp. It is broad and high and has a large four-light W window. The arch towards the nave has polygonal responds with concave sides. This typically Late Perp motif is taken up in the S arcade and the S chapel as well. The piers are octagonal, the arches four-centred. The aisle windows not as tellingly Late Perp. The aisle and chapel are embattled. The aisle piers are relatively slender. That of the chapel is short and stubby. The nave roof is single-framed and no doubt Dec, but the tie-beams must be Late Perp strengthening – FONT. Norman, cauldron-shaped, with nine rosettes connected by clasps. The font is similar to that at Bayton near by. – PULPIT. Stone, with red stone inlay. Probably of the time of *Preedy*'s restoration, which was in 1861. – STAINED GLASS. Chancel N and one window in the S chapel evidently by *Gibbs*. – ARCHITECTURAL FRAGMENTS. Norman bits in the N wall inside, the motifs identical with those of the N doorway. So they probably come from a former S doorway. – PLATE. Salver 1723; Cup 1732; Flagon 1740. – MONUMENTS. Incised slab to Richard Smith, 'quondam rector huius ecclesiae', † 1554 (S chapel). Still entirely Gothic. – Big tomb-chest with shields in quatrefoils between chancel and S chapel. Nash records the inscription to Thomas Conyngsby which mentions his son Sir Humphrey 'who built this isle and steeple of the church A.D. 1510'. So here is the rare case of dated Perp in Worcestershire.

The STOCKS and WHIPPING POST are at the W end of the church.

* Professor Zarnecki believes this arch to be the work of a Herefordshire mason, very close to Shobdon. The date of the arch at Rock would be *c.*1160. Mr Stratford adds the similarity to Rowlstone, and is of the opinion that the N doorway is later and was done locally after the Herefordshire master had left.

ROMSLEY

9070

ST KENELM, 1¼ m. NW of the village centre. Still in an entirely rural setting despite its nearness to Birmingham. According to a disproved legend St Kenelm, the boy King of Mercia, was murdered here in 819. He was neither boy nor king. Below the E end of the church is an undercroft containing the holy spring which rose where he had been killed. The blocked arch in the S wall of the chancel led to the stairway down. (The undercroft itself contains nothing ancient. VCH) Nave and chancel in one, of red sandstone, C12, but the charming, thin Perp W
41 tower is grey. It stands forward from the Norman W wall on two buttresses connected high up by an arch. Big animals at the W angles, also of the church itself. One-light bell-openings with canopies flanked by blank canopied windows. Panelled parapet. Perp timber porch with tracery and leaf in the spandrels. Norman of *c.*1150 is the S doorway, with a bad but impressive tympanum of Christ seated and wearing a crown, and angels holding his glory. The ribbed draperies are inspired by the Herefordshire School of carvers (cf. especially Fownhope). The composition of the tympanum is standard Romanesque, but the broad border of very loose interlace is in the Anglo-Saxon tradition. Arch with beakheads in one moulding,* a kind of completely stylized version of the same motif in another. The heads have become just oblong, beaded flaps. The arches are red, the tympanum is brown sandstone. Norman also one chancel N window, later altered, and the flat buttresses. The chancel was remodelled in the C14. – SCULPTURE. Small bad figure of a Saint, high up, outside, on the S wall. It is probably C12. – PAINTING. To the l. of the chancel N window one figure, all that remains of an early C14 cycle. – PLATE. Cup 1592; Almsdish possibly early C18; Paten 1750.

(HORSEPOOL FARMHOUSE, Hunnington, 1¼ m. E. Late C18, stuccoed, with two Venetian windows to each floor. Between the upper ones is a blocked ogee-headed window. Wing with one Venetian window above and one below. MHLG)

ROUS LENCH

0050

ST PETER. Nave and N aisle and chancel. The neo-Norman bellcote takes the place of a timber bell-turret formerly supported

* The only complete beakhead in the county. Round Christ's raised right hand there is a ring. Is this a misunderstood rendering of an orb? (N. Stratford)

inside the nave. The church is basically Norman, see the two
scallop capitals of the N doorway, the three window-heads kept
in the N chapel (one with a radiating pattern, one with zigzag,
and one with foliage), and the S doorway. This has one order of
spiral-fluted columns and in the arch zigzag at r. angles to the
wall. Mr Neil Stratford queries the genuineness of the motif.
Above it, also Norman, and framed by colonnettes with leaf
decoration and an arch with flat zigzag decoration, is an out-
standing relief of Christ seated and blessing. His almond- 15
shaped glory is cusped along the sides. The date is most
probably *c.*1140–50 (cf. the Prior's Door at Ely*). The chancel
arch and the three-bay N arcade are Late Norman too. The
piers are round, the capitals round, of many scallops, the
arches single-stepped or without any step. The chancel was
rebuilt or lengthened in the later C13. The former E window
with plate tracery is now the N aisle W window. Then, in
1884–5, *Preedy* built the N chapel and added the ornate apse
at the E end of the N aisle. All this is super-Norman or rather
Romanesque, especially the Italian-looking ALTAR CANOPY in
the apse. The apse has skylights to make it more dramatic. The
N aisle wall was rebuilt too, but some part of the N doorway
is original. – PULPITS. Both are Elizabethan and have been
brought in. The panels have two tiers of the usual blank
arches. – SCREEN. Fancy Gothic, probably of *c.*1885. This and
the contemporary chancel CHAIRS and KNEELING DESKS of
Elizabethan type are black and gold. – SCULPTURE. Anglo-
Danish stone with untidy interlace, two affronted birds, and,
below one of them, a striding little man. The surface round
the corner is carved too. What was this then? It cannot have
been a lintel. Was it part of a pillar? Or of a sepulchral slab?
– Many architectural FRAGMENTS. They include Norman
window heads, one with intertwined tendrils. – PAINTING.
Late C16 or early C17 Venetian picture of the Feast in the
House of Simon. Inspired by Tintoretto. – PLATE. Cup and
Paten, 1570; Paten by *F. Garthorne*, 1693; three-legged Paten
by *W.*, 1727; Flagon by *Robert Brown*, 1745. – MONUMENTS
Edward Rous † 1611 and his wife † 1580. Big tomb-chest with
two recumbent effigies. His feet are placed against a big head.
Small kneelers against the chest. Back cartouche with strap-
work. – Sir John Rous † 1645. Tomb-chest with black columns

*Mr Stratford believes in Northamptonshire as a source common to both. He bases his view on comparisons between ornamental detail at Castor, as early as *c.*1120, with the Ely transept and Rous Lench.

and a straight top with obelisks and a coat of arms. No effigy. – Frances Rous, daughter of *Thomas Archer* of Umberslade in Warwickshire, the architect. The monument is of 1719 and not good. Seated lady holding her heart. She sits by an urn with two doves on the top. Corinthian columns l. and r., attic with the medallion of the husband held by putti. At the top an open segmental pediment. – Also tablets to Sir Thomas † 1676 and Sir Edward † 1677.

ROUS LENCH COURT. The Rous family held Rous Lench from 1382 to 1721. It then came via the female line to the Rouse Boughtons, and in 1876 to the Rev. W. K. W. Chafy, who died in 1916. Rous Lench Court is a big, picturesque black and white house, largely of *c.*1840. Before the C19 it was yet bigger. It is said to have consisted of ranges round two courtyards. What remains is no more than the S and W sides of the entrance courtyard. Of the early C16 is the W range (to the road) with the gateway and a stone chimneypiece in an upper room. The S range is early C17, except for the E projection to the N, which is entirely of *c.*1840. On the upper floor is a splendid stone chimneypiece from Shaw in the North Riding. It reached the house *via* Hearst's celebrated collection destined for America. There is also an extensive collection of sculpture, furniture, and architectural fragments. The gardens have terraces and topiary, and at the top, accessible from the road, is a TOWER of brick, with machicolations and a higher round stair-turret. It was built by Dr Chafy and reminds one of an Italian Palazzo Pubblico.

The VILLAGE GREEN shows the munificence of Sir Charles Rouse Boughton and Dr Chafy. The prevalent style is C16 to C17, with brick as well as half-timber features. Dr Chafy's LETTER BOX is the most startling item, blown up into a little house the size of a moderate dovecote. The SCHOOL is of 1864 and more original in its treatment of Gothic motifs. Other dates inscribed are 1862 and 1872.

ROWLEY REGIS *see* BIRMINGHAM OUTER WESTERN SUBURBS

RUBERY

9070

ST CHAD. 1956–7 by *Lavender, Twentyman & Percy*. In sight of heavy high blocks of flats for Birmingham people. The church has a low-pitched roof, the square brick campanile stands separate from it. The side walls of the church have a window grid all the way along. The E wall is blank and simply patterned inside, but there is side light on the altar. Attached on the r. side of the altar an octagonal chapel, on the l. vestry, cloakrooms, etc.

RUBERY HILL HOSPITAL. 1882 by *Martin & Chamberlain*. It cost £140,000.*

CHADWICH MANOR, 1¼ m. SW, in the fork between the M5 and A38. Five-bay brick house of the late C17. Segment-headed windows, hipped roof, flat quoins. The central bay projects a little and has its own quoins. Gateposts with big balls.

RUSHOCK

8070

ST MICHAEL. Built in 1758 by *Roger Eykyn*, restored in 1872. But the first of the two dates does not seem to make sense. The E window is clearly 1872, and while the gables and square pinnacles could be 1758, can the Y-tracery be so early, and can the W tower with its ogee-arched S doorway, or must there have been intermediate activity about 1800? After all, Rushock would be earlier even than the extremely advanced Croome d'Abitot.

RUSHOCK COURT FARMHOUSE. An outbuilding is puzzling. Brick with stone dressings, a doorway with stone hood on brackets, and a big window in a broad surround. What was this built for?

SALWARPE

8060

ST MICHAEL. Perp W tower, nave and aisles, and chancel. Victorian Dec windows, but also in the N aisle original ones and, inside, a Dec tomb recess. The chancel was rebuilt in 1848, but the SEDILIA with two round arches seem to be *c.*1530. The arcades are puzzling. Three bays plus a separate W bay. The separation is marked by a square pier on the S side, a broad oblong pier on the N side. That extra breadth indicates perhaps that over the NW bay there was originally a tower. The springer of a transver search in the aisle would confirm that. The VCH suggests instead a tower over the nave E part. *See* p. 377 The arcades have round piers with round abaci and pointed, single-step arches. That indicates a date *c.*1200. The square and oblong piers probably mark the place of a former W wall, but if so, the details of the W bay with its responds can be only slightly later than the arcades. The arches anyway are the same. The Perp arch between tower and nave is broadly

* The building is actually in Warwickshire.

panelled. – SCREEN. In the S aisle E bay, Perp, of single-light divisions. – STAINED GLASS. E window apparently by *Hardman*. – TILES. Some of the C15 at the W end of the N aisle. – (PURSE. Of C13 or early C14 silk with affronted and addossed quadrupeds, including unicorns.) – PLATE. Cup and Cover Paten originally probably of 1571; Flagon given by Elizabeth Talbot (*see* below); Paten, second half C17; Dish, 1820. – MONUMENTS. Priest, chancel N, holding a chalice. Fine soft folds to his garb. Probably late C14. Two angels by his pillow. – Thomas Talbot † 1613. Tablet, chancel S, with two kneelers facing one another across a prayer-desk. Kneeling children in the 'predella'. – Tablet, S aisle E, to Olave Talbot † 1681, with twisted columns. – Below a tomb-chest to the same and her mother Elizabeth † 1689. Black and white marble. No effigy,
66 but two white charity girls against the front of the chest and an inscription from Acts 9:36, 37, 39: 'This Woman was full of Good workes & Alms-deeds' etc.

SALWARPE COURT. Spectacular, many-gabled black and white house of the late C15 or early C16 belonging to the Talbots. All close vertical studding and much later brickwork painted so as to appear black-and-white. The finest details are not on the broad front, i.e. the SE, but on the short SW (solar) side. Bay with upper overhang and bargeboarded gable with carved decoration. The back also is worth looking at. The BARN is contemporary with the house.

COOKS HILL. A cruck house of four bays with two-bay hall and complete central truss. The house is very much altered, with an inserted first floor and fireplace occupying most of the lower bay of the hall (FWBC).

0030

SEDGEBERROW

ST MARY. Consecrated in 1331, but over-restored by *Butterfield* in 1866–8. The E window e.g., if it is medieval, must be late C14. The tracery is a Perp variety of reticulated. Original the W tower, which is hexagonal and thin from the start. Also original the N doorway. But by Butterfield most of the windows. There is no structural division between nave and chancel. The interior of the church is high and quite wide. – REREDOS. By *Butterfield*, ornate and successful. Tripartite with Dec canopies. The back wall entirely geometrical patterns of stone and tile mosaic. – SCREEN. Also obviously by *Butterfield*. Stone base and high, wide-open wooden screen. – STAINED

GLASS. The E window by *Mrs Barber*, the vicar's wife, 1878. – In one chancel N window a seated Saint; early C14. – PLATE. Cup by *I. B.* and Cover Paten, 1639.

SEVERNBANK *see* SEVERN STOKE

SEVERN END *see* HANLEY CASTLE

SEVERN STOKE

8040

ST DENYS. The nave has one small Norman window high up and a Norman buttress. The big N tower was begun *c.*1300 – see the bottom window to the N. The top has the stair-turret higher than the tower itself. Dec the S transept, according to its windows. The S window is interesting, as the top roundel with a quatrefoil is a C13 motif apparently still considered permissible. Also Dec the S aisle. The four-bay arcade has square piers with semicircular projections and typically Dec arches. The arch from aisle into transept conforms. The chancel E window is Early Perp. – STAINED GLASS. In the S transept fragments of the original glass. – TILES. A few in the recess in the nave N wall. This recess is puzzling anyway. Is it a blocked doorway? – Are the Norman ARCHITECTURAL FRAGMENTS re-used? – PLATE. Cup of 1571 with Cover inscribed 1737; Flagon of 1619 by *I. L.* with Christ as the Good Shepherd engraved; Salver Paten, probably *c.*1619. – MONUMENT. James Barker † 1851. By *C. Lewis* of Cheltenham. With a low, broad urn.

SEVERNBANK, ⅝ m. S. Early C19, stuccoed. One side has two canted bay windows and an iron veranda, another a bow window. The former side is two-storeyed, the latter three-storeyed, and as the house is castellated, that looks from certain angles as if it were a tower.

SHAKENHURST *see* BAYTON

SHELL *see* HIMBLETON

SHELSLEY BEAUCHAMP

7060

ALL SAINTS. The tower is ascribed to the C14 (VCH). It is of red sandstone, half green thanks to lichens. The rest is by *Cranston*, 1846–7. It is a remarkably competent job for a relatively unknown architect. Nave and aisle in the style of 1300, chancel in a slightly earlier E.E. style. Exterior and interior keep up this piece of made-up history. – PLATE. Cup and Cover Paten of 1570; Flagon by *I. B.*, 1634; Paten, *c.*1710. – MONUMENT. Francis Galton † 1902. Small tablet, over-richly E.E. It looks 1860 rather than 1900.

OLD RECTORY. Late C18. Dated plans are at the County Record Office. The name of the architect, *Thomas Johnson*, is mentioned (Canon J. S. Leatherbarrow).

7060

SHELSLEY WALSH

ST ANDREW. Built of tufa. Nave and chancel and timber bell-turret. The nave is Norman, the chancel C13, but the latter with all the features renewed. In the nave a tiny S window and a N doorway. This has one order of columns with scallop capitals, an uncarved tympanum, and an arch with zigzag at r. angles to the wall. The chancel is remarkable by its roof, with tie-beams, collar-beams, and large foiled openings in the top triangle. Are the latter medieval? – SCREEN and PARCLOSE SCREEN. All one composition, with one-light divisions and very handsomely decorated top rails. Above the screen is the original ROOD BEAM, also with its original decoration. – TILES. C15, in the chancel floor. – PLATE. Cup *c.*1571 and Cover Paten *c.*1576. – MONUMENT. Francis Walsh † 1596, a tomb-chest without effigy, entirely of wood (cf. the Walsh monument at Stockton-on-Teme). Tapering pilasters and panels with the usual blank arches enclosing in this case shields.

8060

SHRAWLEY

ST MARY. A Norman church, perhaps of two periods, *c.*1120–30 and *c.*1170–80. The chancel has a zigzag sill frieze on the S side and on it three windows, the middle one set in a buttress.* On the N side the frieze is rope. The window profiles are of a very small sunk continuous chamfer. The zigzag frieze continued in the nave on the S side. It is the S doorway with its waterleaf capital and its complicated arch decoration that cannot be earlier than 1180. The door arch itself, however, is segmental, as is that of the small chancel doorway. The latter has a billet hood-mould. The N nave doorway has trumpet instead of waterleaf capitals, and that also is late. The W tower seems to be C17 work. In the nave C18 or early C19 S windows. – CROSS BASE in the churchyard. The base has big angle spurs.

* For this motif see the towers of Cropthorne and Fladbury.

At the entrance to the churchyard is a square brick house with pointed windows and a big hipped roof. It looks like a Nonconformist chapel.

SHURNOCK *see* FECKENHAM

SMETHWICK *see* BIRMINGHAM OUTER WESTERN SUBURBS

SOUTH LITTLETON

0040

ST MICHAEL. Perp W tower. In the chancel (S) one small late C13 two-light window, in the nave (S) one late C13 single-light window. Also in the nave (S) a plain Norman doorway. The one noteworthy detail is the hood-moulds on heads of the chancel (S) doorway and the neighbouring windows. The tower arch is a re-used window-head. – FONT. Norman, round, with tapering sides. A band of arrow-heads, and a rope band. Also three rosettes and a cross. – PULPIT. Perp. – BENCH ENDS. With tracery panels. – PILLAR PISCINA. C12, defaced. – TILES. C15, in a chancel (N) recess. – STAINED GLASS. Bits in one chancel (N) window. – PLATE. Cup and Paten Cover by *I. F., c.*1571.

HATHAWAYS. Opposite the church. A very pleasant brick house. The W part, dated 1721 on the weathervane, is of five by three bays with wooden cross windows. The doorway is not original. Hipped roof and on it a cupola or belvedere and l. and r. of it two broad blocks of two chimneystacks connected by an open arch.* It makes a fine skyline. The E end of the house is supposed to be pre-Reformation, the gabled middle part Elizabethan. (Good staircase.)

SOUTHSTONE ROCK HERMITAGE *see* STANFORD-ON-TEME

SPETCHLEY

8050

ALL SAINTS. Some evidence of the early C14 in nave and chancel, but most of the features are late C16 or even C17, including the W tower with its round-arched entrance, and the very surprising domestic transomed bay window in the chancel, which houses a monument. The Berkeley Chapel on the S side was built in 1614, but windows of *c.*1300 were re-used. The chancel arch is of two continuous chamfers. – STAINED GLASS.

*Mr T. Nicols tells me that a date 1685 is recorded for the start of this part of the house.

In the S chapel evidently by *Hardman*: E 1857, S 1876.– TILES. Some by the altar steps. – PLATE. Chalice, Cover Paten, and Flagon, by *R. T.*, *c.*1680; two Salver Patens on foot, by *D. B.*, 1688. – MONUMENTS. In the 'bay window' plain tomb-chest with pilasters, probably to a Sheldon, and probably late C16. – Between chancel and chapel Rowland Berkeley † 1611 and wife. Alabaster, and of high quality. Recumbent effigies on a tomb-chest with diagonally projecting corners. On these obelisks. Over the effigies coffered arch on two groups of three square fluted pillars. – Sergeant Robert Berkeley † 1656. In full robes. Black and white marble. Careful, somewhat pedantic detailing of the fur. – Elizabeth Berkeley † 1708 and her husband. Marble reredos-type monument with standing putti l. and r.

SPETCHLEY PARK. The estate was Lyttelton property in the C15, Sheldon in the C16, and was then bought by Rowland Berkeley. It is still Berkeley property. The present house is by *Tasker*, 1811–*c.*18. The preceding mansion had stood somewhat to the S.* It is a dignified, spacious mansion of smooth Bath stone with a long S front and a shorter W front. In the
92 latter is the entrance. Giant portico of four unfluted Ionic columns and just one more window l. and r. Two storeys. No ornament except the window surrounds. The S side is as reticent. Central semicircular projection with unfluted Ionic giant pilasters. Then three windows l. and three r. and angle accents with a pedimented tripartite window on the ground floor and a long tablet instead of a window on the upper floor. The original ground level of the house was about 2 ft higher, but it was very soon lowered. The plan of the house is plain but impressive. The three main rooms are along the S front. Behind, continuing the entrance lobby, a hall screened to W and E by pairs of red scagliola columns, and then the spacious staircase with a specially fine iron handrail. E of all this is the CHAPEL (R.C.), running the whole height and nearly the whole depth of the house, with the altar wall to the S. This has a blank 'Venetian' motif with a segmental arch.

In the grounds across the main (A) road a pretty iron FOOTBRIDGE. (Also in the grounds a ROOT HOUSE, with a conical thatched roof. *C.L.*)

CATHOLIC SCHOOL. 1841 by *Pugin*. H-shaped, with the

*Captain Berkeley told me that his mother and St John Hope had excavated its foundations *c.*1912, and that plans had been made and deposited in a safe place, where they were lost.

teacher's house in one wing and classrooms in the other and the centre. Red brick with blue brick ornamental crosses. The only accents are a gawky bell-turret and the Perp main window of the classroom in the wing.*

SPRINGHILL HOUSE *see* BROADWAY

STAMBERMILL *see* STOURBRIDGE

STANBROOK ABBEY *see* POWICK

STANFORD-ON-TEME 7060

ST MARY. Above the road and the grounds of Stanford Court. Built in 1768–9 by *James Rose*. Of good ashlar work. W tower, nave, transepts, and short chancel. Y-tracery and in the E window intersecting tracery. The W tower also has one of the typical large quatrefoils. White ceiling on a big coving. – STAINED GLASS. The E window of 1893 a piece of terrible ham-acting. – PLATE. Cup and Cover Paten 1571; Flagon 1718; Paten 1722; Set of 1769. – MONUMENTS. Sir Humphrey Salway † 1493 and wife. A very good alabaster monument. 42
Recumbent effigies, his feet against a lion's long tail; tomb-chest with kneeling children under crocketed ogees, busy and pretty. – Thomas Winnington † 1746. Standing monument. Sarcophagus on lions' feet, bust at the top. The sculptor is not known. – Edward Winnington and wife † 1791 and 1784, two identical tablets without figures. – Also Edith and Thomas E. Winnington, † 1864 and † 1869, two identical brass monuments with kneeling figures.

STANFORD COURT. The house was burnt in 1886 and rebuilt. Is the long brick front with projecting wings and quoins of even length all Victorian then? Or does it represent pretty exactly what was there? The back is ashlar-faced, has a bow window, and was not affected by the fire. Next to the house fifteen-bay brick stables. Below, a large lake.

SOUTHSTONE ROCK HERMITAGE, 1½ m. S of Stanford Bridge. With remains of a chapel of St John.

STOCKTON-ON-TEME 7060

ST ANDREW. Norman nave of *c.*1130–40 with C14 timber porch, brick chancel of 1718, and timber bell-turret. The *pièce de resistance* is the S doorway, with one order of columns

*I owe information on this building to Mrs Phoebe Stanton.

carrying block capitals, with a thin rib up the angle, big spurs to the base, and an arch with a roll and thin saltire crosses. The chancel arch is of the same build. Single-scallop capitals and a roll. – SCULPTURE. Small Norman panels by the chancel arch: the Lamb and Cross (a roundel) and a lion. Also above the S doorway a large quadruped.* – TILES. C15, in the chancel. – PLATE. Cup and Cover Paten of 1571. – MONUMENTS. C13 coffin lid with a cross with branch stumps all the way along and a Lombardic inscription to Radulphus Ecclesie Stoctone Rector. – Brass of William Parker † 1508, 18 in. figure. – Thomas Walshe † 1593. Entirely of wood (cf. the Walsh monument at Shelsley Walsh). Tomb-chest and back wall and canopy, all very oddly detailed. The columns or balusters, also used horizontally, are particularly baffling.

STOCKTON HOUSE, S of the church. Late C17, brick, with an elaborately shaped gable-end.

6060

STOKE BLISS

CHURCH. Nave and chancel and SW tower with shingled broach spire. The chancel (see the one S lancet) and the S aisle are E.E. The arcade is of four bays and has round piers with moulded capitals and double-chamfered arches – all much restored. In 1854 all the rest was done, notably the tower. The plate tracery is of course Victorian too. But the attractive conceit of the cross-gable over the aisle SE window is probably genuine late C13 work, introduced to give light to the rood screen. – FONT. Norman, drum-shaped, with plain arched panels of the type familiar from Purbeck marble fonts. – SCREEN. Perp, of one-light divisions. – PULPIT. Dated 1631. With the typical broad blank arches and upright lozenges of early C17 woodwork. – READING DESK. Dated 1635, and also with the blank arches. – In addition small frontal figures such as one knows them from bed-heads and overmantels. – PLATE. Flagon of 1805.

HYDE FARM, 1½ m. SW. The outside of the house betrays nothing of the medieval work it has preserved inside. This is one of the earliest hall and cross-wing houses in Worcestershire, and the more complete and monumental of the only two base-cruck halls in the county. The timbers of the base-cruck truss are enormous and heavily moulded. The purlins are very slender (an early feature), and each bay of the hall had an intermediate

*Mr Stratford believes that the same workmen did the sculpture at Eastham, Knighton, and Martley.

truss of which the lower section of the principal rafters has been cut back. There are two tiers of purlins and heavily cusped wind-braces. The timbers in the spandrel above the base-cruck collar are also cusped. Each of the enormous knee-braces had a capital carved in its lower vertical section; the carving is continued into the cruck, concealing the join between the two members. The spere-truss is of much lighter construction but of the same date. The solar wing is hardly less interesting than the hall but very small. Its timbers have greater refinement. The date of the hall building must be *c.*1250. The STABLES opposite the house are C16, with a jettied first floor carried round the gable wall supported by attached brackets. It is a four-bay building with very wide timber spacing and a 28 ft span (FWBC).

THE GROVE, 1¼ m. WNW. The house has a big shaped middle gable. It is probably late C17, but the date 1671 (MHLG) is only on a fireback. The windows are Late Georgian.

GARMSLEY CAMP, 1½ m. SW of Bank Street. This is a univallate hillfort of roughly oval plan enclosing 9 acres. Inturned entrances occur on the NE and W.

STOKE PRIOR

9060

ST MICHAEL. Much of the church is of *c.*1200, perhaps some of it a little earlier, some a little later – namely the N arcade, the transeptal N chapel, and then the transeptal S chapel, the S doorway, and the chancel arch – perhaps in that order. The N arcade is of five bays. Round piers with round, plainly moulded capitals and round abaci. Single-step arches. The arch to the N chapel is of the same type, and a totally renewed small N window is in the chapel. To the nave there is an arch with a crocket capital and a capital with broad leaves. The arch is double-chamfered. That is clearly later than the W arch. The S doorway has one order of colonnettes with plain leaf capitals and a round arch with roll mouldings.* To the l. of the l. capital is a re-used Anglo-Danish stone with close interlace. Unusual Norman hood-mould pattern of lobes. W of the doorway a Norman window. The chancel arch has trumpet capitals and a double-chamfered arch.‡ The S chapel is the base of a tower which is the visual climax of the church. The ground

* Mr Stratford notes a waterleaf capital of a type unique in the county.

‡ Mr Stratford draws attention to a shaft continuing its fillet into the moulded capital. He compares this with the S porch at Halesowen and the early C13 crypt of Hereford Cathedral.

stage, i.e. the chapel, has to W and N trumpet capitals, a moulded capital, and crocket capitals, and the arches have one chamfer and one roll with a fillet. On the S side is a small shafted doorway. To the E the tower is continued in a small chapel with small lancet windows and a rounded tunnel-vault. As the upper stages of the tower were reached, Transitional had given way to E.E. Lancet windows, then blank shafted lancets, then the bell-openings of three shafted lancets, also with continuous rolls. The top is a pointed-trefoiled frieze. Later recessed shingled spire. The whole tower is a splendidly self-contained, sturdy piece. A little later than the tower, i.e. *c.*1250, the S aisle was built. Its windows and the battlements and pinnacles are of course Perp, but the arcade of two bays is typical of *c.*1250. The pier and responds have a round core with four attached shafts, round abaci, and deeply moulded arches. The chancel is E.E. too, see the E buttresses. So is the N vestry. In the chancel the windows were renewed in the early C14. The E window is of five lights with reticulated tracery. In the N chapel also a Dec window. – FONT. Octagonal, Perp. Base with symmetrically arranged crossed leaves. Bowl with panels with rough figures, four of them angels holding shields. One panel has the scene of a baptism. – STAINED GLASS. Fragments in the tower E lancet. – The E window by *Sebastian Evans*, 1860, rather strident in the colours. – MONUMENT. Stone effigy of a priest, C13, in the S aisle.

VICARAGE, to the SE. Brick, five bays, the windows with keystones.

SCHOOL and MASTER'S HOUSE. 1871 at the expense of John Corbett (*see* below and Droitwich). The house is of two storeys, Gothic, the school one-storeyed and symmetrical with round-arched windows.

SALT WORKS. Founded by John Corbett (*see* Droitwich) in 1828 after rock salt had been discovered. It was the principal factory, since Droitwich developed as a spa rather than a centre of industry.

AVONCROFT COLLEGE. The college and Mr Charles have conceived a plan to re-erect timber-framed buildings of interest as a museum or part of a museum. So far one can see a house from Worcester Road, Bromsgrove (a hall and cross-wing house of *c.*1475 with a great timber-framed chimney-stack, probably inserted *c.*1550). This is the only domestic building in Worcestershire where the effect of the open hall can be felt.

TARDEBIGGE FARM, 1¾ m. E. The house is of *c.*1600. It is a hall-type house, but the hall-part was built with two storeys. It consists of the lower bay, which has a fireplace and a stack of slightly later date, the middle bay, comprising the 'house place', and the fireplace bay, at the upper end. At this upper end is also a two-bay cross-wing, and the fireplace structure serves both this wing and the hall. At the lower end is a gable, giving the appearance of a second cross-wing. This and a separate two-storey entrance porch were built later, i.e. *c.*1650. The porch has a staircase that leads directly to the attic, which seems to have been used as a separate flat, perhaps for the parents after the next generation had taken over the farm. The staircase of the main part of the house is under a gable extension of the fireplace bay (FWBC).

STONE

8070

ST MARY. 1831, and typical of the date. W tower with W entrance, big lancet bell-openings, heavy pinnacles, and a recessed spire. Two-light Perp side openings with traceried transoms. Chancel 1899. Dull interior. – STAINED GLASS. E window by *Kempe*, early C20. – PLATE. Salver of 1810. – MONUMENTS. Hannah Hill † 1788. In the churchyard. Pedestal with an elegant urn. – Benjamin Gibbons † 1863. By *Peter Hollins*. The elements are still those of Georgian tablets: pedestal, urn, putti heads; but it is all more naturalistic.

STOULTON

9040

ST EDMUND. Wide nave, wide chancel, and W tower. The tower is a rebuilding of 1936–7. Both the nave and the chancel are Norman, of about 1130–40. There are original buttresses and several original small windows. Also both nave doorways are Norman. They both project a little, as a number of Norman doorways do in the county (*see* p. 15). The S doorway has one order of colonnettes with block capitals, and a roll moulding, and above the doorway are two bays of blank arcading with two-scallop capitals (cf. Bockleton, Eastham, and Knighton-on-Teme). The N doorway is simpler but also has the two-bay blank arcading. The N doorway arch is single-stepped. So is the chancel arch, which stands on the simplest imposts. The nave roof is C14, or at least seems to be. Arched braces, forming a depressed arch, go up to the collar-beams. Above, in the top triangle bold tracery of a quatrefoil over two trefoils. – FONT.

Norman, round, with tapering sides. Wavy top band. – COMMUNION RAIL. Jacobean. – HELMET with an arm as the crest, the Acton achievement. Also a short SWORD. Both are said to be Italian of *c.*1470. – STAINED GLASS. In a chancel S window old bits. – PLATE. Cup of 1570 and Cover Paten of 1571; Salver Paten of 1717. – MONUMENT. William Acton of Lower Wolverton † 1814. By *Crake* of London. Standing woman by an urn. On the pedestal roundel with initials.

LOWER WOLVERTON HALL, 1⅝ m. NE. Early C18, brick, of seven bays and three storeys. Absolutely plain. The substantial doorway round the corner with Tuscan columns and a broken pediment is probably Later Georgian.

9080

STOURBRIDGE

Both Old Swinford and Wollaston are older than Stourbridge. But Stourbridge came into its own with the development of the glass industry. This was first introduced by refugees from Hungary in 1556 and grew first slowly, but in the C19 rapidly. Yet there is little to indicate a sense of civic pride.

ST THOMAS. 1728–36, brick, with stone dressings, perhaps by one of the *Parkers*, local masons. There is no evidence for an attribution to White. It is a solid, competent Early Georgian church – a pity it is not more prominently placed! Square W tower, the parapet partly balustraded with curving-up towards the corners. The nave is of four bays with round-headed windows. The original entrances towards the E, i.e. the street, are blocked. The apse was added tactfully in 1890 by *W. H.*
76 *Bidlake*. Inside there are four bays with Tuscan columns on high pedestals, BOX PEWS,* and two galleries. The plaster vaults are panelled in a restless rhythm, in the aisles they are transverse tunnels. The W tower is open to the nave, probably an alteration of 1890. – The N chancel SCREEN, in a quite successful mixed Classical and Gothic, is also by *Bidlake*. – PLATE. Salver, probably of 1697; Cups of 1742 and 1749.

CHRIST CHURCH, High Street, The Lye. 1843, with pointed windows. Wide nave, transepts, short chancel, W tower. Some of the windows were re-done in Victorian times. – Some BOX PEWS. – The STAINED GLASS in the W roundel evidently of the time when the church was built.

ST JAMES, Bridgnorth Road, Wollaston. By *G. Bidlake*, 1860, and memorable specially for its unified composition with

*These are of 1836.

SCHOOL and PARSONAGE. All three are of blue (engineering) bricks and all three are of decidedly personal details, 'rogue architecture' as Goodhart-Rendel would have called it. Totally asymmetrical the two secular buildings. Note particularly the wilful chimney in the wall of the school towards the nave. The church has a NW porch tower. The details are of *c*.1300. The interior is disappointing. No aisles, but transepts.

ST JOHN EVANGELIST, St John's Road. 1860 by *Street*, a decidedly dour building with its self-consciously bald plate tracery. Red brick, no tower, just a tiny bell-turret. Very odd façade. Inside, round piers with Early Gothic capitals and square abaci. Clerestory with rere-arches. The W lancets have very deep embrasures.

ST MARK, Stourbridge Road, Stambermill. 1870 by *J. Smith*, a local architect. Nave and chancel in one. Bell-turret small, towards the E. Polygonal apse. Late C13 details. Really of no architectural value.

OUR LADY AND ALL SAINTS (R.C.), New Road. By *E. W. Pugin*, the steeple by *G. H. Cox*, the former 1864, the latter 1890. Brick, and dominated by its spire, though the details of this are undistinguished. Pugin Junior's interior looks starved, with its very thin granite columns. All the details are 'Second Pointed'.

CONGREGATIONAL CHAPEL, Lower High Street. 1810, but the long side to the street of 1841. Brick and stone dressings. Five bays, ground stage and two upper tiers, tied together by giant arches.

EBENEZER METHODIST CHAPEL, High Street, The Lye. Red and yellow brick, two tiers of arched windows. The façade with the rising Lombard frieze of S. Pietro in Ciel d'Oro at Pavia.

METHODIST CHURCH (former – now SCHOOL HOUSE), New Road. 1886. Brick in the Romanesque style. NW tower, with quite a lavish portal.

PRESBYTERIAN CHURCH, Lower High Street. 1788. The church lies back from the street. Brick, of three bays with a three-bay pediment and a closed-in porch also pedimented. The E end is altered. – WEST GALLERY and BOX PEWS. – Also a number of tablets.

UNITARIAN CHAPEL, High Street, The Lye. 1861. Gothic, and sadly underfed, with its thin asymmetrical turret.

TOWN HALL, Market Street. By *Thomas Robinson*, 1887. It cost £4,500. Red brick, quite big, but unspectacularly placed.

Roughly symmetrical, but composed so that the tower breaks the symmetry.

LIBRARY, Hagley Road and Church Street. 1905 by *F. Woodward*. Red brick and terracotta. Tudor with Baroque touches, and the typical bulgy columns of *c.*1900. Very asymmetrical composition.

KING EDWARD GRAMMAR SCHOOL, Lower High Street. 1862 by *Thomas Smith*, with additions, especially that N of the old building which dates from 1908 The old building (former hall) is Gothic and has a picturesque tower, the building of 1908 and 1911 is in a chaster Elizabethan with very long transomed windows. New hall by *Webb & Gray*, 1930–1.

SECONDARY MODERN SCHOOL, Park Road West, Wollaston. 1957–8 by *Yorke, Rosenberg & Mardall*. A satisfactory, straightforward job.

MARKET HALL, Market Street and New Street. Opened in 1827. Three-bay façade with giant columns for the upper floors. Stuccoed.

PERAMBULATION. The best street is LOWER HIGH STREET, with the Grammar School, the two chapels, and the two best houses, Nos 7 and 8, both of brick, both decidedly provincial, but both very enjoyable. The one, STOURHURST, has two canted bay windows with Venetian windows wrapped round them. In the centre a tripartite lunette window. Wild top parapet (cf. Broome House) with two broken pediments flanking a segmental one with a round window. Doorway with segmental pediment on columns. The date is probably *c.*1760. Its neighbour is all Gothic, and so probably a little later. All the windows have ogee heads. Even the parapet sprouts out in two ogee gables with finials. In the attic quatrefoil windows. Doorway with clustered shafts instead of columns. To the l. STABLES, also all ogee. S of the Lower High Street a triangle of streets with little more. In the HIGH STREET, which winds nicely, are many old, but few remarkable buildings. The exceptions are (the TALBOT INN, early C17 and refronted in the C18, with some C17 plaster work, and) Nos 122–4, a five-bay Georgian house, badly mauled, but with a nice middle window and a tripartite lunette window over. High parapet and three-bay pediment. In NEW ROAD No. 19, a three-bay house with a nice doorway, in MARKET STREET No. 63, three-storeyed, Georgian and quite plain. COVENTRY STREET is crossed by the fine ten-arched VIADUCT of 1882. Brick and stone, by *Rowbotham* of Wolverhampton.

STOURPORT 8070

Stourport is the only town in England built in consequence of a canal. The Staffordshire and Worcestershire Canal was built in 1766–71 by *Brindley*, designer of the first of the English canals, the Bridgewater Canal of 1761. Stourport was created in the place where the Stour joins the Severn.

ST MICHAEL. Designed by *Sir George Gilbert Scott* in 1875 and started after his death in 1881. The work was carried on by Sir George's son *John Oldrid Scott*. The consecration took place only in 1910, and there was then no w steeple nor a chancel. Nor are these two essential parts of the ambitious composition in existence now. The nave with its six-bay arcades and three-light clerestory windows is impressive in scale and competent in detail. To the w a new chapel nestles under the very high tower arch. Heavy s porch. Rood-loft turret (what for ?) at the E end of the s aisle. The bulk of the money needed for the nave was given by the incumbent, Benjamin Gibbons. The church replaces one of brick built in 1782 by *James Rose*.

CIVIC CENTRE, New Street. By *Andrews & Hazzard* of Birmingham, 1963 etc. A three-storeyed office range with curtain walling, and on one of its sides the Hall, on the other the circular Council Chamber, both with narrow slit windows.

In the WAR MEMORIAL GARDENS is stonework from the gardens of Great Witley Court.*

POWER STATION. By *Farmer & Dark*, 1946–7. An addition to buildings of 1925 and 1936. The addition is worth mentioning as one of the first not to continue Giles Scott's brick tradition of Battersea.

PERAMBULATION. Stourport is a pleasant town, more pleasant probably now that the canal barges have been replaced by pleasure boats, and the basins look gay. The happiest spot is the basin w of MART LANE. Across it one sees the former central WAREHOUSE, early C19, red brick, quite a long front with a cupola and at its s end the back of the TONTINE INN.‡ The inn was opened in 1788 by the Canal Company. The separate houses were used by hop merchants. Its front faces a lawn at the foot of which is the Severn. The composition is a terrace of five houses, the inn – unfortunately with a

* Information given me by Mr R. J. Collins.

‡ Tontine is a financial scheme by which subscribers receive annuities out of profits.

Victorian porch – in the middle. Seven widely spaced bays, two and a half storeys, brick. At the N end of Mart Lane to the E in LICHFIELD ROAD a few Georgian houses. More in YORK STREET to the W. The POLICE STATION has a specially nice doorcase with Roman Doric columns, a head above the door, and a frieze with wreaths. On the other side No. 21 has a Venetian doorway with pediment. Now down BRIDGE STREET with more minor Georgian houses – No. 13 has the best doorcase – to the BRIDGE. This is of iron and was built in 1870. It is not of special value. The abutments are of stone, and there is a causeway of brick from Bridge Street. On the W a public park by the river. Stourport is anxious to make itself attractive. At the top of Bridge Street, i.e. the corner of NEW STREET, the TOWN HALL, very minor, the front with tripartite arcading, the middle arch much wider. The N side of New Street is a consistent terrace of Georgian houses, quite something with its diversity of entrances. The HIGH STREET is the N continuation of Bridge Street. Nos 19 and 20 have pretty doorcases. Behind the street is the METHODIST CHAPEL. Three bays, stuccoed. The porch and the lower window details show that the Georgian discipline was going. Yet the building is supposed to be of 1787 for its centre and of 1812 for the chancel and the side parts with the galleries. At the top of the High Street the SWAN INN, *c.*1840 probably with its Tuscan porch between canted bay windows. Finally, NE of the Swan beyond the new road widening, in MITTON STREET No. 41 – the only noteworthy pre-Canal house, timber-framed and of *c.*1600.

PARSONS CHAIN COMPANY, Worcester Road. 1960–2 by *S. T. Walker & Partners* of Birmingham.

(LICKHILL MANOR, 1½ m. NW. A three-storeyed house of seven bays. NMR)

5 REDSTONE ROCK HERMITAGE, 1½ m. S, on the W bank of the Severn. A once inhabited cave (cf. Wolverley, p. 292, Areley Kings, p. 71, and Stanford-on-Teme, p. 263).

BLACKSTONE ROCK, 2 m. NW, on the E bank of the Severn, overlooking Ribbesford. Also a cave.

9040

STRENSHAM

ST PHILIP AND ST JAMES, Lower Strensham. As a building the church is not of much interest. Perp W tower with higher oblong stair-turret. C14 windows. The evidence in the chancel confused. Very wide nave with wagon roof and tie-beams. Against one an angel ready to take off. – FONT. Circular and Norman, and decorated with arcading. – Two-decker PULPIT; C18. – FAMILY PEW with Jacobean panels. – Early C16 BENCHES, a large set. – Nave PANELLING, linenfold, i.e. early C16, with hat-pegs. – WEST GALLERY. This is decorated with twenty-three painted saints from the former SCREEN and from what else? The painting is rustic work of *c.*1490–1500. – The woodwork also probably from the screen. Leaf spandrels and posts with canopies. – TILES of the C15 in the nave. – PLATE. Cup and Paten, 1571, by *F. R.*; Flagon 1663, by *D. R.*; pair of Candlesticks, 1672, by *T. I.*; Paten, 1692, by *D. B.* – MONUMENTS. On the chancel floor two excellent brasses: Robert Russell † 1390, 4 ft 7 in figure, and John Russell † 1405, 4 ft 1 in., plus a canopy. – In the chancel also brasses to Robert Russell † 1502 and wife (3 ft) and to Sir John † 1562 and wife, kneeling 12½ in. figures. – Sir Thomas Russell † 1632 and wife. Standing alabaster monument with two recumbent effigies. The tomb-chest is open to the front and shows the coffin. L. and r. of this the bases of the columns. On them strapwork and skulls. The columns carry a straight top with above an open segmental pediment. Behind the effigies arch with ribbonwork in the spandrels. Delightfully crisp decoration. – Sir Francis Russell † 1705 by *Edward Stanton*. Large standing marble monument. Semi-reclining effigy in a somewhat twisted position. At his head his wife kneels and gesticulates. Reredos with columns and open segmental pediment. Putti in clouds hold his coronet, an almost blasphemous piece of composition. – Mrs Anne Guise † 1734. Standing monument, the lady semi-reclining on the sarcophagus. High marble back wall. – Mrs Dauncey † 1733, tablet with urn and obelisk. Attributed to *White*. – Sir Charles Trubshaw Withers † 1804. Tablet. Coloured marbles. Two small seated allegories. – Samuel Butler Memorial. By *Ashton*. Gothic, perhaps of the 1830s.

MOAT FARMHOUSE, Lower Strensham. C18. Stone. Three-bay centre and two-bay wings. Hipped roof.

RUSSELL ALMSHOUSES, Upper Strensham. Centre and two short wings. Brick. Quite humble.

STRENSHAM COURT. 1824. Large, two-storeyed ashlar-faced house in the Grecian taste with a deep tetrastyle giant portico of unfluted Ionic columns.*

*An ICE HOUSE is reported in the grounds.

Strensham church, brass to Robert Russell †1390

SUCKLEY

7050

ST JOHN BAPTIST. 1878–9 by *Hopkins*. A big elephant-grey church in the Late Geometrical style. The E window has purely geometrical tracery, the W window is rather like 1300. W tower with pairs of two-light bell-openings. Pyramid roof. S aisle and N transept. Richly decorated corbels for the chancel arch, with fern, birds, etc. In the chancel a genuine C14 recess with ball-flower. – FONT. Norman. Round, with tapering sides and a chain of decorated lozenges (cf. Middle Littleton). – PULPIT. With Jacobean blank-arch panels. – STAINED GLASS. In the chancel by *Kempe*, *c*.1900–5. – PLATE. Cup by *H. W.* and Cover Paten of 1571. – MONUMENTS. Many tablets – more than twelve in the tower.

WHITE HOUSE, 1 m. N. Queen Anne. Of three storeys. Brick, whitened. Segment-headed windows. The doorway has a lovely apsidal hood on carved brackets. Foliage and a basket of flowers and a cherub's head in the hood. The house was originally seven bays wide, and the doorway was in the middle.

LOWER TUNDRIDGE FARMHOUSE, 1 m. SE. Very large, late timber-framed farmhouse, the ground floor of close studding, the upper floor with square panels. L-plan with three-bay rectangular front block on high stone plinth, making four storeys – cellar, ground, first, and high attic floor. Most of the windows have original ovolo mullions and transoms, projecting beyond the wall-face, but they are mutilated and spoilt in their effect – as is the house – by their red-tiled pent-roofs. The design of the chimneystacks, as well as the symmetrical main front, is transitional between Jacobean and Georgian. From *c*.1700 houses of identical plan and proportions were built in brick, but the windows became vertically elongated and a central front door was added (FWBC).

SWINFORD *see* OLD SWINFORD

TARDEBIGGE

9060

ST BARTHOLOMEW. 1777 by *Francis Hiorn*, the chancel added in 1879–80 by *Rowe*. Hiorn's tower is not easily forgotten. It is slender, crowned by a high needle spire, and has a decidedly Baroque bell-stage with concave walls and pairs of columns jutting forward at the angles. One-storeyed attachments l. and r. The body of the church, and especially the interior, is uneventful. Five bays, round-headed windows. The E apse by

Rowe fits remarkably, in spite of modestly medieval capitals. – WOODWORK in the chancel. Pleasant, of 1907. – STAINED GLASS. The Pentecost in the E window is robust and quite monumental. – In a N window glass of 1894 in that somewhat German Renaissance style which was considered particularly suitable for Georgian churches. – PLATE. Set of 1790. – MONUMENTS. Lady Mary Cookes † 1693 and her husband. Very large tablet. Twisted columns and between an oval area with the two three-quarter figures in relief. The inscription reads:

> Mary the one Thing Neceſsary Sought,
> Not what the Rabbies, but what Jesus Taught,
> Soe did our Mary, make't Her Greateſt Care,
> T'obey what ye other Mary, once did Heare
> But Tir'd with th' Eearthly Caſe, her Soul Inſpir'd
> With Love Divine, A Nobler Seat Required,
> Mounted on Cherubs Wings, through Æthers Way
> And Cloath'd with Light of never failing day,
> Sailing by all the Sparkling Orbs of Night
> See Stopp'd at laſt, where's Intellectuall Light,
> Harke how she Sings, with all th' Celeſtiall Choire
> Anthems of Praiſe in Tune to Davids Lyre
> Not Taught by Art, Inſpir'd from above
> She Chants forth Praiſes, to the GOD of Love.

Other Archer, sixth Earl of Plymouth. By *Chantrey*, 1835. White marble. Seated mourning woman in profile. To her r. pedestal with urn, and on the ground book and chalice.

PARSONAGE. White, early C19. (Mr Colvin reports alterations by *Thomas Cundy* in 1815.)

HEWELL GRANGE, ¾ m. E. 1884–91 by *Bodley & Garner* for the Earl of Plymouth (of the Windsor family). The house replaces one by *Cundy*, of which only the four LODGES of the main gates remain. The grounds were laid out by *Repton*. Bodley & Garner's house is of red sandstone, in the Jacobean style except for certain decorative details which are rather Quattrocento or Early French Renaissance. Entrance side long with wings stepped forward. Centre porte-cochère. Cupola over the
97 centre. The garden side is similar but has two turrets and a centre loggia. Three storeys. The windows are mullioned and transomed. The gables are boldly shaped. Bay windows and a middle oriel on the entrance side are semicircular or have semicircularly projecting centres. The interior receives you in a prodigious entrance hall filling at least half the total space of

the house. It is two storeys in height, with colonnaded galleries on three sides. On the short side they are one even run, on the long sides they are in twos. Below, the hall ends l. and r. in screens: six columns and a centre rising in an arch. Columns of black fossiliferous limestone. Behind the l. screen the hall extends right to the end windows. Behind the r. screen follows the generous staircase, of Jacobean detail but a type rather of *c.*1700. It leads to a first-floor landing filling all the area between the staircase and the other end of the house. The details of the hall are even more decidedly Renaissance than the outside. (The chapel has a wooden ceiling by *Detmar Blow & Billerey* and marble and lapis lazuli paving by *Farmer & Brindley.*) The rooms of the house are insignificant in comparison with this overwhelming display of the hall. Garden with trimmed hedges and a WELLHEAD from the Palazzo Marcello in Venice.

CATTESPOOLE, 1½ m. NE. Timber-framed, of *c.*1600. Gabled front, l. and r. gables over projecting wings. One of the few houses still with the beautiful natural colours of its materials.

TUTNALL HALL, 1 m. NW. Early C18. Brick, of seven bays and two and a half storeys. A Warwickshire and Shropshire type with giant pilasters at the angles and flanking the three middle bays. The pilasters are clumsy in the height of their bases and the bulgy friezes. The absence of a proper parapet is a pity too. Windows with keystones.

TARDEBIGGE FARM, *see* Stoke Prior, p. 267.

TENBURY WELLS

5060

Tenbury before the C19 was merely a coaching town on one of the main London to North Wales roads. Then, in 1839, mineral springs were discovered, and a pump room was built. For a while the little town flourished, but soon it sank back into its comfortable tranquillity.

ST MARY. The church appears entirely Victorian, and it is indeed largely the work of *Henry Woodyer*; 1865. The restoration cost £3,000. It was a restoration; for the W tower is Late Norman – see the twin N bell-openings including one waterleaf capital – and the tower parapet is C17. The chancel is medieval too, as is proved by the EASTER SEPULCHRE in the N wall, which, with its canopy, must be of the C14. The aisle arcades with their quatrefoil piers probably also represent what was there. Woodyer really comes into his own only with the W opening into the organ chamber. Doorway and arch separated by a pier below, large reticulated opening above. – SCULPTURE. Parts of an Anglo-Saxon cross shaft with interlace (N aisle). – ARCHITECTURAL FRAGMENTS. Outside the church a trumpet capital from a respond and smaller waterleaf capitals. They belonged no doubt to the church which went with the Norman tower.* – STAINED GLASS. The E window is by *Hardman*. – PLATE. Chalice of 1698; Paten of 1729. – MONUMENTS. In the Easter Sepulchre miniature effigy of a cross-legged late C13 Knight holding his heart. No doubt the memorial of a heart burial. – Thomas Archer and wife, put up in 1581. Alabaster effigies, richly detailed. Tomb-chest with tapering pilasters. Ovals in the panels. – William Godson † 1822. By *Bacon Jun. & Manning*. Large obelisk with rays, clouds, and an angel. Below, a woman has thrown herself over a broken column.

ST MICHAEL (R.C.), 2 m. SW. Built in 1856 to *Woodyer*'s design and at the expense of the Rev. Sir Frederick Gore Ouseley. It is a large church, and would be yet more impressive had it received its intended crossing tower. Nave and aisles, transepts, and a high polygonal apse. Four-bay arcades and round piers of blue stone and Early Gothic capitals. The style of the details is *c*.1300. Woodyer is recognizable primarily by his steep roofs, his steep arches, and his steep porch entrance. Typically High Victorian is the two-bay arcade to the chancel chapels. The two arches are taken in by one giant arch, and a blank foiled roundel is placed into the spandrel. – FONT COVER. A very high wooden canopy. – STAINED GLASS. In the sanctuary by *Hardman*.

A wooden cloister connects the church with ST MICHAEL'S COLLEGE, built at the same time, also by *Woodyer*. It is essentially one oblong range with a short lower wing towards the church. A low tower in the re-entrant angle. In this building Woodyer's idiosyncrasies come out much more strongly, especially in the crazily steep narrow dormers. Odd also on the S front the buttressing of the four W and the three E bays. A handsome four bays of stone cloister run along part of the side towards the church.

THE TOWN. There is not much to be seen at Tenbury, but it is pleasant to walk in the streets of the little town. Its N end is the BRIDGE into Shropshire. The three N arches are medieval and heavily ribbed on their underside. In TEME STREET nothing

* Mr Neil Stratford drew my attention to these pieces.

except the remains of the BATHS behind the Crow Hotel, built in 1862 (architect *James Cranston*),* and much like Gothicky or Chinesey fair stuff, i.e. without seriousness or taste. In MARKET STREET is the ROYAL OAK, Jacobean probably, a flat, timber-framed façade decorated from top to bottom with cusped concave-sided lozenges. In the MARKET SQUARE the oval MARKET HOUSE of 1811, and opposite it a late C18 pair of houses of together eleven bays. Doorways with Gothick clustered shafts. Down CROSS STREET, to finish with, where the KING'S HEAD is timber-framed and has an overhang on brackets, CORNWALL HOUSE is of brick and has a big, shaped end-gable, and PEMBROKE HOUSE is timber-framed again and stands nicely across the vista.

(KYREWOOD HOUSE, ¾ m. ESE. Georgian, of brick, three bays to the road, five to the garden. Doorway with pilasters and pediment. The house is supposed to have been built in 1721. Fine staircase in an almost circular hall with a glazed dome and some plasterwork.‡)

THORNGROVE *see* GRIMLEY

THROCKMORTON

9040

CHURCH. Nave, S aisle, central tower, and chancel. The S arcade of five bays is C13, very irregular in the height and width of the double-chamfered arches. The low, narrow middle arch corresponds to the S doorway. This also has two continuous chamfers. In the central tower and the chancel windows of *c.*1300, much redone at the restoration of 1880. The best preserved window is in the nave on the N side: three stepped, cusped lancet lights. – PLATE. Cup and Cover Paten, *c.*1571; Paten, *c.*1635.

COURT FARM. A splendid timber-framed late medieval hall and solar of *c.*1500. The hall part is of three bays plus screens passage and gallery bay with the original four-centred doorhead. There was, in addition, a service bay, now gone. The three-bay hall range, though now floored, still has parts of the spere-truss and the almost complete central truss which is an open collar-truss with the feet of the principals tenoned into post-head timbers. The latter have the appearance of the ends of a sawn off tie-beam. They are in fact original, but a device more frequently found in Shropshire than Worcestershire. A large window occupied most of the upper bay wall-frame. The third

*So Mr R. J. Collins tells me.

‡This entry was kindly supplied by Mr S. P. Thomas.

bay of the hall range was floored. The positions of the rails of the front wall-frame show very clearly the original internal arrangement. The solar wing is remarkable for its cusped timbers in the front and second trusses. In the front they make trefoils the right way up and upside down. The extremely refined mouldings of the timbers beneath the central truss of the great chamber and the lack of structural discipline in the design of the trusses themselves point to a late date. The fireplaces of the solar wing are probably contemporary with the wing, and the present shaft may be a reproduction of the original – a type that preceded the great brick-shafts of *c.*1570 onwards (FWBC).

9050

TIBBERTON

ST PETER AD VINCULA. 1868 by *Hopkins*. Nave and chancel with timber bell-turret. Brick-faced interior with some yellow and black decoration. – PLATE. Cup and Cover Paten of 1571 by *H. W.* – MONUMENTS. Three characteristic tablets with urns, commemorating deaths in 1797, 1804, and 1817.

RECTORY FARMHOUSE. Large timber-framed house of the C17, consisting of, in the main range, upper bay, narrow fireplace bay with cluster of four diagonal brick shafts on the ridge line, and the house-place bay, all of two tall storeys and attic. On the N side of the fireplace structure was formerly the entrance with a porch the full height of the house, and on the S side, in the same bay, the original staircase, only partly surviving. At the lower end of the main range, a two-bay service cross-wing, containing the original kitchen. A great seven-bay weatherboarded barn, contemporary with the house, and nice C18 brick stables surround the fold (FWBC).

7070

TRIMPLEY

HOLY TRINITY. 1844 by *H. Eginton*. Nave and chancel in one, apse, bellcote – all neo-Norman. The façade is quite ornate, with its W portal, arcading above, rose window with odd ropy detail, and bellcote.

TUTNALL HALL *see* TARDEBIGGE

7080

UPPER ARLEY

ST PETER. (Fragments of Norman ornament in the nave S wall show the existence of a church of that date.) The present church, however, is of the early C14, see some Dec windows and the N arcade inside (quatrefoil piers with thin shafts in the diagonals), and the chancel arch. The N chapel arcade is imitation. The chancel was largely rebuilt in 1885. Short nave. The early C16 clerestory is almost a copy of that of the Kidderminster parish church. Good nave roof. The tower is post-medieval, see the wide arch to the nave. The bell-openings are C18 anyway. – COMMUNION RAIL. The two halves project in a curve. Early Gothick, i.e. *c.*1750–75. – PAINTING. The wall painting above the chancel arch is almost entirely unrecognizable. – STAINED GLASS. E window by *Kempe*, 1887. – PLATE. Set of 1816. – MONUMENTS. Cross-legged Knight, early C14. The effigy must once have been a fine one. – Sir Henry Lyttleton † 1693. Tablet with, at the foot, a still life of skull, trumpet, and torch. – Earl of Mountnorris and Viscount Valentia, both † 1841, two nearly identical tablets by *J. Stephens*.

(HIGHTREES FARMHOUSE, 3 m. NE. C16 timber-framed house with both close studding and ornamental framing. MHLG)

UPPER STRENSHAM *see* STRENSHAM

UPPER WICK 8050

A number of Outer Worcester houses, especially STANFIELD, and W of it the MANOR HOUSE, both brick, of five bays, and also WICK EPISCOPI, ¼ m. E of Stanfield, of six bays with a Tuscan porch.

UPTON-ON-SEVERN 8040

OLD CHURCH. Of the old church, close to the Severn, only the tower remains. The rest was – sad to report – pulled down in
1937. The tower must be of *c.*1300. This is what the long, slim 80
two-light transomed bell-openings with their Y-tracery indicate and the arch to the nave with its continuous chamfers does not contradict. In 1756–7 the medieval church was replaced, and this in its turn was abandoned in 1879 (*see* below). On the S side is just enough of the nave to say that there was a doorway with a Gibbs surround. But one major feature remains of the mid C18, and this of the greatest value to Upton: the cupola on top of the tower. This was built in 1769–70 by *Anthony Keck*. It looks un-English, with its octagon stage, its keyed-in round windows, its copper-covered cupola and little lantern. It might be in Germany.

ST PETER AND ST PAUL, at the W end of the town. 1878–9 by

Arthur Blomfield, large, brown, rockfaced, in the style of 1300.* The slender steeple is a fine sight. Five-bay arcades, five-light E window. The treatment of the N side of the chancel differs from that of the S. – PLATE. Paten by *W. L.*, *c.*1614; Set by *Richard Williams*, 1715. – MONUMENTS. Fragmentary C14 effigy of a Knight; cross-legged. – Inscription and tablets to G. E. Martin and his wife, by *Eric Gill*, *c.*1906 and *c.*1914.

ST JOSEPH (R.C.), Berryfield. Built in 1850.

GOOD SHEPHERD, Hook Common, 2 m. W of Upton-on-Severn. 1870 by *G. R. Clarke*. Stone, nave with E bellcote, and chancel. Plate-traceried windows. Scissor-braced roof.

Upton is a charming little town, as it presents itself from the river and develops on a walk which does not take long. The new BRIDGE is an extremely fine piece of 1939–40 (by *B. C. Hammond*, the County Surveyor). At its end the High Street starts. But it is worth turning S first along WATERSIDE to pass some minor warehouses and see the two best houses in Upton, both Early Georgian, both of five bays and three storeys (plus basement), and both with segment-headed windows, whether one prefers the excellent stone doorway with Gibbs surround of WATERSIDE HOUSE or the Venetian window and the arched window above of THE MALTHOUSE. The HIGH STREET, soon after the start, has the timber-framed ANCHOR INN of 1601 on the l. (partly imitation). Then turn for a moment into CHURCH STREET with minor timber-framed and Georgian brick houses. The best is again early C18, a terrace of even height yet partly two-storeyed, partly two-and-half-storeyed. Parapet with vases. Back to the HIGH STREET and now another timber-framed house. This has three storeys and three gables. The date 1604 is not original but fits the evidence. Opposite a nice mid-Georgian house of only one bay with a Venetian window and quoins. Opposite again the WHITE LION of three storeys, stuccoed, and with giant pilasters, a parapet with urns, and a deep porch with a large lion on. The r. hand addition has a Venetian window. The TALBOT HOTEL, small, though of two storeys, has a projecting pedimented centre, a Venetian doorway, and a Venetian window. Both these hotels are probably mid-Georgian. The Talbot makes a fine S *point de vue* from NEW STREET. In New Street No. 11 is late C18, of three storeys with two two-storeyed canted bay windows, the whole a little bleak, No. 8 has a shallow bow window flanked by doors, and No. 18 is two houses tied together by a

*It cost £12,934 5*s.* 8*d.*

big parapet with balls. Back to the Talbot and on in the direction of the High Street, i.e. along OLD STREET. Here first the former TOWN HALL, built in 1832. It is stuccoed and has four Greek Doric demi-columns below, Doric pilasters above. The BAPTIST CHAPEL lies back, on the opposite side. It is an inconspicuous building of 1734. Three bays, stuccoed, arched windows, two small top gables. Finally the RECTORY behind the new church, dated 1787. Three storeys, three bays, two two-storeyed canted bay windows, and two lunette windows above them. Doorway with broken pediment.

HILL SCHOOL, 1 m. W. By *Sir F. Gibberd*; nothing special.

UPTON SNODSBURY 9050

ST KENELM. Nearly all of 1873–4 by *W. J. Hopkins*. But the tall W tower is Perp. Also in the chancel on the S side an entertaining three-light window of the early C14. Three stepped lancet lights, but also two cunningly introduced ogee curves. In the nave three widely spaced small C13 lancets, probably trustworthy. Late Perp S doorway and low four-bay S arcade. Octagonal piers. The octagonal capitals are decorated with shields. Four-centred arches. The roof of the aisle is original too. – FONT. Octagonal, Perp, with quatrefoil panels enclosing the Signs of the Evangelists, heads, and flowers. – SCREEN. Only the tracery of the single-light divisions is original. – SOUTH DOOR. Handsomely cross-battened. – STAINED GLASS. Bits in the chancel N.

UPTON WARREN 9060

ST MICHAEL. The S tower must be mid-C13. No-one would re-set the bell-openings, which are of two lights with a roll moulding to each and plate tracery. But the tower ground stage has a Dec arch to the church and two Dec windows. A consecration in 1300 is recorded. The chancel masonry may be C17. A stone with the date 1664 survives. A rebuilding of the chancel took place in 1724 (see the E window), and the nave with its totally bare W wall and its Y-tracery in the side windows is of 1798. – Of the same time the WEST GALLERY. – STAINED GLASS. The E window by *Taylor & O'Connor*, 1880, uncommonly horrible. – PLATE. Cup and Cover Paten of 1571.

WARLEY *see* BIRMINGHAM OUTER WESTERN SUBURBS

8050

WARNDON

ST NICHOLAS. The church has a timber-framed W tower (cf. Dormston, Kington, and Pirton). It is very closely timbered in the three stages of the flank walls and the ground storey of the W wall. The panels above this have curved braces. Dating is difficult, but this tower, like the porch mentioned in Mr Charles's introduction, *could* be of the same date as the church. The body of the church is pebble-dashed. Norman S and N doorways, with plain continuous rolls. The E window of three stepped lancet lights is late C13. The small straight-headed windows of the church are Perp and have pretty tracery. The porch is of timber and could be C15 as well. – BOX PEWS. – COMMUNION RAIL. Three-sided, with tall balusters; C17. – STOVE. Early C19 or Early Victorian. Cast iron and wholly Gothic. – (SCULPTURE. In the vestry some cherubs and a pelican said to be from Worcester Cathedral.) – STAINED GLASS. C15 fragments in the heads of N and S windows. In the E window a Virgin of the early C14, similar to that at Eaton Bishop in Herefordshire, and other fragments. – PLATE. Chalice of 1669.

WARNDON FARM, next to the church, is an early C17 brick building with some stone mullioned windows. (Internally, however, it is timber-framed. The plan is of T-shape and consists of a two-storey hall part and a solar wing. The hall has a fireplace structure dividing the two bays and emerging above the roof ridge as a cluster of four diagonal stacks. Warndon Farm is perhaps the earliest brick-built farmhouse in the county. FWBC)

0060

WEBHEATH

ST PHILIP. 1869–70 by *F. Preedy*. Wide nave and chancel. Late C13 tracery. – STAINED GLASS. One S window by *Capronnier* of Brussels; 1871. The style is typically French, quite un-English.

NORGROVE COURT, 1 m. SSW. Mid C17, of brick, with cross-windows and a big hipped roof – early, if the house is really mid C17. The MHLG says *c.*1649. The fenestration is very odd. On the one side in a rhythm of 2–1–2–1–2 with the 1–axes given French windows on the upper floor. On the opposite side the fenestration is quite irregular. The bricks are laid English bond. The house ought to be investigated. (In a room inside a splendid stucco chimneypiece with an overmantel of broad strapwork. The staircase of the house has cut-out flat balusters. VCH and NMR)

WELLAND

7030

ST JAMES. 1875 by *J. W. Hugall*. Red 'crazy-paving' walls. SW porch tower with an uninspired spire. The details late C13 to early C14. Round piers of buff and blue stone striped. Early Gothic capitals. – STAINED GLASS. The E window probably by *Hardman*. – One S aisle window by *Kempe*, 1886. – PLATE. Cup by *I. P.*, 1571; Flagon, 1582; Steeple Cup and Cover by *F. Terry*, 1613. – MONUMENT. Thomas Evans † 1671. Elaborate tablet with scrolls and an open curved pediment.

SCHOOL, SCHOOLMASTER'S HOUSE, and PARSONAGE are all near by and all probably also of *c*.1875.

WELLAND COURT. Brick, mid-C18. Five bays with a one-bay pediment. Stone doorway with pediment and stone Venetian window over.

WOODSIDE FARM, ½ m. NE. Of *c*.1700. Timber-framed with three asymmetrical gables. The centre part of the house has close studding.

WEST MALVERN

7004

ST JAMES. 1870–1 by *Street*. The style is Second or Middle Pointed. S tower with transverse saddleback roof. Five stepped E lancets always have an elevating effect. Low Baptistery of 1924–6 by *Gillespie*. – COMMUNION RAIL. Of brass. By *Sir G. G. Scott*. It was given to the church by Westminster Abbey, patrons of the living, in 1870. It had until then been in Henry VII's Chapel. – STAINED GLASS. Mostly by *Hardman*, but one S aisle window by *Wailes*.

ST JAMES'S SCHOOL. A large mansion of *c*.1850 spectacularly enlarged *c*.1890 by the Dowager Lady Howard de Walden, handled in a subdued Italianate, not at all showy except perhaps for the two-storeyed, one-bay extension to the W. Splendid terraces also to the W. The extensive STABLING is across Park Road. Lady Howard de Walden spent much money on creating footpaths in the hills.

(BRAND LODGE. By *Ernest Newton*, and very typical of him. Centre and cross-gabled wings, a semicircular porch in the middle, and metal-faced shallow polygonal bay windows in the middles of the wings. NMR)

8060
WESTWOOD PARK

The estate was founded in the C12 as an abbey for monks and nuns according to the rule of Fontevrault. It later became a normal Benedictine nunnery. After the Dissolution it came to the Pakingtons, and Sir John Pakington, probably after his wedding in 1598 (according to Habington before 1600), built himself a hunting lodge in the wood. His principal home was Hampton Lovett. After this had been burnt in the Civil War, Sir John Pakington, grandson of the other Sir John, added the wings and made other alterations. The house, of brick with red sandstone dressings, lies in large grounds. A straight avenue leads from the E to the gatehouse, above which, as one approaches, towers the compact house. Originally there were more straight avenues, and they radiated from the house. The GATEHOUSE has two lodges with mullioned and transomed windows, shaped gables, and an arch with openwork strap decoration and the Pakingtons' stars and wheatsheaves, also in openwork. There is a broad wooden cupola on top, its roof of a convex–concave outline. All this, judging from the wings of the house, with which it goes perfectly, must be of *c.*1660–70, though it is conservative for such a date. In the spacious forecourt are two pavilions, again with convex–concave roofs. The windows are of the cross type. According to Kip (*c.*1700) there were originally four such pavilions, the other two connected with a back court corresponding to the forecourt. All four continued along the lines of the wings of the house.

67 The wings are the strangest feature of the HOUSE. They were attached diagonally to the angles of the compact shooting lodge. The joining was done so well that no change of plan, or indeed break of style, is noticed. This of course is largely due to the conservatism of the work of *c.*1660–70. Even the bricks were still laid English bond. The centre of *c.*1598–1600 is more or less square in plan but highly varied in outline, with a passion for canted bay windows. The windows have mullions and transoms. The height is exceptional: three storeys to the front, four to the back. To the SE lies the hall, behind it were service rooms and the staircase, and behind that the kitchen and probably a parlour, all this neatly fitted into the basic square. Such compact plans are rare in Elizabethan and Jacobean architecture, but they do exist (cf. e.g. Barlborough in Derbyshire and such hunting lodges as Sherborne and Cranborne). How much of the decoration of this centre block is of *c.*1600, how much of

c.1660–70 is not certain. The shaped gables and the parapets e.g. could just be of c.1600, though one would prefer a Jacobean date, but they may be just as well (and more probably are) a remodelling of the type when the wings were built. At any rate the wings take up these motifs without hesitation. One is in a similar quandary concerning the porch. Mr Hussey calls it Sir John I, the VCH Sir John III. It is tripartite, with attached columns and the arches arranged à la Arch of Constantine. Strapwork cartouches and an eagle above the middle arch. Above the porch in the centre of the wall is a square panel with a shield in a garland, and that is the first indication of a turn from a belated Jacobean to the Inigo-Jones–Webb–May–Wren tradition. The wings carry at their ends pavilion roofs of a concave–convex–concave outline.* The only thing which distinguishes them stylistically from the earlier work is that there is more wall and less window. To the SW and NE the wings have projecting chimneybreasts.

The porch leads straight into the GREAT HALL, which occupies the whole of this part of the basic square, i.e. about two-fifths of it. It is now entered in its middle, which means a C17 alteration of the traditional entry arrangement and would be exceedingly early if it is original. But if the porch is of c.1660, then at that date the entry might also have been shifted. The plasterwork and other decoration of the hall is not original. Behind it lies the impressive STAIRCASE. This must be of c.1670 (when the small outer projection on the NE side was also made), and it is on an exceptional plan. It runs up in two flights separated by a landing, but the flights are in line and not broken at an angle. The effect is, on its limited scale, comparable to that at Althorp. The newel posts are columns rising much higher than the balustrade and crowned by balls. Thick, still vertically symmetrical balusters. The door surrounds are of c.1670 too. The GREAT CHAMBER above the hall was probably always the most spectacular room. It has a gorgeous wooden chimneypiece of c.1600, with columns, a dragon frieze, and a broad top frieze of broad strapwork. But the ceiling, equally gorgeous, is of c.1675 and eminently 71
characteristic of that date in composition as well as the use of wreaths. The room has four canted bay windows, two to the SE, and one each to SW and NE. Plasterwork of the same date is in the wings.

* But Kip shows plain, steep pyramid roofs. The roofs as they are now were done by *Sir Reginald Blomfield*.

WHEATFIELD *see* POWICK

WHITE HOUSE *see* SUCKLEY

9050

WHITE LADIES ASTON

So called because the Cistercian priory of Whistones, in the N suburbs of Worcester, held a manor at Aston from the mid C13 to the Dissolution.

ST JOHN BAPTIST. Nave and chancel and a tall weather-boarded bell-turret with spire. It stands on heavy timbers inside the nave (cf. Mamble), and could hardly have been built *after* the construction of the nave. The nave has a simple Norman S doorway of which only the imposts are original. In the chancel a Norman window, also on the S side. The chancel was probably Norman too, but is severely altered. The N aisle is of 1861. – FONT. Twelve-sided, with thin rolls along the edges. What date is that? – PAINTING. On the tympanum above the chancel arch by *Mrs Anderson*, *c*.1920. – PLATE. Cup and Cover Paten by *I. P.*, 1571.

ASTON HALL, at the S end of the village. Probably of *c*.1600, with a remarkable brick chimney with sunk lozenges in a chain and sunk oblongs (cf. Priory House, Droitwich).

8050

WHITTINGTON

ST PHILIP AND ST JAMES. 1842 by *A. E. Perkins*. Chalk, rock-faced. Nave and chancel and a thin stone bell-turret. Lancet windows. – BOX PEWS.

7060

WICHENFORD

ST LAWRENCE. The general impression is Victorian, but there are a few Norman fragments loose inside,* the chancel is C13, the lower part of the tower Dec, and the nave also Dec. It is a sizeable church, and the W tower received its present spire at the hands of *A. E. Perkins* in 1863. – PLATE. Cup and Cover Paten, *c*.1571; Almsdish by *Peter Taylor*, 1747. – MONUMENTS. John Washbourne † 1615. Tomb-chest with recumbent effigies. The children kneel against the chest. A superstructure has probably disappeared. – John and Anthony Washbourne. Erected in 1632. Anthony was the father of John, and John was the father of the John of the other monument.

* Mr Stratford compares them with Rock.

Large standing monument, all of wood and really very bad. How can an old and distinguished family have been satisfied with such a performance? Two Knights on two benches, the lower with little headroom. Above and behind two kneeling figures in front of flat arches. Straight top.

WICHENFORD COURT. A perfect example of the type of house customary in the provinces about 1670–80. Seven by three bays, hipped roof, wooden mullion-and-transom-cross windows. Nothing more than that. (Inside one wooden overmantel with Jacobean panels. VCH)

WICK

9040

ST BARTHOLOMEW. Much of the church is Norman, though the exterior tells more of the Victorian restorations and alterations of 1861 (by *Whitfield Dawkes*) and of 1893. The three-bay N arcade looks fairly early Norman and could be, if one were to assume that the unmoulded arches were later pointed. The piers are round, the capitals very elementarily moulded, the abaci square. There are several Norman windows, and the inner S doorway is Norman. But is the blocked W arch Norman too? The nave has a Perp wagon roof. – COMMUNION RAIL. Jacobean, with knobs. – STAINED GLASS. In the chancel by *Kempe*, probably *c.*1890. – PLATE. Cup and Paten Cover of 1571. – In the churchyard the LYCHGATE is said to be by *Bodley*, and he is also credited with the top of the CHURCHYARD CROSS, though the VCH calls it 1911.

WICK MANOR. This eminently picturesque large house just NW of the church is in fact entirely an evocation. It has all the motifs of genuine Worcestershire timber-framing and groups them suggestively. It was done in 1923 round a Georgian core.

A COTTAGE on the N side of the village street has an exposed cruck truss. Yet the timbers look Elizabethan at the earliest. On the same side of the street is a very attractive house of *c.*1840 with Early Tudor windows and bargeboarded gables, very similar to one at Wyre Piddle.

WICKHAMFORD

0040

ST JOHN BAPTIST. Originally unbuttressed C17 W tower. C13 is the chancel – see the side lancets. The E window and the chancel arch are Dec. In the nave N wall a Dec, in the nave S wall a late C17 window. The interior is in a most satisfying state, full of incident and not demonstratively restored.* It is

*Restoration by *G. C. Lees Milne*, 1949.

worthy of note that the chancel never received stalls. Above the chancel arch is a beam with pretty Perp cresting, and above that a tympanum with the arms of Charles II. – FONT. With bits of C17 woodwork stuck on. – The same applies to the PULPIT. – Below the pulpit the lower tiers of a real three-decker. – Under the tower wooden panels with tracery, probably from a Perp PULPIT. – BOX PEWS. With applied C16 linenfold panels. – Jacobean chancel PANELLING. – WEST GALLERY with three panels of beautiful late C17 carvings from a London church. – PEW by the pulpit. Six small Flemish panels. – COMMUNION RAIL. C18. – PAINTING. Wall painting of the Virgin (E wall). No detail can be recognized. The VCH calls it late C13. – PLATE. Cup and Cover Paten 1571. – MONUMENTS. In the chancel the splendid
61 double monument of Sir Samuel and Sir Edward Sandys, both † 1626, and their wives. Alabaster. Two tomb-chests, that of the son just a little lower than that of the father. Recumbent effigies. Against both kneeling children. Five black columns carry four arches. Four wall arches. Straight canopy, its underside decorated with quatrefoils in niches, a remarkable Gothic survival (cf. Inkberrow). Top achievements. – (Lees Milne memorial tablet. By *Reynolds Stone*, 1966.)

MANOR HOUSE, by the church. Highly picturesque. Dated C16 by the VCH. (Inside a C17 chimneypiece of wood.)

8070

WILDEN

ALL SAINTS. 1880 by *W. J. Hopkins*, built at the expense of Alfred Baldwin. Brick, lancet windows and some with geometrical tracery. Double bellcote. All that is not promising, and so it is unexpected to discover inside that the church is truly memorable as a shrine of *Morris* windows. It is probably the only church provided with Morris glass in all its windows. Admittedly it is all of 1900–14, i.e. of after both *Morris*'s and *Burne-Jones*'s deaths, but the cartoons used were all older, and the unity of effect remains prodigious. The choice of Morris's is understandable if one remembers that Alfred Baldwin's wife was a sister of Lady Burne-Jones. – EMBROIDERY. A piece with a big leaf pattern. No particulars seem to be known. – MONUMENT. Alfred Baldwin † 1908. Tablet with a strapwork surround. The Baldwins' ironworks were at Wilden.

WITLEY COURT *see* GREAT WITLEY

WOLLASTON *see* STOURBRIDGE

WOLVERLEY

8070

Wolverley is perhaps the village with the most personal character in the county. The centre is amazingly secluded, and it is dominated by the group of the school buildings on the one hand – themselves a powerful surprise – and by the red church on its steep rock on the other. The church is reached by steps and a ramp cut into the red sandstone.

ST JOHN BAPTIST. Built in 1772. It is most certainly not an attractive building; in fact it looks at first rather like an Early Victorian town hall. But it has a strong personality, as has the village. Red brick, W tower, nave and chancel, all big and blunt. The architect – this is quite clear – knew what he wanted. All the windows are arched, and all are set in blank arches. The chancel E window is a group of three stepped round-headed lights, again an Early Victorian rather than Georgian idea. Battlements on nave and tower. Inside there are big square piers carrying arches. Instead of capitals and abaci just blocks – which is the same in the blank arches outside. Three galleries. – FONT. Six-cornered, Gothick, i.e. probably of the time of the church. – STAINED GLASS. In the chancel (S) two windows by *Morris & Co.*, designed by *J. H. Dearle*, 1899.* – PLATE. Cup and Paten of 1661. – MONUMENTS. Late C14 effigy of a Knight. The legs are broken off, but the feet against a lion are preserved. The helmet helps in the dating. – An unusual number of worth-while tablets. Humphrey Bate † 1741, specially pretty. – Mrs Sarah Hurtle † 1771. Of coloured marbles. Two putti by an urn. The composition, though not the details, still Rococo. – John Hurtle † 1792. Urn before obelisk. By *J. Nelson* of Shrewsbury. – Helen Knight † 1801. Small, by *Flaxman*. Stiffly semi-reclining female figure in relief. She is praying. Little Gothic quatrefoils in the top spandrels, though the relief is entirely classical. – Mary Smith † 1804. Of coloured marbles, again with an urn before an obelisk. – John Smith † 1824. With a heavily draped urn. By *Hollins* of Birmingham. – John Hancocks † 1849. Also urn and drapery.

SEBRIGHT SCHOOL. The old buildings, not all school buildings now, form a spacious group, entirely symmetrical. In the centre, alone of ashlar stone, is a three-bay Gothic composition 93
with three giant pointed arches and two outer staircases leading

* So Mr Sewter kindly informed me.

to a platform on the first floor behind them, where there was access to the school room. Large doorway and two very large Perp three-light windows, all behind the giant Gothic portico. The date 1620 means the endowment of the school. To the l. and r. and in line are two much lower three-bay cottages each with a little quatrefoil in the middle, and then projecting diagonally are two more buildings, one of them dated 1829, which must be roughly speaking the date of the whole. One is clearly a school building, the other may have been the master's house. Neither is Gothic at all. The school has five bays with big round-arched windows and a little top gable. In the house there are instead two storeys, and only the upper windows have round arches. Both houses have giant angle pilasters.

KNIGHT HOUSE, at the N end of the village, up the hill. Of *c.*1760, and a substantial building. Brick. Seven bays and two and a half storeys plus a parapet – a completely flat front. Fine if conventional doorway with Tuscan columns, a triglyph frieze, and a pediment. Good brick outbuildings, the ground-floor windows arched and set in blank arches. The stables have as their centre a three-bay pediment.

(BLAKES HALL, 1⅜ m. N. Cut into the solid red rock is a circular ICE HOUSE, 8½ ft in diameter and 12 ft high. *B.A.S.T.*, LXXII)

Also cut into the rock are CAVE COTTAGES, two at Drakelow, 1 m. WNW of Wolverley and 1¼ m. N of Franche. (Another is at Vale's Rock, Kingsford. MHLG)

BAXTER MEMORIAL. An obelisk a little up a wooded hillside to the E of the Drakelow–Kinver road, 1¼ m. NW of Wolverley. It was erected in the third quarter of the C19.

WOODBURY HILL *see* GREAT WITLEY

WOODMANTON FARM *see* CLIFTON-ON-TEME

WOODNORTON *see* NORTON

WOODSIDE FARM *see* WELLAND

WORCESTER 8050

INTRODUCTION

The site of Worcester has been occupied for more than 2,000 years. The first settlement, on a ridge of sand and gravel overlooking an ancient ford close to the present cathedral, dates from the Early Iron Age, the C5 or C4 BC. Later in the Iron Age the village was defended by a massive bank and ditch, which followed the line of the later Roman defences.

There is some evidence of a Roman fort, probably of the C1 A.D., S of the cathedral, and at about this time the settlement was refortified. In the later C2 or early C3 these defences, though still enclosing the same small area, were enormously strengthened with a new ditch nearly a hundred feet across. At the same time a suburb, with a suggestion of elegant buildings, was developing north of the town, in the area now between Dolday and Angel Place. This suburb was replaced in the later C3 by an extensive iron smelting factory, which produced enough slag for Andrew Yarranton to re-smelt thousands of tons of it in the C17.*

In the C7 Ravenna Cosmography, Roman Worcester is called Vertis, but there is no corroborative evidence for this name, and

*ROMAN REMAINS have come to light from time to time below the town. In 1829 a circular foundation 30 ft in diameter was found in Britannia Square and in the Pitchcroft Lane area extensive traces of iron smelting were recorded. More recently a ditch of defensive form was sectioned in Fish Street. The finds so far have been too fragmentary to allow the nature of the site to be assessed, but in all probability it began life in the C1 as a fort and later developed into a small market centre (D. Simpson).

no apparent connexion between it and Weogorna caestre, from which Worcester derives.

There is at present a gap in the history of the town between the late C4 and the late C7, when the see was founded and the minster of St Peter built. Between 872 and 899 Aethelred, Earl of the Mercians, and Aethelflaed, his wife, built a burh, a fortification of unknown extent which enclosed at least the minster and the market place, and was large enough for Aethelred to be given, in 904, a 'haga', or enclosure, of about eight acres within the burh.

The minster of St Mary, on the site of the present cathedral, was built by Oswald alongside St Peter soon after 960, and Wulstan added a bell-tower in the 1050s. The two minsters probably existed side by side until Wulstan rebuilt St Mary in 1084.

Before September 1069 Urse d'Abitot, Sheriff of Worcestershire, built a motte and bailey castle in the south-western corner of the town. It is not clear how much of the timber defences of this early castle were rebuilt in stone, but it declined in importance during the C13 and was 'wholly destroyed' by the beginning of the C14.

Domesday Book records 131 burgesses, or chief householders, in Worcester. This is a greater number than that for instance at Nottingham, which had 120. There were by this time at least three churches apart from the cathedral – St Andrew, St Helen, and St Martin – and it seems probable that the urban area, if not the fortifications, had extended as far as St Martin before 1100. There were also three houses *ultra Sabrinem*, over the Severn, which suggests that a suburb was emerging at St John's.

In 1189 Worcester received its first royal charter and in the early C13 grants of murage were levied to pay for the building and repair of the sandstone walls whose outline can still be traced on the ground. Recent excavation has shown that the ditch surrounding these walls was flat-bottomed, water-filled, and some 40 ft wide.

The importance of Worcester in the C13 is indicated by the settlements of Greyfriars and Blackfriars. The Franciscans came in 1239 and had their house E of Friar Street, the Dominicans came in 1347, and their house stood by Broad Street and Angel Lane. The prosperity of the town in the late Middle Ages was due to cloth-making. Leland writes: 'The welthe of the towne stands the most on draping, and noe towne of England, at this present tyme, makes so many cloathes yearly.' The late C16 brought a decline, but in the C18 Worcester enjoyed a comfortable affluence, as is proved by Defoe, who writes that 'the people generally (are) esteemed very rich, being full of business', and Lord Torrington in 1784, in spite of his usual bickering, calls Worcester 'well built'. As its industries he mentions china, glove-making, and carpet-making. This wealth of the town is reflected in what remains in one's memory as the most characteristic feature of Worcester: its four C18 churches, all begun between 1730 and 1770.

The C19 saw no great expansion, though architecturally the usual feelers of Late Georgian and Early Victorian terraces and villas can be followed and will be followed in the Outer Perambulation. In addition, with the coming of the Canal in 1815 and of the railway in 1850, the Shrub Hill area filled in with industry. But in spite of that C20 Worcester was a cathedral town first and foremost, and that makes it totally incomprehensible that the Council should have permitted the act of self-mutilation which is the driving of the busiest fast-traffic road through in a place a few yards from the cathedral. The crime is the planners', not the architects', and the planners would of course have been powerless without the consent of the City Council.

Worcester has a population of just under 70,000.

THE CATHEDRAL

INTRODUCTION

Worcester Cathedral from the W, looking across the Severn, is a 4
superb sight. Looking from the E is out of the question now that the new road and the roundabout have removed all peace. Looking closely at the exterior turns into a disappointment, at least for the historian: nearly the whole is smooth Victorian work directed by thorough restorers.

The cathedral goes back in all probability to the late C7. It was rebuilt when Oswald had been made bishop in 961. He also introduced (or re-introduced) Benedictine monks. His church was badly damaged by the Danes in 1041. St Wulstan, bishop at the time of the Conquest, rebuilt it. He was the only Saxon bishop to remain in office, and the reason was that he supported William. He began the present building in 1084. The monks re-entered the choir in 1089, a synod took place in the crypt in 1092. The next relevant dates are the fall of the crossing tower in 1175,* the canonization of Wulstan in 1203,

*'Turris nova corruit' (*Ann. Wig.*, Rolls Series, *Ann. Monast.*, IV, 1869, p. 383). That must mean the crossing tower.

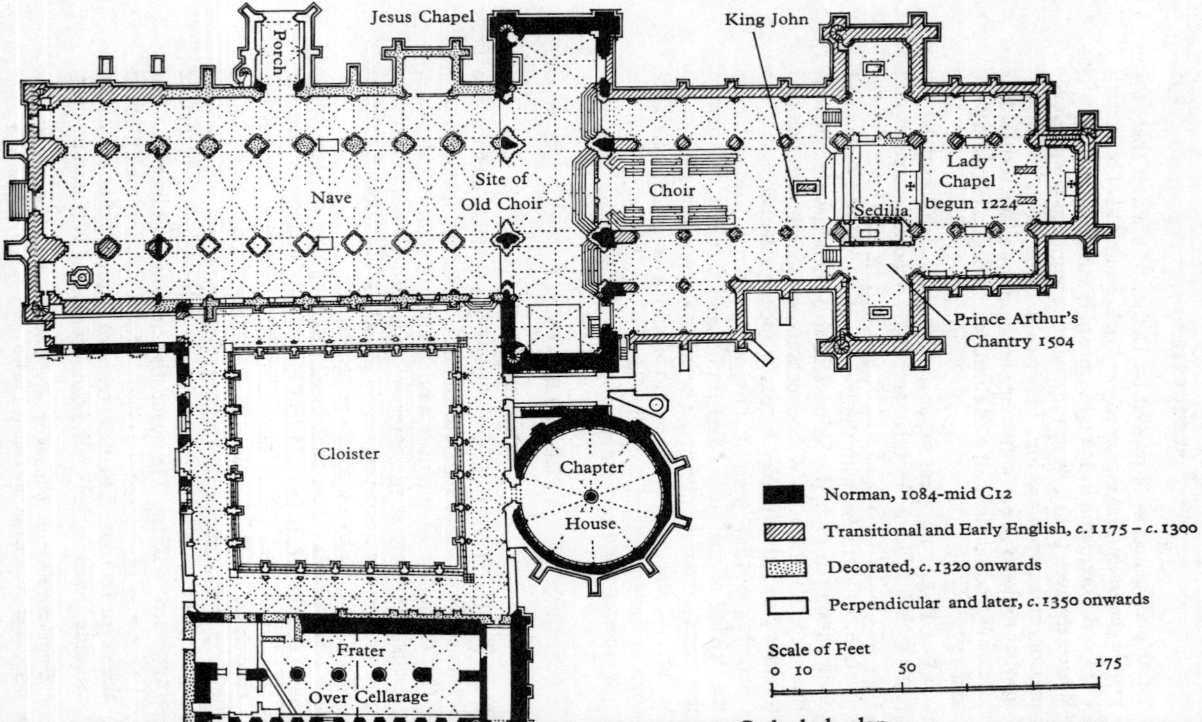

Worcester Cathedral, plan

a fire in the same year, the death of King John in 1216, a solemn rededication in 1218 in the presence of Henry III, and then – oddly enough almost immediately – the beginning of the new E end ('novum opus frontis'*) under Bishop William of Blois in 1224. After that there is a shortage of dates till one comes to the C14. The individual C14 dates will be referred to when needed. The general restoration was begun by *Perkins* in 1857 and continued by *Scott* in 1864. The renewal was complete in 1874.

The cathedral is 425 ft long. It is built in its Norman parts of oolitic limestone from the Cotswolds with sandstone, including the red variety from Alveley, in the Transitional part of Highley sandstone, in the C14 work again of Alveley sandstone, and in the C19 restoration mostly of sandstone from near Ombersley.

THE EXTERIOR

Let it be said once more that the surface of the exterior is entirely mid-Victorian, and that many windows are too. The shape of the E end of Wulstan's cathedral can be guessed from that of the crypt, of which Wulstan said: 'quam ego a fundamentis aedificavi'. It must have had a chancel with apse and ambulatory, but seems to have had no radiating chapels. This is the scheme of Jumièges of *c.*1030–65. Attached to the transepts were apsed side chapels, and there seem to have been turrets at the springing points of the nave of the ambulatory, rather as at Canterbury.‡ However, the part E of the transepts has been replaced by the E.E. work. So the examination should start at the TRANSEPTS. The N transept has its flat buttresses. They have nook-shafts with fillets, i.e. are not of Wulstan's time, but Late Norman or Transitional. The angles carry octagonal shafted turrets. The great N window is Victorian. The E and W sides are blank, except for Perp windows high up. In the S transept the S window is also Victorian. The very long Perp window in the W wall is impressive.

Next the CHANCEL, begun in 1224. It consists of four bays, then an E transept, on the pattern of Canterbury, Wells, and Lincoln, and then three bays of retrochoir with a Lady Chapel only projecting by one narrow bay. The new E end has a total length which places the crossing tower just half-way between W and E wall. The fenestration of the E parts is very beautiful and

* *Frons* was used for the chancel end in other medieval documents too.

‡ That would be the 'duae minores turres' which, the *Ann. Wig.* tell us, fell in 1222 (*ib.*, IV, p. 415).

harmonious, but it is nearly all *Perkins*'s, who had no qualms in replacing a large Perp E window and Perp aisle and clerestory windows by his correct E.E., guided to a certain extent by the indications he could obtain from the interior. Only the E transept E and end windows are original and were sufficient for Perkins to develop his long, slender lancets. The big flying buttress on the N side dates from the C18. The early buttresses are still flat. On the S side of the chancel at its W end projects a two-bay chapel of the same style and period as the rest.

The NAVE was probably begun about 1320 and not vaulted until 1377.* Its S side one cannot see in its totality, because of the cloister. But in the cloister it is patent that the lower parts of the walls with the flat buttresses are Norman. For the entrances to the cloister *see* Cloister, below. The upper parts are all Victorian. Flowing tracery in the aisle windows. Then small, two-light, straight-headed windows marking the Library, i.e. a room made in the C15 above the S aisle in the former aisle roof and outside the triforium. The clerestory has three-light windows with straight shanks. The W end, i.e. the last two bays, introduce to a different phase. There is Norman walling here, and flat buttresses and a Norman corbel table. Two round-arched aisle windows are outlined inside (*see* below). More of nave details is to be seen on the N side. Here the aisle windows are of three lights, with the five-petal-flower motif in the tracery. The projecting Jesus Chapel has a more florid Dec design. The clerestory windows are Dec too. So is the NORTH PORCH, dated by Dr Hopkins 1386. It is two-storeyed. Its façade is all Victorian, with its many corny statues (by *Hardman*). The walls are panelled and have a top quatrefoil frieze. The sides are completely blank. The interior is of two bays, vaulted with oblong tierceron stars on Purbeck marble shafts. The shafts carry sparse nobbly capitals. But look at the inner portal and you see two long thin Norman columns with block capitals – part of the Norman N portal or porch. At Tewkesbury there is just such a portal still fully preserved. The Tewkesbury porch in front of it is tunnel-vaulted. Above the Worcester doorway is the re-used head of a Dec five-petal

*Bishop Cobham (1317–27) was, we know from Leland, responsible for the N aisle vault and was buried in the aisle, but the dates for 1370–90 are less precise than they seem. They come from the notebooks of Prebendary Dr Hopkins, who must have had access to rolls now lost. If he says: nave vault 1377, is that its beginning or its completion or an average in-between date? The same question must be asked for other dates coming from him.

window. The last two bays of the nave prove again to be Norman, see the clerestory windows (later filled in with two-light reticulation tracery) and the flat buttresses. Also the wall is thicker here.

The WEST FRONT is almost entirely Victorian. The W window is of 1865. But traces of the N and S doorways and part of the arch of the middle doorway are original. The arch has zigzag and thin roll mouldings. The sculpture is by *Boulton*.

The CROSSING TOWER was re-built in 1374, after the Norman crossing tower had fallen in 1175. It is in two stages, the lower of seven very slim bays with transom. Only two contain windows; the rest is blank. The sills climb up the roof-lines of the adjoining parts. All the bays carry crocketed gables. The upper stage, above a band of quatrefoils, has two-light bell-openings with transom and bays for statuary under canopies l., r., and between. The tracery of the upper windows is Dec, that of the lower however Perp, and it seems likely, especially if one considers the interior, that there has been interference. The details, however, are all shown already in Britton's *Cathedral Antiquities*, i.e. in 1836.

THE INTERIOR

The great asset of Worcester is the unity of its interior. Although the C13 and the C14 have contributed about evenly, the C14 designers were so conformist that the century and a half hardly tells until one begins to study the detail. Chronologically however, the evidence starts of course with Wulstan's time, and
for this one must go first into the CRYPT. Here is Early 7
Norman work at its most impressive. The crypt consists of a centre of four vessels separated by columns, and seven bays long plus the *corona* or semicircle of apse columns. Around this space went an outer ambulatory, now shored off. It was separated from the centre by thick square piers about $6\frac{1}{2}$ ft thick. The straight ambulatory part is divided into two vessels, nine bays long. Moreover there is the crypt under the Norman S chancel chapel, again in two vessels. It has an E.E. continuation, and the rib-vault of this seems to indicate the existence of an apse above. It is a straightforward quadripartite vault, but in the middle of the W side, from the Norman middle column spring three radiating ribs to touch the centre of the E.E. vault and the middles of the two diagonal ribs up to it from the angles. All the Early Norman columns have plain capitals, mostly block type and single-scallop type, but also one

of the rare form of a single-trumpet-scallop.* Some abaci have billet enrichment. The vaults are plainly groined, and there are no transverse arches at all.

Chronologically next one ought to inspect the TRANSEPTS, and the very W end of the chancel, though Early Norman evidence is rare here. It consists of the following: One strong shaft of the W respond on the S side of the chancel, with a block capital and a base like many in the crypt. In the first bay of the chancel N side is the start of a gallery or triforium arch. In the aisle roofs one can see on the S as well as the N side the jambs of the triforium arches. On the S side there is also the jamb to the transept. Standing in the S transept one sees more plainly the whole arch into the former transept E chapel. The capitals are of block type but with foliage trails, and they are drastically re-done.‡ The arch has big rolls and square mouldings. Above are the traces of an upper chapel arch. Such upper chapels were not rare in England (*see* e.g. Canterbury). There is no reason to date the capitals later than *c.*1130,§ but what else there is of Norman evidence in the transept is definitely Late Norman, i.e. of after the fall of the tower in 1175. It is a shafted window with zigzag at r. angles and a kind of outer stylized beakhead. The crocket capitals make a date before *c.*1190 impossible. In the W wall is the start of blank trefoiled arcading. In the S wall is a much larger window with the same details and with keeled shafts. The keeling links this up with the major vaulting-shafts of the transept. They were, as Willis said, 'engrafted' into the walls. The buttresses outside (*see* above) were provided at the same time. The shafts are tripartite and show clearly that they were intended for rib-vaults different from the present ones. They survive up to their stiff-leaf capi-

*To the best of my knowledge this shape exists neither in Germany, whence the block capital was imported, nor in France, and Mr Stratford agrees.

‡Mr Stratford convincingly connects them with the early C12 crypt at Canterbury and also with the work of *c.*1120 etc. at Romsey (chancel E bays and S transept). Note their profuse decoration of acanthus foliage of the Winchester type, a dragon, and an angel.

§Here are Mr Stratford's thoughts on the dating: The S transept S wall seems to have been begun at the same time as the slype (*see* p. 306), i.e. immediately after 1084, but at a low level work must have been stopped until *c.*1120–40, when the E arch just discussed was built. At that time stone courses in two alternating colours were favoured (SW turret stair, E arch). This seems reasonable, as from the functional point of view completion of the chancel was so much more important. For further evidence of the decoration of the Early Norman structure *see* Furnishings and Sculpture, p. 314.

tals, but the present vault standing on them dates from *c.*1375 and has liernes. Of that time also the Perp elements. Very impressive the three-tier W window of four lights with detached mullions to the inside and some openwork cusping. Impressive also the seven-light and five-light stone grilles in the E wall at triforium level. Other bays have blank panelling. The S window is Victorian. The arches to the chancel and nave aisles are C14 again. But what is the date of the Late Norman work? If the crossing tower fell in 1175, it seems quite likely that vaulting was introduced in the damaged transepts and that the new windows came in at the same time. However, the repairs cannot have been done at once. The W bays of the nave, to which we shall turn presently, are a little earlier in their details and yet seem to be of *c.*1185. The upper parts of the S transepts* with their sophisticated varieties of zigzag seem to go with the W bays of the nave, but they have also, as we have seen, stiff-leaf capitals and in the hood of the triforium dogtooth as well. It is true that in the Canterbury choir of 1174–85 dogtooth and zigzag appear side by side, but in the West Country the earliest occurrence of both motifs together is in the retrochoir of Hereford Cathedral *c.*1190–1200. A further question is whether a development can be recognized between the E and the W walls. In favour of a later date for the W than the E is the fact that the triforium opening in the W walls has a trefoiled head. That would be surprising before 1200 (cf. Lichfield, choir aisles, W bays, *c.*1200–10). The N transept differs in many ways. The arch to the Norman E chapel is here all Victorian and without telling details. The vaulting-shafts are very similar but not quite the same,‡ but the vault is much simpler, just of diagonal and ridge-ribs. If this is really of 1376, it would be surprising. It looks C13, not C14. Can the donation in 1281 of a Bishop of Ely towards the rebuilding of the tower have anything to do with it? The arch to the chancel aisle is like the one in the S transept, but the arch to the nave aisle is early C14, not late. We shall come back to that. The Perp wall treatment differs from that in the S transept. It is much less enterprising. The N window is again Victorian.

Now, before going into the chancel, one ought to see what is

*I am using here notes from Mr Stratford.

‡Willis points out that the remodelling of *c.*1180–90 was done first on the N, then on the S side. The shafts on the N side are like those of the W bays of the nave (*see* below), those on the S side have deeper hollows between the shafts.

12 inside those two WEST BAYS OF THE NAVE which had promised Norman work outside. They are treated like this: The E piers were begun with demi-shafts on a flat surface but continued at triforium level with five vaulting-shafts. The W piers have the vaulting-shafts from the start. So here is Early *v.* Late Norman. To the arcade arches there are a continuous quarter roll and thin shafts, some of them keeled. The arch continues the quarter roll and then has steps. The arches are pointed. The treatment of the triforium is idiosyncratic. Three stepped round arches with a continuous quarter roll. Attached shafts with trumpet and crocket capitals. Arches with zigzag at r. angles and three paterae in relief above them. The whole is set in a pointed arch with a continuous quarter roll. Tripartite stepped clerestory, pointed–round–pointed. Again continuous quarter rolls, again zigzag. The vaulting-shafts are arranged for wall-arches, transverse arches, and diagonal ribs. The Perp vault put in in the C14 contradicts them. In the S aisle the original vault is preserved, the earliest rib-vault in the cathedral. The wall-shafts are as in the nave, and the capitals are trumpet-scallop. In the N aisle the vault is Perp, as in the bays further E. This work at the W end of the then Norman nave is neither dated not datable. It should, except for the lower parts of the E piers, be of *c.*1185.*

22 The CHANCEL is the architecturally most rewarding part of the building. It is uniform in style and almost a building in itself, with its four bays W and three bays E of the transepts. It is most thrilling in the Lady Chapel bay and the E transept, where verticalism is unchecked. The whole 'novum opus' belongs to a more sumptuous period than that preceding it. Purbeck marble was lavished over it, on the pattern of Canterbury and Lincoln. Work proceeded from E to W, and there is – though hardly noticeable – a joint W of the chancel transept. E of the joint the aisles have blank pointed-trefoiled arcading. The shafts are Purbeck in the Lady Chapel, stone otherwise. The capitals are all leaf crockets. In the spandrels is sculpture, foliage, and genre (i.e. little animals and monsters) and figure

*Mr Stratford points to diagonally set zigzag in the triforium arches and its reflexion at Bredon and Bricklehampton, and to the parallels with the leaf paterae in the Glastonbury Lady Chapel, the nave and N porch of Wells, the nave of St David's, and the W front of Llandaff. The Lady Chapel of Glastonbury is particularly important, as it is datable to 1184–6. It has crocket capitals just like the W bays at Worcester, i.e. a French type of capital. Another instance, specially French, is in the W bay of the chancel of Abbey Dore in Herefordshire.

scenes, many religious. The majority are Victorian (by *Boulton*) but some, especially in the Lady Chapel, in the S aisle E wall, the N aisle N wall, and most especially in the SE transept, are well preserved. The figures are thin and agile. You find a Knight fighting a Centaur (Lady Chapel), the Angel with the Last Trump, the dead clambering out of their graves, the Expulsion from Paradise, St Michael with the Scales, the Tor- 24
tures of Hell, a Knight and a Lion, Sagittarius (all SE transept), and (on the N side) the Annunciation, the Nativity, the Visitation. What conveys that irresistible *excelsior* to the Lady Chapel and the transepts is that, though windows are in two tiers, Purbeck shafts run up all the way. In the retrochoir aisles are also detached Purbeck shafts in front of the windows. The aisles are rib-vaulted with small bosses. The piers of the retrochoir have eight Purbeck and eight subsidiary stone shafts and crocket capitals. Only one N capital shows mature stiff-leaf. The arches have many mouldings. The triforium is very odd and very English. There are two layers of arcading. In the front 23
are for each bay two-light openings with much Purbeck marble and with sculpture in the spandrels. The sub-arches grow out of the super-arches in anticipation of what was to be Y-tracery, i.e. the sub-arches have only their inner shank entirely to themselves. Behind that detached arcading runs an even blank stone arcade which keeps to its own rhythm. Tripartite stepped clerestory with detached Purbeck shafts. The vaulting-shafts in the Lady Chapel rise from the ground, in the retrochoir from the arcade spandrels. They have head corbels here, and capitals first at triforium sill level and then again at clerestory sill. Quadripartite vault, just with a longitudinal ridge-rib. In the E transepts triforium, clerestory, and vault are the same. The E crossing piers have to the inside four Purbeck and three stone shafts, and yet there is no space for the diagonal ribs. The vault has of course ridge-ribs longitudinally as well as transversely.

The chancel W of the E transepts is to all intents and purposes the same. If differences are sought out, it is at once visible that the blank aisle arcading ceases and that capitals are getting richer in their displays of stiff-leaf. There is also the fact that head-stops on hood-moulds only come into the interior now. Moreover, the arch soffits differ. W of the E transepts there is a hollow in the arch, where E of them there was a roll. That the chancel should be a little later than the retrochoir stands to reason. The new work was of course started outside the Norman chancel, and this was pulled down only when the new work reached that far W. The S chapel or vestry has two bays with quadripartite vaults. The capitals are of the rich type, the windows Purbeck-shafted, except for parts of the E window, which is played down for some unknown reason. In the N chancel aisle is a pretty little oriel. This belonged to the Sacrist's Lodging, and the small Perp doorway in the aisle led to it.

At the CROSSING the display of Purbeck marble is over. The piers are Perp, of *c.*1374, with broad hollows between the shafts. Small individual capitals. Odd lierne-vault. (The upper stages of the tower have to the inside two-light windows and blank windows, with two transoms below, with one above, and all with Y–tracery, i.e. a motif of 1300 rather than 1350.)

33 With the crossing we have anticipated. The NAVE was started forty years earlier. But it was not a start from scratch. We have already seen that the N porch contains part of a Norman portal, and evidently an early one, that the W wall is Norman, and that the S wall (inside the cloister walk) is Norman too. We can see now that this S wall towards the S aisle is provided between the E and the W exits to the cloister with completely unmoulded and undecorated wide niches, 31 in. deep. They are unique in England.* Their position shows that the present piers are where the Norman piers had been. As regards the post-Norman work in the nave, the arch between N aisle and N transept must be early C14, and indeed, as we have seen, Bishop Cobham (1317–27) vaulted the N aisle. That probably refers just to the beginning; for the arcade E respond is already like the rest of the N aisle. That the Jesus Chapel has the most elaborate window tracery has already been said. The N aisle is of seven bays to the start of the Norman W bays. The arcade piers are very complex, but still starting out from the triple vaulting-shaft. The centre one has a fillet now. In the diagonals are two keels. The arches of course are as complex. The capitals are treated as one band with thick nobbly leaves. The triforium is based on that of the C13 but

*And, according to Professor Bandmann and Professor Kubach, unique in the Empire too. Otronian inner niches are familiar, but they are smaller and curved in section. As for England, the tall, narrow, and shallow niches at Tewkesbury in the same place I consider something morphologically different. The nearest parallel I have myself come across is at Villers-Saint-Paul, N of Paris and SE of Beauvais, and there they are probably of the first half of the C12.

has none of the subtle background arcading. The clerestory is stepped tripartite.

The S arcade is clearly later. There are different bases and thin leaf capitals instead of the band of leaf, the triforium has smaller capitals too, and the clerestory is generally thinner in its forms. So N went up before S, perhaps to leave the monastic side alone as long as possible. But the last two C14 bays on the N side before the Late Norman bays are reached, change to the thinner clerestory details too, though they are not quite like those on the S side. Then finally vaulting took place. The vault preceded those of crossing and S transept; for it has only diagonal and ridge-ribs and no tiercerons or liernes. This vault extends over the Late Norman W bays. The E bay of the nave is in its upper details disturbed by flying buttresses for the crossing tower, which was begun in 1374. The N aisle and the Jesus Chapel have a vault like the nave, the S aisle a more elaborate lierne-vault. That confirms the sequence postulated for the arcades.

THE CLOISTER

The present cloister was built in the C14 and C15, starting with 34
the E walk, and ending with the W walk. The time taken was about a century. One enters from the church by a doorway at the E end of the cloister which, with its capitals and fine arch mouldings, looks *c.*1300 at the latest. The doorway from the church at the W end of the cloister is smaller and Perp. The most striking motif, the chains of reticulation units in the window embrasures and some transverse arches, is applied to all walks but the western. The windows themselves are Victorian. The vault is of the same type with a central octagon of lierne ribs in all four walks, but there again the W is different in details. It is the bosses which distinguish walk from walk. In the E walk there are not over-many, and they are small and nearly all leaves and heads. The S has the finest bosses, all figures and scenes. The centre bay shows the Coronation of the Virgin. The W range again has small leaf bosses. The N bosses are quite different, with applied figures of angels instead of real bosses. It must be assumed that, though W was actually last in its walk, N was vaulted last, probably held up by the new work in the nave.

However, basically the cloister is Norman, as a closer and more extensive examination of the ranges around will at once show. The E wall has clearly Norman masonry, and as one enters the SLYPE, the first room in the E range, one is back in Wulstan's time. One enters through a doorway of the C14 with a niche l. and r., but the blind arcading in two bays of three arches each has columns with block capitals, single-scallop and single trumpet capitals just like the crypt, and there are among the capitals even bulbous Anglo-Saxon ones, probably re-used, although an 'overlap' is not impossible. After all, Wulstan was an Anglo-Saxon, not a Norman. The bulbous capitals are similar to C10 capitals in the Wipertus Crypt at Quedlinburg and also the C11 capitals at Great Paxton in Huntingdonshire. One bulbous base also survives, but on the opposite side. After the slype the cloister E range continues with two large rectangular recesses, probably the receptacles for the Norman library. The chapter house entrance belongs to the C14 again. There are here two niches l. and two r. Perp panel tracery above, quite possibly the earliest in the cathedral.

10 But the CHAPTER HOUSE itself is Norman again, and no later than say 1120–5. It is particularly memorable among English chapter houses as being round, with a middle column. This was taken up before the end of the century at Wells and at the beginning of the C13 at Lincoln, though in both cases the polygon was preferred to the circle. Worcester started a style of chapter houses entirely confined to Britain. Willis suggested that the idea at Worcester was inspired by the apse of the crypt, with its radiating ribs. The exterior of the chapter house was re-cased with Norman stones in the late C14, as the large four-light Perp windows show. But inside is wall arcading with arches both normally round and intersecting. A billet frieze runs above. Wall-shafts reach to the vault and carry block capitals. The middle column has the most elementary capital possible, the shape of Early Norman imposts,* and the vault has radial ribs in the form of semicircles and cells between of a tripartite kind. It is surprising and may have been interfered with, but essentially such a vault must always have been there.

Continuing along the cloister, one passes a plain single-chamfered doorway and then, turning the corner, the C13 doorway which leads into the usual tunnel-vaulted passage to the S. In the passage is a low doorway with a segmental arch to the refectory undercroft. The S exit has a portal of *c.*1200.

* Cf. the Tewkesbury chancel piers. But the base must be a C13 recarving.

There are four orders of colonnettes, and in the round arch one order of pellets and one of individual affronted small leaves. The main room on the S side is, again as usual, the REFECTORY.* The refectory stands on an Early Norman undercroft with flat buttresses and small round-headed windows to the S. They have outside a roll moulding round their heads which continues as a base frieze. The undercroft has short, round piers along its middle and is groin-vaulted with two odd extra groins to indicate the way in from the small outer doorway. These extra groins stand on two differing trumpet-scallop capitals, probably re-used. But, above, the refectory is of the mid C14. It has large windows mostly with reticulation but also with a three-leaf motif. The windows are shafted inside, and the shafts are fluted. The vaulting-shafts have fillets. The reading pulpit was on the N side, and its window bay is distinguished by a tiny rib-vault with an angel boss. The doorway to the stair up to it has a round head. At the E end of the refectory is a magnificently bold carved composition unfortunately largely chopped off. Its centre is an over-life-size
Christ in Majesty in an elongated quatrefoil glory surrounded 20
by the Signs of the Evangelists. The date of this must be *c.*1220–30, as the drapery demonstrates. The composition is French in type. If it were complete, this piece would be among the two or three best of their date in England. The C14 must have appreciated it, or else it would not have been re-used. The friezes below, with heads and beasts, and above, as well as the thinly vaulted niches l. and r., are a C14 addition.

The cloister wall towards the refectory is not to be deciphered with certainty. The main C14 doorway was near the W end. Hood-mould with leaf and three small animals. But before that one passes two large blocked Norman arches and another doorway to the undercroft.

The W range of the cloister is completely exceptional among English monastic cathedrals in that it had the DORMITORY running E–W to a line far forward of the cathedral front. The normal position for the dormitory is of course in the E range on the upper floor. The INFIRMARY incidentally was also here, a separate building more or less in front of the cathedral, but not in axis. The normal place for the infirmary is somewhere E of the E range. The W wall of the cloister against which the

*This is part of the KING'S SCHOOL, and access can only be obtained from the S side.

dormitory stood is most obscure. Looked at from the W,* it is a kind of masonry not found anywhere else in the cathedral precinct. With its irregular narrow bands of lias it has been attributed to a Saxon date, and that is probably correct, as a Norman arch cuts into it. Seen from the cloister, one has first the wide two-bay LAVATORIUM of the monks, C14 of course, and then a deep Perp niche with a four-centred arch and a Perp doorway. This was the main dormitory entrance. But it replaced a Norman one of which a high arch with a big roll moulding is still visible. The smaller round-headed doorway belongs to the Late Norman work, with its continuous filleted roll. This Late Norman work appears once more in the portal to the PASSAGE in the N bay of this range. It has a continuous quarter roll, shafts with trumpet-scallop capitals, and an arch with undercut zigzag at r. angles to the wall. The passage is rib-vaulted in four bays, on triple corbels with scallop capitals not rising at the same level. The middle always starts a little lower. The abaci are canted, the ribs single-chamfered.‡ The W exit again has a continuous quarter-circle. It is reasonable to presume that the passage was built at the same time as the immediately adjoining W bays of the nave. Just inside the passage is the doorway to the LIBRARY, which is in the roof space over the S aisle. It was prepared for this or some other purpose in the C15, by adding to the height of the outer wall and introducing the small paired windows already observed. It is known that Bishop Carpenter founded a library about the middle of the C15. The dormitory was continued to the W by the REREDORTER or lavatory, and of this remarkably much is preserved. It is uncommonly difficult to work out the DORMITORY ruins. As the dormitory projected over the steep fall of the ground to the river, large substructures were necessary. So the range was four-storeyed, but of the top floor, which was the dormitory itself, little evidence remains. It was 123 ft long and was rebuilt in 1375–7. The Late Norman passage just S of the W end of the cathedral led to it. To the reredorter belong the five small lancets still visible. They were in its S wall. Along the reredorter ran the necessary drainage channel. Below the dormitory was a sub-vault, about 9 ft below the cloister level. It was eight bays long and subdivided into parallel naves by oblong piers and columns. It had groin-vaults and transverse

*I.e., from the headmaster's private garden.

‡One capital has short broad leaves, cf. the nave of Abbey Dore (N. Stratford).

arches of *c.*1110–20, but was re-made in the period *c.*1375 with single-chamfered ribs. The W wall, i.e. the E wall of the reredorter, however, is again of *c.*1110–20. Below the reredorter was an additional part of the infirmary, hardly a very satisfactory idea. It was five by two bays in size plus a four-bay S addition with Norman flat buttresses. Below the infirmary level of the reredorter is another sub-vault. The N part of this has round piers with moulded capitals and single-chamfered ribs between cells made of very large bricks. The S part had an open arcade, probably a kind of cloister walk; but this was filled in in the C14.

Finally E of the E range are the ruins of the GUESTEN HALL. This was built *c.*1320, and the remaining windows indeed exhibit flowing tracery of the first order, the best in the cathedral. The hall was of five bays. Three had large transomed windows; the two on the r. were higher up and had a small doorway under. Here another building adjoined the hall. On the opposite side were four bays of windows plus a porch. The fine roof has been removed to Holy Trinity (*see* p. 322).*

FURNISHINGS

They will be discussed from E to W, and always S before N.

LADY CHAPEL AND RETROCHOIR. TRIPTYCH. Small alabaster Virgin in the middle and painted wings. C15. – ORGAN CASE. Small and partly early C18. – PAINTING. The vaults of the whole E vessel were painted by *Hardman*. – STAINED GLASS. The E window with scenes in medallions is by *Hardman*, designed by *John Hardman Powell*. – MONUMENTS. Bishop William of Blois † 1236. Purbeck marble, his feet against stiff-leaf, and stiff-leaf by the sides of his head. The head is in quite high relief. – Bishop, said to be Walter de Cantelupe † 1266, but the Purbeck effigy is flatter than the former and probably earlier. – Mrs Digby. By *Chantrey*, 1825. White marble. Seated figure on a couch. On the short sides of the base praying angels in shallow relief. – Earl of Dudley. By *J. Forsyth*, 1888. White marble effigy on an alabaster base with open arcading. – Lord Lyttelton. By *Forsyth*, 1878. White marble effigy on an alabaster tomb-chest. – Prior Moore (?). He had made preparation for his tomb *c.*1525. This is at the back of the high altar. – The whole back is filled by the

* For illustrations in the original state see Dollman, *Anc. Mon. Arch.*, I, 1861.

memorial to Dean Peel; 1877. Alabaster surface with incised cross and the Signs of the Evangelists.

SOUTH RETROCHOIR AISLE AND SOUTH-EAST TRANSEPT. STAINED GLASS. By *Hardman*. – MONUMENTS. Cross-legged Knight, mid-C13. – Tomb-chest of Sir Gryffyth Ryce † 1523. On the tomb-chest, which, with its shields in cusped quatrefoils, is still pre-Renaissance, two brasses by *Hardman*. – Lady. Flat, defaced Purbeck effigy, *c*.1300. – Purbeck Lady in higher relief, also *c*.1300. – The following two in the substructure of Prince Arthur's Chantry. Bishop Giffard † 1302. Canopy over the head of the bishop. Against the tomb-chest exquisite allegories which would deserve attention. – Lady, probably of the Giffard family, *c*.1300.

NORTH RETROCHOIR AISLE AND NORTH-EAST TRANSEPT. SCREEN. Stone, of three-light divisions and with a dainty quatrefoil frieze. This is genuine C15 work, though re-set. – STAINED GLASS. The E window by *Hardman*; good. – MONUMENTS. Bishop, Purbeck marble, *c*.1300. – Lady, mid-C13, very fine. The lid of the tomb-chest is raised a little above a base with a stiff-leaf border. The lady stands on a stiff-leaf corbel. – Cross-legged Knight, early C14. – Bishop de Braunsford † 1349 (?). The recess has plenty of ballflower decoration. – Bishop de Cobham † 1327. The modelling of the face is remarkably sensitive. The recess fits an early C14 date.

CHANCEL. REREDOS. Designed by *Scott* and made by *Farmer & Brindley* for £1,500. Shrine with five figures, very opulent. – PULPIT. By *Stephen Baldwin*, 1642.* Octagonal, with the Signs of the Evangelists, Tables of the Law, the Eye of God, etc. Altered and restored in 1874. – SCREENS. All of *Scott*'s restoration. Wood and iron as well as stone. – COMMUNION RAIL. Iron. – BISHOP'S THRONE. This is part of *G. G. Scott*'s work. – So are the ORGAN CASES, and so are the STALLS, but they incorporate the MISERICORDS of the stalls of 1379. There are 37 in all. They represent e.g. an old man stirring a pot, a man playing a flute, an angel playing a viol, a knight holding a dagger, a butcher slaughtering an ox, the Circumcision, Presentation of Samuel, a woman writing (?), a sower, knights tilting, an angel playing a lute, a huntsman blowing a horn, a knight fighting two griffins, three reapers, three ploughmen, three mowers, Abraham and Isaac, the Temptation of Eve, the Expulsion from Paradise, Moses des-

*So Mr Philip Styles kindly informs me.

cending from Sinai, the Judgement of Solomon, Samson and the Lion, a man beating down acorns, a lion and a dragon fighting, a sow with piglets, a knight hawking, a monster, a sphinx, a cockatrice, a naked woman riding on a goat, Adam delving and Eve spinning, a stag beneath a tree, a dragon. Some of these scenes clearly mean Labours of the Months, others may belong to the Bestiary. – The LIGHTS on the stalls are by *Jack Penton* and recent. – The elaborate gilt iron SCREENS in the two W bays are by *Skidmore* of Coventry. – MONUMENT. King John, made probably *c.*1230. The tomb-chest dates from *c.*1529 and still has no Renaissance detail.
Shields in enriched quatrefoils. The effigy is of Purbeck marble 21
and one of the finest of its time in England. The drapery is as good as that of any French contemporary effigy. Two Bishops by his head. – PRINCE ARTHUR'S CHANTRY. Prince Arthur, Henry VIII's elder brother, died in 1502, but work started only in 1504. To the choir the chantry has six bays, the E bay of two lights, the next of two, the third again of two both rising higher, then two of three, the second with the ogee-headed entrance, and the last blank, of two, and again rising higher. The two higher bays are enriched by small statuary, and there is plenty of small statuary inside. In many cases the heads were spared by the Reformers. The high openings have instead of transoms cusped arches, and on them cusped arches reversed. It is a controlled, not at all haphazard composition. The
interior has a lierne-vault in two bays with two pendants 44
oddly buttressed or shored. Reredos crowded with figures and canopies. The tomb-chest of the prince stands in the middle. It is quite simple, with shields in quatrefoils. From the retro-choir aisle the chantry is one storey higher: the basement, where the two Giffard monuments are incorporated. There is above them a broad band of Tudor roses, portcullis, other flowers, and angels.

SOUTH CHANCEL AISLE, STAINED GLASS. The kneeling king is a copy of a representation at Malvern Priory and said to be early C19. – MONUMENTS. Mrs Rae, 1772, by *I. F. Moore*. Of coloured marbles. Sarcophagus with a curly top on which two putti. Above, against an obelisk, the portrait medallion flanked by palm fronds. – William Burslem † 1820. By *Westmacott Jun.* White tablet with a seated angel in profile.

NORTH CHANCEL AISLE. SCULPTURE. Canopy with a forti- 45
fied city. This, representing the Heavenly Jerusalem, was originally under the canopy at the top of the pulpit. – MONUMENTS.

Bishop Maddox † 1759. By *Prince Hoare*. Standing monument of black and white marble. Sarcophagus with relief of the Good Samaritan. On the r. a decently draped female with an upturned torch. An urn above in front of an obelisk. Very staid – no doubt in deliberate contrast to Bishop Hough's monument of 1746. – Rev. Dr Marriott † 1807. By *T. King* of Bath. Pretty tablet with an altar and a weeping willow.

CROSSING. CHOIR SCREEN. Of iron, wide open. Designed by *Scott*.

SOUTH TRANSEPT. STAINED GLASS. The S window by *G. Rogers*, designed by *Preedy* in 1853. – MONUMENTS. Bishop Philpott † 1892. By *Sir Thomas Brock*. Seated white figure, one hand raised. – Mrs Hall (of Jamaica and Bevere) † 1794. Standing white monument. Pensive seated woman by a wreathed urn. Good.

NORTH TRANSEPT. STAINED GLASS. The great N window by *Lavers & Barraud*, 1866. – MONUMENTS. Bishop Hough.
84 By *Roubiliac*, 1746. A Rococo composition, i.e. one in which symmetry is artfully avoided. On the l. a standing female figure raising a piece of drapery to reveal a relief on the sarcophagus which shows the scene of the eviction of Hough from Magdalen College after he had been elected president. James II wanted a Catholic president. On the r. a small seated cherub holding a medallion with the portrait of Mrs Hough. Above, on the sarcophagus, the Bishop rises in a diagonal, or rather serpentine movement. Obelisk at the back. – Bishop Fleetwood † 1683. The very reverse. No figures at all. Just a reredos or aedicule. Two columns and an open segmental pediment. Black and white marble. – Bishop Stillingfleet † 1699. Also of the reredos type. Two putto heads rather unconvincingly lift a drapery from the inscription. – Sir Thomas Street † 1696, but done by *Wilton c.*1775–80. An exquisitely chaste reredos and an Adamish urn like a wine-cooler. A putto hovering above.

NAVE. PULPIT. Designed by *Scott* and carved by *Forsyth*. – LECTERN. A gilt angel, 1894 by *Hardman*. – STAINED GLASS. The great W window 1874 by *Hardman*, designed by *Scott*. – MONUMENTS. Robert Wilde † 1608. Two recumbent effigies. Tomb-chest with decorated strips instead of pilasters. Various inscriptions have been removed. – A Beauchamp and his wife, *c.*1400. Tomb-chest with shields in ogee-headed panels. The effigies are impressive. Her head rests against a swan. – Dean Eedes † 1596. Effigy on a high tomb-chest with garish leaf decoration. Canopy of four incorrectly detailed columns. Cambered heads, vault inside with diagonal and ridge-ribs. – Bishop Thornborough † 1641, but erected in 1627. The monument is not at all complete, but even what remains shows that this was a much more correctly classical job.

SOUTH AISLE, from E. Mostly STAINED GLASS. In some of the windows fragments of C14 glass. Also in the window above the cloister doorway glass by *Lavers & Westlake*, 1893. Not very good. – FONT. By *Bodley*. – MONUMENTS. Bishop Thomas † 1689. Not large and very simple. No figures, no display, not even twisted columns or garlands. – Thomas James † 1804. A pair of urns. – A prior; C14. In a late C13 recess. – Bishop Parrie † 1616. Recumbent effigy. In another such recess. – Sir Thomas Lyttelton † 1481. Tomb-chest, badly retooled. The brass is missing. – Mrs Warren † 1792. By *Ricketts*. Weeping putto by an urn. – John Bromley † 1674. Standing monument, narrow. With an urn on top. – Sir Thomas Lyttelton † 1650 and his wife † 1666. By *Thomas Stanton*. Also standing, also narrow. Black and white marble; classical. – Bishop Freake † 1591. Signed by *Anthony Tolly*. High tomb-chest with caryatids, shields, and strapwork. Arch and back tablet. Has this never had an effigy? – Bishop Blandford † 1675. Standing monument, of noble simplicity. High Tuscan columns and an open curly pediment. No figures at all. – Col. Sir Henry Walton Ellis † 1815 at Waterloo. Large, white, standing monument. He sinks from his horse and is received by an angel. A kneeling soldier on the r. By *Bacon Jun.* – FONT. Of the *Scott* time, with high cover. – MONUMENTS. Richard Woolfe † 1877. Sgraffito plate of very good design. – Richard Jolly † 1803. White standing monument by *Bacon Sen.* Mother and three children weeping at the sarcophagus. Of very fine quality, as Bacon could be. – Bishop Gauden † 1662. Black and white. Demi-figure in an oval recess. Segmental pediment at the top. A little heavy, but the decoration is nicely done. This was originally at the back of the high altar. – Bishop Johnson † 1774. By *Nollekens* the bust, by *Robert Adam* the composition. – STAINED GLASS. The W window typical *Clayton & Bell*; 1872.

NORTH AISLE. In the E bay STAINED GLASS with 1862 as the date of commemoration. It is by *Lavers & Barraud*, and the best Victorian glass in the cathedral. Slender stylized figures in a very intense style. – MONUMENTS. Bishop Bollingham † 1576. The base is Perp and has probably nothing to do with the effigy. He is lying on his back supporting with his belly and thighs the weight of the quite large block with the inscription etc. He was, we read among other things, 'a painful preacher of the truthe'. – SCREEN to the Jesus Chapel. Of stone, in two tiers. Probably by *R. A. Briggs*, *c.*1895. – PAINTINGS (in the Jesus Chapel). Head of Christ, attributed to *Tiarini*. – Holy Family, by a Flemish follower of Leonardo da Vinci. – STAINED GLASS in the Jesus Chapel, 1849 by *Wailes*. Individual ogee-headed panels in two tiers. – SCULPTURE. A fine C13 corbel with two tumblers. – Above, big ROYAL ARMS, later C17, probably brought in from outside. – MONUMENTS. John Moore † 1613 and members of his family. Three large kneeling men and behind them, in a fan-vaulted recess, three large kneeling women. Coupled columns. The urns must be an C18 addition. – Mrs Godfreye † 1613. Standing monument. She kneels, quite small; in a recess with two columns and an arch. – Monument to those fallen in 1845 and 1846 by the Sutlej river. By *Westmacott Jun.* Standing monument of white marble. A soldier stands, hand on breast, by the side of a large flag. Classical style. – Tablet of *c.*1640. Corpse in a winding-sheet, yet propped up on the elbow. Oval medallion surrounded by a wreath. The commemorative inscription was no doubt painted on. Two putti on the open segmental top pediment. Inscription: Μακαριοι οι νεκροι etc. – Bishop Hurd † 1808. By *W. H. Stephens*. Simple and without figures. Classical and a little dry.

SCULPTURE. In the gallery over the W bays of the SOUTH AISLE are nineteen pieces of stone diapered with rows of small arches. Such wall areas exist also at Christchurch (Hants) and Castor (Soke of Peterborough; before 1124).

In the CLOISTER N wall totally defaced MONUMENT to a priest.

PLATE. Silver gilt Paten of *c.*1250 from the grave of Bishop Walter de Cantelupe, engraved with the hand of God. – Two Cups of 1638, originally secular, by *R. S.* – Two Cups, two Cover Patens, two Flagons, silver-gilt, by *R. A.*, 1661. – Silver-gilt Mace given in 1662. – Cocoanut Audit Cup, by *W. M.*, *c.*1690 – Almsdish, by *W. K.*, 1690; Chalice, probably German. – Also a Salver from St Andrew's 1693 by *Robert Timbrell*.

THE PRECINCT

Worcester Cathedral has not got a real precinct. Ever since in 1794 a road was cut through its NE angle, it has lost its seclusion, and the new channelling of all the through-traffic along just that corner has made things infinitely worse. The former Bishop's Palace, with which one naturally starts, no longer has anything to do with the cathedral. It is just a large house behind a wall, next to the Technical College, and along that ferocious traffic route.

BISHOP'S PALACE. The building, as one approaches the main entrance, seems entirely of Bishop Hough's time, say of *c.*1730. It is of red and buff stone, eleven bays long, with a three-bay centre carrying a rather gross segmental pediment on flat Doric angle pilasters, windows with segmental heads, and a surprisingly insignificant doorway. Inside, one has at once a staircase with three balusters to the tread, one of them with a long, shallow twist and unusually richly carved tread-ends. But move up that stair or move down into the basement, and you are in a C13 house against whose E side the range of *c.*1730 has been built. The C13 parts are due to Bishop Giffard, who received a licence to crenellate his house in 1271. They consist of the following. Hall undercroft with four bays of rib-vaulting. The ribs form quadripartite bays, but have a longitudinal ridge-rib in addition. A lancet window remains in the N wall, and at the NE corner was the spiral staircase up to the hall. The HALL itself is much re-done. Roof with moulded beams on arched braces. To the E is a large Perp doorway with a steep arch with continuous mouldings. Chimneypiece with broad bands and two allegorical figures. To the S is a smaller doorway originally probably to the porch. Below this and connected by a C13 doorway with the hall undercroft is another undercroft, this of two rib-vaulted bays. N of the W half of the hall undercroft are two smaller rib-vaulted C13 chambers, and E of one of them a C15 room. The CHAPEL of the palace lies W of the former hall porch. What remains is only its chancel (with a trefoil-headed PISCINA). The large blocked W arch led to the nave. S of the chapel are the rib-vaulted undercrofts of one L-shaped building of four bays in the N–S, two bays in the E–W wing. It has narrow lancet windows to the W. Above, all is altered, but two two-light C14 windows are preserved. The whole is confusing and has little of standard C13 domestic planning. The river-front has partly C13, partly C18 masonry.

Between the Bishop's Palace and the cathedral is COLLEGE YARD, a friendly L-shaped group of Georgian houses looking at the trees in the yard which screen the traffic. No. 10 stands on its own, separated by its grand gates with fine piers. The house dates from 1687 and has its original staircase with good sturdy balusters. N of the chancel originally stood a large octagonal CAMPANILE of the C14, also called Clocherium. Immediately E of it was the parish church of St Michael.

On the S side the precinct is a real precinct. COLLEGE GREEN still gives you the sense of the close. From the outside world one enters it by the Great Gate known as the EDGAR TOWER. It was begun in the early C14 and completed after licence to crenellate had been obtained in 1368–9. It has to the outside, where again all detail is Victorian, two polygonal turrets, two two-light windows and canopied niches l. and r., and three tiers of canopied niches between the windows. To the inside the arrangement is similar. The archway itself has continuous chamfers, to the outside separated by the portcullis groove. Inside, it is divided into two bays by a cross wall which alone makes the distinction between pedestrians and carriages. The inner vault has diagonal and ridge-ribs, the outer has liernes. Original, battened DOOR. Inside, on the upper floor, is a little landing with a rib-vault. Two turret rooms also have small rib-vaults. In the main upper room is a small doorway with a shouldered lintel, the shoulders being double-curved.

W of the Edgar Tower is the DEANERY, a good house of *c*.1730, seven bays, with rusticated angle pilasters. The doorway has a Gibbs surround with pediment. The pretty staircase is reached by a pair of arches. It has slender turned balusters and carved tread-ends. All along the S side are nice quiet houses, with their ornamental doorcases, and what the KING'S SCHOOL has added does not do any harm. The range facing W is Gothic of 1910; the ranges round the corner are of 1899 and the conversion of the Canons' Stables of 1907–9. All three buildings are by *Alfred Hill Parker*. The N side is the Refectory, for which *see* above, p. 307.

There is nothing to be added except the little street called COLLEGE PRECINCT which is just outside the E wall of the cathedral, i.e. really in the town. It consists of small houses and makes a pretty picture. It is in this area that the perambulation is going to start (*see* p. 326).

THE TOWN

CHURCHES

ST ALBAN, Deansway. Small, of nave and chancel in one, N aisle, and a bellcote. Norman, but over-restored. Norman S wall with a blocked doorway, a small blocked window, and a neo-Norman doorway and two neo-Norman windows. The neo-Norman work is of 1821. The N arcade is Late Norman: round piers and round abaci, double-chamfered arches, flat leaf capital decoration, coarse dogtooth in the hood-mould. The chancel details (e.g. E window of three stepped lancets) are E.E., but much re-done. – PLATE. *See* All Saints. – MONUMENT. Large tablet with an elaborate surround to Edmund Wyatt † 1684.

ALL SAINTS. A fine introduction to Worcester, as one crosses
the bridge from the Welsh side. Perp W tower, with charac-
teristic arch to the nave. But the higher parts belong to the
new church, built in 1739–42. The most likely designer is
Richard Squire. The tower has a stage with paired rusticated
pilaster strips, and then the bell-stage with paired pilasters.
The bell-openings are arched twins. Balustrade and pinnacles.
The body of the church is six bays long. In the second from the
W, on the N side, is the main entrance, with fluted Doric pilas-
ters, a triglyph frieze, and a segmental pediment. The E is the
real façade, with a very large arched window, coupled fluted
Doric pilasters, a triglyph frieze, and a broken-back pediment.
The aisles end in (former) E entrances. Six-bay interior with
Tuscan columns, a segmental vault, and flat aisle ceilings. – 77
REREDOS, not high, tripartite, with Corinthian pilasters and a
segmental pediment. – The PAINTING above is by *Josiah
Rushton* of the Royal Worcester Porcelain Works; 1867. –
PULPIT. With some C17 panels. – Good gilt iron SCREEN
between chancel and chancel aisles. It is by *Sir Aston Webb*
and seems to date from the time of Webb's restoration of the
church, i.e. *c.*1889. – SWORD REST. Of wrought iron, C18, 82
good. – COMMUNION RAIL. Of the time of the church. –
STAINED GLASS. C15 fragments in the W and the N aisle W
windows. – PLATE. Cup and Cover Paten 1571; Chalice by
T. H., 1619 (from St Alban); Chalice and Cover Paten by
I. M., 1635; Chalice, 1639; Ewer, by *T. I.*, *c.*1690; Paten
by *George Wickes*, 1726; Almsdish by *John Gorham*, 1770.–
MONUMENTS. Edward Hurdman † 1621 and wife. Two big
kneeling figures by a prayer-desk. The context has been de-
stroyed. – Many tablets, especially attractive one † 1676 and
one † 1683. Both have twisted columns. The former is to
Samuel Mathew and has a frontal demi-figure.

ST ANDREW, Deansway. Only the Perp tower has been allowed to remain. It now stands in a public garden. The tower has an excellently slim recessed spire, 155 ft high. It was built or rebuilt by *Nathaniel Wilkinson* in 1751 and has a Corinthian capital at the top instead of a finial. Its original top (replaced by a copy) stands in the same public garden. The arches to E, N, and S are high and have fine Perp mouldings. Lierne-vault inside. To the E the springers of the first bay of the arcades.

ST BARNABAS, Church Road, Rainbow Hill. 1884–5 by *Ernest Day* (cost *c.*£4,000). Red brick, mostly with lancet windows. No tower, wide apse. Exposed brick inside.

ST CLEMENT, Henwick Road. 1822–3 by *Thomas Lee Jun.*, but apparently to a design by an otherwise unknown *Thomas Ingleman* (Colvin). The amazing thing is that it is neo-Norman, a choice entirely exceptional before 1830 and fashionable only in the forties. Ornate, rather crude façade with embraced W tower. The chancel was enlarged by *Preedy* in 1879. Inside, the three galleries have been preserved. – PLATE. Cup and Cover Paten by *H. W.*, 1571; Chalice (replica of the former) and Paten, by *W. Bellchambers*, 1828.

ST CUTHBERT'S CHAPEL, Manor Farm, Lower Wick. No more exists now than a few feet of red sandstone masonry.

ST GEORGE, St George's Square. 1893–5 by (Sir) *Aston Webb*, a key work of his early and best period. The church is placed spectacularly at the far end of the long square. The façade is basically of the type of Windsor and King's College, i.e. with a large Perp window and two turrets. But nothing, except the window tracery, is really imitative. Brick and some stone bands. The centre is a giant niche à la Tewkesbury. The arch is almost round. On the entrance level the niche is filled in. The top of the façade is straight, and the turrets stand on that straight top, instead of one being prepared for them from the ground. Small spires on the turrets. Excellent interior, also of brick and stone. Nave and aisles are separated by three wide arches, almost round. Just one thin triangular shaft runs up the piers to the roof. Clerestory with lancets, two for each bay. Large transepts with two long two-light windows each. The chancel is distinguished by the use of a greater amount of stone. The side chapels or rooms are separated by lower and smaller panelled arches. The tracery in the five-light E window is more personal than that of the W window. – STAINED GLASS. E window and aisle and chapel windows by *Kempe*, *c.*1900. – PLATE. This includes a Paten by *Jno. Bodington*, 1709; Set by *Edward, John, Edward Jun., and Wm. Barnard*, 1830.

ST GEORGE (R.C.), Sansome Place. 1829 by *Henry Rowe*. The ambitious façade of the type of Roman Baroque façades is an addition of 1887, probably by *S. J. Nicholl*, who re-did the chancel in 1880. The façade is of three bays, of ashlar, with on the upper stage angle pilasters, but coupled attached columns for the centre. Top pediment. Plain interior.

ST HELEN, High Street. Now the County Record Office. The street end is of 1857–63 (by *Preedy*). It fits its function of being part of the street. Large E window, evidently Victorian. But there are other details which are definitely Gothick, probably of *c*.1800. This would fit the date of the W tower, which was rebuilt in 1813. The side and tower windows were again all Victorian, but the tower has preserved an original quatrefoil. Perp interior. The piers have canted projections, and the tower arch is of the same design. – REREDOS. By *Preedy*, 1867. Of alabaster. – MONUMENT. John Nash † 1662. Standing monument with stiffly reclining figure, the head propped by the arm. Twisted columns, an odd open pediment with a small segmental pediment set in. Garlands in the pediment. Flat back arch with putti in the spandrels. A provincial job. – Many minor tablets.

ST JOHN IN BEDWARDINE, St John's. The oldest part of the church is the N arcade. It is later C12. Three bays, round piers with multi-scallop capitals, and square abaci. The arches were re-done when a new wide N aisle was built in 1841 by *Parsons*. W rose window, two-light N windows with narrowly set buttresses. The chancel and the N chapel were extended in 1884 by *Ewan Christian*. He added the monumental screen to the N aisle. The chapel arcade is Dec with a continuous two-wave moulding. The S arcade and the chancel arch are Perp. The piers have four canted projections. The arches are double-chamfered. – The three GALLERIES are preserved from Parsons' time. – STAINED GLASS. Small fragments in the chancel side windows. – MONUMENT. Abel Gower † 1669. Tablet with twisted columns, two female allegorical figures between them and the inscription, two putti on the open curly pediment.

ST MARTIN, Cornmarket. 1768–72 by *Anthony Keck*. The silly Gothic tracery in the E window is by *Hopkins*, 1855–62. The church is of brick with stone dressings. The W tower carries a balustrade. The sides of five bays, the arched windows with rusticated surrounds of alternating size. The E end is a façade, with three arched windows and a large pediment all across.

Interior of nave and aisles. Unfluted Ionic columns each with its bit of entablature. Groin-vaulted aisles, flat nave ceiling with penetrations from the arcades. – WEST GALLERY. – PLATE. Alms Bowl, 1638; Flagon by *Rebecca Emes & E. Barnard*, 1813.

ST MARTIN, London Road. By *G. H. Fellowes Prynne*, 1903–11. Large red stone church, rockfaced, and with no break in the roof between nave and chancel. The junction is marked only by a small turret. No tower. The chancel on an undercroft. Well grouped additions to the S. Wide interior of brick and stone striped. Narrow passage aisles, but two-bay-deep transepts. They are, however, not emphasized in the run of the arcades. The arches die against the piers. The W Baptistery is of 1960–1 (by *F. Potter & Associates*). – PLATE. Cup and Cover Paten, 1570.

ST MARY MAGDALENE, Northfield Street. By *F. W. Preedy*, 1876–7. It cost £13,000. Late C13 in style. SW tower, the bell-stage octagonal with big pinnacles to connect with the spire. Spacious interior with the usual short round piers.

ST NICHOLAS, The Cross. 1730–5 by *Humphrey Hollins*. The W tower is embraced by the two staircase bays. The result is a façade which could be given some grandeur. Giant pilasters, doubled for the portal bay. The doorway has Tuscan attached columns and a broken-back pediment. A horizontal oval over it. The side bays have niches and roundels over. The coupled giant pilasters carry a large open segmental pediment with a shield. The tower has variety from stage to stage, first a square with stepped corners, then a square with recessed rounded corners, then an octagonal stage, and then the double-curved cap with a lantern. The design of the tower was cribbed from Gibbs's *Book of Architecture*, which had only come out in 1728. The body of the church is of four bays. Round-arched windows, the arches keyed in. The interior is disappointing, just a rectangle with an apse. – The three GALLERIES, the PULPIT, and the COMMUNION RAILS, all partly or wholly of iron, are of *Hopkins*'s restoration of 1867. – FONT. A baluster of Baroque shape, especially the fluted outward-curving stem. Four cherubs' heads on the bowl. – PLATE. Paten by *T. C.*, 1684; Paten by *John Robinson*, 1740; two Chalices by *Peter & Wm. Bateman*, 1807; two Tankards, also 1807.

ST PAUL, Spring Gardens. 1885 by *A. E. Street*. Large, of red brick, with black brick trim. Bellcote on the nave E gable. Lancets and plate tracery.

ST PETER THE GREAT, St Peter's Street. 1836–8 by *John Mills*. Brick with stucco dressings. Lean N tower, high three-light windows, four-centred arches, wide nave, ceiling striped by plaster ribs. – WEST GALLERY. – The ORGAN CASE is Gothic, but looks earlier than the church. – PLATE. Chalice, C17; Paten and Almsdish, by *S. I.*, 1721. – MONUMENT. Mrs Allcroft † 1831. Kneeling woman by an urn. By *J. Marsh* of London.

ST STEPHEN, St Stephen's Street. 1861–2 by *Preedy*. Large, of red sandstone, with a clumsy tower. Goodhart-Rendel felt that it badly needed a spire. Windows with plate tracery. Aisles and a clerestory of two short two-light windows per bay, with a stubby round detached column between. – STAINED GLASS. The E and W windows look *Hardman*'s.

ST SWITHUN, Church Street, just off the High Street. Plain Perp tower with nice C18 combinations of classical arches and ogee gables. This and the rest of 1734–6 are probably by the *Woodwards* of Chipping Campden. The sides are of six narrowly spaced bays with giant fluted Doric pilasters and windows with keyed-in round arches. The E side is the real façade. A richly appointed Venetian window and a large 75
broken-back pediment. Clock on top. The interior is marvellous. It is aisleless and has a segmental vault with ribs which must be meant to be Gothic; for the little wall corbels on which they stand are imitation Gothic. Bosses also are a Gothic motif. The chancel space is divided from side spaces by screen walls half-way up carrying two Roman Doric columns. – (ALTAR TABLE. This is a beautiful wrought-iron piece.) – FONT. A baluster. – BOX PEWS. – The PULPIT is wholly delightful. It rises very high above the pews and is reached by a winding staircase. It has its back wall and tester with plenty of frills. – The WEST GALLERY stands on square fluted wooden pillars. – MAYOR'S CHAIR, and rising from its back the scrolly SWORD REST. – STAINED GLASS. The E window was designed by *Eginton*. – PLATE. Chalice 1794. – MONUMENTS. Joseph Withers and wife, of *c*.1770. By *Bacon*. Big putto, his hand on the double profile medallion. The putto is placed before an urn which is placed before an obelisk. – Henry Hope † 1753. By *Squire*. Conservative for its date.

HOLY TRINITY, Shrub Hill. 1863–5 by *Hopkins*. A large and

prosperous-looking building, though without a tower. It is surprising in this industrial neighbourhood, and is in fact to
50 be demolished. What will then happen to its ROOF, the splendid roof of the Guesten House of the cathedral, which was demolished in 1859? It had to be reduced in span and increased in pitch for its new home. It is a five-bay triple purlin roof with a complex pattern of three tiers of cusped and curved wind-braces forming circles. The trusses are open collar trusses with the collars set very high and braced to the principal rafters by long slender arch-braces. The roof is the most elegant of medieval carpentry in the county.* Its date is 1326. The church has a S aisle, ample transepts and a wide polygonal apse. It is a restrained and dignified job. A new home must be found for the roof, and any congregation for a future church ought to be ready to make a sacrifice for it. – FONT by *Forsyth*, REREDOS and PULPIT by *Boulton*, the latter two 1863–5. Those whom Scott used in the cathedral, Hopkins used here.

HOLY TRINITY AND ST MATTHEW, Ronkswood Estate. 1964–5 by *Maurice W. Jones*. Circular, with a spike. Inside, the walls are conical. Windows along the walls, except by the chancel, only at the bottom, and a strip right at the top. The windowless part is in a chequerboard pattern.

BAPTIST CHURCH, Sansome Walk. 1863–4 by *Pritchett & Son* of Darlington. A full-dress church, with a SW tower, even if it is a thin one. Large transepts. The style is of *c*.1300.

CONGREGATIONAL CHURCH, Angel Place. 1858 by *Paulton & Woodman*. It cost £6,000. Italianate, and of some grandeur. Five bays, ashlar-faced. Giant semicircular portico of Corinthian columns.

COUNTESS OF HUNTINGDON'S CHAPEL, Bridport, off Deansway. 1804, enlarged 1815. An odd plan is the result. A three-bay chapel with a hipped roof and behind it, transversely, a large oblong part apsed at both ends. The interior has galleries on thin shafts and a flat ceiling.

FRIENDS' MEETING HOUSE, Sansome Place. 1701. A plain one-storey cottage. Pedimented porch and two bays l., two bays r.

PUBLIC BUILDINGS

CASTLE. There is virtually nothing left of Worcester Castle. The site of the great motte, still to be seen on C18 engravings

*Description by Mr Charles.

but levelled in 1833, is now a terraced garden between the King's School and the river, and though fragments of sandstone walls incorporated into near-by buildings are probably part of the C13 stone castle or the later medieval prison, they are no longer coherent.

SHIRE HALL, Foregate Street. 1834–5 by *Charles Day* and *Henry Rowe*, the former of Bristol, the latter the town architect of Worcester. This is an impeccable Grecian design, in the Smirke taste, of fine ashlar stone. It has a giant portico of six fluted Ionic columns with a pediment and excellent Schinkelish detail. Two detached single-storey wings frame it and come forward towards the street. Inside large *salle des pas perdus* all across the building. It has a plainly coffered segmental ceiling and three large windows each end. Balcony in the far wall with iron handrail.

GUILDHALL, High Street. The Guildhall was built in 1721–3. 73
The designer was probably *Thomas White*, who submitted a design in 1718 and signed the carved trophy in the pediment. It is a splendid town hall, as splendid as any of the C18 in England, but it is just a little barbaric in its splendour. It is of brick with ample stone dressings, nine bays in the centre and with three-bay wings, two bays deep. The centre is of two storeys, the wings, though of the same height, of two and a half. The windows are all segment-headed and with a rather clumsy roll moulding in the surround. The centre of the centre is of three bays, framed by giant Corinthian pilasters and carrying an enormous segmental pediment with the trumpet-blast of White's bellicose trophy. Three statues on top, the middle one being Justice. Between the giant pilasters is a grand doorway with Corinthian columns against rustication and a pediment broken back in the centre. There are niches l. and r. with the statues of Charles I and Charles II, and above the doorway is Queen Anne, also in a niche. The side parts of the centre have oblong panels with carved garlands and other motifs. The high and long entrance hall is disappointing, but on the top floor is the more rewarding Assembly Room. It has shallow apses at both ends screened by columns – a favourite Adam motif introduced in this case by *George Byfield* in 1791. The ceiling is coved and painted. The decoration is in a light Italian style and dates from the restoration under *Scott* and the municipal architect *Henry Rowe* in 1878–80. – CORPORATION PLATE. Sword, C16; Sword of State, late C17; four Maces, 1760–1.

TECHNICAL COLLEGE, Deansway. By *R. Sheppard, Robson & Partners*, begun in 1960. A good design, if one looks at it independent of its surroundings. It has the massiveness which seems to be the hallmark of the sixties, but it is compact, unified, and not gimmicky. What turns one against it with some violence is its position on the Severn, only separated from the cathedral by the Bishop's Palace. It presses its C20 point home, and perhaps one does not like to be reminded that what in the past had been the force of the House of God is now that of the House of Technology. A lower, larger wing reaches N, and there is more to come. Read on.

POLICE HEADQUARTERS, Deansway. Completed in 1941 and designed by *Sir Percy Thomas*. Those who object to the new Technical College ought to answer honestly whether they prefer this anaemic neo-Georgianism.

FIRE STATION, Deansway. 1941 by *G. R. Acton*. What applied to the former applies here. Historicism is surely not the solution to building near a cathedral (or anywhere) in the mid C20.

VICTORIA INSTITUTE, Foregate Street. Now museum, art gallery, and library. 1896 by *J. W. Simpson* and *Milner Allen*. Cost: *c.*£25,000. Red brick and terracotta, a resourceful and animated, totally asymmetrical composition in a mixed Tudor and Baroque style. At the r. hand corner a turret, the l. half with a large Elizabethan twelve-light window below, the four middle lights under an arch. Above a long row of Henry VIII windows, of 4 plus 2 plus 4 plus 2 lights.

SCHOOL OF ART AND SCIENCE (former), Sansome Walk. In the same style and no doubt by the same architect as the Victoria Institute. The façade is in its own way as successful.

ROYAL INFIRMARY, Castle Street. Built in 1767–70 by *Anthony Keck*. Red brick. The original part is the block near the NE corner facing E. It is of seven bays with a three-bay pediment. Some enlargements of 1849, but mostly C20.

HILLBOROUGH HOSPITAL, Tallow Hill, the former HOUSE OF INDUSTRY. 1793–4 by *George Byfield*, but now all of *c.*1895.

ALICE OTTLEY SCHOOL, Upper Tything. The headmistress's house is the most ambitious private house in Worcester,
74 BRITANNIA HOUSE, perhaps by *Thomas White*, who certainly carved the Britannia which gave the house its name. It is not dated, but must belong to the time of the Guildhall. Brick with

stone dressings. Five bays, two storeys. Four rusticated giant pilasters. Doorway with pilasters and a pediment with lush decoration below. Even lusher leaf decoration round the middle window. Panelled parapet raised in the middle segmentally to house the seated Britannia. The windows have aprons in the form of fluted segments. Staircase with fine twisted and columnar balusters, three to the tread.

ROYAL GRAMMAR SCHOOL, Upper Tything. The school has behind and beside the genuinely scholastic buildings two other ones. One faces the street, PRIORY HOUSE, a five-bay brick house, with decorated keystones. The other, behind it, is partly of venerable age indeed. There was on the site the Cistercian Nunnery called WHITELADIES, founded by Bishop Cantelupe *c.*1250. Of their chapel the E wall is preserved, of red sandstone, with two lancet windows and two smaller recesses. This wall forms the W wall of a long domestic range of the early C18. Eleven bays, two storeys, segment-headed windows. The doorway is later. The first building for the school faces the street. Three bays, rather tight. Brick and stone, tall, straight-headed Gothic windows, but big shaped gables. This is by *A. E. Perkins*, 1868. The best building of the school dates from 1914–15 and contains the Perrins Hall and Library. It is neo-Jacobean, red brick and yellow stone, asymmetrically arranged. The scale is quite bold. The architect was *Alfred Hill Parker*.

GIRLS' GRAMMAR SCHOOL, Spetchley Road. By *Rusman & Cousins*, completed 1962. A good, straightforward group.

SWAN THEATRE, Severn Terrace. 1963–5 by *Henry Gorst*. Done as lightly and as inexpensively as if it were for an exhibition.

SHRUB HILL STATION. 1865, probably by the engineer *Edward Wilson*. A remarkably good building. Thirteen bays long and two storeys high, all faced with engineering bricks. The detail is still indebted to Georgian. On the platform a part of the building with a faience exterior.

SEVERN BRIDGE. 1771–80 to the design of *John Gwynne* of Shrewsbury. It cost £30,000 then. How could it? It has five segmental arches. It was widened in 1931, and so the masonry is not old. Balustraded parapet.*

* Information received from the City Library.

PERAMBULATIONS

They are divided into Inner and Outer Worcester. Outer Worcester is taken as meaning N of The Tything, E of Shrub Hill, SE of Sidbury, and outside the very centre of St John's in Bedwardine.

INNER WORCESTER

The following is divided into (*a*) The Walls, (*b*) S, SE, and E of the cathedral, (*c*) N of the cathedral, which contains of course the bulk of the material, (*d*) the Shrub Hill area.

(*a*) *The Walls*

Compared with such cities as York and Chester or even Newcastle, Worcester has little to offer. Those who want to see low bits and pieces can trace a stretch running N–S between NEW STREET and Bowling Green Terrace, then just S of the dog-leg of Little Charles Street, just W of Talbot Street, and so to the canal. A shorter stretch is W of the HIGH STREET and runs W. It is parallel to and S of The Butts, i.e. just N of where the house of the Blackfriars was situated.*

(*b*) *South, South East, and East of the Cathedral*

There is no break between College Precinct and Edgar Street and Severn Street. SEVERN STREET runs in a bend down to the river, and the DIGLIS HOTEL, mid-Georgian, faces the river. It is of brick, four bays with a two-bay pediment and an Ionic porch round the corner. But before one reaches it, one has to pass the ROYAL WORCESTER PORCELAIN WORKS. (One of their buildings is C18. It is of one storey only.) The building towards the street is of *c.*1860. It is of red and yellow

* I owe all this information to Mr J. Matley Moore.

brick, as are the industrial buildings in the Shrub Hill area. Two storeys, giant segmental arches.

EDGAR STREET has quite a number of pretty brick houses. No. 13 has a Venetian window on the second floor. No. 3 is dated 1732. It has five bays and three storeys. The keystones of the windows are a little decorated. No. 7 looks early C18, three bays and three and a half storeys. The doorway is later.

SIDBURY has suffered much from the new road, and Commandery Road is entirely new. The effect is that the few pre-Georgian houses look out of place. No. 57 has two gables, and the bargeboards seem to be original. No. 79 is Elizabethan with overhang and close studding on the upper floor. Near to it is the entry to the Commandery.

The COMMANDERY was originally the Hospital of St Wulstan. It was founded by St Wulstan in 1085 just outside the town walls. Of the chapel of the hospital remains of early C14 quatrefoil piers are re-set in the garden. The present building is of the late C15. It is called Commandery because from the late C13 the masters of the hospital called themselves preceptors or commanders. The building is timber-framed. The great hall is impressive in size and detail. It has wall-shafts and arched braces to tie-beams, with tracery. Originally there were hammerbeams, not tie-beams. Tracery has been introduced above the braces to the collar-beams as well. The screens passage is preserved and has plain muntins. The screen is treated in the spere way. The high-table end has a coving with
bosses. Fine oriel window with arched window lights and a 51
small boss. In the windows pretty late C15 STAINED GLASS with birds, a wheat-ear, a flower, etc. At the entry to the oriel and at the side entry to the staircase two fine STALL ENDS, probably from the chapel. One has a lion, the other a dog. Good Elizabethan staircase with rising square balusters and newel-posts with geometrical decoration. One upstairs room has a Jacobean overmantel with religious scenes. The solar has moulded beams and arched braces with tracery. Also on the first floor a room with eminently interesting WALL PAINTINGS of religious subjects (Martyrdom of St Erasmus, Martyrdom of St Thomas Becket, Weighing of Souls, Crucifixion, Saints). The Trinity on the ceiling. The paintings seem to be early C16.

(c) *To the North*

DEANSWAY, to the NW, is just one confusion. Some of it is Cathedral Precinct, or should be. The other features are the new public buildings, and the new open space by St Andrew's tower. There is only one Georgian house left as a reminder of the former scale: No. 5, of five bays, with an elaborate late C18 doorway. This short walk ends by the bridge.

The next expedition should be up Friar Street; for in that direction one finds the best of Worcester's black and white houses. To reach Friar Street from the cathedral one crosses the new road (when one can), and actually first enters the top houses of SIDBURY. On the W side it looks as if all was going to come down to expose the back with the car-parking ramp of the high block of the new central development, on which more soon. On the opposite side No. 11 is timber-framed and has a C15 doorway with traceried spandrels. After that FRIAR STREET starts. TUDOR HOUSE on the W side is mid-C16. It has an overhang and close studding. Four (restored) first-floor oriels. Inside a nice, minor Elizabethan plaster ceiling, and also, at the time of writing, four excellent stone bosses of the Evangelists, or perhaps four parts of a quatrefoil stone. What can their date be? Opposite are the LASLETT ALMS-HOUSES, a spacious job of brick and half-timbering, designed in 1912 by *Lewis, Sheppard & Son* of Worcester. Then Nos 26–32, C16, with overhang. No. 32 has a pretty painted ceiling with strawberry trail, of the time of the house.

The GREYFRIARS follows next, one of the finest timber-framed buildings in the county. It seems to have been the guest-house of the friary, of which nothing else is preserved. The Franciscans came in 1239. The old orders never liked their coming. Florence of Worcester wrote: 'O dolor, o plus quam dolor, o pestis truculenta. Fratres minores venerunt in Angliam.' It dates from *c.*1480 and is on an unusual plan, with a shallow-curved, 69-ft-long façade to the street and an archway into a small courtyard flanked by original wings, once much larger. The wings, the one on the r. with a very deep jetty once typical of such rear courts at Worcester, are probably Elizabethan. The archway has thin buttress-shafts and leaf spandrels. The main façade has two gables and a long straight range between them. The first-floor jetty is supported on coved brackets between the finely moulded wall-posts. Close studding above. Gables with bargeboards. In the centre long twelve-light window, restored. Under the gable eight-light window, modern, but perhaps reproducing the C17 appearance. A drawing by John Britton shows that the building now looks very much as it did when he drew it early in the C19. The hall is on the ground floor, to the r. of the archway, and access is from an entrance in the courtyard. The street wall of the hall is not original. There were, before the restoration, shop-windows here. The finest room is on the first floor, oddly enough not corresponding to the hall, but partly above the archway. It is reached by an Elizabethan staircase and has a pretty Elizabethan plaster frieze. It was ceiled from the start, which is unexpected and interesting. The roof structure was never left visible. The garden is surely the most beautiful in the city, and the building quite the best kept of Worcester's rapidly diminishing number of framed buildings.

The adjoining house is Jacobean, with two big gables and oriels on brackets under. The continuation is NEW STREET. Nos 5–7, on the E side, is NASH'S HOUSE. It is a three-storey-and-attic town-house of the C16, jettied at each floor level with close-timbered wall-frame and continuous windows on the street front. The window pattern consists of a large window in the centre of each bay and high-level windows on either side. The mullions of many of these still exist. The first-floor jetty has been additionally supported in the last century by cast-iron columns. Until recently there was a two-bay block of early date at the back with a gap of approximately 6 ft between the buildings. A square framed structure straddled the gap and half the width of the rear block. The timbers of its top storey, five floors above the street level, were heavily smoke-blackened and there was a smoke outlet in the form of a cupola. The roof was gabled in all four directions. The use of this building was that of a shot tower. Unfortunately it was demolished with the rear block when the main building was restored.

Opposite Nash's House is the MARKET HALL of 1849, three bays, with Greek Doric columns *in antis*. On the E side the opening to the recently rebuilt Nash and Wyatt Almshouses. Then Nos 15 and 16 with Georgian doorcases and the OLD PHEASANT INN, Elizabethan with two overhangs. The elaborate brackets of the archway must be later C17. So to the CORNMARKET. At the corner the fine No. 4. Timber-framed, but with two Late Georgian bowed shop windows. The adjoining No. 5 is dated 1577. It has a very graceful Adamish doorway. Nos 8–9 are a reproduction. If the original house had the motif of the fluted segment aprons below the windows, then it can be attributed to *Thomas White* on the strength of his Britannia House (*see* p. 324). The PUBLIC HALL on the

N side, stuccoed, in a quiet Italianate style, still Georgian in spirit, is being demolished at the time of writing. It is or was of 1848–9, by *Hopkins*. A little NW of here, in TRINITY STREET, another timber-framed Elizabethan house. This is small, with two gables and an upper balcony with timber posts supporting the jutting of the gables. The house originally stood across the road. That ends this timber expedition.

The main N walk is along the spine of Worcester, the line High Street–Cross–Foregate–Foregate Street–Tything–Upper Tything. But before one reaches the High Street, one must now take in the new central development. It is not easy to be fair to it. But one should not forget that this development in this place is hara-kiri by the city, not murder by the architects. They are *Shingler, Risdon Associates*, and they have made a good job of it. The part by the cathedral and the unfortunate roundabout are only three storeys high, and their façades – of course of engineering bricks – vary enough to prevent boredom, yet sufficiently to give either side a character. The high block – anyway only six storeys – is pushed back, and from the HIGH STREET one approaches it by a pedestrian shopping alley. It is the GIFFARD HOTEL, and the consultants on this are *Russell, Hodgson & Leigh*. The work is very satisfying throughout, neither gimmicky nor modish. So the SE end of the High Street is this new development. Opposite, there is first FISH STREET, with the timber-framed Jacobean FARRIER'S ARMS with overhang and close studding. Then, in the High Street, the first house of note: No. 95 (Messrs Stallard), with a good High Victorian shop front, with Gothic motifs. Below are extensive wine cellars, tunnel-vaulted in brick. The new building N of this is going to preserve one medieval stone cellar. Then Nos 83–84, brick, three-storeyed, the ground floor – as in all these houses – newer shop fronts. Opposite all is C20. The most notable building is the CADENA CAFÉ, large, of red brick and brown terracotta, with a corner turret. Down CHURCH STREET, just S of the Cadena, to allow a moment for the original GRAMMAR SCHOOL, or what is left of it, half-hidden behind the tower of St Swithun. It is of 1735 and one-storeyed, with arched windows. On the W side of the High Street No. 66 is Early Georgian and has five bays and three storeys with a one-bay projection, stressed by even quoins of rustication and a pediment. No. 61 is the corner of Broad Street. It dates from *c.*1700 and has three by five bays, with a hipped roof and dormers.

In BROAD STREET No. 61 is one of the collector's pieces at Worcester, a four-storeyed mid-Georgian brick house of only one bay width. The big quoins emphasize the narrowness. A Venetian window on every floor, and then, on top of it all, a domed little BELVEDERE with pointed windows in three directions and access to a room in the back gable on the fourth. In this room and the dome sparse Gothick decoration. On the opposite side the MIDLAND BANK, in a dignified Italian, though not of the distinction of Lloyds Bank (*see* below). The Midland Bank is by *H. L. Florence* and dates from 1876 – a late date.

The continuation of the High Street is THE CROSS. This short stretch of road is dominated by St Nicholas and the extremely fine LLOYDS BANK, 1861–2 by *Elmslie*. It cost about £14,000. It is of four generously spaced bays and three storeys, ashlar-faced. The portal has two pairs of granite columns, and all first-floor windows are in aedicules. It is the provincial bank at its most confidence-inspiring. But first, a little S of this, a good early C18 brick house of three and a half storeys, with quoins, window surrounds, swags below the windows, and a later doorway, and then, at the end of THE AVENUE, the City Department of Health, a house odd to the avenue, wholly delightful to the back. That back, to Trinity Street, shows this to be Worcester's premier Gothic Revival house, of a date hardly later than the 1770s, with doorway and all windows Venetian, but with the higher middle light ogee-headed. Having realized at the back that the house is not a C19 folly, one may well think that underlying some of the evidently Victorian work on the front, such as the pediment with its kind of pinnacle, there is an early C18 house with giant fluted pilasters and fluted keystones.

At the end of The Cross turn l. into ANGEL STREET. The SHAKESPEARE HOTEL has splendidly bold early C19 lettering, and the former CORN EXCHANGE of 1848 is a mighty job, only five bays, but with truly colossal pairs of Tuscan columns *in antis*. Arched windows l. and r.

Back to The Cross and on into THE FOREGATE. This part of the street is unfortunately cut by the railway arch, a sign of what the free enterprise of railway building in the mid C19 was allowed to do to towns, just as the development by the cathedral is a sign of what free enterprise allows the car to inflict on us now. First on the E side two large buildings of red brick and terracotta, the first more Baroque, the second with a dash of the Loire. This latter is the HOP MARKET HOTEL dated 1900. It is, according to Mr Collins, by *Alfred B. Rowe* (of Henry Rowe & Son). Some Tudor touches are also noticeable. On the W side an early C18 brick house of three storeys with giant angle pilasters, and then the Berkeley Hospital.

The BERKELEY HOSPITAL was founded in 1697, and the building is dated 1703. To Foregate there are two five-bay blocks of two storeys with hipped roofs. Brick and stone dressings, moulded window surrounds. Small doorways with open curly pediments to the opening between the two blocks. This leads into the courtyard with the almspeople's houses. Each has a doorway flanked by two windows. The CHAPEL in the middle at the far end is of five bays with arched windows and a big doorway with open segmental pediment on carved brackets. Above, a niche with the statue of the founder and a composite curvy pediment. Hipped roof and lantern. It is a surprise to find in the chapel that one has entered it in the middle of one of the long sides. Plain interior. Fine gatepiers and iron gates.

The Berkeley Hospital is at the corner of SHAW STREET. In Shaw Street it is worth looking at two pairs of early C19 houses each with a combined doorway, i.e. three Greek Doric columns and a pediment. The Greeks would not have done it.

FOREGATE STREET is the street richest in Georgian buildings. It starts with VICTORIA HOUSE (W) of ten bays and three and a half storeys, late C18 and quite plain. This was once the Hop Pole Inn. Then the STAR HOTEL, probably of *c.*1850, stuccoed, of three and a half storeys and nine bays plus the l. hand archway with tripartite windows above it. After the railway arch, in PIERPOINT STREET the AUCTION MART of *c.*1825, stuccoed, of five bays with six giant fluted pilasters and a notable frieze above the entrance. Pierpoint Street leads to SANSOME WALK, where Nos 4 and 6 are part of a mid-C18 seven-bay house. Doorways with segmental pediments on brackets. No. 15 is early C18, of five bays.

Back to Foregate Street. No. 49, again W, is of only two bays, but three storeys, and has giant fluted pilasters and a nice first-floor iron balcony. Nos 44–45 is two houses of three storeys, with decorated keystones to the windows. Those of No. 44 are more lively. No. 43 is more ambitious, of five bays with the surround of the middle window curving out at the foot and a pediment on fat corbels. Then follows a whole stretch of Georgian properties. Two of them have good doorways with Tuscan columns and broken pediment, that of No. 42 with a sun face in the pediment in the William Kent taste, but nice Adamish detail otherwise. No. 39 has a pretty iron balcony, No. 37 is the pedimented centre of a once larger house. No. 33 has an early C18 doorcase with fluted Corinthian pilasters, the best of them so far. Nos 29–30 is a nine-bay terrace, the main part of seven bays with a Gibbs surround to the doorway, i.e. Early Georgian.

Turn l. into CASTLE STREET for some minor Georgian houses and the surprisingly ambitious AUSTIN HOUSE of 1939 by *J. C. S. Soutar*, a garage, car repair shop, and car showroom, with a tower of tapering sides and a pretty, rather Swedish open lantern.

After Castle Street the spine road becomes THE TYTHING. The change is only one of name. No. 58 is of four bays and three and a half storeys with quoins. Then Messrs KAY & CO.'s offices, 1938 by *Braxton Sinclair*, an imitation of the Georgian taken remarkably seriously. More nice genuine Georgian doorways, before KAY & CO.'s main premises are reached. They date from 1907 and are by *J. W. Simpson & Maxwell Ayrton*, the best building at Worcester by far of that date. The compact façade is as successful as the long utilitarian side, yet made true architecture by the fenestration and the gables. The best detail is the lettering over the main entrance.

Upper Tything belongs to Outer Worcester.

(*d*) *The Shrub Hill Area*

The canal and the railway made this the industrial suburb. For the station *see* p. 325. The GREAT WESTERN HOTEL must belong to the station job. It is also all engineering bricks, five bays, two and a half storeys, and with a Tuscan porch, i.e. still entirely Georgian. An early factory is that of HARDY & PADMORE in Foundry Street, established in 1814. The long brick front has arched windows, except for the top half-storeys with oculus windows. Typical Early Victorian factory buildings around are of red and yellow brick. Such are HEENAN & FROUDE'S by Shrub Hill Station, one of six bays with a six-bay pediment, another of twelve bays. The main building, in Shrub Hill, is long and has a five-bay pediment. It was built as the Worcester Engine Works in 1864. The architect was *Thomas Dickson* (of the engineering firm *E. Wilson*).* A similar building is in Pheasant Street, off St Martin's Street.

*Mr R. J. Collins provided me with these facts.

OUTER WORCESTER

As in most towns, these outer districts do not make up a proper perambulation. The only exception is to the N, where Upper Tything simply continues The Tything.

The noteworthy buildings in UPPER TYTHING are Public Buildings (*see* p. 324), although Britannia House was of course built as a private house. The only other building that will be noticed at once is ST OSWALD'S HOSPITAL of 1873–4 by *H. Rowe*. The premises are spacious and include a CHAPEL, the size of a small church. The W bay is separated from the rest by an arch as a kind of narthex. Semicircular apse, but Second Pointed style. Opposite Britannia House one ought to turn W at once to see BRITANNIA SQUARE, a large area with a spacious open green in which the main house is placed. This and all the other houses are stuccoed and in the same style. Building began about 1820. By 1822 some of the houses on the E side were up. Many of the houses in the square are semi-detached, of four bays, two-storeyed, with giant pilasters. The middle house alone is of five bays and three storeys. It has giant pilasters too, and the ground-floor pairs of side windows are set under blank segmental arches. Other houses, e.g. Nos 37 and 49, are of five bays too, but two-storeyed. One has a Greek Doric, the other a Tuscan porch. The same types continue along ALBANY TERRACE. But No. 4, THE ALBANY, is singled out for more ornate treatment, and that betrays at once the provincial quality of the whole. The detail is all debased Greco-Egyptian, especially the capitals. Back to Upper Tything for the QUEEN ELIZABETH ALMSHOUSES, by *Gibbons*, of *Lord & Parker* of Worcester, 1876–7.

BARBOURNE ROAD starts with a late C18 terrace. The houses were of some consequence, as three of the five are of five bays each. Then, opposite, a five-bay Georgian former country house, OLD BASKERVILLE, and, remaining on that side, a house with a Tuscan porch, and then a few more. Presently, on the other, E, side ST GEORGE'S SQUARE, another Britannia Square, but the brick houses not stuccoed, and the square itself of a form which makes it easier to take it in. It is long, relatively narrow, and ends in a semicircle. Aston Webb's church is a set piece at the end which could not be bettered. The houses are mostly semi-detached and of two bays each. They have two and a half storeys. There are also three-bay detached houses with porches. All round this area, i.e. BARBOURNE, much was built about 1865. *The Builder* in 1866 says that 'within the last year or two a little town has sprung up'.

Farther out at the fork of the Droitwich and Ombersley roads a polygonal TOLLHOUSE. Then in the DROITWICH ROAD the fine GATEPIERS of the former PERDISWELL HALL. They have beautiful *Coade* stone reliefs of Navigation and Agriculture, dated 1788. The STABLES are stuccoed, with a pediment and blank arches round the side windows. The house was demolished in 1956.

WEST of Worcester proper, in and around ST JOHN'S IN BEDWARDINE, there is little to pick out: Messrs BERROW'S two buildings in HYLTON ROAD, the earlier with a series of monopitch roofs by *Henry Gorst*, the newer, of precast concrete parts with a very curious, typically sixties-looking staircase feature, 1964–5 by *Austin Smith, Salmon, Lord*. Then close to St John's church, in ST JOHN'S, a five-bay house with fluted keystones and an arched middle window. More such houses in Upper Wick (for which *see* p. 281) and also on the way to Lower Wick. In the MALVERN ROAD first, on the l., a terrace, Late Georgian, with segment-headed windows. Then, on the r., in its own garden, PITMASTON HOUSE, five-bay Georgian, but some time in the mid C19 gothicized and provided with rather heavy Gothic additions.

To the NORTH-EAST is a development similar to, and probably contemporary with, Britannia Square, in the Lansdowne area and especially LANSDOWNE CRESCENT. The best houses are BISHOP'S HOUSE and THE HOMESTEAD, both with giant pilasters and blank arches above the ground-floor windows filled with a shell motif. The former house has a Greek Doric porch, the latter a conservatory. The whole length of the Crescent are stuccoed houses no doubt put up as one job. They have ample front gardens and a fine view over Worcester.

The Late Georgian and Early Victorian development has left more traces than in any other direction in that to the SOUTH-EAST. Here there is, still at the very end of Sidbury, the LOCH RYAN HOTEL, stuccoed, of five bays, with a pedimented three-bay projection. Doorway with broken pediment on Ionic columns. This looks late C18. Then an earlier Georgian brick terrace in BATH ROAD. The first house is dated 1740. Five bays, two storeys, decorated keystones, doorway with Tuscan columns. The terrace opposite is probably late C18. Off LONDON ROAD Nos 1–2 BATTENHALL PLACE are early C19, with the principal (once no doubt the middle) window distinguished by a blank arch with a fan motif. Then, in London Road, ST MARY'S TERRACE, early C19, red, of three storeys. The middle window of each house is arched. A little farther out is the LARK HILL development, stuccoed like Lansdowne Crescent and Britannia Square. One house on the l. is of three bays with a Tuscan porch, a group on the r. has giant pilasters and pretty verandas.

In PERRY WOOD WALK is the new office building of the METAL BOX COMPANY, 1963–4 by *Howell, Killick, Partridge & Amis*, a good, vigorous, if decidedly restless job in the idiom of the sixties.

7070

WRIBBENHALL

Wribbenhall is really Bewdley across the river. Just as on the other side the three main streets go straight from the bridge, and l. and r. along the Severn. Only everything is smaller.

From the bridge one sees beyond a new car showroom a late C18 or early C19 WAREHOUSE with segment-headed windows, then some gardens behind which a long Georgian terrace (on which *see* below). Then a nice group to the corner of the Kidderminster road including a timber-framed cottage of the C16 and a red-brick Elizabethan or Jacobean house. Before turning the corner one should look into the STOURPORT ROAD, which starts along the river. No. 1 is of five bays and three storeys with segment-headed windows. The river front here is in a nice contrast to Bewdley's Severnside opposite; for while Severnside has no trees at all, here they are an integral part of the picture. In KIDDERMINSTER ROAD a timber-framed house with two moulded bressumers, then a four-bay Georgian façade to an older timber-framed house and the BLACK BOY, also C18 over older timber-framing. Turn l. into a nameless passage to yet another C16 timber-framed house and to a fifteen-bay red-brick early C18 terrace of two storeys with hipped roof.

ALL SAINTS. 1878 by *Arthur Blomfield*. Rockfaced red sandstone with a SE tower above the vestry. Style of *c*.1300. – Iron SCREEN. – STAINED GLASS. E probably by *Hardman*.

SECONDARY MODERN SCHOOL, Stourport Road. By *Yorke, Rosenberg & Mardall*, 1954–5. A pleasant design, with much wood-slatting, a curved brick screen wall, and a bold water tower. In the hall WALL PAINTINGS by *Michael Rothenstein*

WYCHBOLD

9060

ST MARY. Quite a big church, built in 1888–9 at the expense of John Corbett (*see* Droitwich) by *Lewis Shepherd* of Worcester. SE tower in the Dec style and with an original late C13 doorway with moulded capitals and a deeply moulded arch. The tower E window also seems original. The church has transepts and no aisles, and the interior is brick-faced.

WYCHBURY HILL *see* HAGLEY

WYRE PIDDLE

9040

CHURCH. Early Norman chancel arch, as elementary as any. The rest mostly C19-looking, but in fact old. The bellcote over the E end of the nave e.g. looks E.E. The churchyard slopes down to the Avon. – PILLAR PISCINA. C12, the top a single-scallop capital. – Next to it a stone SHELF supported by an E.E. stiff-leaf capital. – FONT. Norman, drum-shaped, with a band of vertical single zigzags and another of normal zigzag. Scallops on the underside.* – (SCULPTURE. In the vestry two large animal heads, probably corbels.) – STAINED GLASS. Many fragments in the W window. – TILES. C15; in the chancel. – PLATE. Reconstructed Cup, the stem Elizabethan; Flagon by *R. S.*, 1640; Plate by *W. M.*, 1673.

HOUSE. Built *c.*1625–50, but radically remodelled *c.*1840–50, with straight-headed windows in the style of *c.*1500, hood-moulds, and bargeboarded gables (cf. a larger house at Wick).

WYTHALL

0070

ST MARY. 1862 by *F. Preedy*, the splendid central tower of 1903. Without the tower there would not be much to the building. It is in an aggressive style inspired by Butterfield. Red brick, with black-brick and stone pattern. The brick is exposed inside as well. The jambs of windows and arches inside are emphasized by saw-tooth brick cutting. The pier capitals inside have Early French Gothic foliage. Flat E end, S transept, S aisle. Now the tower. It is very high, of darker brick, and in its 101
upper parts all open so that one can see through it. On each side are two very high two-light openings, richly shafted. The top is a saddleback roof with an odd flèche in the middle and

*Almost identical with the Abberton font (Neil Stratford).

an equally odd polygonal stair-turret running up one corner. The inspiration comes from the C13 in Normandy. The design is of a very high quality and is indeed *W. H. Bidlake*'s.

SCHOOL. In the churchyard. Dated 1840. Brick, with pointed windows and on the raised centre a pedimental gable.

GLOSSARY

ABACUS: flat slab on the top of a capital (q.v.).

ABUTMENT: solid masonry placed to resist the lateral pressure of a vault.

ACANTHUS: plant with thick fleshy and scalloped leaves used as part of the decoration of a Corinthian capital (q.v.) and in some types of leaf carving.

ACHIEVEMENT OF ARMS: in heraldry, a complete display of armorial bearings.

ACROTERION: foliage-carved block on the end or top of a classical pediment.

ADDORSED: two human figures, animals, or birds, etc., placed symmetrically so that they turn their backs to each other.

AEDICULE, AEDICULA: framing of a window or door by columns and a pediment (q.v.).

AFFRONTED: two human figures, animals, or birds, etc., placed symmetrically so that they face each other.

AGGER: Latin term for the built-up foundations of Roman roads; also sometimes applied to the banks of hill-forts or other earthworks.

AMBULATORY: semicircular or polygonal aisle enclosing an apse (q.v.).

ANNULET: *see* Shaft-ring.

ANSE DE PANIER: *see* Arch, Basket.

ANTEPENDIUM: covering of the front of an altar, usually by textiles or metalwork.

ANTIS, IN: *see* Portico.

APSE: vaulted semicircular or polygonal end of a chancel or a chapel.

ARABESQUE: light and fanciful surface decoration using combinations of flowing lines, tendrils, etc., interspersed with vases, animals, etc.

ARCADE: range of arches supported on piers or columns, free-standing: or, BLIND ARCADE, the same attached to a wall.

ARCH: round-headed, i.e. semicircular; pointed, i.e. consisting of two curves, each drawn from one centre, and meeting in a point at the top; segmental, i.e. in the form of a segment;

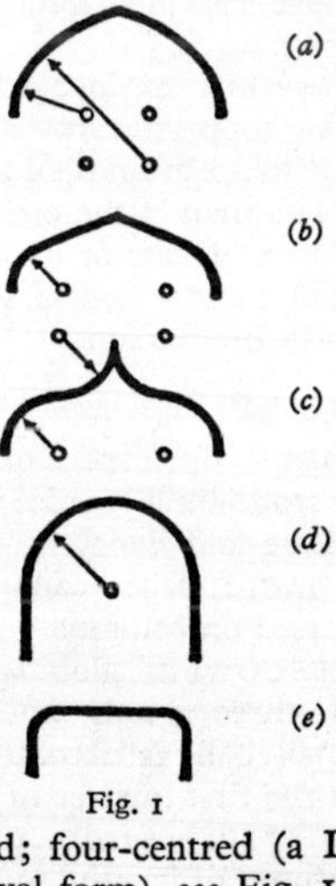

Fig. 1

pointed; four-centred (a Late Medieval form), *see* Fig. 1(*a*); Tudor (also a Late Medieval form), *see* Fig. 1(*b*); Ogee (introduced *c.*1300 and specially popular in the C14), *see* Fig. 1(*c*); Stilted, *see* Fig. 1(*d*); Basket, with lintel connected to the jambs by concave quadrant curves, *see* Fig. 1(*e*) for one example; Diaphragm, a transverse arch with solid spandrels carrying not a vault but a principal beam of a timber roof.

ARCHITRAVE: lowest of the three main parts of the entablature (q.v.) of an order (q.v.) (*see* Fig. 12).

ARCHIVOLT: under-surface of an arch (also called Soffit).

ARRIS: sharp edge at the meeting of two surfaces.

ASHLAR: masonry of large blocks wrought to even faces and square edges.

ATLANTES: male counterparts of caryatids (q.v.).

ATRIUM: inner court of a Roman house, also open court in front of a church.

ATTACHED: *see* Engaged.

ATTIC: topmost storey of a house, if distance from floor to ceiling is less than in the others.

AUMBRY: recess or cupboard to hold sacred vessels for Mass and Communion.

BAILEY: open space or court of a stone-built castle; *see* also Motte-and-Bailey.

BALDACCHINO: canopy supported on columns.

BALLFLOWER: globular flower of three petals enclosing a small ball. A decoration used in the first quarter of the C14.

BALUSTER: small pillar or column of fanciful outline.

BALUSTRADE: series of balusters supporting a handrail or coping (q.v.).

BARBICAN: outwork defending the entrance to a castle.

BARGEBOARDS: projecting decorated boards placed against the incline of the gable of a building and hiding the horizontal roof timbers.

BARROW: *see* Bell, Bowl, Disc, Long, *and* Pond Barrow.

BASILICA: in medieval architecture an aisled church with a clerestory.

BASKET ARCH: *see* Arch (Fig. 1*e*).

BASTION: projection at the angle of a fortification.

BATTER: inclined face of a wall.

BATTLEMENT: parapet with a series of indentations or embrasures with raised portions or merlons between (also called Crenellation).

BAYS: internal compartments of a building; each divided from the other not by solid walls but by divisions only marked in the side walls (columns, pilasters, etc.) or the ceiling (beams, etc.). Also external divisions of a building by fenestration.

BAY-WINDOW: angular or curved projection of a house front with ample fenestration. If curved, also called bow-window: if on an upper floor only, also called oriel or oriel window.

BEAKER FOLK: Late New Stone Age warrior invaders from the Continent who buried their dead in round barrows and introduced the first metal tools and weapons to Britain.

BEAKHEAD: Norman ornamental motif consisting of a row of bird or beast heads with beaks biting usually into a roll moulding.

BELFRY: turret on a roof to hang bells in.

BELGAE: Aristocratic warrior bands who settled in Britain in two main waves in the C I B.C. In Britain their culture is termed Iron Age C.

BELL BARROW: Early Bronze Age round barrow in which the mound is separated from its encircling ditch by a flat platform or berm (q.v.).

BELLCOTE: framework on a roof to hang bells from.

BERM: level area separating ditch from bank on a hill-fort or barrow.

BILLET FRIEZE: Norman ornamental motif made up of short raised rectangles placed at regular intervals.

BIVALLATE: Of a hill-fort: defended by two concentric banks and ditches.

BLOCK CAPITAL: Romanesque capital cut from a cube by having the lower angles rounded off to the circular shaft below (also called Cushion Capital) (Fig. 2).

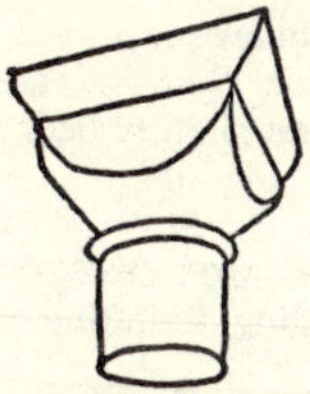

Fig. 2

BOND, ENGLISH or FLEMISH: *see* Brickwork.

BOSS: knob or projection usually placed to cover the intersection of ribs in a vault.

BOWL BARROW: round barrow surrounded by a quarry ditch. Introduced in Late Neolithic times, the form continued until the Saxon period.

BOW-WINDOW: *see* Bay-Window.

BOX: A small country house, e.g. a shooting box. A convenient term to describe a compact minor dwelling, e.g. a rectory.

BOX PEW: pew with a high wooden enclosure.

BRACES: *see* Roof.

BRACKET: small supporting piece of stone, etc., to carry a projecting horizontal.

BRESSUMER: beam in a timber-framed building to support the, usually projecting, superstructure.

BRICKWORK: *Header:* brick laid so that the end only appears on the face of the wall. *Stretcher:* brick laid so that the side only appears on the face of the wall. *English Bond:* method of laying bricks so that alternate courses or layers on the face of the wall are composed of headers or stretchers only (Fig. 3*a*). *Flemish Bond:* method of laying bricks so that alternate headers and stretchers appear in each course on the face of the wall (Fig. 3*b*).

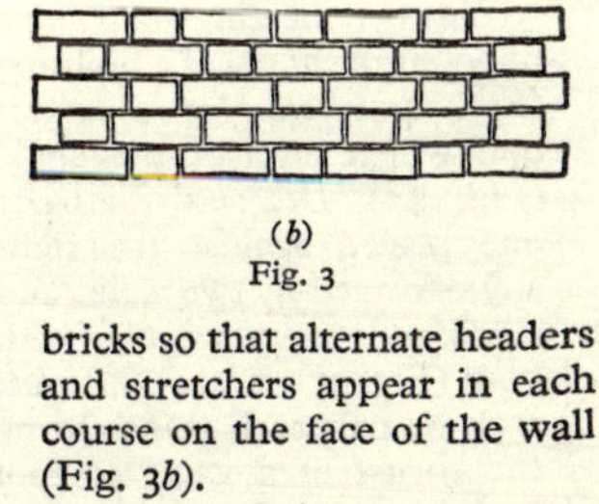

(*a*)

(*b*)

Fig. 3

BROACH: *see* Spire.

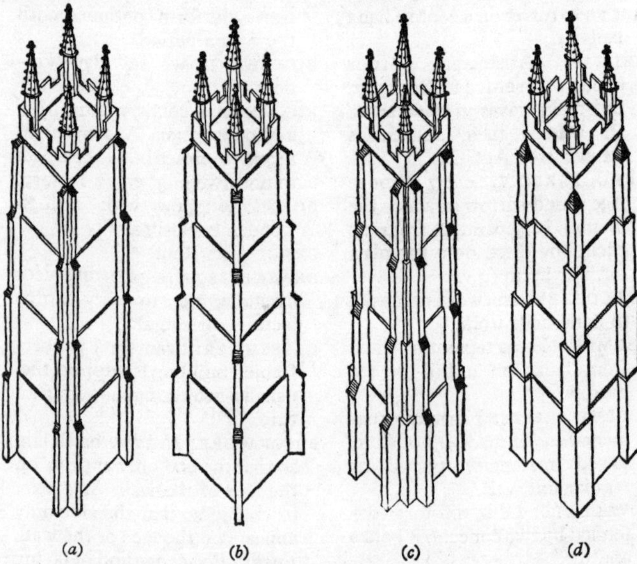

Fig. 4

BROKEN PEDIMENT: *see* Pediment.

BRONZE AGE: In Britain, the period from *c.*1800 to 600 B.C.

BUCRANIUM: ox skull.

BUTTRESS: mass of brickwork or masonry projecting from or built against a wall to give additional strength. *Angle Buttresses:* two meeting at an angle of 90° at the angle of a building (Fig. 4*a*). *Clasping Buttress:* one which encases the angle (Fig. 4*d*). *Diagonal Buttress:* one placed against the right angle formed by two walls, and more or less equiangular with both (Fig. 4*b*). *Flying Buttress:* arch or half arch transmitting the thrust of a vault or roof from the upper part of a wall to an outer support or buttress. *Setback Buttress:* angle buttress set slightly back from the angle (Fig. 4*c*).

CABLE MOULDING: Norman moulding imitating a twisted cord.

CAIRN: a mound of stones usually covering a burial.

CAMBER: slight rise or upward curve of an otherwise horizontal structure.

CAMPANILE: isolated bell tower.

CANOPY: projection or hood over an altar, pulpit, niche, statue, etc.

CAP: in a windmill the crowning feature.

CAPITAL: head or top part of a column.

CARTOUCHE: tablet with an ornate frame, usually enclosing an inscription.

CARYATID: whole female figure supporting an entablature or other similar member. *Termini Caryatids:* female busts or demi-figures or three-quarter figures supporting an entablature or other similar member and placed at the top of termini pilasters (q.v.). Cf. Atlantes.

CASTELLATED: decorated with battlements.

CELURE: panelled and adorned part of a wagon-roof above the rood or the altar.

CENSER: vessel for the burning of incense.

CENTERING: wooden framework used in arch and vault construction and removed when the mortar has set.

CHALICE: cup used in the Communion service or at Mass. *See also* Recusant Chalice.

CHAMBERED TOMB: burial mound of the New Stone Age having a stone-built chamber and entrance passage covered by an earthen barrow or stone cairn. The form was introduced to Britain from the Mediterranean.

CHAMFER: surface made by cutting across the square angle of a stone block, piece of wood, etc., usually at an angle of 45° to the other two surfaces.

CHANCEL: that part of the E end of a church in which the altar is placed, usually applied to the whole continuation of the nave E of the crossing.

CHANCEL ARCH: arch at the W end of the chancel.

CHANTRY CHAPEL: chapel attached to, or inside, a church, endowed for the saying of Masses for the soul of the founder or some other individual.

CHEVET: French term for the E end of a church (chancel, ambulatory, and radiating chapels).

CHEVRON: Norman moulding forming a zigzag.

CHOIR: that part of the church where divine service is sung.

CIBORIUM: a baldacchino.

CINQUEFOIL: *see* Foil.

CIST: stone-lined or slab-built grave. First appears in Late Neolithic times. It continued to be used in the Early Christian period.

CLAPPER BRIDGE: bridge made of large slabs of stone, some built up to make rough piers and other longer ones laid on top to make the roadway.

CLASSIC: here used to mean the moment of highest achievement of a style.

CLASSICAL: here used as the term for Greek and Roman architecture and any subsequent styles inspired by it.

CLERESTORY: upper storey of the nave walls of a church, pierced by windows.

COADE STONE: artificial (cast) stone made in the late C18 and the early C19 by Coade and Sealy in London.

COB: walling material made of mixed clay and straw.

COFFERING: decorating a ceiling with sunk square or polygonal ornamental panels.

COLLAR-BEAM: *see* Roof.

COLONNADE: range of columns.

COLONNETTE: small column.

COLUMNA ROSTRATA: column decorated with carved prows of ships to celebrate a naval victory.

COMPOSITE: *see* Order.

CONSOLE: bracket (q.v.) with a compound curved outline.

COPING: capping or covering to a wall.

CORBEL: block of stone projecting from a wall, supporting some feature on its horizontal top surface.

CORBEL TABLE: series of corbels, occurring just below the roof eaves externally or internally, often seen in Norman buildings.

CORINTHIAN: *see* Order.

CORNICE: in classical architecture the top section of the entablature (q.v.). Also for a projecting decorative feature along the top of a wall, arch, etc.

CORRIDOR VILLA: *see* Villa.

COUNTERSCARP BANK: small bank on the down-hill or outer side of a hill-fort ditch.

COURTYARD VILLA: *see* Villa.

COVE, COVING: concave undersurface in the nature of a hollow moulding but on a larger scale.

COVER PATEN: cover to a Communion cup, suitable for use as a paten or plate for the consecrated bread.

CRADLE ROOF: *see* Wagon roof.

CRENELLATION: *see* Battlement.

CREST, CRESTING: ornamental finish along the top of a screen, etc.

CRINKLE-CRANKLE WALL: undulating wall.

CROCKET, CROCKETING: decorative features placed on the sloping sides of spires, pinnacles, gables, etc., in Gothic architecture, carved in various leaf shapes and placed at regular intervals.

CROCKET CAPITAL: *see* Fig. 5. An Early Gothic form.

CROMLECH: word of Celtic origin still occasionally used of single free-standing stones ascribed to the Neolithic or Bronze Age periods.

Fig. 5

CROSSING: space at the intersection of nave, chancel, and transepts.

CROSS-WINDOWS: windows with one mullion and one transom.

CRUCK: big curved beam supporting both walls and roof of a cottage.

CRYPT: underground room usually below the E end of a church.

CUPOLA: small polygonal or circular domed turret crowning a roof.

CURTAIN WALL: connecting wall between the towers of a castle.

CUSHION CAPITAL: *see* Block Capital.

CUSP: projecting point between the foils in a foiled Gothic arch.

DADO: decorative covering of the lower part of a wall.

DAGGER: tracery motif of the Dec style. It is a lancet shape rounded or pointed at the head, pointed at the foot, and cusped inside (*see* Fig. 6).

Fig. 6

DAIS: raised platform at one end of a room.

DEC ('DECORATED'): historical division of English Gothic architecture covering the period from *c.*1290 to *c.*1350.

DEMI-COLUMNS: columns half sunk into a wall.

DIAPER WORK: surface decoration composed of square or lozenge shapes.

DIAPHRAGM ARCH: *see* Arch.

DISC BARROW: Bronze Age round barrow with inconspicuous central mound surrounded by bank and ditch.

DOGTOOTH: typical E.E. ornament consisting of a series of four-cornered stars placed diagonally and raised pyramidally (Fig. 7).

Fig. 7

DOMICAL VAULT: *see* Vault.

DONJON: *see* Keep.

DORIC: *see* Order.

DORMER (WINDOW): window placed vertically in the sloping plane of a roof.

DRIPSTONE: *see* Hood-mould.

DRUM: circular or polygonal vertical wall of a dome or cupola.

E.E. ('EARLY ENGLISH'): historical division of English Gothic architecture roughly covering the C13.

EASTER SEPULCHRE: recess with tomb-chest, usually in the wall of a chancel, the tomb-chest to receive an effigy of Christ for Easter celebrations.

EAVES: underpart of a sloping roof overhanging a wall.

EAVES CORNICE: cornice below the eaves of a roof.

ECHINUS: Convex or projecting moulding supporting the abacus of a Greek Doric capital, sometimes bearing an egg and dart pattern.

EMBATTLED: *see* Battlement.

EMBRASURE: small opening in the wall or parapet of a fortified building, usually splayed on the inside.

ENCAUSTIC TILES: earthenware glazed and decorated tiles used for paving.

ENGAGED COLUMNS: columns attached to, or partly sunk into, a wall.

ENGLISH BOND: *see* Brickwork.

ENTABLATURE: in classical architecture the whole of the horizontal members above a column (that is architrave, frieze, and cornice) (*see* Fig. 12).

ENTASIS: very slight convex deviation from a straight line; used on Greek columns and sometimes on spires to prevent an optical illusion of concavity.

ENTRESOL: *see* Mezzanine.

EPITAPH: hanging wall monument.

ESCUTCHEON: shield for armorial bearings.

EXEDRA: the apsidal end of a room. *See* Apse.

FAN-VAULT: *see* Vault.

FERETORY: place behind the

high altar where the chief shrine of a church is kept.

FESTOON: carved garland of flowers and fruit suspended at both ends.

FILLET: narrow flat band running down a shaft or along a roll moulding.

FINIAL: top of a canopy, gable, pinnacle.

FLAGON: vessel for the wine used in the Communion service.

FLAMBOYANT: properly the latest phase of French Gothic architecture where the window tracery takes on wavy undulating lines.

FLÈCHE: slender wooden spire on the centre of a roof (also called Spirelet).

FLEMISH BOND: *see* Brickwork.

FLEURON: decorative carved flower or leaf.

FLUSHWORK: decorative use of flint in conjunction with dressed stone so as to form patterns: tracery, initials, etc.

FLUTING: vertical channelling in the shaft of a column.

FLYING BUTTRESS: *see* Buttress.

FOIL: lobe formed by the cusping (q.v.) of a circle or an arch. Trefoil, quatrefoil, cinquefoil, multifoil, express the number of leaf shapes to be seen.

FOLIATED: carved with leaf shapes.

FOSSE: ditch.

FOUR-CENTRED ARCH: *see* Arch.

FRATER: refectory or dining hall of a monastery.

FRESCO: wall painting on wet plaster.

FRIEZE: middle division of a classical entablature (q.v.) (*see* Fig. 12).

FRONTAL: covering for the front of an altar.

GABLE: *Dutch gable:* A gable with curved sides crowned by a pediment, characteristic of *c.*1630–50 (Fig. 8*a*). *Shaped gable:* A gable with multicurved sides characteristic of *c.*1600–50 (Fig. 8*b*).

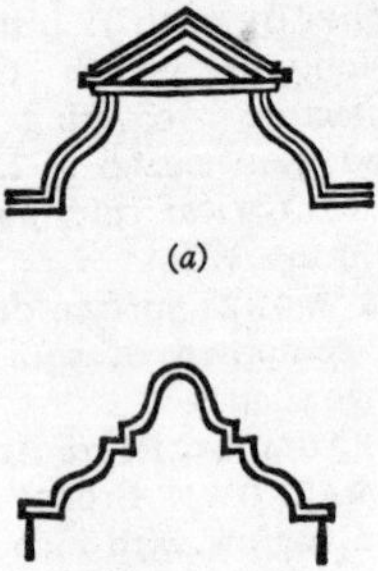

(*a*)

(*b*)

Fig. 8

GADROONED: enriched with a series of convex ridges, the opposite of fluting.

GALILEE: chapel or vestibule usually at the W end of a church enclosing the porch. Also called Narthex (q.v.).

GALLERY: in church architecture upper storey above an aisle, opened in arches to the nave. Also called Tribune and often erroneously Triforium (q.v.).

GALLERY GRAVE: chambered tomb (q.v.) in which there is little or no differentiation between the entrance passage and the actual burial chamber(s).

GARDEROBE: lavatory or privy in a medieval building.

GARGOYLE: water spout projecting from the parapet of a wall or tower; carved into a human or animal shape.

GAZEBO: lookout tower or raised

summer house in a picturesque garden.

'GEOMETRICAL': *see* Tracery.

'GIBBS SURROUND': of a doorway or window. An C18 motif consisting of a surround with alternating larger and smaller blocks of stone, quoin-wise, or intermittent large blocks, sometimes with a narrow raised band connecting them up the verticals and along the face of the arch (Fig. 9).

Fig. 9

GROIN: sharp edge at the meeting of two cells of a cross-vault.

GROIN-VAULT: *see* Vault.

GROTESQUE: fanciful ornamental decoration: *see* also Arabesque.

HAGIOSCOPE: *see* Squint.

HALF-TIMBERING: *see* Timber-Framing.

HALL CHURCH: church in which nave and aisles are of equal height or approximately so.

HAMMERBEAM: *see* Roof.

HANAP: large metal cup, generally made for domestic use, standing on an elaborate base and stem; with a very ornate cover frequently crowned with a little steeple.

HEADERS: *see* Brickwork.

HERRINGBONE WORK: brick, stone, or tile construction where the component blocks are laid diagonally instead of flat. Alternate courses lie in opposing directions to make a zigzag pattern up the face of the wall.

HEXASTYLE: having six detached columns.

HILL-FORT: Iron Age earthwork enclosed by a ditch and bank system; in the later part of the period the defences multiplied in size and complexity. They vary from about an acre to over 30 acres in area, and are usually built with careful regard to natural elevations or promontories.

HIPPED ROOF: *see* Roof.

HOOD-MOULD: projecting moulding above an arch or a lintel to throw off water (also called Dripstone or Label).

ICONOGRAPHY: the science of the subject matter of works of the visual arts.

IMPOST: bracket in a wall, usually formed of mouldings, on which the ends of an arch rest.

INDENT: shape chiselled out in a stone slab to receive a brass.

INGLENOOK: bench or seat built in beside a fireplace, sometimes covered by the chimneybreast, occasionally lit by small windows on each side of the fire.

INTERCOLUMNIATION: the space between columns.

IONIC: *see* Order (Fig. 12).

IRON AGE: in Britain the period from *c.* 600 B.C. to the coming of the Romans. The term is also used for those un-Romanized native communities which survived until the Saxon incursions.

JAMB: straight side of an archway, doorway, or window.

KEEL MOULDING: moulding whose outline is in section like that of the keel of a ship.

KEEP: massive tower of a Norman castle.

KEYSTONE: middle stone in an arch or a rib-vault.

KING-POST: *see* Roof (Fig. 14).

KNEELER: horizontal decorative projection at the base of a gable.

KNOP: a knob-like thickening in the stem of a chalice.

LABEL: *see* Hood-mould.

LABEL STOP: ornamental boss at the end of a hood-mould (q.v.).

LACED WINDOWS: windows pulled visually together by strips, usually in brick of a different colour, which continue vertically the lines of the vertical parts of the window surrounds. The motif is typical of *c.* 1720.

LANCET WINDOW: slender pointed-arched window.

LANTERN: in architecture, a small circular or polygonal turret with windows all round crowning a roof (*see* Cupola) or a dome.

LANTERN CROSS: churchyard cross with lantern-shaped top usually with sculptured representations on the sides of the top.

LEAN-TO ROOF: roof with one slope only, built against a higher wall.

LESENE or PILASTER STRIP: pilaster without base or capital.

LIERNE: *see* Vault (Fig. 21).

LINENFOLD: Tudor panelling ornamented with a conventional representation of a piece of linen laid in vertical folds. The piece is repeated in each panel.

LINTEL: horizontal beam or stone bridging an opening.

LOGGIA: recessed colonnade (q.v.).

LONG AND SHORT WORK: Saxon quoins (q.v.) consisting of stones placed with the long sides alternately upright and horizontal.

LONG BARROW: unchambered Neolithic communal burial mound, wedge-shaped in plan, with the burial and occasional other structures massed at the broader end, from which the mound itself tapers in height; quarry ditches flank the mound.

LOUVRE: opening, often with lantern (q.v.) over, in the roof of a room to let the smoke from a central hearth escape.

LOWER PALAEOLITHIC: *see* Palaeolithic.

LOZENGE: diamond shape.

LUCARNE: small opening to let light in.

LUNETTE: tympanum (q.v.) or semicircular opening.

LYCH GATE: wooden gate structure with a roof and open sides placed at the entrance to a churchyard to provide space for the reception of a coffin. The word *lych* is Saxon and means a corpse.

LYNCHET: long terraced strip of soil accumulating on the downward side of prehistoric and medieval fields due to soil creep from continuous ploughing along the contours.

MACHICOLATION: projecting gallery on brackets constructed on the outside of castle towers or walls. The gallery has holes in the floor to drop missiles through.

MAJOLICA: ornamented glazed earthenware.

MANSARD: *see* Roof.

MATHEMATICAL TILES: Small facing tiles the size of brick headers, applied to timber-framed walls to make them appear brick-built.

MEGALITHIC TOMB: stone-built burial chamber of the New Stone Age covered by an earth or stone mound. The form was introduced to Britain from the Mediterranean area.

MERLON: *see* Battlement.

MESOLITHIC: 'Middle Stone' Age; the post-glacial period of hunting and fishing communities dating in Britain from *c.* 8000 B.C. to the arrival of Neolithic communities, with which they must have considerably overlapped.

METOPE: in classical architecture of the Doric order (q.v.) the space in the frieze between the triglyphs (Fig. 12).

MEZZANINE: low storey placed between two higher ones.

MISERERE: *see* Misericord.

MISERICORD: bracket placed on the underside of a hinged choir stall seat which, when turned up, provided the occupant of the seat with a support during long periods of standing (also called Miserere).

MODILLION: small bracket of which large numbers (modillion frieze) are often placed below a cornice (q.v.) in classical architecture.

MOTTE: steep mound forming the main feature of C11 and C12 castles.

MOTTE-AND-BAILEY: post-Roman and Norman defence system consisting of an earthen mound (the motte) topped with a wooden tower eccentrically placed within a bailey (q.v.), with enclosure ditch and palisade, and with the rare addition of an internal bank.

MOUCHETTE: tracery motif in curvilinear tracery, a curved dagger (q.v.), specially popular in the early C14 (Fig. 10).

Fig. 10

MULLIONS: vertical posts or uprights dividing a window into 'lights'.

MULTIVALLATE: Of a hill-fort: defended by three or more concentric banks and ditches.

MUNTIN: post as a rule moulded and part of a screen.

NAIL-HEAD: E.E. ornamental motif, consisting of small pyramids regularly repeated (Fig. 11).

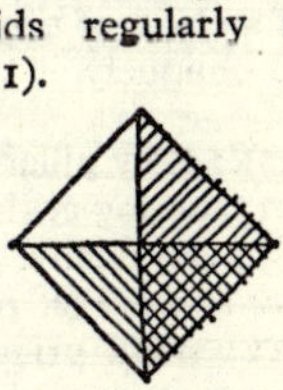

Fig. 11

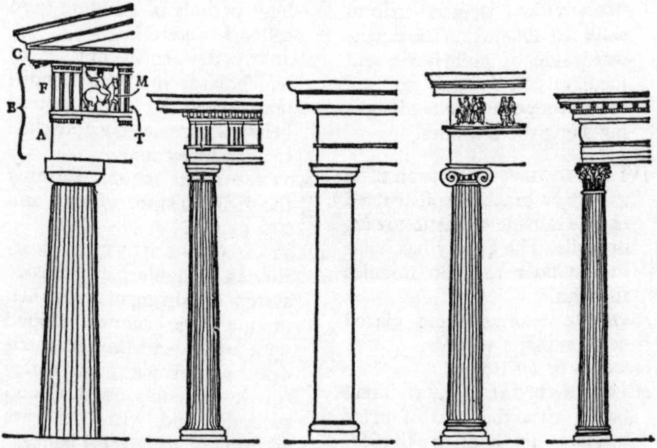

Fig. 12. Orders of Columns (Greek Doric, Roman Doric, Tuscan Doric, Ionic, Corinthian) E, Entablature; C, Cornice; F, Frieze; A, Architrave; M, Metope; T, Triglyph.

NARTHEX: enclosed vestibule or covered porch at the main entrance to a church (*see* Galilee).

NEOLITHIC: 'New Stone' Age, dating in Britain from the appearance from the Continent of the first settled farming communities *c.* 3500 B.C. until the introduction of the Bronze Age.

NEWEL: central post in a circular or winding staircase; also the principal post when a flight of stairs meets a landing.

NOOK-SHAFT: shaft set in the angle of a pier or respond or wall, or the angle of the jamb of a window or doorway.

NUTMEG MOULDING: consisting of a chain of tiny triangles placed obliquely.

OBELISK: lofty pillar of square section tapering at the top and ending pyramidally.

OGEE: *see* Arch (Fig. 1c).

ORATORY: small private chapel in a house.

ORDER: (1) *of a doorway or window:* series of concentric steps receding towards the opening; (2) *in classical architecture:* column with base, shaft, capital, and entablature (q.v.) according to one of the following styles: Greek Doric, Roman Doric, Tuscan Doric, Ionic, Corinthian, Composite. The established details are very elaborate, and some specialist architectural work should be consulted for further guidance (*see* Fig. 12).

ORIEL: *see* Bay-Window.

OVERHANG: projection of the upper storey of a house.

OVERSAILING COURSES: series of stone or brick courses, each one projecting beyond the one below it.

OVOLO: convex moulding.

PALAEOLITHIC: 'Old Stone' Age; the first period of human culture, commencing in the

Ice Age and immediately prior to the Mesolithic; the Lower Palaeolithic is the older phase, the Upper Palaeolithic the later.

PALIMPSEST: (1) *of a brass:* where a metal plate has been re-used by turning over and engraving on the back; (2) *of a wall painting:* where one overlaps and partly obscures an earlier one.

PALLADIAN: architecture following the ideas and principles of Andrea Palladio, 1518–80.

PANTILE: tile of curved S-shaped section.

PARAPET: low wall placed to protect any spot where there is a sudden drop, for example on a bridge, quay, hillside, housetop, etc.

PARGETTING: plaster work with patterns and ornaments either in relief or engraved on it.

PARVIS: term wrongly applied to a room over a church porch. These rooms were often used as a schoolroom or as a store room.

PATEN: plate to hold the bread at Communion or Mass.

PATERA: small flat circular or oval ornament in classical architecture.

PEDIMENT: low-pitched gable used in classical, Renaissance, and neo-classical architecture above a portico and above doors, windows, etc. It may be straight-sided or curved segmentally. *Broken Pediment:* one where the centre portion of the base is left open. *Open Pediment:* one where the centre portion of the sloping sides is left out.

PENDANT: boss (q.v.) elongated so that it seems to hang down.

PENDENTIF: concave triangular spandrel used to lead from the angle of two walls to the base of a circular dome. It is constructed as part of the hemisphere over a diameter the size of the diagonal of the basic square (Fig. 13).

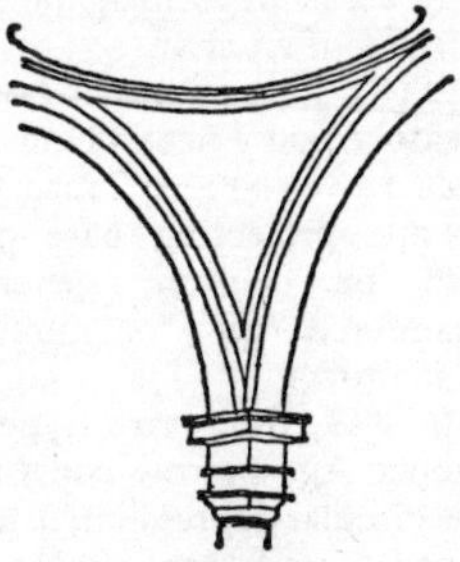

Fig. 13

PERP (PERPENDICULAR): historical division of English Gothic architecture covering the period from *c.*1335–50 to *c.*1530.

PIANO NOBILE: principal storey of a house with the reception rooms; usually the first floor.

PIAZZA: open space surrounded by buildings; in C17 and C18 England sometimes used to mean a long colonnade or loggia.

PIER: strong, solid support, frequently square in section or of composite section (compound pier).

PIETRA DURA: ornamental or scenic inlay by means of thin slabs of stone.

PILASTER: shallow pier attached to a wall. *Termini Pilasters:* pilasters with sides tapering downwards.

PILLAR PISCINA: free-standing piscina on a pillar.

PINNACLE: ornamental form crowning a spire, tower, buttress, etc., usually of steep pyramidal, conical, or some similar shape.

PISCINA: basin for washing the Communion or Mass vessels, provided with a drain. Generally set in or against the wall to the S of an altar.

PLAISANCE: summer-house, pleasure house near a mansion.

PLATE TRACERY: *see* Tracery.

PLINTH: projecting base of a wall or column, generally chamfered (q.v.) or moulded at the top.

POND BARROW: rare type of Bronze Age barrow consisting of a circular depression, usually paved, and containing a number of cremation burials.

POPPYHEAD: ornament of leaf and flower type used to decorate the tops of bench- or stall-ends.

PORTCULLIS: gate constructed to rise and fall in vertical grooves; used in gateways of castles.

PORTE COCHÈRE: porch large enough to admit wheeled vehicles.

PORTICO: centre-piece of a house or a church with classical detached or attached columns and a pediment. A portico is called *prostyle* or *in antis* according to whether it projects from or recedes into a building. In a portico *in antis* the columns range with the side walls.

POSTERN: small gateway at the back of a building.

PREDELLA: in an altarpiece the horizontal strip below the main representation, often used for a number of subsidiary representations in a row.

PRESBYTERY: the part of the church lying E of the choir. It is the part where the altar is placed.

PRINCIPAL: *see* Roof (Fig. 14).

PRIORY: monastic house whose head is a prior or prioress, not an abbot or abbess.

PROSTYLE: with free-standing columns in a row.

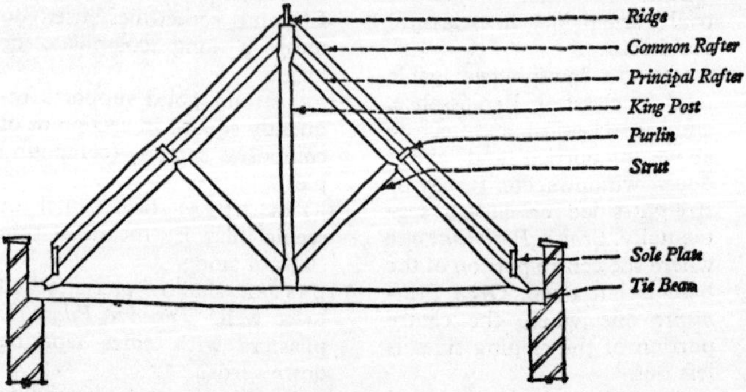

Fig. 14

PULPITUM: stone screen in a major church provided to shut off the choir from the nave and also as a backing for the return choir stalls.

PULVINATED FRIEZE: frieze with a bold convex moulding.

PURLIN: *see* Roof (Figs. 14, 15).

PUTHOLE or PUTLOCK HOLE: putlocks are the short horizontal timbers on which during construction the boards of scaffolding rest. Putholes or putlock holes are the holes in the wall for putlocks, which often are not filled in after construction is complete.

PUTTO: small naked boy.

QUADRANGLE: inner courtyard in a large building.

QUARRY: in stained-glass work, a small diamond- or square-shaped piece of glass set diagonally.

QUATREFOIL: *see* Foil.

QUEEN-POSTS: *see* Roof (Fig. 15).

QUOINS: dressed stones at the angles of a building. Sometimes all the stones are of the same size; more often they are alternately large and small.

RADIATING CHAPELS: chapels projecting radially from an ambulatory or an apse.

RAFTER: *see* Roof.

RAMPART: stone wall or wall of earth surrounding a castle, fortress, or fortified city.

RAMPART-WALK: path along the inner face of a rampart.

REBATE: continuous rectangular notch cut on an edge.

REBUS: pun, a play on words. The literal translation and illustration of a name for artistic and heraldic purposes (Belton = bell, tun).

RECUSANT CHALICE: chalice made after the Reformation and before Catholic Emancipation for Roman Catholic use.

REEDING: decoration with parallel convex mouldings touching one another.

REFECTORY: dining hall; *see* Frater.

RENDERING: plastering of an outer wall.

REPOUSSÉ: decoration of metal work by relief designs, formed by beating the metal from the back.

REREDOS: structure behind and above an altar.

RESPOND: half-pier bonded into a wall and carrying one end of an arch.

RETABLE: altarpiece, a picture or piece of carving, standing behind and attached to an altar.

RETICULATION: *see* Tracery (Fig. 20*e*).

REVEAL: that part of a jamb (q.v.) which lies between the glass or door and the outer surface of the wall.

RIB-VAULT: *see* Vault.

ROCOCO: latest phase of the Baroque style, current in most Continental countries between *c.*1720 and *c.*1760.

ROLL MOULDING: moulding of semicircular or more than semicircular section.

ROMANESQUE: that style in architecture which was current in the C11 and C12 and preceded the Gothic style (in England often called Norman). (Some scholars extend the use of the term Romanesque back to the C10 or C9.)

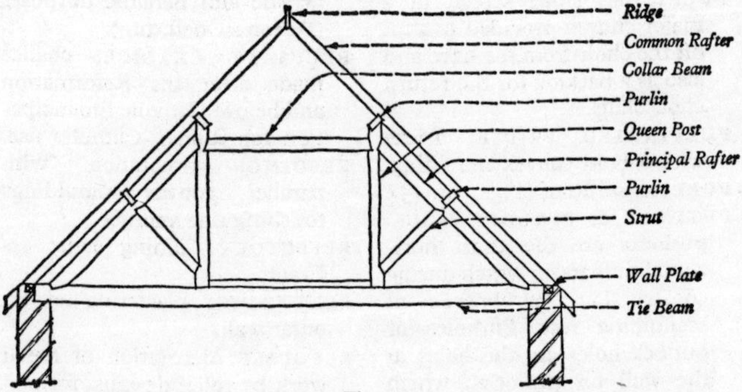

Fig. 15

ROMANO-BRITISH: A somewhat vague term applied to the period and cultural features of Britain affected by the Roman occupation of the C1–5 A.D.

ROOD: cross or crucifix.

ROOD LOFT: singing gallery on the top of the rood screen, often supported by a coving.

ROOD SCREEN: *see* Screen.

ROOD STAIRS: stairs to give access to the rood loft.

ROOF: *Single-framed:* if consisting entirely of transverse members (such as rafters with or without braces, collars, tie-beams, king-posts or queen-posts, etc.) not tied together longitudinally. *Double-framed:* if longitudinal members (such as a ridge beam and purlins) are employed. As a rule in such cases the rafters are divided into stronger principals and weaker subsidiary rafters. *Hipped:* roof with sloped instead of vertical ends. *Mansard:* roof with a double slope, the

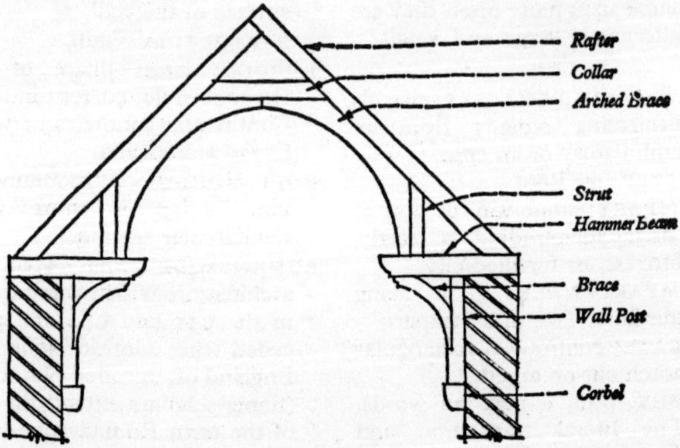

Fig. 16

lower slope being larger and steeper than the upper. *Saddle-back:* tower roof shaped like an ordinary gabled timber roof. The following members have special names: *Rafter:* roof-timber sloping up from the wall plate to the ridge. *Principal:* principal rafter, usually corresponding to the main bay divisions of the nave or chancel below. *Wall Plate:* timber laid longitudinally on the top of a wall. *Purlin:* longitudinal member laid parallel with wall plate and ridge beam some way up the slope of the roof. *Tie-beam:* beam connecting the two slopes of a roof across at its foot, usually at the height of the wall plate, to prevent the roof from spreading. *Collar-beam:* tie-beam applied higher up the slope of the roof. *Strut:* upright timber connecting the tie-beam with the rafter above it. *King-post:* upright timber connecting a tie-beam and collar-beam with the ridge beam. *Queen-posts:* two struts placed symmetrically on a tie-beam or collar-beam. *Braces:* inclined timbers inserted to strengthen others. Usually braces connect a collar-beam with the rafters below or a tie-beam with the wall below. Braces can be straight or curved (also called arched). *Hammer-beam:* beam projecting at right angles, usually from the top of a wall, to carry arched braces or struts and arched braces. (*See* Figs. 14, 15, 16.)

ROSE WINDOW (or WHEEL WINDOW): circular window with patterned tracery arranged to radiate from the centre.

ROTUNDA: building circular in plan.

RUBBLE: building stones, not square or hewn, nor laid in regular courses.

RUSTICATION: *rock-faced* if the surfaces of large blocks of ashlar stone are left rough like rock; *smooth* if the ashlar blocks are smooth and separated by V-joints; *banded* if the separation by V-joints applies only to the horizontals.

S

SADDLEBACK: *see* Roof.

SALTIRE CROSS: equal-limbed cross placed diagonally.

SANCTUARY: (1) area around the main altar of a church (*see* Presbytery); (2) sacred site consisting of wood or stone uprights enclosed by a circular bank and ditch. Beginning in the Neolithic, they were elaborated in the succeeding Bronze Age. The best known examples are Stonehenge and Avebury.

SARCOPHAGUS: elaborately carved coffin.

SCAGLIOLA: material composed of cement and colouring matter to imitate marble.

SCALLOPED CAPITAL: development of the block capital (q.v.) in which the single semi-circular surface is elaborated into a series of truncated cones (Fig. 17).

Fig. 17

SCARP: artificial cutting away of the ground to form a steep slope.

SCREEN: *Parclose screen:* screen separating a chapel from the rest of a church. *Rood screen:* screen below the rood (q.v.), usually at the W end of a chancel.

SCREENS PASSAGE: passage between the entrances to kitchen, buttery, etc., and the screen behind which lies the hall of a medieval house.

SEDILIA: seats for the priests (usually three) on the S side of the chancel of a church.

SEGMENTAL ARCH: *see* Arch.

SET-OFF: *see* Weathering.

SEXPARTITE: *see* Vault.

SGRAFFITO: pattern incised into plaster so as to expose a dark surface underneath.

SHAFT-RING: motif of the C12 and C13 consisting of a ring round a circular pier or a shaft attached to a pier.

SHEILA-NA-GIG: fertility figure, usually with legs wide open.

SILL: lower horizontal part of the frame of a window.

SLATEHANGING: the covering of walls by overlapping rows of slates, on a timber substructure.

SOFFIT: underside of an arch, lintel, etc.

SOLAR: upper living-room of a medieval house.

SOPRAPORTE: painting above the door of a room, usual in the C17 and C18.

SOUNDING BOARD: horizontal board or canopy over a pulpit. Also called Tester.

SPANDREL: triangular surface between one side of an arch, the horizontal drawn from its apex, and the vertical drawn from its springer; also the surface between two arches.

SPERE-TRUSS: roof truss on two free-standing posts to mask the division between screens passage and hall. The screen itself, where a spere-truss exists, was originally movable.

SPIRE: tall pyramidal or conical pointed erection often built on top of a tower, turret, etc. *Broach Spire:* a broach is a sloping half-pyramid of masonry or wood introduced at the base of each of the four oblique faces of a tapering octagonal spire with the object of effecting the transition from the square to the octagon. The *splayed foot spire* is a variation of the broach form found principally in the south-eastern counties. In this form the four cardinal faces are splayed out near their base, to cover the corners, while the oblique (or intermediate) faces taper away to a point. *Needle Spire:* thin spire rising from the centre of a tower roof, well inside the parapet.

SPIRELET: *see* Flèche.

SPLAY: chamfer, usually of the jamb of a window.

SPRINGING: level at which an arch rises from its supports.

SQUINCH: arch or system of concentric arches thrown across the angle between two walls to support a superstructure, for example a dome (Fig. 18).

SQUINT: a hole cut in a wall or through a pier to allow a view of the main altar of a church from places whence it could not otherwise be seen (also called Hagioscope).

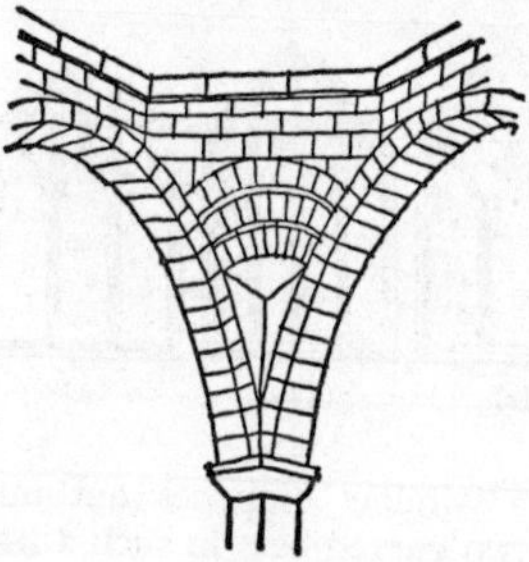
Fig. 18

STALL: carved seat, one of a row, made of wood or stone.

STAUNCHION: upright iron or steel member.

STEEPLE: the tower of a church together with a spire, cupola, etc.

STIFF-LEAF: E.E. type of foliage of many-lobed shapes (Fig. 19).

Fig. 19

STILTED: *see* Arch.

STOREY-POSTS: the principal posts of a timber-framed wall.

STOUP: vessel for the reception of holy water, usually placed near a door.

STRAINER ARCH: arch inserted across a room to prevent the walls from leaning.

STRAPWORK: C16 decoration consisting of interlaced bands, and forms similar to fretwork or cut and bent leather.

STRETCHER: *see* Brickwork.

STRING COURSE: projecting horizontal band or moulding set in the surface of a wall.

STRUT: *see* Roof.

STUCCO: plaster work.

STUDS: the subsidiary vertical timber members of a timber-framed wall.

SWAG: festoon formed by a carved piece of cloth suspended from both ends.

TABERNACLE: richly ornamented niche or free-standing canopy. Usually contains the Holy Sacrament.

TARSIA: inlay in various woods.

TAZZA: shallow bowl on a foot.

TERMINAL FIGURES (TERMS, TERMINI): upper part of a human figure growing out of a pier, pilaster, etc., which tapers towards the base. *See also* Caryatid, Pilaster.

TERRACOTTA: burnt clay, unglazed.

TESSELLATED PAVEMENT: mosaic flooring, particularly Roman, consisting of small 'tesserae' or cubes of glass, stone, or brick.

TESSERAE: *see* Tessellated Pavement.

TESTER: *see* Sounding Board.

TETRASTYLE: having four detached columns.

THREE-DECKER PULPIT: pulpit with Clerk's Stall below and Reading Desk below the Clerk's Stall.

TIE-BEAM: *see* Roof (Figs. 14, 15).

TIERCERON: *see* Vault (Fig. 21).

TILEHANGING: *see* Slatehanging.

TIMBER-FRAMING: method of construction where walls are built of timber framework with the spaces filled in by plaster

(a) (b) (c) (d) (e) (f) (g)

Fig. 20

or brickwork. Sometimes the timber is covered over with plaster or boarding laid horizontally.

TOMB-CHEST: chest-shaped stone coffin, the most usual medieval form of funeral monument.

TOUCH: soft black marble quarried near Tournai.

TOURELLE: turret corbelled out from the wall.

TRACERY: intersecting ribwork in the upper part of a window, or used decoratively in blank arches, on vaults, etc. *Plate tracery: see* Fig. 20(*a*). Early form of tracery where decoratively shaped openings are cut through the solid stone infilling in a window head. *Bar tracery:* a form introduced into England *c.*1250. Intersecting ribwork made up of slender shafts, continuing the lines of the mullions of windows up to a decorative mesh in the head of the window. *Geometrical tracery: see* Fig. 20(*b*). Tracery characteristic of *c.* 1250–1310 consisting chiefly of circles or foiled circles. *Y-tracery: see* Fig. 20(*c*). Tracery consisting of a mullion which branches into two forming a Y shape; typical of *c.* 1300. *Intersecting tracery: see* Fig. 20(*d*). Tracery in which each mullion of a window branches out into two curved bars in such a way that every one of them is drawn with the same radius from a different centre. The result is that every light of the window is a lancet and every two, three, four, etc., lights together form a pointed arch. This treatment also is typical of *c.* 1300. *Reticulated tracery: see* Fig. 20(*e*). Tracery typical of the early C14 consisting entirely of circles drawn at top and bottom into ogee shapes so that a net-like appearance results. *Panel tracery: see* Fig. 20(*f*) and (*g*). Perp tracery, which is formed of upright straight-sided panels above lights of a window.

TRANSEPT: transverse portion of a cross-shaped church.

TRANSOM: horizontal bar across the openings of a window.

TRANSVERSE ARCH: *see* Vault.

TRIBUNE: *see* Gallery.

TRICIPUT, SIGNUM TRICIPUT: sign of the Trinity expressed by three faces belonging to one head.

TRIFORIUM: arcaded wall passage or blank arcading facing the nave at the height of the aisle roof and below the clerestory (q.v.) windows. (*See* Gallery.)

TRIGLYPHS: blocks with vertical

grooves separating the metopes (q.v.) in the Doric frieze (Fig. 12).

TROPHY: sculptured group of arms or armour, used as a memorial of victory.

TRUMEAU: stone mullion (q.v.) supporting the tympanum (q.v.) of a wide doorway.

TUMULUS: *see* Barrow.

TURRET: very small tower, round or polygonal in plan.

TUSCAN: *see* Order.

TYMPANUM: space between the lintel of a doorway and the arch above it.

UNDERCROFT: vaulted room, sometimes underground, below a church or chapel.

UNIVALLATE: of a hill-fort: defended by a single bank and ditch.

UPPER PALAEOLITHIC: *see* Palaeolithic.

VAULT: *Barrel-vault: see* Tunnel-vault. *Cross-vault: see* Groin-vault. *Domical vault:* square or polygonal dome rising direct on a square or polygonal bay, the curved surfaces separated by groins (q.v.). *Fan-vault:* late medieval vault where all ribs springing from one springer are of the same length, the same distance from the next, and the same curvature. *Groin-vault* or *Cross-vault:* vault of two tunnel-vaults of identical shape intersecting each other at r. angles. Chiefly Norman and Renaissance. *Lierne:* tertiary rib, that is, rib which does not spring either from one of the main springers or from the central boss. Introduced in the C14, continues to the C16. *Quadripartite vault:* one wherein one bay of vaulting is divided into four parts. *Rib-vault:* vault with diagonal ribs projecting along the groins. *Ridge-rib:* rib along the longitudinal or transverse ridge of a vault. Introduced in the early C13. *Sexpartite vault:* one wherein one bay of quadripartite vaulting is divided into two parts transversely so that each bay of vaulting has six parts. *Tierceron:* secondary rib, that is, rib which issues from one of the main springers or the central boss and leads to a place on a ridge-rib. Introduced in the early C13. *Transverse arch:* arch separating one bay of a vault from the next. *Tunnel-vault* or *Barrel-vault:* vault of semicircular or pointed section. Chiefly Norman and Renaissance. (*See* Fig. 21.)

VAULTING SHAFT: vertical member leading to the springer of a vault.

VENETIAN WINDOW: window with three openings, the central one arched and wider than the outside ones. Current in England chiefly in the C17–18.

VERANDA: open gallery or balcony with a roof on light, usually metal, supports.

VESICA: oval with pointed head and foot.

VESTIBULE: anteroom or entrance hall.

VILLA: (1) according to Gwilt (1842) 'a country house for the residence of opulent persons'; (2) Romano-British country houses cum farms, to which the description given in (1)

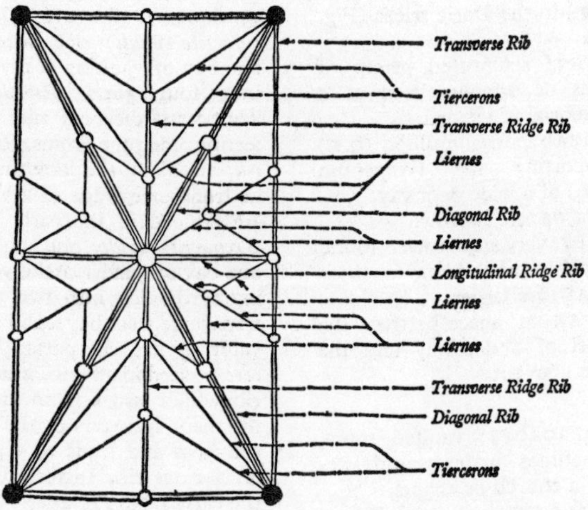

Fig. 21

more or less applies. They developed with the growth of urbanization. The basic type is the simple corridor pattern with rooms opening off a single passage; the next stage is the addition of wings. The court-yard villa fills a square plan with subsidiary buildings and an enclosure wall with a gate facing the main corridor block.

VITRIFIED: made similar to glass.

VITRUVIAN OPENING: A door or window which diminishes towards the top, as advocated by Vitruvius, bk. IV, chapter VI.

VOLUTE: spiral scroll, one of the component parts of an Ionic column (*see* Order).

VOUSSOIR: wedge-shaped stone used in arch construction.

WAGON ROOF: roof in which by closely set rafters with arched braces the appearance of the inside of a canvas tilt over a wagon is achieved. Wagon roofs can be panelled or plastered (ceiled) or left uncovered.

WAINSCOT: timber lining to walls.

WALL PLATE: *see* Roof.

WATERLEAF: leaf shape used in later C12 capitals. The water-leaf is a broad, unribbed, tapering leaf curving up towards the angle of the abacus and turned in at the top (Fig. 22).

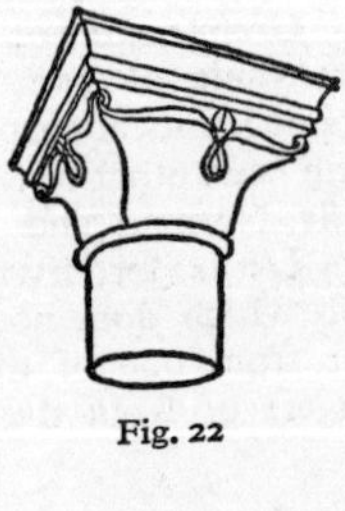

Fig. 22

WEALDEN HOUSE: timber-framed house with the hall in the centre and wings projecting only slightly and only on the jutting upper floor. The roof, however, runs through without a break between wings and hall, and the eaves of the hall part are therefore exceptionally deep. They are supported by diagonal, usually curved, braces starting from the short inner sides of the overhanging wings and rising parallel with the front wall of the hall towards the centre of the eaves.

WEATHERBOARDING: overlapping horizontal boards, covering a timber-framed wall.

WEATHERING: sloped horizontal surface on sills, buttresses, etc., to throw off water.

WEEPERS: small figures placed in niches along the sides of some medieval tombs (also called Mourners).

WHEEL WINDOW: *see* Rose Window.

INDEX OF PLATES

INDEX OF ARTISTS

INDEX OF PLACES

ADDENDUM

(FEBRUARY 1968)

p. 257 [Salwarpe, St Michael.] However, the Rev. A. H. Doyle tells me that some irregular facing in the S aisle indicates that there was once a springer there as well, and hence an arch as on the N side.

NOTES

NOTES

NOTES

NOTES